The Circular Economy Handbook

Peter Lacy · Jessica Long ·
Wesley Spindler

The Circular Economy Handbook

Realizing the Circular Advantage

Peter Lacy
Accenture
London, UK

Jessica Long
Accenture
Washington, D.C., USA

Wesley Spindler
Accenture
London, UK

ISBN 978-1-349-95967-9   ISBN 978-1-349-95968-6   (eBook)
https://doi.org/10.1057/978-1-349-95968-6

This Palgrave Macmillan imprint is published by the registered company Springer Nature Limited
The registered company address is: The Campus, 4 Crinan Street, London, N1 9XW, United Kingdom

To the World Economic Forum, Forum of Young Global Leaders, and members of the Platform for Accelerating the Circular Economy (PACE), in recognition of their support and work in progressing the transformation to a more circular economy.

To all the pioneering changemakers, organizations, and partners, who have been a constant inspiration to us—demonstrating what it means to be responsible leaders as we pave a new path forward.

And to our families, especially—Lucy, Jack, Sam, Gay, Jenny, Bethan, Aida, Felicity, Isabel, Sophie, Lincoln, Archie, Chris and Trish—without them, we surely would not be the individuals we are today, striving to make our small contribution to a brighter future for all.

Foreword by Frans van Houten

We must standardize and scale up the circular economy to achieve a global leap in prosperity.

The daily toll of environmental harm being inflicted on our population and planet is a heavy burden. In the simplest terms, it is the most important issue of our times. How we systematically reverse the tide of wastefulness and reduce carbon emissions must be at the forefront of our collective thinking as individuals, organizations, and institutions. For my part, I am convinced the circular transformation is a sustainable path in decoupling economic development from unsustainable resource consumption.

Six years ago, Philips made a strategic decision to embed circular thinking throughout our business, as a competitive necessity, and with the conviction that companies solving the problem of resource constraints will gain an advantage. The misconception is that circularity adds costs. My experience is that circular innovation unlocks new value by increasing customer preference and generating superior margins. Moreover, by ingraining green thinking with a strong sense of purpose and a commitment to meaningful innovation, the culture and attractiveness of Philips as an employer and partner have benefitted immeasurably.

In many respects, the fundamental challenge remains. How do we embed circularity in *everything* we do, while also bringing employees, customers and suppliers with us on this vital transformation? We set firm goals and ambitious targets designed to stretch the boundaries of what we can achieve. It is our objective to "close-the-loop" on all large medical equipment by 2020. We will extend this to all medical equipment by 2025 and embed this approach throughout our consumer businesses.

Considering progress and next steps, Philips is driven by the necessary passion, expertise, and innovation capabilities to unlock latent circular value. Often, it demands intensive efforts and commitments on behalf of our employees and partners to meet the standards we set ourselves. Circular ecosystems and business models must be an integral part of our DNA. By embracing lean and continuous improvement, our priority now is to *optimize, standardize and scale-up* circularity throughout all aspects of the global supply chain.

I see a similar evolution in other companies—at large corporations and small and medium-sized enterprises (SMEs)—in both the public and private sectors, and across key initiatives in e-waste, plastics and capital equipment. We can be proud of our achievements. Yet the urgency of the challenge demands that we go faster, execute more effectively, and stretch targets even further. How we act as a global coalition of leaders to scale up, measure impact and set new standards is what will drive universal change.

I congratulate the authors of this handbook on delivering practical guidelines, clear strategies and instructive case studies to galvanize and grow the circular economy. The tipping point at which we will inflict irreversible damage on future generations is fast approaching. It is the responsibility of business leaders, at all levels, to translate this shared wisdom into an all-pervading and operationally effective circular economy.

Amsterdam, Netherlands

Frans van Houten
CEO & Chairman, Philips
Co-Chair, Platform for Accelerating
the Circular Economy (PACE)

Foreword by David Rosenberg

"Our house is on fire." Famed Swedish climate activist Greta Thunberg said this in Davos in 2019, and her vivid picture is not an overstatement. We need to act with urgency to change the course of our planet's trajectory. Commercial leaders must step up and drive impact.

The Circular Economy Handbook is an essential guide for companies who are striving to do the right thing for the planet, investors, and all stakeholders by embracing circular economy principles. In an area where issues can be complex and the trade-offs seemingly prohibitive, the good news is that there are examples of successful circular economy businesses. This book lays out different forms of success with case studies that explain inspirational, easily embraced business models. It is one thing to want to do the right thing; knowing how to do it is the critical part.

This book provides a much-needed blueprint on how a business can start a circular economy journey. What are the right questions to ask? What are the right problems to solve? What should be your long-term goals as well as shorter-term milestones? Where to prioritize? This handbook addresses these questions, showing how to get started and succeed.

Bill McDonough, the co-author of *Cradle to Cradle*, inspired me to build companies to solve problems that were not being solved fast enough. I co-founded AeroFarms, a fully controlled environment vertical farming company, with the goal of growing plants in closed-loop water systems. We set a goal of zero waste before we knew how to achieve that goal. Embedding circular economy principles into the fabric of the company empowered employees to find opportunities for impact. In just one example, our employees identified a solution that cut our energy footprint by over 30%.

In another example, we developed a cloth growth media (materials that plants grow in) that replaces dirt and consists of 100% recycled materials and is 100% reusable.

Peter Lacy and I co-founded the Circular Economy Taskforce at the World Economic Forum to inspire the business community to incorporate circular economy principles into their everyday business models. We set up The Circulars, a circular economy award program to recognize leading companies in this area. More than five years down the line, a number of the insights and inspiring stories captured from The Circulars are reflected in this handbook, a testament to the power of the program and the progress of the circular economy more broadly.

The Circular Economy Handbook will help the world accelerate new circular business models.

It illustrates the broader business design and how to get there. As Michael Braungart, co-author of *Cradle to Cradle*, states, we as members of the planet want to get to a place where people do not say "environmentally smart" but rather just "smart." In the same way, the goal is to transition from "circular economy business models" to every business model being circular in nature.

For now, we need the compelling examples, smart strategies, and instructive business models this book provides, and we need it urgently, because our house is on fire.

Jersey City, NJ, USA

David Rosenberg
Co-Founder & CEO, AeroFarms
Co-Chair, The Circulars

Foreword by Naoko Ishii

The circular economy is a topic whose time has come. There is now growing worldwide recognition among many governments, businesses, civil society organizations and financial institutions that not only does the financial and ecological survival of our planet depend on shifting to a circular economy, but this shift provides tremendous economic and societal opportunities and benefits.

The World Economic Forum has reported that implementing the circular economy worldwide could yield material cost savings of up to $1 trillion a year by 2025. Building on this awareness, *The Circular Economy Handbook* is a timely, necessary "how to" guide to circularity for leaders in both the public and private sectors. By conveying opportunities and insights on how to scale investments, the publication shows that a circular economy can be good both for the environment and for business. Public–private partnership will be crucial to success on that journey.

Our current global economic model is essentially linear: we extract, we manufacture, we consume, we throw away. It has been estimated that only 9% of the resources that are extracted return to the production system as input into new products after their first use. This economic model is on a collision course with nature, and it must change. To bring about that change, governments, businesses, civil society organizations and financiers all have a role to play. No one actor can do it singlehandedly.

Recognizing the need for a global platform to catalyze private–public collaboration toward a circular economy, the Global Environment Facility co-chairs the Platform for Accelerating the Circular Economy (PACE), together with Philips and hosted by the World Resources Institute. It brings together leaders from both the public and private sectors to take concerted action.

It is my firm belief that tomorrow's economy will be radically different from yesterday's economy. In this respect, the circular economy is nothing less than a blueprint for a fundamental transformation of our economic system—a transformation that is urgently needed, entirely possible, and desirable.

The Circular Economy Handbook: Realizing the Circular Advantage is an important addition to our collective toolbox to help realize this goal.

Washington, USA

Naoko Ishii
CEO & Chairperson
Global Environment Facility
Co-Chair, Platform for Accelerating
the Circular Economy (PACE)

Foreword by Ellen MacArthur and Andrew Morlet

Since the launch of the first report (Towards The Circular Economy, Ellen MacArthur Foundation) quantifying the opportunity of a circular economy at the World Economic Forum in 2012, the idea has been taken up at an extraordinary rate. It has captured the imagination of business leaders, emerging innovators, governments and cities, designers and academics around the world. The attractiveness of the idea is perhaps due to the compelling inherent logic and economic rationale of the circular economy, as well as its value-creation possibilities and competitive advantages. At the same time, the adverse impacts of the one-way, take-make-waste linear system are becoming starkly apparent. By 2050, the size of the global economy is projected to quadruple, and the world population is expected to increase to over 10 billion, with emerging markets accounting for two-thirds of global consumption. We now know that the negative impacts of the linear economy in terms of waste, pollution, finite resource depletion, natural systems degradation and climate change will, on current trend, be catastrophic.

The dire outlook of the linear economy in contrast to the opportunity offered by the circular economy has been clearly demonstrated through research by the Ellen MacArthur Foundation and many others. The publication of *Waste to Wealth* in 2015 provided important evidence of the value creation potential, conservatively estimating this as a $4.5 trillion opportunity by 2030, through the adoption and scale-up across five key business models. This new book reflects the evolution in thinking and case evidence that has emerged around the circular economy in the past five years, with many leading businesses now moving rapidly from initial awareness to substantial engagement and investment.

There is also no doubt that the technologies of the Fourth Industrial Revolution, such as Artificial Intelligence, robotics, additive manufacturing, and the Internet of Things, will play a crucial role in this transition. They will provide new levels of data transparency and insight, unlock new possibilities for design, new biological and technical materials innovation, better material selection, better manufacturing methods, embedded materials intelligence, and scalable asset tracking and recovery. Taken together, this phenomenon is leading to the potential for new business models and better products that safely, effectively, and efficiently fit within systems that work, economically, environmentally, and societally. If guided by the vision of a circular economy, this next wave of technology-enabled innovation holds enormous promise for circular economic transformation and accelerated transition.

The opportunities presented by a circular economy are gaining substantial media coverage and gaining the attention of government and city regulators, as well as asset managers and investors. Businesses that lead this agenda, and create value based on circular economic principles, will seize the advantage, while those who remain stuck in the paradigm of extractive, linear economics will find themselves increasingly challenged.

This new book provides compelling new case examples and invaluable guidance on approaches, tools, and enabling technologies for the practical adoption of circular economy principles in business. It is a very welcome addition to the field.

Cowes, UK

Ellen MacArthur
Founder & Chair of Trustees
The Ellen MacArthur Foundation

Andrew Morlet
CEO, The Ellen MacArthur
Foundation

Foreword by William McDonough

One might say the linear, "take, make, waste" production model of the first industrial revolution has used unprincipled commerce as a weapon to wage unintentional war with the planet. Fortunately, today we see a multitude of business and social leaders embracing the aspirations of the *Cradle to Cradle* circular economy, applying its principles to go beyond merely reducing, minimizing, and avoiding waste to approach the state of natural systems in which there is no waste at all.

Before the publication of *Cradle to Cradle: Remaking the Way We Make Things*, in 2002, I had the privilege of working with companies who were pioneers in this thinking, including furniture manufacturer Herman Miller (beginning in 1994) and flooring company Shaw Industries Group (1999). We worked together on rethinking and, ultimately, redesigning products, practices, and even corporate visions and goals, setting a new standard for what was to come. From 2014 to 2016, I served as the inaugural chair of the Global Meta-Council on the Circular Economy for the World Economic Forum, which allowed me to see firsthand, and play a role, in the movement toward wide-scale implementation of circular economy practices.

There has been amazing progress made over the past 25 years. Yet, if we consider how most products are conceived and marketed today, it is clear that we still have a long way to go. For example, companies and regulators often refer to a product's "lifecycle" and its "end of life" to signal environmental responsibility. In fact, the "life" of a product is often a very short story about sophisticated birth—attended by global supply chains—and crude, even hazardous death in refuse piles; burial on land, in rivers, and at sea; or cremation in burn piles and toxic "waste to energy"' plants. These are old stories of "throwing things away" in a world with more than enough. But now, as we recognize the constraints placed on growth by limited resources, we can see that "away has gone away." Rather than designing for "end of life" in a flawed system, let's design for "end of use" or "next use" in a system that is safe, circular, and beneficial.

Cradle to Cradle circular economy practices allow us to do that. They represent a fundamental shift in the first principle underlying the terms of commerce itself. They move us beyond the simplistic, self-centered question, "How much can I get for how little I give?"—the quantification of economic value in a shrinking world of limits and fear—and instead put first the richly informed and generous question, "How much can we give for all that we get?"—a new commercial qualification of human values in an ever-expanding world of abundance and hope.

From my perspective, *The Circular Economy Handbook: Realizing the Circular Advantage* is an incredibly valuable tool. By addressing every link in economic value chains, as well as the means to a shared prosperity, it provides outstanding support for the growing interest in and implementation of circular economy design. For those who follow this handbook, I hope that they see a shift of not just business models and systems, but also of mindset and language as they explore the principles and practices of the *Cradle to Cradle* circular economy.

Charlottesville, VA, USA

William McDonough
Chief Executive, McDonough
Innovation

Acknowledgements

There have been countless individuals and teams who have contributed to shaping our thinking on the circular economy topic, and ultimately influenced the insights of this handbook—it's truly been a collaborative effort, and for that we are eternally thankful.

In particular, we would like to call out our main contributors—Alden Hayashi, whose way with words has brought a coherence and readability to the manuscript that we could never have obtained without his efforts; and Jenna Trescott, Christopher Hook, and Zeina Lamah, three great minds who worked tirelessly next to us to bring life and logic to the content.

We would also like to thank the members of the Accenture Team who dedicated great time and attention to the handbook's research and manuscript development over many months and iterations:

Akshay Kasera, Alvise Lisca, Alyssa Di Cara, Anna Töndevold, Belinda Deng, Cathy McAndrew, Daniel Newton, Dave Spelman, Jay Thakkar, Joshua Curtis, Katharine Chung, Kritika Choudhary, Lieke Vossen, Michael Lieder, Michiel Frenaij, Nazneen Shaikh, Palash Gupta, Priyanka Abbi, Ragini Ahluwalia, Rebecca Caseby, Ritesh Bhangale, Rohit Bhat, Shrestha Padhy, Sophie Wilson, Sriharsha Vavilala, Sukanya Deshmukh, Sundeep Singh, Sytze Dijkstra, and Tony Murdzhev.

Finally, we would like to recognize all the individuals who have shared their perspectives with us through reviews, interviews, words of support, and ongoing collaboration. Their critiques, stories, and pioneering leadership have brought a richness to the content and to the circular movement more broadly. Thank you for your dedication to the cause:

Adam Lowry, Amy Brown, Andrew Morlet, Andrew Winston, Antonia Gawel, Bea Perez, Chris Riley, Christophe Beck, David Rosenberg, Dominic Waughray, Doug Baker, Ellen MacArthur, Eric Soubeiran, Erika Chan, Ernst Siewers, Feike Sijbesma, Flemming Besenbacher, Frans van Houten, Gonzalo Muñoz, J. Jon Imaz, James Quincey, Jamie Butterworth, Jean-Pascal Tricoire, Jennifer Silberman, John Atcheson, John Kern, John Pflueger, Joost van Dun, Karl-Johan Persson, Katharina Stenholm, Katherine Garrett-Cox, Laurent Auguste, Leon Wijnands, Lisa Brady, Luca Meini, Marc Delaye, Marc Zornes, Mark Cutifani, Massimiano Tellini, Matanya Horowitz, Matthew Silver, Michael Goltzman, Naoko Ishii, Nishant Parekh, Noel Kinder, Peter Desmond, Reinier Mommaal, Rick Ridgeway, Robert Bernard, Saori Dubourg, Shiva Dustdar, Stephen Roberts, Tobias Webb, Tom Szaky, Tony Milikin, Virginie Helias, William McDonough, and Zhao Kai.

Praise for *"The Circular Economy Handbook"*

"The climate emergency makes the switch to a circular economy ever more urgent. The circular economy is happening, but not quickly enough. This practical handbook can accelerate the transition by helping business leaders to rethink their propositions and scale-up their circular solutions. It's also a call to action—the systems change we need is only achievable if we all contribute. This book will hopefully inspire many to move forward on the path to true impact."
—Ralph Hamers, *CEO ING Group*

"Our generation has the unique opportunity to reconcile the paradox between progress for all and a sustainable future for our planet, thanks to a step change in efficiency. Digital technologies are there to help, to shift the way we manage energy, provided we rethink the way we design buildings, industries, cities. *The Circular Economy Handbook* demonstrates how digitization and circular models go hand in hand to enable this efficiency."
—Jean-Pascal Tricoire, *Chairman and CEO, Schneider Electric*

"We believe that waste will come to be seen as a precious commodity, shaping new business models and defining commercial opportunities hitherto unimagined. Act now and be part of this systemic transformation in our economy, our lives, our relationship to the environment. This handbook, with its deep practical insights supported by extensive knowledge and research, is a timely contribution to the field and essential reading for the conscious, contemporary leader."
—Antoine Frérot, *Chairman and CEO, Veolia. Author of* Water: Towards a culture of responsibility *(2011)*

"There cannot be an effective circular economy without private sector's engagement and innovation. Raising awareness on circular economy opportunities and empowering companies from different industries to become circular leaders is a crucial way to accelerate the transition."
—Karmenu Vella, *Commissioner for Environment, Maritime Affairs and Fisheries, European Commission*

"The business case for the circular economy is crystal clear. Whilst many are already realizing value from the concept, our world is still only 9% circular. This new handbook will play an important role in scaling up the circular economy as it provides practical guidance for companies and puts a much-needed spotlight on the disruptive technologies needed to drive the transition. Nature is already circular, now it's up to us to do the same."
—Feike Sijbesma, *CEO, Royal DSM*

"*The Circular Economy Handbook* provides private sector leaders with an overall framework as well as specific implementation guidance for revamping their business processes to make them more circular and consequently sustainable."
—Bea Perez, *Senior Vice President & Chief Communications, Public Affairs, Sustainability & Marketing Assets Officer, The Coca-Cola Company*

"Climate change is on everyone's lips. But given material and land use account for close to half of global emissions, we cannot solve the climate crisis without a clear focus on the circular economy. Circularity is the tool needed to deliver real decoupling of economic growth and resource usage. In *The Circular Economy Handbook*, the authors demonstrate there is a path forward for sustainable business by providing actionable insights and practical strategies for making a successful circular transition."
—Ida Auken, *MP, Chairman of the Parliament's Energy and Climate Committee, Former Minister for The Environment, Denmark*

"Organizations great and small are pivoting towards the circular economy. To craft our path forward, the private sector must step forward and join hands with governments, civil society and consumers in leading the change. *The Circular Economy Handbook* arrives at a critical juncture in the history of humankind, as we devise entirely new modes of making, consuming and living. Channelling our energies together, with the grace of new technologies, we can catalyse such a transformation."
—Gonzalo Muñoz, *Founder, TriCiclos*

"*The Circular Economy Handbook's* predecessor, *Waste to Wealth*, has been an important resource for our circular economy strategy, showing that closed loop systems and upcycled materials can be drivers for growth. Now, this handbook goes one step further and provides practical insights on the role that innovation, technology and collaboration will play in securing a competitive advantage from circularity. It is a critical contribution to a rapidly growing school of thought, now more important than ever."

—Tony Milikin, *Chief Sustainability and Procurement Officer,*
Anheuser-Busch InBev

"In China, whilst policy-makers have made circular economy a priority as a top-down initiative, citizens are looking forward to seeing a much bigger bottom-up movement from business. *The Circular Economy Handbook* is timely piece to support this critical movement. Since its publication in 2015, I have introduced its predecessor, *Waste to Wealth*, to officials, business leaders and researchers in China. I look forward to doing the same with the handbook."

—Zhu Dajian, *Professor and Director, Institute of Governance for*
Sustainability, Tongji University, Shanghai

"We cannot solve tomorrow's problems with today's solutions, and the stakes are getting higher and higher as we fail to make real progress on the issues of our generation; climate change, unemployment and poverty in our developing economies. This handbook makes a valuable contribution by illustrating the powerful role digitisation and circular economies can play and by encouraging business leaders to not only push out on disruptive technologies, but also to re-invent their core businesses."

—Rob Shuter, *Group CEO and President, MTN Group*

"The 'take, make, waste' mindset is difficult to break away from, but we are fast approaching a point of no return. The *Circular Economy Handbook* offers concrete direction for how to make the transition circular. It calls out that retrofitting small-scale circular initiatives into business–as-usual environments simply won't deliver the change we need to see. I hope the Handbook becomes a practical companion for senior executives on their change journey. The time to act is now."

—Lise Kingo, *CEO and Executive Director, United Nations Global Compact*

"The Fourth Industrial Revolution will impact every aspect of our lives. In order to thrive within this new global dynamic, we need to adopt new business models and norms. The circular economy is one approach that can enable us to keep pace with technological innovation, support integrated and sustainable ecosystems, and move us towards a brighter future. *The Circular Economy Handbook* is an essential guide for organizations of all types looking to capitalize on the circular opportunity."

—Professor Klaus Schwab, *Founder and Executive Chairman, World Economic Forum*

"The need to develop new business models to adapt to climate urgency, resource constraints and social imperatives is at the top of my personal agenda. The circular economy reinvents the way we create and share value for society at large, by extracting the highest possible value from materials. *The Circular Economy Handbook* represents a major contribution, helping us to move from concept to action, by scaling up and mainstreaming new business models in a pragmatic way."

—Ilham Kadri, *CEO, Solvay*

Contents

Abbreviations

4IR	4th Industrial Revolution
ACEA	European Automobile Manufacturers' Association
ACT	Australian Capital Territory
AI	Artificial Intelligence
B2B	Business-to-Business
B2C	Business-to-Consumer
C2B	Consumer-to-Business
CCU	Carbon Capture and Utilization
CCUS	Carbon Capture, Utilization, and Storage
Cefic	European Chemical Industry Council
CFCs	Chlorofluorocarbons
CLP	Closed Loop Partners
CO2	Carbon dioxide
CO2e	Carbon-dioxide-equivalent
COP	Conference of the Parties
CORFO	Chilean Economic Development Agency
CPG	Consumer Packaged Goods
CSR	Corporate Social Responsibility
CTO	Chief Technology Officer
D2C	Direct-to-Consumer
DAC	Direct Air Capture
DC	Direct Current
EACs	Environmental Attribute Certificates
EIB	European Investment Bank
EJ	Exajoules
EOR	Enhanced Oil Recovery
EPA	Environmental Protection Agency

EPR	Extended Producer Responsibility
ESG	Environmental, Social, and Governance
EU	European Union
EV	Electric Vehicle
FMCG	Fast-Moving Consumer Goods
GDP	Gross Domestic Product
GE	General Electric
GHGs	Greenhouse Gases
GM	Genetically Modified
GPS	Global Positioning Systems
HFCs	Hydrofluorocarbons
HNWI	High Net Worth Individuals
HP	Hewlett-Packard
ICT	Information and Communication Technology
IEA	International Energy Agency
IFF	International Flavors & Fragrances
IIoT	Industrial Internet of Things
ILO	International Labour Organization
IoT	Internet of Things
IPCC	Intergovernmental Panel on Climate Change
IRENA	International Renewable Energy Agency
IT	Information Technology
KPIs	Key Performance Indicator
LaaS	Light-as-a-Service
LCAs	Lifecycle Assessments
LSEV	Low Speed Electric Vehicle
M&A	Mergers and Acquisitions
M&IE	Machinery and Industrial Equipment
M2M	Machine-to-Machine
MRI	Magnetic Resonance Imaging
NFC	Near-Field Communication
NGOs	Non-Governmental Organizations
NT	Northern Territory
O&G	Oil and Gas
OECD	Organization for Economic Co-operation and Development
OEMs	Original Equipment Manufacturers
OPEC	Organization of the Petroleum Exporting Countries
P&G	Procter & Gamble
PACE	Platform for Accelerating the Circular Economy
PCs	Personal Computers
PE	Polyethylene
PET	Polyethylene Terephthalate

PP	Polypropylene
PPAs	Power Purchase Agreements
PUE	Power Usage Effectiveness
PV	Photovoltaic
QR	Quick Response
R&D	Research and Development
RCRA	Resource Conservation and Recovery Act
RFID	Radio-Frequency Identification
ROI	Return on Investment
rPET	Recycled PET
SaaS	Software-as-a-Service
SDGs	Sustainable Development Goals
SEZs	Special Economic Zones
SFK	Smart Factory Kunshan
SKUs	Stock Keeping Units
SMEs	Small and Medium-Sized Enterprises
TFEC	Total Final Energy Consumption
TNC	The Nature Conservancy
TPU	Thermoplastic Polyurethane
UK	United Kingdom
UN	United Nations
UNDP	United Nations Development Programme
UNEP	United Nations Environment Programme
UNIDO	United Nations Industrial Development Organization
UNITAR	United Nations Institute for Training and Research
UPS	United Parcel Service
US	United States
USDA	United States Department of Agriculture
V2G	Vehicle-to-Grid
VAT	Value-Added Tax
VOCs	Volatile Organic Compounds
Volvo CE	Volvo Construction Equipment
VR/AR	Virtual Reality/Augmented Reality
WBCSD	World Business Council for Sustainable Development
WEEE	Waste Electrical and Electronic Equipment
WEF	World Economic Forum
WHO	World Health Organization
WWF	World Wildlife Fund

List of Figures

List of Tables

xxxii   List of Tables

1

Introduction:
The Path to Transformation Is Circular

Businesses today are competing in a rapidly shifting global context. Complex and interconnected challenges are changing the face of how companies need to think, work, and innovate. Rising geopolitical and geo-economic tensions, the pace and scale of technological change, along with the urgency of the climate crisis, resource scarcity and a myriad of other social and environmental issues are dramatically altering the landscape. The good news is, with the circular economy we have an unprecedented opportunity to transform some of these challenges to opportunities, creating financial and economic value for business and society. In fact, not only can business step up to these obstacles and help reshape our economic system, our research shows the value at stake is massive: $4.5 trillion of upside, even at conservative estimates. In seizing the circular advantage, we believe business can spur innovation, create new markets and wisely pivot our current global direction toward one that is more sustainable and resilient. It's time to act now. In this book, we show leaders how they can do exactly that.

A Critical State

Let's first set the context, starting with the key macro-trends. According to the United Nations (UN), the world population will top 9.2 billion by 2050.[1] Half the world's population (3.6 billion) is now considered middle class, set to expand to 5.3 billion by 2030.[2] As living standards rise, so will consumption and demand for more resource-intensive goods (e.g., meat,

© The Author(s) 2020
P. Lacy et al., *The Circular Economy Handbook*,
https://doi.org/10.1057/978-1-349-95968-6_1

housing, and vehicles), based on current trends. By 2030, global demand is expected to increase 35% for food, 40% for water, and 50% for energy.[3] This competition for resources is set against a backdrop of persistent economic inequality and intensifying geopolitical tensions.[4]

Even as we have become more efficient at extracting value from raw materials, those improvements have not kept pace with the rise in consumption. The hard truth is this: We are now consuming about 1.75 times the earth's carrying capacity, meaning we are using 75% more natural resources than we are regenerating each year. This appetite for scarce resources is only expected to grow in coming decades.[5] For example, the production of mined metal commodities is expected to jump 250% by 2030 to satisfy demand and other commodities are under similar pressure.[6]

This does not bode well, especially for two of our most precious resources: clean water and fresh air. According to the World Health Organization (WHO), 785 million people currently lack access to drinking water and, by 2025, fully half of the world's population will be living in a water-stressed area.[7] Already about four billion people suffer from severe water scarcity at least one month a year. The number of people at risk of floods is predicted to rise from around 1.2 billion today to 1.6 billion in 2050.[8,9] In addition, ocean pollution is headed toward levels which until recently were thought unimaginable by most of us: By 2050, there will be more plastics (by weight) in the oceans than fish.[10] The air we breathe is also under assault. Air pollution kills an estimated seven million people a year, a number equivalent to that of smoking tobacco, and air pollution-related mortality is escalating in most parts of the world.[11,12]

We're also witnessing a devastating loss of biodiversity and habitat. Since 1970, human activities have wiped out 60% of mammals, birds, fish, and reptiles, one-fifth of the world's coral reefs, and 13 million hectares of forest.[13,14] This loss could threaten the global food supply, with already about one-fifth of the earth's vegetated surface becoming less productive over the past two decades.[15] In 2017 alone, 39 million acres of tree cover was lost in the tropics. This is an area the size of Bangladesh, representing 40 football fields of trees *every minute* for the entire year.[16] And in 2018, fires were deliberately set in Indonesia to clear land for agriculture, resulting in the destruction of over 10,000 square miles of forests, a blanket of toxic haze over large parts of Southeast Asia that lasted for weeks, illnesses of hundreds of thousands (and over 100,000 estimated deaths), and $30 billion in economic losses.[17]

Then we come to climate change. Perhaps the most overarching and interlinked challenge with far-reaching social and environmental implications casting a looming shadow over the other macro-trends. In October 2018, a report by the Intergovernmental Panel on Climate Change (IPCC) presented details of a dire scenario: If global warming continues at the current rate, temperatures will likely increase by 1.5 °C between 2030 and 2052, and the planet could potentially be three to five degrees warmer by 2100.[18,19] Unfortunately, there's only about 12 years left to keep warming to even the 1.5 °C level. Any increase above that significantly raises the risks of droughts, floods, extreme weather events, and poverty for hundreds of millions of people. According to an IPCC study, the estimated economic impact for a warming of 1.5 °C by 2100 would be $54 trillion. For a warming of 2 °C, it would be $69 trillion.[20] The bottom line is that urgent changes are necessary to head off disaster.

Another core macro-trend which has a ripple effect across all other trends, is the unprecedented technological change we have witnessed in the Fourth Industrial Revolution (4IR), characterized by various technologies such as machine learning and artificial intelligence (AI), that are disrupting just about every industry across the globe. 4IR is unlike past industrial revolutions because of the breadth, pace, and scale of new technologies that have the potential to decouple growth from resource use. Disruptive technologies, as we explore in this book, play a key role as an amplifier in scaling and making circular business models more effective and efficient. However, to achieve these benefits, the technologies must be deployed with intent and managed properly to minimize any unintended consequences, including adverse environmental impacts, the displacement of employees, the risks of cyberthreats, and ethical concerns.

Heeding the Call to Action

The scale of the challenge is undeniable, but the outlook isn't all bleak. In the past few years, we have reached an inflection point on climate change, for instance. Around the world, organizations and individuals are waking up to the fact that we are heading toward irreparable damage. Fortunately, there is now growing recognition that climate action is critical to long-term socio-economic success, and many governments have been heeding the call to action. To date, 185 parties have ratified the Paris Agreement, which aims to keep global warming this century to well below 2 °C above the pre-industrial levels and to pursue efforts to limit the temperature increase further to 1.5 °C.[21] In addition, businesses have been joining the battle, with many of the world's largest and most influential companies committing to 100% renewable power.[22] The investor community is also joining the conversation. The fossil-fuels divestment campaign has grown from $50 billion worth of assets (from 181 institutions) in 2014 to nearly $8 trillion (from more than 1000 institutions) at the end of 2018.[23] Public activism has also been on the rise, especially among the young. Almost half of 18- to 24-year-olds identified environmental issues as one of our three most pressing concerns, compared with 27% of the general population.[24] In 2019, hundreds of thousands of students in more than 1600 cities joined a classroom strike to bring attention to climate change issues.[25]

Broadening Beyond Climate

As concern over climate change has intensified, the focus has spread toward broader issues of sustainability and resource usage. While it's critical to focus on reducing carbon emissions through means such as energy efficiency, zero-carbon production, and renewable energy, focusing only on the production and consumption of energy solves for just half of global greenhouse gas (GHG) emissions. Therefore, it is equally important to address how we manufacture and use products, which comprises the remaining half (approximately) of GHG emissions.[26,27] That calls for a transformation across the entire economic system. Nothing less will meet the urgency of the moment, if the world is to achieve the UN Sustainable Development Goals (SDGs) by 2030 and stay within the boundaries underlined by the Paris Agreement.[28] Promisingly, various stakeholder groups are increasing focus on the health and well-being of our planet and its inhabitants. There has been particular concern about the volume and rate of extraction of natural resources, and the irresponsible usage (overconsumption) and disposal of products and materials. Issues like ocean health, plastics, e-waste, and food waste have become hot topics, galvanizing attention on the world stage and carrying both social and environmental impacts.

Growing concern has spurred an uptick in action. Governments around the world have been setting aggressive targets. The European Union (EU) has announced a commitment to banning some common single-use plastic items, such as cutlery and straws, by 2021 and a collection-rate target for plastic bottles of 90% by 2029.[29] India has said it would phase out disposable packaging by 2022, while China, Indonesia, Malaysia, Thailand, and Vietnam have closed their doors to the importing of plastic waste.[30,31] Consumer habits are also shifting, with just under a third of millennials globally now using various asset-sharing services, for example.[32] Most companies are well aware of the changes in government policies and consumer behavior, and many have been working to stay ahead of the curve with new goals, such as increasing the usage of recycled materials, zero waste to landfill targets, or commitments to 100% reusable and recyclable packaging.

The Circular Economy Advantage: A New Economic System and Business Strategy

Think the above are all environmental issues? Wrong. These are business issues both directly and indirectly. Turning from the macro-trends, we look at the microeconomics and the business strategies available to leaders. We know that achieving such ambitious goals will not be easy. But the flip side of every challenge is an opportunity. The global economy depends on business stepping up in the face of global pressures, with new forms of innovation and value creation. The "circular" economy offers a powerful way forward: a massive transformation from the traditional "linear" ways of doing business to new principles of circularity (see "The Linear Versus the Circular Economy"). In essence, companies must reject the "take, make, waste" approach in favor of keeping products and resources in use for as long as possible and, at end of use, cycling (or "looping") their components and materials back into the system in zero-waste value chains. In other words, a circular economy eliminates the concept of waste altogether, fundamentally changing the way we produce and consume, creating a healthier, thriving ecosystem that circulates value throughout the economy and society. In doing so, it fundamentally decouples economic growth from resource usage and recouples economic growth with societal progress—presenting a much-needed solutions framework for tackling our global challenges.

 The Linear Versus the Circular Economy

A **linear economy** refers to the traditional industrial model that follows a "take, make, waste" process in which raw materials are extracted, turned into products, and after being used or consumed, the products are typically thrown away as non-recyclable waste (or at most, they are recycled or downcycled). This is our mainstream economic model today.

In a **circular economy**, growth is decoupled from the consumption of scarce resources. Products and materials are kept within productive use for as long as possible, and when they reach end of use, they are effectively cycled (or looped) back into the system. Arriving at true circularity means rethinking and transforming full value chains to create a system in which waste is designed out entirely and the goal is net positivity (adding instead of extracting resources) through restorative models. The circular and continuous flow of both technical and biological materials through "value circles" is illustrated by The Circular Economy Systems Diagram (see Fig. 1.1).

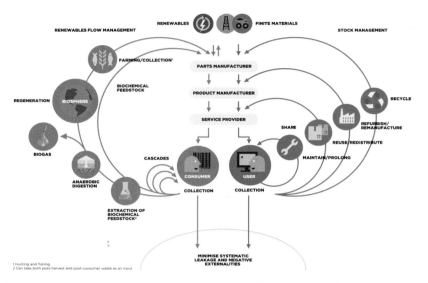

Fig. 1.1 Circular economy systems diagram[34] (*Source* Ellen MacArthur Foundation, SUN, and McKinsey Center for Business and Environment; Drawing from Braungart & McDonough, Cradle to Cradle [C2C])

Moving to a circular economy has the potential to do more than deliver the disruptive changes needed to secure a sustainable future. It will also open exciting new possibilities for businesses to enter new markets with innovative products and services, clearing the path to long-term growth. Equally important, it is an opportunity for companies to rethink the resource use of their operations and supply chains and the associated contribution to their cost base. Further benefits include the impact on brand, trust, and reputation that comes with clarity of purpose in attracting talent or delighting consumers. In short, the circular economy can help protect the environment and address societal challenges while also enabling organizations to achieve competitive advantage.

That advantage will be based on finding ways to not just balance but positively connect and reinforce the three foundational components of the new framework of competitive agility as defined by Accenture: growth and customers, profitability, and sustainability and trust (see Fig. 1.2).[33]

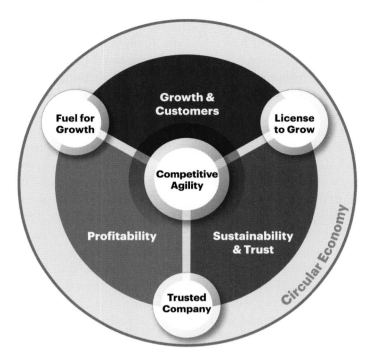

Fig. 1.2 Competitive agility framework

We first articulated the competitive advantage that could be gained through the circular economy in *Waste to Wealth*. Published in 2015, the book described the significant opportunity for value capture that was on the table for organizations that incorporate five new circular business models and ten enabling technologies into their business construct. Since then, we've come a long way—Accenture Strategy has analyzed more than 1500 circular case studies via The Circulars program, the world's premier circular economy award initiative run in collaboration with the World Economic Forum, an international organization that engages the political, business and other leaders of society to shape global, regional, and industry agendas.[35] In addition, we've worked for and collaborated with companies and partners, many of which have been interviewed for this book, to deliver leading circular economy strategies around the globe. From this work, we have found that, although significant progress has been made, *it is not enough*. Specifically, although organizations have proven the business case for circularity through the adoption of circular business models and disruptive technologies, those efforts have generally focused on "quick wins," small-scale initiatives, or programs that could be retrofitted into business-as-usual environments. But competitive advantage is about fundamentally reengineering the business. **More must be done to reach the full value potential of the circular economy**.

So, what's needed? We found that true impact and scale will only be delivered when companies deploy circular business models and Fourth Industrial Revolution (4IR) technologies in a holistic manner to capture new growth opportunities while also strengthening their core business (see "What is the Fourth Industrial Revolution?"). We refer to this as a "wise pivot"—a term that our colleagues Omar Abbosh, Paul Nunes, and Larry Downes have written extensively about in the context of digital transformation in particular.[36] To accomplish that pivot within the circular context, companies must do three things simultaneously: (1) transform the existing value chain to remove waste and increase efficiencies to drive up investment capacity, (2) grow the core business organically by embedding circular offerings to sustain the fuel for investments, and (3) invest in and scale entirely new, disruptive circular businesses.

 What Is the Fourth Industrial Revolution?

The First Industrial Revolution used water and steam power to mechanize production. The Second Industrial Revolution relied on electric power to create mass production. The Third Industrial Revolution deployed electronics and information technology to automate production. Now a Fourth Industrial Revolution is building on the third, the digital revolution that has been occurring since the middle of the last century. It is characterized by a fusion of technologies that is blurring the lines between the physical, digital, and biological spheres. The diversity and combinatorial potential of these technologies has the power to bring about constant, exponential change to businesses and to societies around the world.[37]

Of course, we recognize this is not simple nor straightforward, but the stakes couldn't be higher. Not only are we talking about the creation of an economic system that puts people and nature first, we are also referring to enormous economic value at risk of not being captured. In *Waste to Wealth*, Accenture estimated this value at $4.5 trillion by 2030. This is between 4 and 5% of the projected global Gross Domestic Product (GDP), more than the entire German economy today (the world's fourth largest).[38] Since 2015, when the book was published, we have revisited these calculations and found no substantial change in the scale of that opportunity. In fact, this estimate is probably fairly conservative. It assumes that we have until 2050 to get to a "one-planet economy"; it expects that we can continue to become more efficient at extracting value from resources; and it does not account for the likely cascading effects that resource shortages would have on the global economy.

Based on our experience, our extensive research, and our close work with our partners at the World Economic Forum, we know that the opportunity is not only huge but entirely within reach. The bottom line is that we have just a decade to make substantial progress toward a circular transition, much of which must be pioneered by the private sector. Considerable investments are needed to implement and scale circular solutions, and **the time to act is now**. But how, exactly, should companies proceed?

The Way Forward

Given the seriousness of these challenges, there's been no shortage of proposed solutions and approaches, leading to considerable confusion for many companies. Do businesses need to completely overhaul themselves, revamp everything from top to bottom, or would less drastic changes suffice? We believe *both* transformation and incremental change will need to happen in parallel, given that some organizations are ready to disrupt and move fast while others need to move more slowly. The purpose of *The Circular Economy Handbook* is not to advise companies where on the spectrum they should fall, but to bring a deep level of pragmatism to all organizations, regardless of their starting point. The book, therefore, is designed as a practical guide to support executives with useful strategies and actionable insights through illustration of our key learnings and numerous case studies. The goal is for readers to learn how to scale the circular economy within their organizations and drive competitive advantage throughout their value chains. For easy referral, we have organized *The Circular Economy Handbook* in three major sections:

Part I. Where Are We Now?—Setting the Foundation

First, we provide an update on the five *circular business models* that were first introduced in *Waste to Wealth*: Circular Inputs, Sharing Platform, Product as a Service, Product Use Extension, and Resource Recovery. Each of these circular models can help companies address the four types of waste (resources, capacity, lifecycles, and embedded value). We also identify the five key enablers that are crucial to accelerate adoption: consumer engagement, design, reverse logistics, disruptive technologies, and ecosystems. We then highlight the *disruptive technologies* of the Fourth Industrial Revolution that are essential for circular impact. These technologies fall into three categories—digital, physical, and biological—and can enable the circular business models through increased efficiency, greater innovation, enhanced information transparency, and reduced reliance on resource-intensive materials, especially when the technologies are used in combination.

Part II. Where Do We Need to Be?—Scaling Industry Impact

The circular economy cuts across our entire economic system, but each industry has unique challenges and will experience the transition differently. In this section, we provide a profile on 10 major *industries*, identifying their biggest waste pools and challenges, along with the areas that present the greatest opportunities. We also highlight examples of enabling technologies and obstacles for players in the industry to overcome in their circular journey. In addition, we examine strategies for how leading companies can realize the value in their bottom line with a set of initiatives to illustrate the scale of impact that can be attained by incorporating circularity within an industry value chain. We hope that by providing profiles on a range of industries, one can learn leading practices that cut across different sectors of the economy.

Part III. How Do We Get There?—Making the Pivot

Companies need to learn how to implement and scale circular initiatives. This requires the transformation and growth of the core business, while scaling new initiatives in parallel. To accomplish that, organizations must implement a "wise pivot" and they need to advance their circular maturity across four dimensions:[36]

- *Operations*: Addressing the value lost through operations and by-products of business processes with respect to energy, emissions, water, and waste.
- *Products & Services*: Rethinking the design, lifecycle, and end of use of a product or service to optimize its usage, eliminate waste, and close product loops.

- *Culture & Organization*: Embedding circular principles into the fabric of an organization through redefined working practices, policies, and procedures.
- *Ecosystem*: Collaborating and partnering with public- and private-sector actors to create an enabling environment for collective transformation. This includes examining the essential role of *Investment* and *Policy*, which are detailed in two "deep dive" chapters.

Although companies may be inclined to focus first on the dimensions within their immediate control, it is important they consider all four dimensions holistically in their maturity journeys to capture that systems-change mindset. Only then will they be able to capture the highest levels of value from their circular initiatives.

*   *   *

As we discussed at the start of this chapter, the social and environmental pressures we face are daunting. But the circular economy offers us an alternative. It can help us address environmental challenges before they reach a global tipping point, with societies and organizations thriving in parallel. Our hope is that this book will help you chart your own organization's path and enable you to navigate through it, armed with the knowledge to make the transition from a linear to a circular business, and to deploy circular business models that can deliver the disruptive changes needed to secure a sustainable future and inclusive growth. That journey begins in the following chapter, with a better understanding of waste and the five business models that can help transform it into a valuable resource.

Notes

1. Australian Academy of Science, "Population and Environment: A Global Challenge," https://www.science.org.au/curious/earth-environment/population-environment (accessed August 9, 2019).
2. *Financial Times*, "More Than Half the World's Population Is Now Middle Class," https://www.ft.com/content/e3fa475c-c2e9-11e8-95b1-d36dfef1b89a (accessed August 9, 2019).
3. European Commission, "Growing Consumerism," https://ec.europa.eu/knowledge4policy/foresight/topic/growing-consumerism_en (accessed August 9, 2019).
4. World Economic Forum in partnership with Marsh & McLennan Companies and Zurich Insurance Group, "The Global Risks Report 2019

14th Edition," http://www3.weforum.org/docs/WEF_Global_Risks_Report_
2019.pdf (accessed August 30, 2019).

5. Earth Overshoot Day, "Global Footprint Network," 2019, https://www.
overshootday.org/newsroom/past-earth-overshoot-days/ (accessed August
12, 2019).

6. Prasad Modak, "Environmental Management Towards Sustainability," CRC
Press, 2017.

7. World Health Organization, "Drinking-Water," June 14, 2019, https://www.
who.int/en/news-room/fact-sheets/detail/drinking-water (accessed August 9,
2019).

8. Mesfin M. Mekonnen and Arjen Y. Hoekstra, "Four Billion People Facing
Severe Water Scarcity," Science Advances, February 12, 2016, https://
advances.sciencemag.org/content/2/2/e1500323/tab-figures-data (accessed
August 9, 2019).

9. UN News, "UN Spotlights Rainwater Recycling, Artificial Wetlands Among
'Green' Solutions to Global Water Crisis," March 19, 2018, https://news.
un.org/en/story/2018/03/1005332 (accessed August 9, 2019).

10. Ellen MacArthur Foundation, "The New Plastics Economy: Rethinking the
Future of Plastics," https://www.ellenmacarthurfoundation.org/assets/down-
loads/EllenMacArthurFoundation_TheNewPlasticsEconomy_Pages.pdf
(accessed August 9, 2019).

11. World Health Organization, "How Air Pollution Is Destroying Our Health,"
October 29, 2018, https://www.who.int/air-pollution/news-and-events/how-
air-pollution-is-destroying-our-health (accessed August 9, 2019).

12. Nat Clim Chang, "Future Global Mortality Changes in Air Pollution
Attributable to Climate Change," The National Center for Biotechnology
Information, July 31, 2017, https://www.ncbi.nlm.nih.gov/pmc/articles/
PMC6150471/ (accessed August 9, 2019).

13. World Wildlife Fund, "A Warning Sign from Our Planet: Nature Needs Life
Support," October 30, 2018, https://www.wwf.org.uk/updates/living-plan-
et-report-2018 (accessed August 9, 2019).

14. The World Counts, "Coral Reef Destruction Facts," https://www.theworld-
counts.com/counters/ocean_ecosystem_facts/coral_reef_destruction_facts
(accessed August 9, 2019).

15. Food and Agriculture Organization of the UN, "The State of the World's
Biodiversity for Food and Agriculture," 2019, http://www.fao.org/
state-of-biodiversity-for-food-agriculture/en/ (accessed August 9, 2019).

16. Mikaela Weisse and Liz Goldman, "2017 Was the Second-Worst Year on
Record for Tropical Tree Cover Loss," Global Forest Watch, June 27, 2018,
https://blog.globalforestwatch.org/data-and-research/2017-was-the-second-
worst-year-on-record-for-tropical-tree-cover-loss (accessed August 9, 2019).

17. Joe Cochrane, "Blazes in South East Asia May Have Led to Deaths of Over
100,000, Study Says," *The New York Times*, September 19, 2016, https://

www.nytimes.com/2016/09/20/world/asia/indonesia-haze-smog-health. html (accessed August 9, 2019).

18. IPCC, "Special Report: Global Warming of 1.5 °C," https://www.ipcc.ch/ sr15/chapter/summary-for-policy-makers/ (accessed August 9, 2019).

19. Reuters, "Global Temperatures on Track for 3–5 Degree Rise by 2100: U.N.," November 29, 2018, https://uk.reuters.com/article/us-climate-change-un/global-temperatures-on-track-for-3-5-degree-rise-by-2100-u-n-idUKKCN1NY186 (accessed August 9, 2019).

20. Ove Hoegh-Guldberg, Daniela Jacob, Michael Taylor, et al., "Impacts of 1.5 °C Global Warming on Natural and Human Systems," IPCC, https://report. ipcc.ch/sr15/pdf/sr15_chapter3.pdf (accessed August 9, 2019).

21. UN Climate Change, "What Is the Paris Agreement?" https://unfccc.int/ process-and-meetings/the-paris-agreement/what-is-the-paris-agreement (accessed August 9, 2019).

22. The Climate Change Group, "The World's Most Influential Companies Committed to 100% Renewable Power," https://www.theclimategroup.org/ RE100 (accessed August 9, 2019).

23. Louise Hazan, Yossi Cadan, Richard Brooks, et al., "1000 Divestment Commitments and Counting," Gofossilfree.org, 2018, https://gofossilfree. org/wp-content/uploads/2018/12/1000divest-WEB-.pdf (accessed August 9, 2019).

24. Damian Carrington, "Public Concern Over Environment Reaches Record High in UK," *The Guardian*, June 5, 2019, https://www.theguardian.com/ environment/2019/jun/05/greta-thunberg-effect-public-concern-over-environment-reaches-record-high (accessed August 9, 2019).

25. Suyin Haynes, "Students from 1600 Cities Just Walked Out of School to Protest Climate Change. It Could Be Greta Thunberg's Biggest Strike Yet," *Time*, May 24, 2019, https://time.com/5595365/global-climate-strikes-greta-thunberg/ (accessed August 9, 2019).

26. Material Economics, "The Circular Economy—A Powerful Force for Climate Mitigation," https://europeanclimate.org/wp-content/uploads/2018/06/ MATERIAL-ECONOMICS-CIRCULAR-ECONOMY-WEBB-SMALL2. pdf (accessed August 30, 2019).

27. United States Environmental Protection Agency, "Global Greenhouse Gas Emissions Data," https://www.epa.gov/ghgemissions/global-greenhouse-gas-emissions-data (accessed September 2, 2019).

28. United Nations Climate Change, "Action on Climate and SDGs," https:// unfccc.int/topics/action-on-climate-and-sdgs/action-on-climate-and-sdgs (accessed September 2, 2019).

29. European Parliament, "Parliament Seals Ban on Throwaway Plastics by 2021," March 27, 2019, http://www.europarl.europa.eu/news/en/press-room/20190321IPR32111/parliament-seals-ban-on-throwaway-plastics-by-2021 (accessed August 9, 2019).

30. Stephen Buranyi, "The Plastic Backlash: What's Behind Our Sudden Rage—And Will It Make a Difference?" *The Guardian*, November 13, 2018, https://www.theguardian.com/environment/2018/nov/13/the-plastic-back-lash-whats-behind-our-sudden-rage-and-will-it-make-a-difference (accessed August 9, 2019).

31. Doug Woodring and Trish Hyde, "From Plastic Waste Trade War to Circular Economy," Urbanet, April 9, 2019, https://www.urbanet.info/from-plastic-waste-trade-war-to-circular-economy/.

32. Robert Williams, "Forrester: Millennials Boost Growth of Sharing Economy," Mobile Marketer, January 30, 2018, https://www.mobile-marketer.com/news/forrester-millennials-boost-growth-of-sharing-economy/515851/ (accessed August 19, 2019).

33. Mark Pearson and Bull Theafilou, "Formula Won: A New Way to Measure Corporate Competitiveness," Accenture Strategy, 2017, https://www.accenture.com/_acnmedia/PDF-57/Accenture-Formula-Won-PoV.pdf#zoom=50 (accessed August 9, 2019).

34. Ellen MacArthur Foundation, "Infographic: Circular Economy System Diagram," https://www.ellenmacarthurfoundation.org/circular-economy/infographic (accessed August 27, 2019).

35. The Circulars in collaboration with Accenture Strategy, "About the Circulars," www.thecirculars.org (accessed August 12, 2019).

36. Accenture, "Make Your Wise Pivot to the New," 2018, https://www.accenture.com/_acnmedia/PDF-79/Accenture-Make-Your-Wise-Pivot.pdf (accessed August 9, 2019).

37. Klaus Schwab, "The Fourth Industrial Revolution: What It Means, How to Respond," World Economic Forum, January 14, 2016 https://www.weforum.org/agenda/2016/01/the-fourth-industrial-revolution-what-it-means-and-how-to-respond/ (accessed August 9, 2019).

38. Accenture Research.

Part I

Where are We Now?—Setting the Foundation

2

The Circular Business Models

In *Waste to Wealth* (2015), we identified a global opportunity worth $4.5 trillion that was up for grabs by redefining the concept of "waste" as a valuable resource. We focused on four distinct types of waste categories from which to capture this value (see Fig. 2.1):

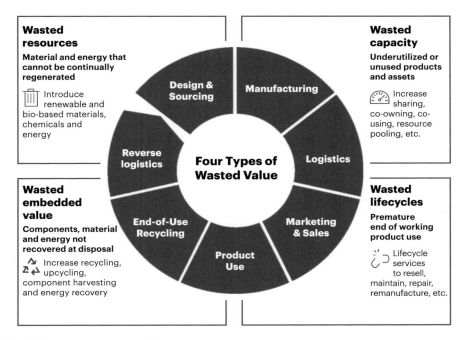

Wasted resources
Material and energy that cannot be continually regenerated

Introduce renewable and bio-based materials, chemicals and energy

Wasted capacity
Underutilized or unused products and assets

Increase sharing, co-owning, co-using, resource pooling, etc.

Wasted embedded value
Components, material and energy not recovered at disposal

Increase recycling, upcycling, component harvesting and energy recovery

Wasted lifecycles
Premature end of working product use

Lifecycle services to resell, maintain, repair, remanufacture, etc.

Design & Sourcing — Manufacturing — Logistics — Marketing & Sales — Product Use — End-of-Use Recycling — Reverse logistics

Four Types of Wasted Value

Fig. 2.1 Four categories of waste

P. Lacy et al., *The Circular Economy Handbook*,
https://doi.org/10.1057/978-1-349-95968-6_2

- **Wasted resources**: Use of materials and energy that cannot be effectively regenerated over time, such as fossil energy and non-recyclable material.
- **Wasted capacity**: Products and assets that are not fully utilized throughout their useful life.
- **Wasted lifecycles**: Products reaching end of use prematurely due to poor design or lack of second-use options.
- **Wasted embedded value**: Components, material, and energy not recovered from waste streams.

To seize the opportunity value of redefining waste, we introduced five business models underpinning the transformation to a circular economy (see Fig. 2.2). Taken individually, or combined, these models help transform traditionally linear "take, make, dispose" approaches of production and consumption into circular approaches that minimize or even eliminate waste, pollution, and inefficiencies. Over the past five years, these models have been widely recognized by various public and private sector organizations as a viable approach for implementing circular economy strategies. However, the scale of adoption has not been equally distributed across the models, and the pace of implementation has been slower than hoped. Our analysis and experience show that there is still more work to be done to fully leverage the benefits of the circular models. The following sections highlight our key learnings and insights over the last several years, drawn from research, direct work with companies on their circular economy efforts, and engagement in multilateral discussions.

Five Ways to Create Circular Value

The uptake of the five circular business models has been disparate across geography, industry, business size and structure, and product type. While progress needs to be made by harnessing *each* of the models to drive true scale and impact within the circular economy, they are not mutually exclusive—the business models have the potential to create the greatest impact when they work together to generate maximum value. For example, Desso, a carpet manufacturer, applies Cradle to Cradle™ principles to design products that are intended to be taken back and recycled under a leasing agreement, thereby combining two circular business models: *Resource Recovery* and *Product as a Service*.[1]

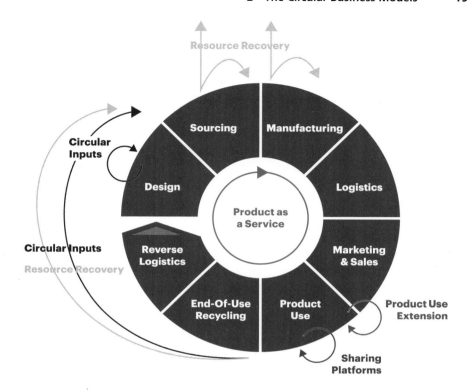

Typical value chain

 CIRCULAR INPUTS
Use of renewable energy,
bio-based or potentially
completely recyclable materials

 SHARING PLATFORMS
Increased usage rates through
collaborative models for usage,
access, or ownership

 PRODUCT USE EXTENSION
Prolongation of product use
through repair, reprocessing,
upgrading and resale

 PRODUCT AS A SERVICE
Offer of product use with retention
of the product at the producer to
increase resource productivity

 RESOURCE RECOVERY
Recovery of usable resources
or energy from waste
or by-products

Fig. 2.2 Circular value loop—the five business models

While three of the models are more focused on production (Circular Inputs, Product Use Extension, and Resource Recovery), the other two

(Sharing Platforms and Product as a Service) target consumption and the relationship between the product and the consumer. Essentially, the models cover the full value chain of circularity. *Circular Inputs* focus on the "ingredients" that go into products at the design, sourcing, and manufacturing stages. These inputs, such as renewable resources, aim to eliminate *wasted resources* (including toxic and single-use materials) and are a stepping stone for all other models. In some of the more advanced examples, Circular Inputs can go beyond zero-waste to be resource-additive (e.g., where waste streams are processed into material streams). *Product Use Extension* focuses on maximizing the use of a product. To do so, companies must start from the very beginning (specifically, product design and responsible sourcing) in order to avoid *wasted lifecycles* and keep products in use for as long as possible. In addition, *Product Use Extension* plays an important role in enabling the *Product as a Service* and *Sharing Platforms* models. The latter two go further by reinventing "product utility" in entirely new ways (e.g., buying a function or service, like mobility, rather than the product itself—a vehicle). This in turn incentivizes companies to derive the maximum value and utilization out of products, addressing *wasted capacity* and *wasted lifecycles*. Once a product reaches end of use, the role of *Resource Recovery* is to return the embedded materials or energy back into the production cycle, thereby "closing the loop" of the product from sourcing to usage and back to sourcing.

As discussed in the Introduction, the ultimate goal of the circular economy is a holistic closure of the entire "take, make, waste" cycle. Obviously, achieving that ambitious target will require a long-term massive shift in the current way of doing business, but significant progress can be made over the short term by focusing on multiple localized value pools. Specifically, within any circular value chain "loop", companies can focus on closing multiple "mini-loops" (see Fig. 2.2); for example, a waste stream from one production step could be re-processed into a useful by-product, or the feedstock for another process could come from a secondary material source. Consider the growing use of food production waste as a source of energy for the facility in which it is produced. Downstream, there are additional marketplace-related mini-loops that help consumers resell used products, from toys and clothing to boats and semi-tractors. These loops can cross-industry boundaries (one industry using the waste of another industry as an input) and geographies, presenting numerous opportunities for the adoption of the five circular business models across the global economy.

To tap into those opportunities, executives need to understand the five circular business models in greater detail. In this chapter, we discuss the current rates of adoption, key success factors, and common obstacles for each of the models, and we provide examples of their deployment.

Circular Inputs

Renewable, recycled, or highly recyclable inputs are used in the production process, enabling partial or total elimination of waste and pollution.

Circular Inputs, also understood as "Circular Supplies" or "Circular Supply Chain," is one of the most adopted circular business models by companies to date. To implement it, an organization must replace a "linear" type of resource in its supply chain with a "circular" alternative. These solutions can be broadly categorized into three groups:

- **Renewable resources**: Inputs that replenish naturally and can be used repeatedly, e.g., water from rain harvesting or desalination processes, wind and solar energy, hydrogen fuel from excess renewable energy, etc.
- **Renewable bio-based materials**: Materials such as bioplastics and microbial agrochemical solutions that are developed from chemistry derived from living organisms.
- **Renewable man-made materials**: Engineered materials based on non-organic chemistry that can be recycled infinitely without a substantial loss of quality or physical properties.

In the short to medium term, a company should identify, prioritize, and implement the substitution of production inputs with circular alternatives where operationally and commercially viable. In the long term though, the goal is to close and dematerialize resource loops completely, thereby eliminating waste, in a continuous collaboration with a broad spectrum of cross-industry and cross-sector stakeholders. In other words, the first part of the *Circular Inputs* journey is about phasing out the use of "linear" resources (and waste), whereas the second stage tosses out the concept of waste altogether as part of a holistic change to production systems.

To date, the adoption of *Circular Inputs* has largely been driven by the replacement of linear feedstocks, such as non-renewable or recyclable resources, with alternatives that have a lesser environmental impact. Amid that activity, legislation and subsidies aimed at "greening" the economy have emerged and become mainstream, with the growing prominence of environmental sustainability in the public dialogue (e.g., the EU's ban of single-use plastics and bee-harming pesticides).[2] Below we discuss two areas that have thus far been critical to the success of the *Circular Inputs* model: renewable energy and material innovation.

Renewable Energy

Growing concern over climate change has helped to spur large-scale financing of renewable energy projects, leading to cheaper, reliable, and improved technologies. As a result, renewables will be the fastest-growing energy source in the electricity sector, forecasted to make up over 70% of global electricity generation growth from 2017 to 2023.[3] That progress aside, we need to reduce or eliminate our reliance on carbon-intensive sources such as fossil fuels at a much faster pace. Unfortunately, several barriers, including technological and financial limitations, inhibit the deployment of renewable energy in new markets, while integrating renewable generation into the grid continues to be an obstacle in established markets.[4] Multinational organizations with heavy energy footprints can lead the way and should consider scaling investments in renewable energy capacity as part of their long-term energy strategies.

Material Innovation

For years, formal and informal media sources have been exposing the environmental damage caused by various material streams—from chlorofluorocarbons in the 1990s to microplastic pollution more recently—leading to heightened public concerns and an awareness of the need for regulatory action. At the same time, resource scarcity has impacted most sectors, from cotton to gold to rare earth minerals. The result has been a tangible increase in research and development activity in the search for alternative solutions, as well as a push by established companies to patent and commercialize new circular materials for inclusion in their future production.[5] Take, for example, Sulapac, a Finnish packaging material manufacturing company, and its biodegradable packaging solution made from wood chips and natural binders as an alternative to traditional single-use packaging made from petroleum-based plastic.[6]

Ultimately, to be successful, a material innovation must be more than just circular; it also needs to satisfy other criteria, including quality standards and cost parity. As such, when considering a new material, companies should focus on functionality, usability, and reusability, and the volume requirements needed to help achieve cost parity. Lifecycle assessments may also help limit any potential unintended environmental impacts, such as the increased energy intensity required to create a reusable material. To help in that analysis, innovations such as the so-called material passports can provide information about materials throughout the lifecycle, facilitating recovery at end of use.[7] A material passport contains data associated with a specific product, including the characteristics of that item's materials, that facilitate the recovery, recycling, or reuse of those resources. To further accelerate the transition to more circular inputs, organizations need to look beyond organizational borders, assessing systemic material flows, opportunities, and barriers. For example, TriCiclos, a circular economy engineering company, through its waste management divisions in Latin America, leveraged its recycling infrastructure network to analyze waste, and that information has helped companies like PepsiCo and The Coca-Cola Company to redesign their packaging and to develop new materials.[8] Engaging with the circular economy at this level requires a culture of collaboration with suppliers, peers, partners, and customers. We will describe this in greater detail in the subsequent chapters on organizational culture and ecosystems.

 Case Study: Nike

Nike, a multinational footwear and apparel company, has achieved a number of successes in material innovation with its own Nike Grind materials, which generate inputs for new footwear, apparel, and surfaces in sport facilities.[9] Using a collection of "waste" materials (recycled athletic footwear and surplus manufacturing scraps), the company has been able to develop new high-performance products. Roughly, 73% of all Nike shoes and apparel contain some recycled material, while 98.2% of manufacturing waste is diverted from landfills.[10] Nike's Flyleather material, for example, is made with at least 50% recycled natural leather fiber from leather scraps, with a similar look, feel, and even smell of virgin leather.[11] Moreover, the material allows for a more efficient cutting process, generating less waste compared with traditional leather. Even more impressive, 100% of the polyester fibers in Flyknit yarn is recycled.[12]

Sharing Platforms

The utilization rates of products and assets are optimized through shared ownership, access, and usage typically enabled by digital technologies.

A *Sharing Platform* enables owners to maximize how assets are used, while building a community and providing customers with affordable and convenient access to products and services. Adoption of this model has occurred across various markets and geographies (albeit with comparatively lower levels of deployment by multinationals), with focus mainly on high-value categories, such as vehicles and accommodation.[13] Although the growth of *Sharing Platforms* as a concept has recently flourished, thanks to the advancement of the platform economy, so far we have found few examples of scaled *Sharing Platforms* with circular principles built-in intentionally.

For large corporations, *Sharing Platforms* often require a substantial change to existing business models or the setup of a new venture to facilitate experimentation. Getting consensus on the strategy, format, functionality, and business model demands a good amount of exploration and finetuning, especially for more risk-averse, established businesses. Consequently, multinational corporations are slower to embrace this model. Instead, start-ups have led the way, radically disrupting their respective industries in the business-to-consumer (B2C) market (e.g., home and ride-sharing platforms like Airbnb, Lyft, and ZipCar) and local small businesses. Over the last few years, though, *Sharing Platforms* have begun to make inroads with big multinationals as well. Marriott, one of the world's largest hotel chains, recently launched Homes & Villas, an Airbnb competitor for premium home-share rentals, while a number of the established rent-a-car companies, including Avis and Enterprise, currently offer "car sharing."[14,15,16] At present, *Sharing Platforms* have proliferated throughout numerous industries, from fashion and accessories to shared workspaces, tools, and machinery, including many examples in the business-to-business space (B2B). In fact, B2B sharing might present the most promising opportunities for large corporations, especially for businesses which maintain high-cost assets that have low utilization rates. For example, Cohealo is a platform for hospitals to share and maximize the efficient use of medical equipment.[17]

In emerging markets, the increased penetration of smartphones has created a strong launchpad for sharing services. India and China, for example, have seen a surge of *Sharing Platforms* with companies like RentSher and Didi Chuxing Technology.[19,20] Smart Factory Kunshan (SFK), a joint venture between a local government in Jiangsu Province and a German firm, helps around 30 early-stage companies access shared production and assembly facilities in their start-up factory, demonstrating adoption rates that, in some cases, are higher than in developed economies.[21,22] This isn't surprising, considering that much of the dramatic expansion in the global middle class over the next several years will occur in Asia.[23] Consumers in these economies increasingly desire services that offer convenience, customization, and cost-savviness, resulting in the growing adoption of *Sharing Platforms*. Accelerating urbanization—characterized by high population density, limited space, and efficient logistics—provides additional support for such models, especially in Asia and Africa, where 90% of urban growth is projected to take place.[24]

Case Study: eRENT

Based in Finland, start-up eRENT provides a Sharing Platform for construction equipment and machinery management. The platform enables customers to rent out and manage different types of equipment aggregated nationally through one digital channel, matching idle assets with new demand and improving the productivity of less efficient industry processes (e.g., booking equipment with rental depots over the phone). The service, which includes heavy-duty equipment as well as smaller handheld tools, is a one-stop shop for entire construction sites. On average, eRENT customers save 20% on equipment and machinery costs, thanks to various technologies including Internet of Things (IoT) tracking.[18]

Product as a Service

Companies retain ownership of a product and sell its benefits on a service basis while remaining responsible for the good's maintenance and treatment at end of use.

With the *Product as a Service* business model, products are used by one or more customers through a lease or pay-for-use arrangement. This approach turns the incentive for product durability and upgrading upside-down, shifting companies' focus from volume (i.e., selling "widgets") to performance (i.e., selling the function of that widget). Popular examples include tire company Michelin's pay-by-the-mile model for cargo fleets and lighting company Signify's offering, Light-as-a-Service (LaaS).[25] *Product as a Service* models are based on the premise that companies can generate additional value from their products by developing long-term relationships with customers, selling additional services (cross-selling or upselling), monetizing usage data, or extracting material value at the end-of-use stage.

Despite the increased potential for value generation, the uptake of the *Product as a Service* model at scale remains limited. Certainly, the shift from selling a product to selling a service is a fundamental change in a company's value proposition that introduces a host of complexities. For one thing, the "servitization" of a product involves the design, planning, and roll-out of multiple additional capabilities, from customer-service desks and account managers to the collection and reverse logistics systems, at the very least. Accordingly, companies need to invest in building out those key capabilities, and the potential costs associated with those efforts need to be absorbed by the pricing model and ultimately may increase the total cost of ownership over the entirety of the product's use. In addition, data ownership concerns can act as a deterrent for potential customers, especially in the business-to-business space, where operational data can offer a significant competitive advantage.

For these reasons, early-stage firms are currently better placed to implement a *Product as a Service* model as they tend to be more agile, less risk-averse, and better positioned to more quickly engage customers and tailor their branding. A critical success factor is developing accounting models that better align to products which are used as a service by several customers, rather than a one-time purchase by a single customer. Such models require a firm to adjust traditional financial expectations to account for longer lifecycles, product ownership and depreciation, takeback, servicing, and evaluation of how the residual value of an asset at the end of its life is integrated into business accounting records. In some cases, it may even warrant the establishment of a new venture and product range designed with the business model in mind.

The subscription model is a clear disrupter within *Product as a Service*. Spurred by the success of subscription-based services in the entertainment industry, adoption has now shifted to fashion, food, and grooming products. Overall, subscription-based services are growing at a rate of 200% annually since 2011, supported by an explosion in product variety and a more seamless experience unleashed by digital technologies.[26] The model works particularly well for premium goods that are highly desirable but not easily affordable, especially where product obsolescence is a significant factor. Consumer electronics are a prime example of such market dynamics, leading to the emergence of companies such as Grover, which rents cell phones, drones, gaming gear, and other electronics devices.[27] While the subscription model raises questions about over-consumption and excess choice, we believe models that appropriately handle returns, use-extension and next-use will be the winners in balancing consumer demand, affordability, and environmental impact.

Product as a Service models at scale remain a challenge for traditional businesses and companies focused on quarterly and annual financial performance. Compelling business case evidence would help organizations better understand the model's benefits (both tangible and intangible) and the financial re-engineering required (e.g., the change in cash flows, balance sheet extensions, credit risk considerations, and long-term uncertainty). Externally, engagement with customers and close collaboration in the service development is crucial.

Case Study: Rent the Runway

Rent the Runway is a US-based e-commerce company that provides an online service for designer dress and accessory rentals. Customers can rent high-end fashion from four to eight days for a fraction of the retail price (10% upwards), opening an entirely new market. Rent the Runway also offers subscription plans, where consumers pay a monthly fee to continuously refresh their wardrobe, and the plans include free shipping, dry cleaning, and rental insurance. The company has found that customers who sign up to their service reduce spending on clothing purchases, and since launching a circular packaging solution in 2015, more than 900 tons of shipping waste have been saved.[28,29] The company was valued at $1 billion in 2019.[30]

Product Use Extension

A product's use in its intended application is purposefully extended through design considerations, repairs, component reconditioning, upgrades, and resale on secondary markets.

With the *Product Use Extension* business model, companies optimize the use of a product in its original form and for its intended application. Consider, for example, how often a mobile phone is replaced for an upgraded model, when all that's really needed is an update to a core feature like the camera or battery. *Product Use Extension* is applied during or at the end of the product's first use. Instead of being disposed of, landfilled, or at best recycled, the item is repaired/reconditioned/updated to extend its use, or it is given a second use in a marketplace for used products. The business model encompasses a number of activities—from repairing, refurbishing, and upgrading, to trading in and reselling—some of which can be viewed as business models in their own right.

An advantage of *Product Use Extension* is that it does not require a wholesale change to a company's existing business model but rather an extension of business capabilities or market channels so that, for example, new revenue streams can be generated through resale. Importantly, by engaging people to extend the use of products they own, companies are able to create additional touch points with their customer base. This enhances customer centricity, develops brand loyalty, and supports the acquisition of additional product feedback. According to Rick Ridgeway, Patagonia's VP of Public Engagement, "Our repair facility is the largest in North America, completing more than 70,000 repairs in 2018 alone." Furthermore, adds Ridgeway, "The Worn Wear platform has attracted new customers to buy Patagonia clothing at a reduced price and strengthened our brand through stronger ties to existing customers. We've been able to use the insights and data collected on broken products to improve R&D, resulting in products of higher quality and improved longevity."

The key organizational challenge for adopting this business model, particularly where relatively low-value products are concerned, comes down to choosing the right format and scope for establishing an internal exploratory venture. At first glance, those decisions may not look that consequential, but implementing a *Product Use Extension* model often means acquiring new capabilities, potential changes to product design (e.g., increased modularity to allow for feature upgrades), and changes to financial models to offset concerns over reduced one-time product sales. Take Vitsoe, for example, a furniture design company that sells a "Universal Shelving System," a modular and upgradeable shelving system that is designed to be long-lasting and upgradeable with new shelves, drawers, and other additions and can be easily dismantled and re-built.[31]

Other innovations are emerging across a variety of industries, including electronics, fashion, and furniture. In the fashion industry, adoption has largely been driven by premium brands or by companies like clothing retail company H&M that is implementing models that shift the design criteria for clothing to focus more on quality, longevity, and the resale of used items to environmentally conscious consumers—for example, H&M launched a pilot in Sweden to sell second-hand clothing.[32] As a result, the fashion resale market is estimated to be growing 24 times faster than traditional retail.[33] The world's biggest producer of affordable design furniture, IKEA, is also making strides with *Product Use Extension* models. In France and Belgium, the company's "Second Life for Furniture" initiative lets customers exchange old items for a store voucher.[34] IKEA also leases office furniture to enterprise clients in Switzerland and is piloting the sale of used furniture in the UK. The leasing scheme will be expanded to many more countries by 2020.[35]

 Case Study: Schneider Electric

The French multinational energy management company Schneider Electric extends the use of its switchboards by replacing switchgear components at the customer site to renew, upgrade, or add new functionalities. Extending the usefulness of equipment can save up to 65% of the cost of new installations. Returned switchboards and accessories can be reused and obsolete components can be refurbished, repaired, or recycled to minimize waste. For example, the switchgear housing, plugs, lights, switches, and extra cabinets can be reused, and cables and wires can be kept for future use. This results in the prevention of carbon dioxide emissions (40 tonnes, equivalent to 8 cars traveling around the world) and a reduction in water (389 kiloliters, equivalent to 7 years of water consumption for an average European consumer) and energy intensity (750,000 megajoules, equivalent to 135 barrels of oil).[36]

Resource Recovery

The value of embedded materials or energy from agricultural and industrial goods is captured through collection, aggregation, and processing at the end of a product's use through recycling, upcycling, or downcycling infrastructures and practices.

Perhaps it should come as no surprise that, as an extension of traditional waste management, *Resource Recovery* has become the most widely adopted business model. *Resource Recovery* focuses on the end stages of the value chain, namely the recovery of materials and resources from products at the end of use that are no longer functional in their current application. Ideally, the recovered resource is used in a way that maintains its highest possible value for the longest period of time, e.g., steel recovered at the end of a vehicle's use that is reused in the making of another vehicle or upcycled in higher-value applications rather than being downcycled into lower-value products. In this context, companies should keep in mind the "hierarchy of waste" when identifying ways to create value from end-of-use products (see Fig. 2.3). Businesses should aim high, keeping in mind that closed-loop solutions are optimal, although they may be complex and not always technically feasible. Solutions that reduce material quality should only be considered as a last resort.

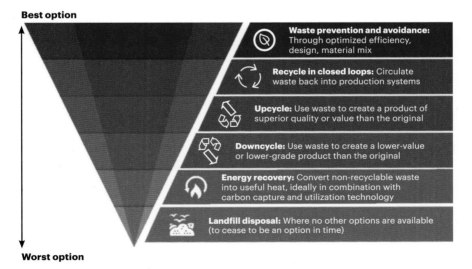

Fig. 2.3 Hierarchy of waste from a circular economy point of view

To date, there's a wide range of organizations that have adopted at least some form of *Resource Recovery*. Companies are recovering everything from valuable metal from electronic waste, to plastic from packaging and even cigarette butts, in the pursuit of generating value from waste streams and manufacturing by-products. Given that most organizations have some form of a waste management strategy, this model requires minimal adaptation of existing business structures and is less disruptive than others.

Even so, the untapped potential for scaling existing solutions is still considerable, from increasing the quantity of collected and processed waste to improving the quality of the recycled output or by-products. In general, the present-day economics and technological capabilities (e.g., for sorting or disassembly) have limited the amount and type of resources that can be recovered under business-as-usual operations. Collection and separation remain costly, and the existing waste-related infrastructure is often ill-equipped to serve the quantity or quality requirements of buyers. But as technology improves (and costs fall), as data become more abundant, and as new innovative solutions automate what previously was labor intensive, organizations will be looking into recovering (and obtaining a greater value of) increasing volumes of wasted resources. *Resource Recovery* models will also gain wider adoption thanks to resource shortages and regulatory changes, such as Extended Producer Responsibility (EPR) levies that require companies to be responsible for the treatment and disposal of their products, as well as increasing consumer pressure to address waste issues. For their part, businesses need to provide incentives to engage consumers, encourage product returns, and foster long-term behavioral change. The incentives could be financial, such as technology company Apple's GiveBack program (for electronics products) and the reGAIN App (for clothing), through which customers can turn in their used products for credit and discount vouchers that can be applied against future purchases.[37,38]

Case Study: Veolia

Veolia, a water, waste, and energy management solutions company, helps its clients to better manage their waste and to recover valuable resources at end of use. As part of that process, the company is constantly developing new technologies for the recycling of packaging and optimization of recycling economic models, with 60% of the company's circular economy revenue attributed to recycling and material recovery. For Selfridges, a leading UK department store, Veolia analyzed the store's waste streams to increase the existing materials being recycled as well as to add new waste streams to recycling. As part of that project, Veolia engineered a way to recycle fibers from used coffee cups so that the resulting material could be used as the main input for the production of the store's classic yellow bags, tripling recycling rates from 15% to 55% and delivering 100% diversion from landfill.[39]

Accelerating the Transition

As highlighted in the previous section, the five business models are being deployed by companies, but numerous barriers are impeding the rate and scale of that adoption. To overcome those obstacles, companies must devote time and attention to the following five key enablers.

Consumer Engagement: Re-Shape What It Means to Consume

"People don't want to buy a quarter-inch drill. They want a quarter-inch hole!" This widely quoted statement, from Theodore Levitt of the Harvard Business School, highlights that it isn't the products themselves that customers need, but the service or experience they provide. In other words, products, in many cases, are merely the delivery mechanism for a desired function or outcome. New, need-based business models such as *Sharing Platforms* and *Product as a Service* support this transition from ownership to access. This shift will become increasingly important for many businesses, as more and more consumers begin seeking products and services that they can access at the tap of a finger.

Another consideration is shifting demand preferences, with 66% of consumers globally stating they are willing to pay more for sustainable brands.[40] Indeed, over the past few years, there has been a growing public awareness of global climate and waste challenges. Accelerated by international dialogues, extreme weather events, and mainstream media coverage, awareness campaigns around waste production, disposal, and carbon dioxide emissions have become commonplace across multiple industries. This has had a large impact on the consciousness of a growing number of consumers, leading to various actions such as the banning of single-use plastic bags at supermarkets. It is worth noting though that consumer interest or intent does not always lead to changes in purchasing behavior, as cost and quality remain key factors for consumer purchasing decisions.

Moreover, the environmental impact of a company's choices is not always easy to understand, requiring organizations to raise levels of transparency and communication. Adam Lowry, Co-Founder of Ripple Foods, the dairy alternatives company, explains that, although there is growing awareness around topics like plastic waste, there is little understanding around the details. "A lot of biodegradable packaging is simply litter, but consumer perception is that plastic is evil," says Lowry. "There is a mismatch in understanding what the best circular materials are, and it's a challenge to change consumer perception." The approach at Ripple Foods is to be completely transparent with how the company makes decisions from a circular economy standpoint and to create feedback loops to improve over time. According to Lowry, "This is a different approach from other brands that simply add a label. Sometimes, branding can create a false sense of understanding with consumers. We try to float indicators of how we've made responsible choices, referencing primary scientific research, and we invite consumers to examine how we've made choices." As companies like Ripple demonstrate, educating consumers is important from a corporate responsibility perspective and can also help increase brand trust and engagement.

Design: Plan for Product Circularity

Until recently, product designs have typically failed to consider end-of-use scenarios as a key input. Since design sits at the start of a product's lifecycle—and circularity, for many, has focused on end of use—it has been a barrier, preventing the efficient use of products and hindering the recovery of their embedded materials at high quality. The majority of low-to-mid value products are designed for short-term use only, often with built-in obsolescence. Take, for instance, a simple cleaning spray bottle. The product might be labeled to indicate that it can be recycled, but the body of the bottle might be made of multiple polymer structures that are unfeasible to separate, and the metallic spring inside the bottle cannot be easily removed for reuse or recycling. Obsolescence is also an issue for high-value products, such as consumer electronics, where design features like seamless edges make disassembly particularly difficult. Given the rapid pace of technology changes, obsolescence is likely to remain a considerable challenge in the coming years, highlighting the need for more circular design practices (see Table 2.1).

Table 2.1 Circular design principles

Objectives	Illustrative principles
Product composition and production—use only circular or more sustainable materials	• Reduce or eliminate the need for materials and packaging • Use recycled/renewable materials and remanufactured components • Reduce SKUs (stock keeping units) and excess inventory waste • Choose alternative, less resource-intensive, and nontoxic materials • Design to eliminate or minimize waste during production processes
Product use—keep in useful life for as long as possible and reduce impact while in use	• Design for durability, modularity, repair/upgradeability, and efficiency while in use • Design to avoid single use and obsolescence • Deploy technologies to extend product use and enable recovery (e.g. for asset monitoring) • Deploy circular business models, designing products for sharing, leasing, and second life
Product recovery—enable materials or components to be easily brought back into a value chain	• Design for end of use disassembly, refurbishment and remanufacture • Choose materials that are recyclable or compostable at end of use

Design approaches need to incorporate circular principles to allow consumers to extend product usage and companies to recover valuable materials and eliminate waste at end of use. The Cradle to Cradle Certified™ Product Program, for instance, provides clear guidelines for evaluating material health, reutilization, renewable energy, carbon management, water stewardship, and social fairness.[41] A fundamental shift in design principles is required to fully enable *Resource Recovery* and *Product Use Extension* practices such as repair, refurbishment, and remanufacturing. For years, such design principles have tended to be considered for high-value goods, although not necessarily under the circular terminology umbrella. In fact, various machinery and equipment are based on modular, serviceable, and upgradeable principles. These include vehicle and aircraft components, information and communication technology (ICT) equipment, healthcare equipment, and so on. According to John Pflueger, Principal Environmental Strategist at Dell, a multinational technology company, "It is critically important to incorporate circular principles in the design phase. We are always seeking ways to make our products easy to repair and disassemble, and that starts with design." In contrast, few mass-produced, retail-distributed products are designed with circular and disassembly considerations. With increasing Extended Producer Responsibility (EPR) legislation, however, such products are slowly gaining the attention of designers and innovation departments at leading organizations. Still, for the majority of those items, current marketplace economics do not yet encourage circular designs. What's needed is a systemic shift across the product value spectrum.

Once design has been adapted for the disassembly and reuse of products, engaging in *Resource Recovery* activities can become an attractive business opportunity. To give an example, Scandinavian industrial group Moelven offers building walls as part of interior solutions that can be taken apart and re-assembled for a different design without requiring any new materials.[42] Given the increasing global volume of waste streams, the use of secondary materials poses a significant sourcing opportunity. Consider the following: 40% of the plastics produced is packaging, used only once and then discarded.[43] If such waste streams can be turned into secondary materials, then alternative sourcing channels could become strategically relevant. Sony's electronics products & solutions segment, for instance, uses up to 99% of recycled plastics in its electronics. An advantage of incorporating these features into design is that plastics can easily be used multiple times which, in turn, has the added benefit of lowering the carbon dioxide emissions in Sony's TV production by 80%.[44]

Reverse Logistics: Create Takeback Loops

Tackling infrastructure gaps so that manufacturers can receive idle, unwanted, damaged, underutilized, or end-of-use products is a priority for scaling circular economy models. Reverse logistics present a key capability, important for nearly all circular business models, particularly *Product as a Service*, *Sharing Platforms*, *Product Use Extension*, and *Resource Recovery*. This is not limited to the collection and aggregation of products and material, but extends to value-adding activities such as sorting, separating, reprocessing, and remarketing. It also includes links to requirements such as value chain tracing capability (to identify and document specific material content) and relevant waste regulations such as cross-border waste handling and EPR legislation.

What is Reverse Logistics?

Reverse logistics is "the process of moving goods from their typical final destination for the purpose of capturing value, or proper disposal."[45] It is a crucial part of a circular value chain, and one of the main differentiators between a traditional value chain and a circular one. Reverse logistics is the process that enables the circular loop (and associated "mini loops") to be closed. Managing the return and recovery of products from the consumer back into the value chain is a key tenet of the circular economy that enables products and materials to be recycled, reused, remanufactured, and so on.

Reverse logistics is at the heart of the complexity within a circular value chain. It hosts the same set of challenges as forward logistics, e.g., information, infrastructure, and capacity constraints; high warehousing and inventory costs; last-mile optimization challenges; and rising customer expectations on delivery speed. In addition, it presents an entirely different layer of complexity linked to the unpredictability of supply (both quantity and quality), the mechanisms to incentivize returns, and often the inadequate national and international networks for resource recovery. To address such issues, logistics company DHL partnered with Cranfield University in the UK and the Ellen MacArthur Foundation, a charity focused on supporting the transition to the circular economy, to develop the Reverse Logistics Maturity Model which structures key problem categories and potential solution approaches into three product-based archetypes: low-value Extended Producer Responsibility, service parts logistics, and advanced industrial products.[46] Such free practical guides spark further adoption of circular business models.

Another approach could be the use of a "white label" solution that supports a company with logistics, storage, and resale. Consider re-commerce company Yerdle, which handles the collection, logistics, repair, storage, and web development of fashion industry clients' secondary markets.[47]

Disruptive Technologies: Accelerate with 4IR Innovations

Fourth Industrial Revolution (4IR) technologies enable the smart use of resources and create new opportunities for the circular economy. Imagine the amount of effort required to share a passenger vehicle 30 years ago, when the vast majority of households had neither mobile devices nor Internet connections. Now, smart mobile devices and other 4IR innovations have drastically decreased the administrative costs of services far below the resource cost, leading to the deployment of various new business models (*Sharing Platforms* and *Product as a Service*). Such technologies also allow companies to track and monitor details of their assets' usability and functionality in real time, resulting in improved efficiencies and long-term value generation (*Product Use Extension*). The service provider Dirkzwager, for example, offers the remote monitoring and management of offshore assets like oil rigs throughout their use cycles.[48] This capability not only helps protect those valuable assets; it also improves the safety of shipping in congested waters, detects early oil spills, and otherwise prevents environmental pollution.

 What Are 4IR Technologies?

4IR technologies refer to the array of digital, physical, and biological technologies that are enabling the Fourth Industrial Revolution (4IR). Within the 4IR, technological breakthroughs are occurring at an exponential rate, disrupting almost every industry and population globally.[49] This will be explored further in the Disruptive Technologies chapter.

Other 4IR innovations help in the recovery of valuable materials (*Resource Recovery*). Consider AMP Robotics, a start-up that has developed a new kind of sorting technology for recycling facilities: the Cortex robot. Powered by advanced artificial intelligence (AI), Cortex can automate the separation of commodities with practically no retrofit or change to existing operations, thereby fundamentally changing the costs of recovering resources from waste. Other technological developments have come from different fields. Cambrian Innovation, a commercial provider of distributed wastewater and resource recovery solutions, has harnessed proprietary bioelectrochemical technologies to convert wastewater into clean water and energy.[50] The model helps industrial manufacturers become more circular. "We take a very data-centric approach, using a combination of proprietary biological treatment technologies and an analytics platform to monitor our plants," explains Matthew Silver, Founder and CEO of Cambrian Innovation. Indeed, digital, physical, and biological technologies have been at the core of solving for circularity and will be explored in greater depth in the following chapter.

Ecosystems: Embrace the Power of External Engagement

The ongoing technology revolution has catapulted the globalization of consumption and production onto a new economic change curve that's defined by the erosion of boundaries between industries and value chains. Automakers like Tesla and Mercedes-Benz are branching out into energy storage; mining companies are slowly repositioning as material stewards; and global e-commerce conglomerates like Amazon have become logistics companies. Indeed, industries have been converging, while old, "linear" relationships are being redrawn into web-like expansive ecosystems. Four major factors have been driving this trend: policy and legislation, investment, knowledge sharing, and practical collaboration—all of which will be explored in more detail in the Ecosystem chapter.

Organizations must thoughtfully consider how they engage with and influence the various forces outside their direct value chains. Consider legislation, such as the industry-specific regulations to extend producer responsibility for the added environmental or social costs incurred over a product's use. Such policies are a strong incentive for manufacturers to incorporate circular design principles and to facilitate sustainable approaches at the end-of-use phase (*Resource Recovery*). Between 1970 and 2015, 400 EPR measures were implemented, with a majority focused on the electronics industry, mostly within Europe.[51] Other policies have focused on consumers. Sweden has significantly reduced the VAT for repairs, encouraging the longer use of everything from bicycles to washing machines and other appliances (*Product Use Extension*).[52] Policy and regulatory-driven inflection points are critical for the adoption of circular business models, and as such, we will discuss them in greater detail in the Role of Policymakers chapter.

The Combinatorial Power of Business Models

To tap into the full potential of circular business models, the models should be considered in combination to enable a multiplier effect in value generation. Companies are thus encouraged to study and hypothesize where each of the five models fits, or could fit, within the organization and under what circumstances. For example, designing products and sourcing materials with a *Product as a Service* model in mind from the start would mean retaining ownership, collecting the product after use, and often disassembling the product for reuse. On the other hand, for a *Product Use Extension* model, it may be enough to design for easy maintenance and recycling. The combinatorial power of the five models can drive competitiveness and, perhaps most importantly, "future proof" organizations for an uncertain, rapidly changing global marketplace. Consider Nike which started with the incremental implementation of *Circular Inputs* and *Resource Recovery* from pre- and post-consumer waste streams. The company then developed its branded by-product under the Nike Grind label and continues its circular ascent through its children shoe-subscription start-up Adventure Club.[9,53]

 Case Study: Dell

Dell offers "PC-as-a-Service" by combining hardware, software, and lifecycle services in exchange for monthly fees. In parallel, an asset resale and recycling initiative allows the company to take back, resell, recycle, or return to lease any excess hardware in an environmentally conscious manner at the end of use. With Dell Reconnect, a partnership with Goodwill in the United States that accepts any brand or type of computer for free, working assets are responsibly refurbished, and others are recycled. Also, a buyback option is offered in some regions for customers to trade in eligible devices from any manufacturer in exchange for payment. When it comes to recovery, the returned plastics are shredded at the manufacturing facilities, melted, and blended. Currently, about 35% of this content is recycled and molded into new parts. As of June 2017, these so-called closed-loop plastics were being used in parts for more than 90 different Dell products. The net benefits of these recycling efforts are estimated at $2 million in savings so far.[54]

Throughout this chapter, we have discussed how the five circular business models have evolved and been adopted. We've shown how they have helped companies transform their traditional, linear ways of doing business into circular approaches that minimize waste, increase efficiencies, and provide platforms for innovation. But how, specifically, have organizations been able to leverage technology to implement and scale those models? In the next chapter, we describe the various 4IR technologies that are enabling the transformation from linear to circular.

 Chapter Takeaways

- The five circular business models provide a proven framework to support the transition to circularity, but adoption of the models has been mixed among multinationals. In general, the models that don't require a major overhaul of existing operations (namely Resource Recovery, Circular Inputs, and Product Use Extension) tend to be deployed more frequently by large corporations than those models that typically require major transformations (specifically, Product as a Service and Sharing Platforms).

- Much work is needed to accelerate the transition of the circular economy through the deployment of those business models, and we have identified five key enablers that cut across all five models and are critical to their adoption: consumer engagement, design, reverse logistics, disruptive technologies, and ecosystems.
- To harness the power of the business models, they should be considered in combination to maximize value creation across the full value chain.

Notes

1. Ellen MacArthur Foundation, "Towards the Circular Economy: Volume 1," 2013, https://www.ellenmacarthurfoundation.org/assets/downloads/publications/Ellen-MacArthur-Foundation-Towards-the-Circular-Economy-vol.1.pdf (accessed August 9, 2019).
2. Damian Carrington, "EU Agrees Total Ban on Bee-Harming Pesticides," *The Guardian*, April 27, 2018, https://www.theguardian.com/environment/2018/apr/27/eu-agrees-total-ban-on-bee-harming-pesticides.
3. IEA, "Renewables 2018 Market Analysis and Forecast from 2018 to 2023," https://www.iea.org/renewables2018/ (accessed August 9, 2019).
4. IRENA, "Renewable Energy Policies in a Time of Transition," 2018, https://www.irena.org/-/media/Files/IRENA/Agency/Publication/2018/Apr/IRENA_IEA_REN21_Policies_2018.pdf (accessed August 9, 2019).
5. Lauren Hepler, "Why Materials Will Make or Break the Circular Economy," GreenBiz.com, February 3, 2016, https://www.greenbiz.com/article/why-materials-will-make-or-break-circular-economy (accessed September 2, 2019).
6. Sulapac, "The Ocean Friendly Straw," https://www.sulapac.com/ (accessed August 9, 2019).
7. Bamb, "Enabling a Circular Building Industry," https://www.bamb2020.eu/ (accessed August 9, 2019).
8. Jennifer Elks, "Nestlé, Coke, Pepsi & Unilever Join Forces to Combat Waste in Chile," Sustainable Brands, https://sustainablebrands.com/read/collaboration-cocreation/nestle-coke-pepsi-unilever-join-forces-to-combat-waste-in-chile (accessed August 16, 2019).
9. Nike Grind, "More Performance. Less Waste," https://www.nikegrind.com/ (accessed September 2, 2019).
10. Nike, "Purpose Moves Us, FY18 Nike Impact Report," https://s3-us-west-2.amazonaws.com/purpose-cms-production01/wp-content/uploads/2019/05/20194957/FY18_Nike_Impact-Report_Final.pdf (accessed September 2, 2019).

11. Nike News, "Nike Flyleather," September 14, 2018, https://news.nike.com/news/what-is-nike-flyleather (accessed September 2, 2019).

12. Nike Purpose, "Waste," https://purpose.nike.com/waste (accessed August 9, 2019).

13. Based on data from entries into the Circular Awards over a 5-year period.

14. Halah Touryala, "World's Largest Hotels 2019: Marriott Leads Again, Hyatt & Accor Rise," Forbes, May 15, 2019, https://www.forbes.com/sites/halah-touryalai/2019/05/15/worlds-largest-hotels-2019/#39d51282796d (accessed August 16, 2019).

15. Avis, https://www.avis.co.uk/ (accessed August 16, 2019).

16. Enterprise Car Club, https://www.enterprisecarclub.co.uk/gb/en/home.html (accessed August 16, 2019).

17. Cohealo, "Make Your Medical Equipment Sweat," https://cohealo.com/ (accessed August 9, 2019).

18. eRent, "Track and Rent Platform," https://www.erent.fi/en/ (accessed August 9, 2019).

19. Online rental company operating in India's biggest urban hubs offering laptops, projectors, wheelchairs, costumes, event supplies and services and even home appliances.

20. Global transportation company offering app-based transportation services and automobile sales, leasing, financing, maintenance, fleet operation, as well as EV-specific services.

21. Start Up Factory China, "German-Chinese Demonstration Center Industry 4.0 in Kunshan on the Way," July 2017, https://www.startupfactory-china.de/en/2017/07/13/jul-2017-smart-manufacturing-demonstration-lab-kunshan/ (accessed August 9, 2019).

22. Judith Wallenstein and Urvesh Shelat, "What's Next for the Sharing Economy?" Boston Consulting Group, October 4, 2017, https://www.bcg.com/en-gb/publications/2017/strategy-technology-digital-whats-next-for-sharing-economy.aspx (accessed August 9, 2019).

23. Homi Kharas, "The Emerging Middle Class in Developing Countries," Brookings Institution, June, 2011, https://siteresources.worldbank.org/EXTABCDE/Resources/7455676-1292528456380/7626791-1303141641402/7878676-1306699356046/Parallel-Sesssion-6-Homi-Kharas.pdf (accessed August 9, 2019).

24. PWC UK, "Rapid Urbanization," https://www.pwc.co.uk/issues/megatrends/rapid-urbanisation.html (accessed August 9, 2019).

25. Philips Lighting, "Light as a Service," http://www.lighting.philips.co.uk/campaigns/art-led-technology (accessed August 9, 2019).

26. Daniel McCarthy and Peter Fader, "Subscription Businesses Are Booming. Here's How to Value Them," Harvard Business Review, December 19, 2017, https://hbr.org/2017/12/subscription-businesses-are-booming-heres-how-to-value-them (accessed August 9, 2019).

27. Thomas Ohr, "Berlin-based Grover Raises €37 Million in Series A Funding to Make Consumer Tech More Accessible," EU-Startups, July 20, 2018, https://www.eu-startups.com/2018/07/berlin-based-grover-raises-e37-million-in-series-a-funding-to-make-consumer-tech-more-accessible/ (accessed August 9, 2019).

28. Rent The Runway, "The Real Sustainable Fashion Movement," https://www.renttherunway.com/sustainable-fashion?action_type=footer_link (accessed August 9, 2019).

29. Samuel Hum, "How Rent The Runway Created a Multi-Million Dollar Clothing Rental Legacy," Referral Candy Blog, November 2018, https://www.referralcandy.com/blog/rent-the-runway-marketing-strategy/ (accessed August 12, 2019).

30. Yola Robert, "Rent The Runway Joins the Unicorn Club at a $1 Billion Valuation," March 25, 2019, https://www.forbes.com/sites/yolarobert1/2019/03/25/rent-the-runway-joins-the-unicorn-club-at-a-1-billion-valuation/#28c6bcda5f0c (accessed August 12, 2019).

31. Vitsoe, "606 Universal Shelving System," https://www.vitsoe.com/gb/606 (accessed August 9, 2019).

32. Reuters, "Fashion Backwards? H&M to Trial Sales of Vintage Garments," April 5, 2019, https://www.reuters.com/article/us-hennes-mauritz-environment/fashion-backwards-hm-to-trial-sales-of-vintage-garments-idUSKCN-1RH1PN (accessed August 9, 2019).

33. ThredUP, "2018 Resale Report," 2018, https://www.thredup.com/resale/ (accessed August 9, 2019).

34. Fast Company, "Ikea Wants You to Stop Throwing Away Your Ikea Furniture," January 28, 2016, https://www.fastcompany.com/3055971/ikea-wants-you-to-stop-throwing-away-your-ikea-furniture (accessed August 9, 2019).

35. Butler, Sarah, "Ikea to Sell Refurbished Furniture to Boost Culture of Recycling," *The Guardian*, 2019, https://www.theguardian.com/business/2019/feb/07/ikea-to-sell-refurbished-furniture-in-bid-to-boost-culture-of-recycling (accessed August 9, 2019).

36. Giovani Zaccaro, "Retrofit Versus Replace: What Should You Do with Our Power Distribution Equipment?" Schneider Electric Blog, March 14, 2018, https://blog.se.com/electricity-companies/2018/03/14/retrofit-versus-replace-what-should-you-do-with-your-power-distribution-equipment/ (accessed August 16, 2019).

37. Apple, "Environmental Responsibility Report, 2018 Progress Report, Covering Fiscal Year 2017," https://www.apple.com/environment/pdf/Apple_Environmental_Responsibility_Report_2018.pdf (accessed August 16, 2019).

38. reGAIN app, "Turn Your Unwanted Clothes into Discount Coupon," https://regain-app.com/ (accessed August 16, 2019).

39. Veolia, "Selfridges—Commercial Waste," https://www.veolia.co.uk/case-studies/selfridges (accessed August 9, 2019).

40. Nielsen, "Consumer-Goods' Brands That Demonstrate Commitment To Sustainability Outperform Those That Don't," 2019, https://www.nielsen. com/eu/en/press-releases/2015/consumer-goods-brands-that-demonstrate-commitment-to-sustainability-outperform/ (accessed August 9, 2019).

41. Cradle to Cradle, "Cradle to Cradle Certified Products Registry," https:// www.c2ccertified.org/products/registry (accessed August 9, 2019).

42. Moelven, "A Circular System," https://www.moelven.com/news/news-archive2/2018/a-circular-system/ (accessed August 9, 2019).

43. Laura Parker, "Fast Facts About Plastic Pollution," National Geographic, December 20, 2018, https://news.nationalgeographic.com/2018/05/plastics-facts-infographics-ocean-pollution/ (accessed August 9, 2019).

44. Sony, "Leading the Development of Recycled Plastics," https://www.sony. co.uk/electronics/sorplas-recycled-plastic (accessed August 9, 2019).

45. Karen Hawks, "What Is Reverse Logistics?" *Reverse Logistics Magazine*, Winter/Spring 2006, http://www.rlmagazine.com/edition01p12. php (accessed August 9, 2019).

46. CE100 in Collaboration with Cranfield University and Deutsche Post DHL Group, "An Introduction to the Reverse Logistics Maturity Model," April 2016, https://www.ellenmacarthurfoundation.org/assets/downloads/ce100/ Reverse-Logistics.pdf (accessed August 9, 2019).

47. Yerdle, "About Us," https://www.yerdlerecommerce.com/about-us (accessed August 16, 2019).

48. Dirkzwager, "Remote Offshore Asset Monitoring," http://www.dirkzwager.com/?mod=content&section=Remote%20Offshore%20Asset%20 Monitoring&id=296 (accessed August 9, 2019).

49. Klaus Schwab, "The Fourth Industrial Revolution: What It Means, How to Respond," World Economic Forum, July 6, 2015, https://www.weforum. org/agenda/2016/01/the-fourth-industrial-revolution-what-it-means-and-how-to-respond/ (accessed August 9, 2019).

50. Unreasonable Group, "Cambrian Innovation," https://unreasonablegroup. com/companies/cambrian-innovation?v=ln30J0CHbQc#overview (accessed August 30, 2019).

51. OECD, "Extended Producer Responsibility: Guidance for Efficient Waste Management," September 2016, https://www.oecd.org/environment/waste/ Extended-producer-responsibility-Policy-Highlights-2016-web.pdf (accessed August 9, 2019).

52. Richard Orange, "Waste Not Want Not: Sweden to Give Tax Breaks for Repairs," *The Guardian*, September 19, 2016, https://www.theguardian. com/world/2016/sep/19/waste-not-want-not-sweden-tax-breaks-repairs (accessed August 9, 2019).

53. Nike Adventure Club, "The Sneaker Club for Adventurous Kids," https:// www.nikeadventureclub.com/ (accessed September 2, 2019).

54. Dell, "Closed-Loop Recycled Content," https://www.dell.com/learn/us/en/ uscorp1/corp-comm/closed-loop-recycled-content (accessed August 9, 2019).

3

Disruptive Technologies

Technology has laid the foundation for every industrial revolution. From steam engines to the internal combustion engine to computers and the Internet, technological innovations have enabled businesses to attain unprecedented increases in performance. The Fourth Industrial Revolution (4IR) is no exception and is characterized by various technologies disrupting just about every industry across the globe. "Much of the technology we need to build a circular economy is already here, and it's rapidly getting better," says Doug Baker, Chairman and CEO of Ecolab. "In the coming years we'll see amazing innovations in big data and machine learning, bio-industrial products, reuse of captured carbon and a host of other advanced technologies."

In the previous chapter, we discussed how five dominant business models are driving the transition from a linear to a circular economy. In this chapter, and throughout the book, we explore the role 4IR innovations are playing in enabling circular business models and in accelerating the transition to a circular economy.

The Fourth Industrial Revolution

The 4IR is unlike any of the past industrial revolutions. For one thing, the previous three industrial revolutions—mechanization, mass production, and automation—had just one or a few game-changing technologies that enabled companies to achieve a "leapfrog" in industrial productivity.

© The Author(s) 2020
P. Lacy et al., *The Circular Economy Handbook*,
https://doi.org/10.1057/978-1-349-95968-6_3

In the Fourth Industrial Revolution, it's not just a handful of technical inventions; an array of technologies and combinations of them are sparking transformational change across global value chains.[1] The range of these innovations across the digital, physical, and biological worlds is breathtaking: everything from artificial intelligence to nanotechnology to cellular and tissue engineering. Along with the range of technologies, the pace at which these new innovations are being developed and scaled is much greater than that of previous industrial revolutions. As Dominic Waughray, Managing Director at the World Economic Forum Centre for Global Public Goods, put it, "The Fourth Industrial Revolution will enable positive transformations towards the circular economy. For example, many technology and value chain innovations are available to transform value chains like electronics, plastics and fashion – from shaping provenance tools, to product passports and an internet of materials. These possibilities have yet to be fully leveraged. Multilateral collaboration is necessary to help unlock the potential of 4IR innovation around the world to help accelerate the circular economy transformation."

Since the First Industrial Revolution, the relationship between economic growth and the use of natural resources has been around 1:1. In other words, as our economy has grown, so has the use of land, water, materials, and other natural resources. This has subjected the environment and the earth's resources to tremendous strain that is not currently sustainable with continued global growth.

4IR technologies are a game changer in the sustainability revolution because they make it possible for business, for the first time, to *decouple production and growth from the use of natural resources*. To accomplish this, these technologies provide four important capabilities. First, they **enable greater efficiencies** and thus reduced wastage. Second, they help **drive innovation** by allowing new entrants to disrupt existing markets while challenging incumbent companies to pivot into new business models and new markets. Third, 4IR technologies **increase information transparency**, allowing companies to gather and analyze data quickly to obtain valuable insights through new levels of visibility (into equipment usage and product, energy, and material flows), connectivity (between machines, customers, and decision-makers), and flexibility (the capability to modify or adapt a device, function, or process) that are key to deploying circular business models. Finally, biological 4IR technologies, in particular, enable us to **move away from the use of traditional limited or resource-intensive materials**.

27 Key Technologies

In 2015, we identified 10 key technologies with a central role in the circular economy. Since then, our list has grown to 27 (see Fig. 3.1 and Table 3.1). Some of the technologies have matured considerably. The Internet of Things (IoT), for example, has become the new standard for devices to connect, interact, and exchange data—capabilities critical to enabling new circular models, such as Product Use Extension and Sharing Platforms. We have also seen broader technologies like track-and-trace systems evolve from barcode to advanced RFID (radio-frequency identification) to blockchain-based systems, allowing product and asset tracking and empowering models such as Resource Recovery.

DIGITAL

Technologies based on computer, electronics and communication sciences, which make use of the increasing volume of information and connectedness of physical resources

Artificial Intelligence		Internet of Things
Machine Learning	Cloud/ Edge	M2M Comm.
Machine Vision	Big Data Analytics	Mobile Devices
Blockchain	Digital Anchors	Digital Twin

PHYSICAL

Technologies based on basic properties of materials, energy, forces of nature and their interactions

3D Printing	Robotics	Energy Storage
Energy Harvesting	Nano-technology	Spectroscopy
Physical Markers	AR/VR	Carbon Capture & Storage
	Material Science	

BIOLOGICAL

Technologies based on biological aspects, including, but not limited to, biological systems and living organisms (or derivatives thereof), to make products and processes for specific uses

Bio-energy	Bio-based Materials	Genetic Engineering
DNA Marking	Cellular & Tissue Engineering	Hydroponics & Aeroponics

Fig. 3.1 Technologies enabling the circular economy

Table 3.1 Overview of 27 technologies for the circular economy

Digital	Description	Example
Artificial intelligence	Enables machines to simulate human intelligence, at scale, and act without explicit instructions	Noodle.ai apps help clients reduce their waste and optimize their operations by leveraging AI to make sense of big data, find trends and key correlations. One of their apps, for example, has helped a client reduce direct labor handling costs by 7% and save in maintenance and transportation costs by the same percentage[2]
Machine learning	Permits machines to perform new tasks after being trained on historical datasets	Topolytics, a data aggregator and analysis business, draws in data from producers of secondary raw materials and from the recycling or reprocessing sector through its "WasteMap" and "WasteTrack" platforms. This generates the most accurate, verifiable dataset for tracking the movements of these materials locally and globally. Machine learning and geospatial analytics then generate insights and reports for the users and processors of the materials[3]
Cloud (and edge) computing	Hosts web-based content and applications in a central location, making them available to many devices at the same time. Devices are connected over a network and can access content and applications in real time (Edge computing hosts the web-based content on the device itself rather than a central location)	Rubicon Global's cloud-based, big data platform connects waste producers with a network of independent waste haulers across the United States, Canada, and 18 additional countries. The result is higher landfill diversion rates, creative reuse of waste material, optimized truck routes, and detailed analysis of waste data[4]
Machine vision	Acquires, processes, analyzes, and understands digital and analog images, enabling the automatic extraction of data from the real world	Cognex Corporation manufactures machine vision systems that provide image-based inspection to help ensure defect-free part shipments for stamping suppliers, delivering increased efficiency and reduced wastage from product returns[5]
Big data analytics	Analyzes extremely large datasets to uncover patterns, trends, and dependencies	Alstom, an integrated transport systems company, uses big data analytics to operate predictive maintenance tools that monitor the condition of trains and transportation infrastructure. This helps minimize unnecessary downtime and boosts utilization[6]

Digital	Description	Example
Internet of Things (IoT)	Deploys wireless devices with embedded sensors that interact and trigger actions	SKF INSIGHT technology (deployed in the railway and wind industries) enables rotating machinery to transmit data on operating conditions to the cloud, from which customers can extract information through a remote diagnostic service and receive reports and warnings. This maximizes the useful life of machinery, cutting total lifecycle costs[7]
Machine-to-machine (M2M) communication	Connects data, analytics, and machines based on sensors and actuators. The technology allows different pieces of equipment or control centers to automatically exchange information without human intervention	Hello Tractor has a "Smart Tractor" sharing platform that connects tractor owners with farmers. The system links SMS message requests with software that identifies nearby tractors with the required usability and functionality. Smart Tractor also provides real-time information about the condition of tractor parts, increasing the usable lifecycle of products[8]
Mobile devices	Combines hardware, operating systems, networks, and software to provide users with real-time access to content	NCC, a construction and property development company, leverages mobile devices for its "Loop Rocks" platform, which enables the smart handling of construction waste. Construction site managers use an app to upload details of excess material for haulers and other players to then pick up those materials, resulting in the more efficient handling of construction waste[9]
Blockchain	Uses digital transaction ledgers that are shared by all parties participating in an established, distributed network of computers. This enhances transparency and secures information sharing as the data is auditable, unchangeable, and open	Provenance allows users to create and store a digital record of assets for anything of value so that those items and materials can be tracked throughout supply chains[10]

(continued)

Table 3.1 (continued)

Digital	Description	Example
Digital anchors	Utilizes a tiny computer to monitor, analyze, communicate, and even act on data. The computer is attached to or embedded in the product to authenticate it and to establish a link between the product and its accompanying data stream. The technology could deploy RFID tags, Near-Field Communication (NFC) tags, Quick Response (QR) codes, or barcodes	Circularise, a Dutch start-up, is creating cryptographic anchors to be attached to products, enabling those items to be traced and linked to a blockchain, thus increasing the reliability and authenticity of those products. The platform enables product-related questions to be directed upstream in the value chain[11]
Digital twin	Deploys a virtual model of a process, product, or service by pairing the virtual and physical worlds. This allows the analysis of data and the monitoring of systems to develop new solutions and to conduct predictive maintenance	General Electric (GE), a multinational conglomerate, uses digital twins that simulate asset performance in different usage scenarios under varying conditions, thereby enabling GE to more efficiently and effectively develop better maintenance solutions[12]

Physical	Description	Example
3D printing	Creates 3D objects by forming successive layers of material under computer control	Daimler Trucks North America, a commercial vehicle manufacturer, is piloting the sale of on-demand 3D-printed plastic parts. This allows delivery of parts that are traditionally difficult to provide due to low or intermittent demand and reduces time-to-repair, production and shipment costs, and wasted materials[13]
Robotics	Applies machines that are programmed to automatically carry out a complex series of actions. The technology is especially suitable for repetitive and rules-based processes using structured data. When combined with machine learning, robots can train themselves	Zenrobotics builds waste-sorting robots that can sort and pick objects with various weights and shapes, and the robots are capable of learning new sorting rules. This increases the efficiency of recycling plants and increases the quantity of materials that can be recycled[14]

Physical	Description	Example
Energy storage and utilization	Prolongs the life of batteries, increases their storage capacity, or replaces existing chemicals-based raw materials with organic substances	Iberdrola, a clean-power company with almost zero emissions, has built the largest pumped-hydro storage plant in Europe. Two reservoirs with over 500 meters of altitude difference are used to produce electricity during peak consumption times. This allows for large amounts of power to be produced quickly without any GHG emissions[15]
Energy harvesting	Captures small amounts of energy that would otherwise be lost as heat, light, sound, vibration, or movement	EnOcean, a German start-up, has developed energy-harvesting wireless switches that rely on kinetic or solar energy for switching applications rather than depending on traditional forms of energy[16]
Nanotechnology	Manipulates matter on an atomic, molecular, or supramolecular scale. Examples include fullerene, carbon nanotubes, and quantum dots	GloNaTech, a Greek nanotechnology company, produces marine coatings containing carbon nanotubes that facilitate the release of microorganisms responsible for biofouling (i.e., the polluting of underwater surfaces by organisms like algae and barnacles). The technology reduces the flow resistance between a ship's body and the water, resulting in lower fuel consumption (and decreased carbon dioxide emissions)[17]
Spectroscopy	Uses different spectra of electromagnetic radiation to analyze a material based on its molecular composition	TOMRA Sorting Recycling, a recycling technology company, has developed equipment that uses near-infrared sensors for sorting trash, increasing recycling efficiency[18]
Physical markers	Helps authenticate a product by requiring a direct link to a database. Physical markers are attached to the products themselves, enabling customers to authenticate more information about that item	Examples of physical markers include watermarks, holograms, optical characteristics, and chemical markers. They increase a product's traceability and enable its authenticity to be verified. For instance, edible QR codes are being developed by several companies to increase transparency and traceability on everything from cows to sushi to produce[19,20]

(continued)

Table 3.1 (continued)

Physical	Description	Example
Virtual reality/ augmented reality	Provides interactive, fully immersive digital reality in a computer-generated or video-enabled environment (VR), or superimposes text, sounds, and graphics on top of the real physical world via wearable devices through use of augmented reality (AR)	ThyssenKrupp, a German industrial engineering and steel company, developed a HoloLens that enables field service engineers to fix elevators by displaying virtual models of the product, information on prior services, and repair guidance. This cuts wastage, boosts the engineers' productivity, and enhances safety[21]
Carbon capture and utilization	Captures waste carbon dioxide from large point sources (such as fossil-fuel power plants), transports it to a storage site, and deposits it where it will not enter the atmosphere. With utilization, new products or processes are enabled by the captured carbon	Graviky, a spinoff from the Massachusetts Institute of Technology, recycles carbon dioxide emissions to produce ink. The company has used this application to clean over 1.6 trillion liters of air[22]
Materials science	Applies chemical engineering and knowledge from other fields to material innovation. Materials science can help design products and processes that minimize the use and generation of hazardous substances	DSM-Niaga, an industrial design and engineering company, redesigns everyday products, so they can be recycled back into the same product. By using the lowest diversity of ingredients possible and clean materials, Niaga® products can be remade over and over again, closing "the loop" for those materials, for example, fully recyclable carpets that can repeatedly be recycled into new carpets[23]

Biological	Description	Example
Bio-energy	Derives energy from biomass, which includes biological material such as plants and animals, wood, waste (hydrogen) gas, and alcohol fuels	Cambrian Innovation, a commercial provider of distributed wastewater and resource recovery solutions, treats wastewater by leveraging electrically active microbes to produce clean water and clean energy in the form of biogas[24]
Bio-based material	Uses substances derived from living organisms to produce new materials. These substances could include biopolymers and other natural fibers created partially or wholly by using plant feedstock	gCycle, a diaper manufacturing company, provides 100% compostable diapers; it replaces oil-based plastic with non-GMO corn biofilm in diapers[25]

Biological	Description	Example
Genetic engineering	Manipulates an organism's genome directly through the use of biotechnology	Genetic engineering has increased crop yields by 22% and reduced pesticide use by 37%, according to a meta-analysis based on 147 studies reporting the impacts of genetically modified (GM) soybean, maize, or cotton.[26] A GM eucalyptus plant approved in 2015 produced 20% more wood and cut time to maturity by 20%[27]
DNA marking	Marks items in ways that are undetectable to the eye, enabling people to differentiate between genuine and counterfeit products and materials	Products like semiconductors or microchips can be tagged with a botanical DNA utilizing ink. This can help with the traceability of products or materials, preventing counterfeiting and allowing circularity by ensuring the information related to a certain material or product, such as its provenance or material composition is verifiable[28]
Cellular and tissue engineering	Applies the principles of cell and tissue growth to produce functional replacements of materials or modifications of existing ones	Cellular production is enabling the production of new foods, such as the world's first cultured hamburger by Dr. Mark Post.[29] A cultured beef burger may deliver the same taste to consumers with a fraction of the environmental costs
Hydroponics and aeroponics	Deploys organic, ecologically responsive, and sustainable approaches to gardening	Aeroponic methods, for example, use 90% less water and far less fertilizer compared with traditional agriculture methods.[30] Robbe's Vertical Farming offers a gardening-as-a-service solution for local wholesalers and supermarket chains to grow their own greens with the company's help and supervision. This means local customers can enjoy the benefits of sustainably grown local vegetables[31]

The 27 technologies fall into three broad categories of continuing advancements and breakthroughs in the use of science and engineering: digital, physical, and biological (see Fig. 3.1).

Although all of these 27 4IR technologies are being used in applications today, not all are being deployed at the same rate or scale. In general, companies have adopted digital innovations more widely than physical or biological technologies. As one proof point, 59% of the 1500 circular companies we analyzed over the last five years via The Circulars award initiative have deployed digital technologies (compared with a 28 and 13% deployment rate for physical and biological technologies, respectively).[32]

The big gap in adoption is correlated with technology maturity and is reflected in substantial differences in investments. In the United States and Europe, investments in the digital industry are about double that of biotech.[33] Thanks to such investments, digital technologies are becoming cheaper and are scaling quickly. Between 2004 and 2014, for example, the cost of IoT sensors plunged by more than half. Such dramatic price drops have resulted in electronic devices that harness digital technologies (laptop computers, tablets, smartphones, and other consumer electronics products) becoming ubiquitous in many regions.[34] Moreover, these devices rely on a virtual world that is less dependent on physical resources to generate and maintain value. As a result, companies have found it relatively easier to implement or retrofit digital technologies into existing processes and operations.

In contrast, many physical and biological technologies are less mature and have not yet been proven or deployed at scale. They have in part been limited by their requirements for substantial capital or considerable R&D timeframes to bring solutions to the mass market. Moreover, those solutions tend to be proprietary, may require significant operational changes for widespread implementation, or necessitate investigation into ethical and regulatory considerations. For example, genetic engineering can stir ethical questions around topics like the potential negative impacts of gene pollution on natural environments.

Applications Across the Circular Value Chain

The 27 4IR technologies have been used in diverse applications throughout the circular value chain. Our assessment of leading circular innovations around the world reveals how leading performers are unlocking business value through innovative technology applications across all stages of the value chain, often by combining several technologies to achieve the desired economic and environmental impact. Figure 3.2 provides additional examples of 4IR applications spanning the circular value chain.

ECOVATIVE - supplies a new form of packaging made of mycelium, or 'mushroom roots', which is compostable at end of life. **Technologies deployed: Bio-based materials**

SIEMENS - re-designs manufacturing processes to be more efficient and flexible using insight from analytics. **Technologies deployed: Digital twin, Big data analytics**

ADIDAS - replicates genetic sequences of spider silk in other ingredients to create nylon replacement. **Technologies deployed: Bio-based materials, Genetic engineering, Material science**

IKEA - optimizes truck and container loads to minimize transportation with smart packing. **Technologies deployed: Big data analytics, Artificial intelligence**

1 2 RETURN - software as a service and framework that streamlines the transportation, processing and settlement of product returns. **Technologies deployed: Cloud, M2M communication**

BANYAN NATION - plastics recycling platform utilizing the informal sector to collect post-consumer plastics and applying cleaning technology to restore plastic to near-virgin quality. **Technologies deployed: Cloud, Big data analytics**

SHARE NOW - BMW and Daimler joint venture for a car sharing platform that offers a product as a service pay as you go solution to urban mobility. **Technologies deployed: Cloud, IoT**

Fig. 3.2   Illustrative applications of 4IR technologies across the circular value chain[35] (*Source* See chapter Notes)

Technology Spotlight

Of the 27 technologies, we will delve deeper into two from each of the three major categories: digital, physical, and biological (see Fig. 3.3). These six technologies are the most frequently embraced by the organizations we analyzed over the last five years. In addition to addressing their application in the circular economy, we will discuss a few important considerations when deploying these technologies.

DIGITAL

59%

IoT
Intelligent connections between things and devices enabling a secure infrastructure that lets information be shared across the business ecosystem

MACHINE LEARNING
The ability for algorithms to learn independently and perform ever-more complex functions, leading to exponential growth in artificial intelligence

PHYSICAL

28%

ROBOTICS
Robotics technology, often couples with digital technology such as AI and Machine Learning, to make processes automated and more efficient

ENERGY HARVESTING
A process, sometimes known as energy scavenging, that captures energy that would otherwise be lost as heat, light, sound or kinetic energy

BIOLOGICAL

13%

BIO-BASED MATERIALS
Plant-based compostable and/or recyclable materials being increasingly used to substitute less circular-friendly materials

BIO-ENERGY
Renewable energy derived from biomass which includes biological material such as plants, wood, waste, hydrogen gas and alcohol fuels

Fig. 3.3 Adoption rates and the six 4IR technologies making the biggest impact within the circular economy (*Source* Peter Lacy, Jessica Long, Wesley Spindler et al., "The Circular Advantage: Moving from Insight to Action—Preview to the Circular Advantage Handbook," https://thecirculars.org/content/resources/The_Circular_Advantage.pdf [accessed August 9, 2019])

Digital: Internet of Things (IoT)

IoT technologies consist of wireless devices with embedded sensors that allow for the interconnectivity of assets or products and the exchange of data generated in a sensor network. These devices could include everything from vehicles to home appliances to industrial equipment, all of which can potentially be monitored and controlled remotely. Consider Philips Healthcare, with a product portfolio that includes hospital assets like magnetic resonance imaging (MRIs), position emission tomography (PET) scanners, and computed tomography (CT) equipment. IoT technology enables Philips to monitor those products remotely, thereby facilitating predictive maintenance and product life extension. This has allowed Philips to deploy a Product as a Service model, in which the company sells the services of those medical devices while retaining product ownership. When a customer has ended its use of a device, the product is returned to Philips for repair, refurbishment, and reuse or recovery. At the beginning of 2018, Philips pledged to take back and repurpose all of the large medical systems equipment (e.g., magnetic resonance imaging or MRI, and computed tomography, CT, scanners) that its customers were prepared to return to the company and to extend those practices across its professional portfolio by 2025. In 2018, after pilot projects in Italy and Greece, Philips successfully launched the roll-out of a global program to achieve its ambitious circular economy goal, together with metrics to monitor progress.[36]

Accenture estimates that the Industrial Internet of Things (IIoT) could add about $14.2 trillion to the global economy by 2030.[37] As companies continue to deploy IoT technologies, they should consider measures to manage cybersecurity risks, interoperability, and data privacy. This could include implementing multi-layered security protections or obtaining customers' consent prior to using their information.[38]

Digital: Machine Learning

With machine learning, an application of artificial intelligence, algorithms learn on their own to improve and perform new functions, all without being specifically programmed to do so. The technology, which often relies on neural networks, can be a tremendous aid in improving the decision-making of even human experts. This is largely due to the vast (and exponentially growing) amounts of data that the technology can analyze with tremendous speed and accuracy. Machine learning can help organizations design circular products, components, and materials through iterative self-learning algorithms that allow rapid prototyping and testing. It can also be used to minimize waste, resource use, and emissions through the deployment of predictive analytics for more precise demand-planning or for analyzing usage patterns to optimize asset management.

Using machine learning, industrial automation leader Siemens has been able to optimize the combustion processes of its gas turbines. Their goal was to minimize emissions, which can be a difficult task requiring careful consideration of various factors, including gas composition, local weather conditions, and the turbine age. Thanks to sophisticated neural networks, Siemens has been able to achieve impressive results, even surpassing the performance of human experts. In a series of tests, after a human expert had set the turbine controls manually, the machine-learning system was able to further reduce the emissions of nitrogen oxide by an additional 20%.[39]

Machine learning has tremendous potential, with the market expected to surpass $23 billion by 2023.[40] To unlock that value, though, companies must overcome various technical challenges. Applications like the Siemens turbine-control system require copious amounts of data for the machine-learning application to yield useful results. While large corporations might possess virtual treasure troves of data, not all of that information might be readily usable. Most of it might need to be "cleaned" first, and much of it might be locked in different formats in the separate storage and processing systems of business-unit siloes. As such, data aggregation and integration can be a very difficult but foundational task for companies looking to apply machine learning to their own processes.[41,42] Additionally, ethical challenges should be carefully managed to ensure algorithmic bias is avoided and data is used appropriately and transparently.

Physical: Robotics

Robotics is especially well suited for automating processes that are repetitive and rules-based. When combined with machine learning, the technology can be trained to perform a complex series of actions. The global robotics market is expected to reach $62 billion by 2024, with numerous applications in the circular economy, such as waste collection, sorting, and pulverization.[43]

A good example that illustrates the power of robotics technology in resource recovery is multinational technology company Apple's development of Liam, a robot that can quickly disassemble the company's iPhone 6s. Two lines of the advanced robot can take apart 2.4 million phones a year, enabling Apple to recover high-quality components and materials that would typically go to waste under traditional recycling techniques. For every 100,000 devices, Liam can recover considerable amounts of aluminum (1900 kilograms), copper (800 kilograms), tin (55 kilograms), rare-earth elements (24 kilograms), tungsten (3.5 kilograms), tantalum (2.5 kilograms), and gold (0.3 kilograms).[44] Apple is already beginning to close the loop with some of those materials. Specifically, recaptured aluminum is re-melted and used to make Macintosh minicomputers in the company's final-assembly facilities.[45] According to Apple, Daisy (Liam's successor) can disassemble up to 200 iPhones an hour (equaling approximately 1.8 million a year), separating parts and removing certain components as it works.[46]

When deploying robotics, companies need to consider several factors, including capital expenditure and returns and the social impact of workforce displacement. A careful assessment of the efficiency gains delivered by harnessing robotics should be undertaken and considered against the initial investment costs of applying the technology. In this analysis, companies should also evaluate the investments needed to re-train and re-position potentially displaced employees.

Physical: Energy Harvesting

Energy harvesting is the use of specialized materials or equipment to capture, store, and supply energy that would otherwise be lost as heat, light, sound, vibration, or movement. Deployment has been somewhat constrained to date (due to conversion efficiencies, source stability, and power-storage capacities), but the technology is advancing, and the global energy-harvesting market is expected to surpass $1 billion by 2025.[47] Applications run the gamut and reflect no shortage of ingenuity: IoT sensors that harvest sunlight to power themselves, antennas that scavenge for radio-frequency energy that is then converted to DC (direct current) electricity, a new type of incandescent light bulb that self-recycles the heat it generates, and so on. Two leading technology institutes in the United States and China have created a "nanogenerator" that simultaneously harnesses wind and solar energy and can be installed on the roof of a home, powering energy-efficient light-emitting diode (LED) lights inside as well as a temperature sensor.[48]

The technology is expected to be even more critical in the future, especially for smaller and low-energy-consumption devices. IoT applications and consumer electronics will drive innovation in this space, using sensors and other electronic devices in environments where the costs associated with providing power have made certain applications difficult.[49,50] Buildings, representing almost 30% of energy worldwide, offer a huge area of opportunity.[51] If companies could harvest the excess energy wasted within a building, it could be used to power devices that would slash overall building energy consumption and deliver substantial economic value to building owners.

Biological: Bio-Based Materials

This technology includes plant-based compostable and recyclable materials that are increasingly being used as substitutes for less-sustainable resources. Bio-based materials can be made from biopolymers and from other natural fibers created partially or wholly through the use of plant feedstock. As mentioned above, Japanese automaker Mazda is a case in point. Instead of using traditional plastics and other environmentally challenging materials for its car interiors, the company has been switching to bio-based plastics.[52] Working with Mitsubishi Chemical Corp., the industrial products arm of the Japanese corporation Mitsubishi, Mazda has developed a new plastic that is not only produced from plant-derived materials but also can be dyed instead of painted, thus reducing the need for volatile organic compounds (VOCs). The automaker also uses bio-fabrics, manufactured entirely from plant-derived fiber, for the upholstery of its vehicle seats, and it has started deploying high-strength, durable bio-plastics for exterior vehicle parts as well.[52] Over the next 20 years, global plastic production is expected to double, and much of that could instead be sourced from new materials that are bio-based as well as from materials and chemicals derived from renewable biological resources.[53]

Companies that intend to develop and scale use of this technology need to consider several factors, including full environmental impact and product recyclability. First, they must understand the provenance of a material being considered. For example, does the feedstock used to create the bio-based material come from a waste stream or from growing a crop on otherwise productive land? Second, bio-based materials are circular *only* if the appropriate waste management systems are available to recycle them back into the value chain or re-absorb them back into the environment. By weighing these and other factors, a company might discover that the use of a particular bio-based material might not necessarily be more environmentally efficient than an oil-derived alternative.[54,55]

Biological: Bio-Energy

Bio-energy technology is used to convert natural and organic matter such as plants, waste, and alcohol fuels into energy. One approach is to extract energy from wastewater through electromethanogenesis (a form of electro-fuel production where methane is produced by direct biological conversion from electrical current and carbon dioxide), anaerobic digestion, or other biological or biochemical processes. Another approach focuses on factory waste gases, for example, by turning carbon emissions into ethanol fuel for cars. Through such applications, bio-energy technologies can provide the foundation for efficient resource recovery, with the global bio-energy market expected to grow by $54 billion from 2018 to 2022.[56]

Consider Enerkem, a Montreal start-up that has developed technology for converting municipal non-recyclable garbage into transportation fuels and other renewable chemicals that can then be used across different industries. At a plant in Rotterdam, Enerkem has plans to gasify 300,000 tons of waste annually to produce more than 200,000 tons of methanol. Without that processing plant, the waste would have been headed for incineration elsewhere, potentially resulting in the release of 300,000 tons of carbon dioxide.[57]

Although technologies like Enerkem's offer win-win solutions—not only extracting biofuel from waste but also avoiding the release of greenhouse gases—scaling them beyond their early maturity calls for incentives and investments in infrastructure. Additionally, it is important to note that converting resources into energy should most often be the last resort in an ideal circular system, only when all other options, such as re-using and recycling, are exhausted. Furthermore, health impacts from the burning of matter as well as GHG emissions must be considered, which can vary depending on the feedstock and technology used. Another key risk of bio-energy production is drawing from virgin resources, such as biofuel crops that are grown on farmland as opposed to marginal land unsuitable for food production, sparking a debate over the wisdom of diverting crops or farmland for energy production. Because of such issues, the successful and responsible application of bio-energy technology is highly dependent on location, local policy, and available feedstock.[58,59]

Combinatorial Effects

While 4IR technologies possess powerful capabilities, there's no one-size-fits-all solution for creating circular value. Technologies can be deployed in various ways depending on the industry, scale, waste stream, and challenges involved. Our analysis, though, uncovered a common thread: the most competitive businesses tended to deploy *combinations* of technologies to achieve the best performance. Of the 27 technologies, a few combinations seemed particularly promising in terms of their potential to disrupt the linear economy and accelerate circular businesses.

Most often we found that companies achieved synergies in the same given area, such as a digital technology combined with other digital technologies.

A firm might, for example, use IoT to monitor, track, and trace the use of a product and then apply big data analytics to mine insights that could be used to generate circular value. The analysis could, for instance, help determine whether any returned products should be refurbished for resale or instead have their parts harvested to obtain the highest value. In one example, Winnow, a technology company working in the hospitality sector, develops artificial intelligence tools to help chefs run more profitable and sustainable kitchens by cutting food waste in half. Using computer vision, the system harvests large volumes of food waste images which are used to train a predictive model. Chefs benefit from accurate analytics which pinpoint where waste occurs in their kitchens helping them cut food costs by 3–8% (ROI of up to 10 times in year one). Clients like IKEA and IHG have already begun rolling out the technology at scale.[60]

Some of the most interesting and powerful combinations, however, emerge from solutions that transcend boundaries between the digital, physical, and biological worlds. Specifically, digital technologies are frequently used as a multiplier to scale an application and accelerate its impact, for example, the use of machine vision and AI to improve the performance of physical technologies, such as robots. Our data indicates that deployment of such digital-physical applications is the most common type of cross-field combination. In contrast, digital-biological combinations currently represent just 8% of circular deployments. That said, digital-biological combinations possess tremendous potential. Consider, for example, indoor farming leader AeroFarms' use of aeroponics and predictive analytics for superior and consistent agricultural productivity that reduces resource consumption and waste generation, while increasing quality output. Similarly, the team at LanzaTech, made up of biologists, chemists, engineers, and computational biologists, leverages technology to amplify impact by combining disciplines. LanzaTech generates a great deal of data in its global facilities that needs to be digitally modeled to improve next-generation products. "It is thanks to this marriage of biology and AI that we are able to predict design flows and accelerate the production of new sustainable chemicals that can be brought into the circular supply chain," explains Jennifer Holmgren, CEO of LanzaTech.

In the future, we believe the greatest impact will come from solutions that fuse all three (digital, physical, and biological) types of technologies. An apt example is tire company Goodyear's new concept tire, Oxygene. In this innovative product, moss would grow within the sidewall of the tire by absorbing moisture from the road, and this would improve traction with the moss also helping to remove carbon dioxide from the air.[61] For a city about the size of Paris, with 2.5 million vehicles, these tires could potentially extract 40,000 tons of carbon dioxide every year.[61] Moreover, the energy harvested from the moss' photosynthesis could then power electronic sensors in the tire that, through IoT, would be able to exchange data with other vehicles as well as with the transportation infrastructure, thus enabling applications for smart mobility.[61] The ability of these technology combinations to solve business and environmental challenges is still being proven—both economically and at scale—but they illustrate the potential power of combined 4IR technologies to fundamentally transform our current value chains.

Managing Unintended Consequences

Applications like Oxygene represent an exciting future for the use of 4IR technologies in circular business models. At the same time, companies need to be cognizant of the potential unintended consequences that can arise from transforming their core businesses with these disruptive new innovations. As with other 4IR linear applications, organizations should employ safeguards to protect consumer data and guard against cyberthreats, and they must focus on opportunities to reskill their workforce to avoid disruption and displacement due to automation.[62,63]

Moreover, executives must also consider the potential system-level impact or ethical considerations of scaling their circular technologies. For instance, studies show that the supply of biomass is under pressure to meet future demand in a sustainable manner.[64] As such, businesses aiming to integrate bio-based materials, bio-chemicals, and bio-fuels as raw material in their supply chain should be aware of the production and environmental footprint of those resources and target more sustainable alternatives where possible. Tetra Pak, the global food-processing and packaging company, has elected to use versatile crops, such as sugarcane bagasse and to rely on sustainably managed forests to derive its bio-based packaging material. Today, Tetra Pak sources 100% of its paperboard from forests that have been certified by the Forest Stewardship Council, and the company works with suppliers, non-governmental organizations, and other stakeholders to promote responsible forest management and to strengthen product traceability through certification and labeling.[65,66]

In our research, the potential unintended consequence companies most often share with us concerns the full environmental footprint of these new circular innovations, that is, that the newer innovations might actually produce greater negative environmental impacts. To make that determination, companies need to perform comparable lifecycle assessments (LCAs) and determine, for example, the point at which scaling is needed to ensure that the new products are circular and that they reduce overall environmental impact.

Future Outlook

Further on the horizon, there are several transformative technologies we expect to open up new opportunities as they are implemented in circular business models, including but not limited to:

Smart digital twin and AR/VR. Digital-twin technology, which refers to a digital replica of physical assets, processes, people, places, systems, and devices, allows for the analysis of data and monitoring of systems to develop new solutions or to conduct predictive maintenance. Water technology company Xylem, for example, developed a digital twin of the city of South Bend, Indiana's sewer system and used AI to analyze and optimize storm water surges to avoid combined sewer overflows that pollute local waterways—preventing more than 1 billion gallons of storm and sewer water from entering the St. Joseph River every year. This helped the city reduce its construction budget by $500 million that would have otherwise been needed to build more underground tunnels to hold excess storm water, conserving energy and lessening human impact on the environment. The solution is also helping protect waterways connected to the river, such as Lake Michigan, which is a critical source for water treatment plants that supply drinking water to Chicago, Grand Rapids, and the region.[67]

Blockchain and cryptographic anchors. Blockchain technology can help ensure a product's authenticity, tracing it from its point of origin to the end user on a secure, immutable distributed ledger. Cryptographic anchors are tamper-proof "digital fingerprints" that can be embedded into products, or parts of products, allowing physical goods to have a traceable digital identity that can be stored on a blockchain, facilitating asset tracking and value recovery at end of use. Blockchain-based communication company, Circularise, for example, developed an open, distributed, and secure communication protocol for the circular economy in combination with cryptographic anchors. Using the technology, a customer can scan a product's anchor to ask questions about that item (whether it contains mercury, for instance) and then automatically receive yes/no answers from a source upstream in the value chain.[68]

Machine vision, machine learning, and robotics. Machine learning and machine vision systems—which acquire, process, analyze, and understand digital images, extracting valuable data quickly from the real world—are improving as they "learn" from additional images. Robotics is being further equipped with machine vision and powered by machine learning to improve their capabilities and intelligence for circular applications. AMP Robotics, for example, is using machine vision to sort waste, and the accuracy of the system has improved over time to 99%.[69]

Breakthroughs in physical and biological technologies. Driven by investments and start-up activity, growth in physical and biological technologies has been steady and promising. "Food tech" is one area with a constant stream of innovation that we expect to continue to spur transformation. Specifically, advances in technologies like robotics, drones, and sensors will continue to shape the next generation of farms while reducing labor, energy, and resource intensity, and we are also on the brink of a revolution in bio-based technologies. Food tech start-up Apeel Sciences, for example, uses plant extracts derived from discarded agricultural by-products to create invisible tasteless coatings that extend the shelf life of fresh products by two to five times.[70] The technology can help grocers reduce waste while improving the appearance and nutritional content of their fruits and vegetables. Lab-grown food could further remove farm dependency altogether, creating food quickly with highly controlled inputs. Consider Memphis Meats, a food technology company, which produces animal cells in the lab to create cell-based meat. The start-up has received over $20 million in funding, with investment from large food corporations like Tyson and Cargill, and, as prices fall, products could be launched commercially within the next few years.[71] Agricultural processes will evolve more broadly as well. Restorative agriculture, a farming technique that aims to increase biodiversity, enrich soils, and enhance ecosystem services, is quickly gaining ground, for instance. Meanwhile, companies like Lystek, a Canadian waste treatment technology company, are taking organic waste from cities and converting it into regenerative soil enhancers.[72]

The fashion industry is embracing a host of emerging and potentially game-changing biological innovations. Every year, the H&M Foundation selects five start-ups pioneering circular fashion technologies for their accelerator program.[73] In 2018 and 2019, there was an uptick in biological innovations, representing three of the five technologies in both years. These start-ups include Crop-A-Porter, which makes textiles from food crop harvest leftovers; Algae Apparel that uses algae as a dye; and Sane Membrane, a biodegradable and mineral-based membrane for outdoor wear.[73] Other innovations have focused on physical technologies, such as Smart Stitch, which makes dissolvable thread; The Regenerator, which separates cotton and polyester blends for recycling; and Petit Pli that makes "clothes that grow" with a child's physical development.[73,74]

While digital technologies play a key role as an amplifier in scaling and making circular business models more effective and efficient, our society and industries continue to focus on producing and consuming physical goods. Therefore, the acceleration of biological and physical technologies we've explored here will be instrumental in creating circular inputs from the outset, enhancing the ability to convert "waste" back into virgin materials and ultimately help to close the loop.

Productivity Leapfrogs

In the past, technological breakthroughs enabled companies to achieve productivity leapfrogs throughout various industries. Today, instead of distinct technological revolutions, we are experiencing constant progress, with new waves of innovation continually making existing technologies obsolete. This has placed relentless demands on companies to stay up to date, but it has also unlocked new opportunities at an exponential rate in ever-shorter time spans. As John Atechson, CEO of Stuffstr, a recirculation platform that aims to accelerate the transition to a circular economy, puts it, "We are constantly improving our algorithm to increase the insights we can attain from data and improve accuracy. Our ability to harness data, which is growing at an epic scale, leads to more recirculation opportunities, ultimately changing consumers' mindset about the linear system."

Without a doubt, 4IR innovations have provided a rich platform for firms to gain considerable competitive advantages in deploying the five circular business models. To unlock the full potential of these technologies, though, companies must implement them holistically across all operating groups and function areas. The technologies must also be channeled purposefully in ways that tap into their nascent synergies and managed properly to minimize unintended consequences, including adverse environmental impacts, displacement of employees, risk of cyberthreats, and ethical concerns. In the next chapter, we'll discuss these and other implications for specific industries.

Chapter Takeaways

- The Fourth Industrial Revolution (4IR) is unlike past industrial revolutions because of the breadth, pace, and scale of new technologies that have the potential to decouple growth from resource use.
- Companies have been deploying a variety of 4IR technologies that can be grouped into three broad categories—digital, physical, and biological—and the focus so far has largely been on digital.
- The technologies used most prominently to enable business and environmental outcomes have been IoT and machine learning (for digital), robotics and energy harvesting (for physical), and bio-based materials and bio-energy (for biological).
- 4IR technologies have been a key enabler of circular business models through increased efficiency, greater innovation, enhanced information transparency, and reduced reliance on resource-intensive materials.
- Deploying combinations of technologies will help businesses achieve the best results. Staying at the forefront of emerging technologies may also accelerate progress toward regenerative and restorative processes that are additive to natural resources.
- To achieve these benefits, the technologies must be woven holistically into the fabric of the organization, deployed with intent, and managed properly to minimize any unintended consequences.

Notes

1. Kalus Schwab, "The Fourth Industrial Revolution: What It Means, How to Respond," World Economic Forum, January 14, 2016, https://www.weforum.org/agenda/2016/01/the-fourth-industrial-revolution-what-it-means-and-how-to-respond/ (accessed August 9, 2019).
2. Noodle.ai, "NFI Industries Teams Up with Noodle.Ai to Bring World-Class Artificial Intelligence to the Transportation and Distribution Industries," 2019, https://noodle.ai/case-studies/nfi (accessed August 9, 2019).
3. Topolytics, "About—Topolytics," http://topolytics.com/about/ (accessed August 17, 2019).
4. Rubicon Global, "About Us," https://www.rubiconglobal.com/about/ (accessed August 17, 2019).
5. Cognex, "Cognex—The Leader in Machine Vision," https://www.cognex.com/en-gb/company (accessed August 17, 2019).
6. Alstom, "Alstom Launches HealthHub, an Innovative Tool for Predictive Maintenance," September 23, 2014, https://www.alstom.com/press-releases-news/2014/9/innotrans2014-alstom-launches-healthhub-an-innovative-tool-for-predictive-maintenance- (accessed August 17, 2019).
7. SKF, "SKF Insight," https://www.skf.com/uk/products/condition-monitoring/skfinsight.html (accessed August 17, 2019).

8. Hello Tractor, "About Hello Tractor," https://www.hellotractor.com/about-us/ (accessed August 17, 2019).

9. NCC, "Digital Construction," https://www.ncc.group/our-offer/customer-values/digital-construction/ (accessed August 17, 2019).

10. Provenance, "About," https://www.provenance.org/about (accessed August 17, 2019).

11. Circularise, "About," https://www.circularise.com/about-1 (accessed August 17, 2019).

12. GE Digital, "Digital Twin," https://www.ge.com/digital/applications/digital-twin (accessed August 17, 2019).

13. Daimler, "NextGenAM—Pilot Project for Automated Metallic 3D Printing Proves a Complete Success," https://media.daimler.com/marsMediaSite/en/instance/ko/NextGenAM--pilot-project-for-automated-metallic-3D-printing-proves-a-complete-success.xhtml?oid=43205447 (accessed August 17, 2019).

14. Zenrobotics, "Robotic Waste Recycling Solutions," https://zenrobotics.com/ (accessed August 17, 2019).

15. Iberdrola, "Do You Know What Pumped-Storage Hydropower Stations Are Used for?" https://www.iberdrola.com/environment/pumped-storage-hydropower (accessed August 17, 2019).

16. EnOcean, "Energy Harvesting," https://www.enocean.com/en/technology/energy-harvesting/ (accessed August 17, 2019).

17. GloNaTech. "Marine Coatings," https://www.glonatech.com/nanotechnology-applications/marine-coatings/ (accessed August 17, 2019).

18. TOMRA, "The Next Big Step in Sensor-Based Waste Sorting," https://www.tomra.com/en-gb/about-us/tomra-innovation/sensor-based-waste-sorting (accessed August 17, 2019).

19. BBC News, "Cow Spray Painted with QR Code to Promote Dairy Farming," June 26, 2012, https://www.bbc.co.uk/news/uk-england-leicestershire-18594155 (accessed August 17, 2019).

20. Nate Hindman and Joe Epstein, "Sushi Chef Creates Edible QR Codes to End 'Fish Fraud' in California Restaurants," Business Insider, July 15, 2013, https://www.businessinsider.com/sushi-with-qr-codes-2013-7?r=US&IR=T (accessed August 17, 2019).

21. Esat Dedezade, "HoloLinc: Thyssenkrupp Rolls Out World's First Mixed Reality Stairlift Solution, Allowing Customers to Visualise and Customise products in Their Own Homes," Microsoft News, October 22, 2018, https://news.microsoft.com/europe/2018/10/22/hololinc-thyssenkrupp-rolls-out-worlds-first-mixed-reality-stairlift-solution-allowing-customers-to-visualise-and-customise-products-in-their-own-homes/ (accessed August 17, 2019).

22. Graviky Labs, "1.6 Trillion Litres of Air Cleaned So Far," http://www.graviky.com/ (accessed August 17, 2019).

23. DSM, "Niaga® Technology," https://www.dsm.com/corporate/science-innovation/resources-circularity/niaga.html (accessed August 17, 2019).

24. Unreasonable Group, "Cambrian Innovation—Meet an Unreasonable Company," https://unreasonablegroup.com/companies/cambrian-innovation?v=ln30J0CHbQc#overview (accessed August 17, 2019).

25. Peter Lacy, "These 5 Disruptive Technologies Are Driving the Circular Economy," World Economic Forum, September 14, 2017, https://www.weforum.org/agenda/2017/09/new-tech-sustainable-circular-economy/ (accessed August 17, 2019).

26. Wilhelm Klümper and Matin Qaim, "A Meta-Analysis of the Impacts of Genetically Modified Crops," *PLoS One*, 9(11), November 2014, https://journals.plos.org/plosone/article/file?id=10.1371/journal.pone.0111629&type=printable (accessed August 17, 2019).

27. Daniel Norero, "GMO Crops Have Been Increasing Yield for 20 Years, with More Progress Ahead," Alliance For Science, February 23, 2018, https://allianceforscience.cornell.edu/blog/2018/02/gmo-crops-increasing-yield-20-years-progress-ahead/ (accessed August 17, 2019).

28. James A. Hayward and Janice Meraglia, "DNA Marking and Authentication: A Unique, Secure Anti-Counterfeiting Program for the Electronics Industry," International Symposium On Microelectronics, 2011, https://adnas.com/wp-content/uploads/2016/07/dna_marking_and_authentication_oct_2011_5.pdf (accessed August 17, 2019).

29. Isha Datar and Daan Luining, "Mark Post's Cultured Beef," New Harvest, November 3, 2015, https://www.new-harvest.org/mark_post_cultured_beef (accessed August 17, 2019).

30. Tessa Naus, "Is Vertical Farming Really Sustainable?" Eit Food, August 29, 2018, https://www.eitfood.eu/blog/post/is-vertical-farming-really-sustainable (accessed August 17, 2019).

31. Bioeconomy, "Robbe's Little Garden's Vertical Farming Boosted by Smart Technology Greenhouses," https://www.bioeconomy.fi/robbes-little-gardens-vertical-farming-boosted-by-smart-technology-greenhouses/ (accessed August 17, 2019).

32. Peter Lacy, Jessica Long, Wesley Spindler et al., "The Circular Advantage: Moving from Insight to Action—Preview to the Circular Advantage Handbook," https://thecirculars.org/content/resources/The_Circular_Advantage.pdf (accessed August 9, 2019).

33. Labiotech, "How Big Is the Investment Gap Between Biotech and Digital? (Smaller Than You Think…)," 2018, https://labiotech.eu/features/gap-between-digital-biotech-investments/ (accessed August 9, 2019).

34. Simon Sharwood, "Developing World Hits 98.7 Per cent Mobile Phone Adoption," The Register, 2017, https://www.theregister.co.uk/2017/08/03/itu_facts_and_figures_2017/ (accessed August 9, 2019).

35. (1) Ecovative: Ecovative Design, "We Grow Materials," https://ecovative-design.com/ (accessed August 27, 2019); (2) Siemens: Siemens, "Efficiently Plan and Communicate Your Manufacturing Processes," https://www.plm.

automation.siemens.com/global/en/products/manufacturing-planning/manufacturing-process-planning.html (accessed August 27, 2019); (3) IKEA: IKEA, "The IKEA Group Approach to Sustainability," https://www.ikea.com/ms/en_JP/pdf/sustainability_report/group_approach_sustainability_fy11.pdf (accessed August 27, 2019); (4) SHARENOW: Your-Now, "Our Car Sharing SHARE NOW," https://www.your-now.com/our-solutions/share-now (accessed August 27, 2019); (5) Banyan Nation: Banyan Nation, "Our Work," http://banyannation.com/#ourwork (accessed August 27, 2019); (6) 12Return, "Returns Management Software," https://www.12return.com/returns-management-platform (accessed August 27, 2019); (7) Adidas: Anthony King, "Spinning Out Spider Silk Research," Royal Society of Chemistry, May 1, 2017, https://www.chemistryworld.com/features/spinning-out-spider-silk-research/3007091.article (accessed August 27, 2019).

36. Deloitte, "Medtech and the Internet of Medical Things—How Connected Medical Devices Are Transforming Health Care," July 2018, https://www2.deloitte.com/content/dam/Deloitte/tw/Documents/life-sciences-health-care/Medtech%20and%20the%20Internet%20of%20Medical%20Things.pdf (accessed August 17, 2019).

37. Accenture, "Winning with the Industrial Internet of Things How to Accelerate the Journey to Productivity and Growth," 2015, https://www.accenture.com/t20160909T042713Z__w__/us-en/_acnmedia/Accenture/Conversion-Assets/DotCom/Documents/Global/PDF/Dualpub_11/Accenture-Industrial-Internet-of-Things-Positioning-Paper-Report-2015.pdfla=en (accessed August 9, 2019).

38. Phil Beecher, "Three IoT Implementation Challenges and How to Overcome Them," IT Pro Portal, 2018, https://www.itproportal.com/features/three-iot-implementation-challenges-and-how-to-overcome-them/ (accessed August 9, 2019).

39. BootUP, "Sustainable Energy Management with Artificial Intelligence," https://www.bootupventures.com/downloads/AI_in_energy.pdf (accessed August 9, 2019).

40. Business Wire, "Machine Learning: Global $23+ Billion Market Trends & Opportunities (2018–2023)," 2018, https://www.businesswire.com/news/home/20181212005361/en/Machine-Learning-Global-23-Billion-Market-Trends (accessed August 9, 2019).

41. Daniel Gutierrez, "Three Barriers to Machine Learning Adoption," insideBIGDATA, 2016, https://insidebigdata.com/2016/09/20/three-barriers-to-machine-learning-adoption/ (accessed August 9, 2019).

42. Lily Fu, "Four Key Barriers to the Widespread Adoption of AI," R&D Magazine, 2018, https://www.rdmag.com/article/2018/05/four-key-barriers-widespread-adoption-ai (accessed August 13, 2019).

43. Zion Market Research, "Global Industrial Robotics Market Will Reach USD 62.19 Billion By 2024: Zion Market Research," 2018, https://www.

globenewswire.com/news-release/2018/10/25/1626970/0/en/Global-Industrial-Robotics-Market-Will-Reach-USD-62-19-Billion-By-2024-Zion-Market-Research.html (accessed August 9, 2019).

44. Apple, "Environmental Responsibility Report—2017 Progress Report, Covering Fiscal Year 2016," 2017, https://images.apple.com/environment/pdf/Apple_Environmental_Responsibility_Report_2017.pdf (accessed August 17, 2019).

45. Lloyd Alter, "The New MacBook Air Is Made from Recycled Aluminum: Is This a Big Deal?" Treehugger, October 20, 2018, https://www.treehugger.com/corporate-responsibility/new-macbook-air-made-recycled-aluminum-big-deal.html (accessed August 17, 2019).

46. Apple, "Apple Expands Global Recycling Programmes," April 18, 2019, https://www.apple.com/uk/newsroom/2019/04/apple-expands-global-recycling-programs/ (accessed August 17, 2019).

47. Market Watch, "Global Energy Harvesting Market 2019—Industry Analysis, Size, Share, Strategies and Forecast to 2023," 2019, https://www.marketwatch.com/press-release/global-energy-harvesting-market-2019-industry-analysis-size-share-strategies-and-forecast-to-2023-2019-03-28 (accessed August 9, 2019).

48. Wang et al., "Efficient Scagenging of Solar and Wind Energies in a Smart City," ACS Publications, May 5, 2016, https://pubs.acs.org/doi/abs/10.1021/acsnano.6b02575 (accessed August 9, 2019).

49. Gene Frantz, Dave Freeman, and Chris Link, "TI Technology Opens New Frontiers for Perpetual Devices," 2018, http://www.ti.com/lit/wp/sszy004/sszy004.pdf (accessed August 9, 2019).

50. Ed Sperling and Kevin Fogarty, "The Limits of Energy Harvesting," Semiconductor Engineering, 2019, https://semiengineering.com/the-limits-of-energy-harvesting/ (accessed August 9, 2019).

51. BP, "Energy Demand by Sector," https://www.bp.com/en/global/corporate/energy-economics/energy-outlook/demand-by-sector.html (accessed August 9, 2019).

52. Mazda, "Bio-Based Plastics," https://www.mazda.com/en/innovation/technology/env/bioplastics/ (accessed August 17, 2019).

53. GRID-Arendal, "Global Plastic Production," 2013, http://www.grida.no/resources/6923 (accessed August 9, 2019).

54. Katherine Martinko, "The Problem with Bioplastics," Treehugger, 2017, https://www.treehugger.com/clean-technology/problem-bioplastics.html (accessed August 9, 2019).

55. Umit Emre Erdogan, "Success and Failure Factors for the Adoption of Bio-Based Packaging," KTH Industrial Engineering and Management, Master of Science thesis, 2013, www.diva-portal.org/smash/get/diva2:636875/FULLTEXT01.pdf (accessed August 9, 2019).

56. Technavio, "Global Bioenergy Market 2018–2022," 2018, https://www.technavio.com/report/global-bio-energy-market-analysis-share-2018 (accessed August 9, 2019).

57. Arlene Karidis, "Enerkem to Make Methanol Through Gasification in Netherlands," Waste360, 2018, www.waste360.com/waste-energy/enerkem-make-methanol-through-gasification-netherlands (accessed August 9, 2019).

58. Bentham Paulos, "Myths and Facts About Biopower (Part 1 of 3)," energy-post.eu, 2017, https://energypost.eu/myths-and-facts-about-biopower-part-1-of-3/ (accessed August 9, 2019).

59. U.S. Energy Information Administration, "Biomass and the Environment," 2019, https://www.eia.gov/energyexplained/index.php?page=biomass_environment (accessed August 9, 2019).

60. Winnow Solutions, "Technology to Run a More Profitable, Sustainable Kitchen," 2019, https://www.winnowsolutions.com/en/benefits (accessed August 9, 2019).

61. PR Newswire, "Goodyear Unveils Oxygene, a Concept Tire Designed to Support Cleaner and More Convenient Urban Mobility," 2018, www.prnewswire.com/news-releases/goodyear-unveils-oxygene-a-concept-tire-designed-to-support-cleaner-and-more-convenient-urban-mobility-675956303.html (accessed August 9, 2019).

62. Centre for the New Economy and Society, "The Future of Jobs Report 2018," World Economic Forum, 2018, www3.weforum.org/docs/WEF_Future_of_Jobs_2018.pdf (accessed August 9, 2019).

63. H. James Wilson, Paul R. Daugherty, and Nicola Morini-Bianzino, "The Jobs That Artificial Intelligence Will Create," *MIT Sloan Management Review*, 2017, https://sloanreview.mit.edu/article/will-ai-create-as-many-jobs-as-it-eliminates/ (accessed August 9, 2019).

64. Therese Bennich and Salim Belyazid, "The Route to Sustainability—Prospects and Challenges of the Bio-Based Economy," Sustainability, 2017, www.mdpi.com/2071-1050/9/6/887/pdf (accessed August 9, 2019).

65. FSC is an international, non-governmental organisation dedicated to promoting responsible management of the world's forests. Forest Stewardship Council, "About Us," https://fsc.org/en/page/about-us (accessed August 27, 2019).

66. Tetra Pak, "FSC® Label Now Visible on 70% of All Tetra Pak packaging in Malaysia," October 6, 2017, https://www.tetrapak.com/my/about/news-archive/fsc-label-now-visible-on-malaysia-packaging (accessed August 9, 2019).

67. Xylem, "City of South Bend, Indiana," 2019, https://www.xylem.com/siteassets/campaigns/stormwater-handbook/combined-sewer-overflow-volume-reduction.pdf (accessed August 9, 2019).

68. Circularise, "The Open, Distributed and Secure Communications Protocol for the Circular Economy," https://www.circularise.com/ (accessed August 9, 2019).

69. Platform for Accelerating the Circular Economy in collaboration with Accenture Strategy, "Harnessing the Fourth Industrial Revolution for the Circular Economy Consumer Electronics and Plastics Packaging," World Economic Forum, January 2019, http://www3.weforum.org/docs/WEF_Harnessing_4IR_Circular_Economy_report_2018.pdf (accessed August 17, 2019).

70. Derek Markham, "Produce Covered with This Invisible Plant-Based Edible Coating Stay Fresh Twice as Long," Treehugger, December 21, 2016, https://www.treehugger.com/green-food/produce-covered-invisible-plant-based-edible-coating-stay-fresh-twice-long.html (accessed August 9, 2019).

71. Chloe Sorvino, "Tyson Invests in Lab-Grown Protein Startup Memphis Meats, Joining Bill Gates and Richard Branson," Forbes, January 29, 2018, https://www.forbes.com/sites/chloesorvino/2018/01/29/exclusive-interview-tyson-invests-in-lab-grown-protein-startup-memphis-meats-joining-bill-gates-and-richard-branson/#23c1e3873351 (accessed August 9, 2019).

72. Lystek, "Lystegro Biofertilizer," 2019, https://lystek.com/solutions/lystegro-biofertilizer/ (accessed August 9, 2019).

73. Accenture and the H&M Foundation, "Circular x Fashion Tech Trend Report 2018," 2018, https://www.accenture.com/t20180327t110326z__w__/us-en/_acnmedia/pdf-74/accenture-gca-circular-fashiontech-trend-report-2018.pdf (accessed August 17, 2019).

74. H&M Foundation, "H&M Foundation Awards 5 Innovations a Total €1 Million Grant for Their Efforts to Make Fashion Sustainable," Cision PR Newswire, April 4, 2019, https://www.prnewswire.com/news-releases/hm-foundation-awards-5-innovations-a-total-1-million-grant-for-their-efforts-to-make-fashion-sustainable-300824787.html (accessed August 17, 2019).

Part II

Where Do We Need to Be?—Scaling Industry Impact

4

Circular Economy: A Tale of 10 Industries

We've outlined the global opportunity to transition from a linear to a circular economy and the underlying business models and technologies that support the transformation. Now we will explore what this shift means across specific industries. We will examine the role that 10 different industries can play in the circular transition and how they can realize significant value through large-scale adoption of circular principles.

There are countless ways to segment industries, and today's digital economy challenges traditional definitions. For this reason, we segmented the industries based on product types and characteristics and the raw materials that are affected by their production and consumption. For example, rather than looking at retail, we considered the various types of products consumers purchase: consumables, clothes, household appliances, information and communication technology (ICT) devices, etc. Each of these differs in terms of the raw materials used, waste streams, useful life, typical price point, and customers' emotional attachment.

What's Driving the Industry Shift to Circularity?

The types and volume of industry-level circular activity vary widely. In general, consumer-facing industries have seen the largest volumes of circular activity, often driven by demands from consumers, governments, and employees. Specifically, the leading players in fast-moving consumer goods (FMCG) have set ambitious circular economy goals, often with a focus on packaging and input waste reduction. The consumer-facing fashion industry

© The Author(s) 2020
P. Lacy et al., *The Circular Economy Handbook*,
https://doi.org/10.1057/978-1-349-95968-6_4

has also seen an uptick in action and commitment on the circular economy, from use of alternative materials to product takeback and reuse. For these industries, rising consumer demand and expectations is a clear driver. According to a 2019 Accenture survey, nearly three-quarters of consumers (72%) say they buy more "environmentally friendly products" today than five years ago. Growing public discourse on issues such as plastics and "disposable" fashion is spurring the "call to action" for brands in these sectors. More recently, however, business-to-business (B2B) industries that are less visible to consumers, such as chemical, and metals and mining companies, are starting to see a push from customers (or from the customers of customers). Indeed, a majority of consumers (83%) believe it is important for companies to design products that are meant to be reused or recycled, and about half (49%) believe that the chemical industry, for example, is the *least concerned* about the impact it has on the environment compared with eight other sectors.[1]

Other industries feel the pressure of regulatory drivers. In the household appliances sector, for instance, increasing regulations on responsible treatment of products at end of use are pushing companies to focus on greater recovery of used machines. In the United States, Environmental Protection Agency (EPA) regulations require technicians who service refrigeration and air-conditioning equipment to follow specific practices to maximize recovery and recycling.[2] The topic of regulation and the implications for businesses will be covered in depth in our section on policy (see Part III, "Policy—The Role of Policymakers").

In some cases, circular economy principles naturally align with how industries have long managed their businesses, such as the focus on multi-decade product lifecycles for machinery and industrial equipment (M&IE) and automotive companies. These industries often have strong after-sales maintenance and services baked into their business models. Therefore, the transition to circularity is a natural extension of business-as-usual.

Uptake of the Circular Business Models

Across industries, a compelling financial case is emerging for the move from linear to circular models of production and consumption. To capture circular value and pivot to new growth areas, most industries adopt a dual focus: applying circular models to their existing value chains, while also incrementally altering the way they do things today. An example is driving efficiencies within operations while experimenting with Product as a Service business models. The typical mix of opportunities across industries includes a change to the product itself (e.g., via Circular Inputs, such as renewable materials), its production (e.g., the use of fewer resources and reduced resource or material waste), and its consumption (e.g., circular models that change the way that customers consume, re-consume, or take control of a product at end of use).

Today, the greatest opportunity for creativity and industry crossover occurs at the intersection of Resource Recovery and Circular Inputs, as each industry tries to figure out what it can and should take back into its value chain versus what it should divert for reuse by others. We are seeing used shoes recycled into sports flooring or car interiors, unwanted plastics transformed into superior road surfaces, and wastewater becoming fuel for public fleets. Although the crossover of Circular Inputs is still limited by technical feasibility, inadequate infrastructures, and unintended impacts, the potential is huge. We'll explore this further in later chapters.

Circular opportunities may also blur industry lines. Many businesses are finding opportunities by enabling circularity for other sectors. Oil and gas companies are getting into the electricity and e-mobility sectors, and chemical companies are embracing their role in textiles and food component innovation. Take, for example, American chemical company Eastman Chemical's circular recycling technology that has the potential to break down polyester-based products into "building blocks" which can, in turn, be used in new products, ultimately helping to solve the textile recycling challenge.[3]

The Barriers and Enablers

On their journeys to close the loop—within an organization, across the industry, and throughout an ecosystem—we see common barriers and enablers. Companies across all industries need to scale innovation, build partnerships, focus on broader supply chain circularity, and support enabling policies and regulations. While circular opportunities will generally address the four types of linear waste covered in Chapter 2 (i.e., wasted resources, wasted capacity, wasted lifecycles, and wasted embedded values), the balance between them will differ.

Resource-intensive production industries like oil and gas refining, metals and mining, or equipment manufacturing need to focus on reducing wasted resources as well as machine downtime (wasted capacity). This means looking at circular and renewable inputs and focusing on efficiencies, utilization, and the foundational reduction and reuse of natural resources, such as water. In more consumption-focused industries, such as consumer electronics and goods, a significant part of the waste profile occurs during product use (wasted capacity) and premature disposal (wasted lifecycles). Thus, in addition to reducing waste during manufacturing processes, these companies can capture value through service-based models that extend product lives or through the recovery of useful material at end of use (wasted embedded values).

It's also important to note that customer demand and appetite for different models will vary by industry. Although there's a general shift toward more simplicity and less consumption, consumer readiness to shift to renting or sharing models for goods or services depends on the perceived value of the product. Research suggests such models are generally easier with goods that are more functional and less sentimental (a lawn mower versus a wedding dress), lower value versus hyper valuable (a stroller versus a piece of art), or those that lack hygienic factors when it comes to reuse (a book versus a toothbrush).[4] When it comes to willingness to pay, consumers are also most likely to pay a premium for food and beverage packaging (containers or wrappers), electronics products (computers, TVs, stereos, etc.) and children's toys that are designed to be reused or recycled, with over 55% willing to pay at least a 10% premium.[5]

Just as existing industry dynamics can be conducive to circular economy practices (e.g., the focus on servicing in M&IE), they can also complicate the transition. In the ICT and fashion industries, consumers have become accustomed to having access to the latest products at the lowest possible costs, either on-demand or delivered within days. This drives the relatively short lifespan for previously longer-lasting devices and clothing. Even products that are durable and have long useful lives become outdated or unwanted prematurely. For instance, mobile phones might technically last for four to five years, but the demand for a quicker refresh of these products limits their ability to generate enough value through disassembly and upcycling versus reselling on secondary markets.

Lastly, although sophisticated advancements are happening across industries, such as AI tools leveraging machine vision to reduce food waste in kitchens or pressurized CO_2 helping to completely eliminate water and chemicals from textile dyeing processes, the opportunities and barriers related to technology and infrastructure have not been uniform, even within a single industry. Moreover, the maturity of technologies and infrastructures has not been uniform across industries. The fashion industry is struggling with the quality and performance of recycled textiles, for example. In oil and gas, greater carbon circularity relies on carbon capture technologies that have yet to prove scalable at a reasonable cost. When it comes to collection at end of use, the FMCG industry is encouraging customers to return their product packaging but because packaging is currently so low-value, companies have been focusing on building out very localized collection and recycling systems. In contrast, ICT devices have very valuable components that require global shipping to centralized locations.

Understanding the Value

Given the specific nuances of different industries, we've decided to look at the value opportunity for each individually, recognizing that many companies might operate across multiple industries, and the lines aren't always clear between them. For each industry, we highlight one key circular value area that companies can pursue over the short and medium term. We determined a key circular theme to help identify a set of tangible opportunities, for example, packaging in FMCG. The opportunity set is then used to determine specific drivers of value grounded in case studies that illuminate the potential scale of the opportunity for individual companies and the industry as a whole.

It is important to note, however, that this is not the only way the industry can create value from the circular economy. For example, we recognize that the potential value opportunities for FMCG companies stretch far beyond optimization of packaging. These value calculations could never hope to be comprehensive and are estimates based on the best currently available information. But they do point to the magnitude of the opportunities available and the imperative for action.

Figure 4.1 summarizes the industries we will cover and the areas of circular value opportunity we will explore in more depth.

To assess the potential scale of any given opportunity, we calculated the impact on operating profit (see Fig. 4.2).[5] It quickly became apparent that these opportunities could generate value in three ways:

1. Value addition through new sources of revenue,
2. Value addition through reducing costs, and
3. Revenue generated for a specific company through value migration.

Value addition is the creation of profit pools where none existed before. This evident in the majority of cases examined. **Value migration** refers to profit shifting between industry participants or from one type of product/service to another. This measures a shift in value rather than new value added to the industry value chain. For example, Company A's circular product resonates with consumers better than Company B's linear equivalent and therefore people switch from B to A. Sometimes value migration occurs between industries as they converge, but this is less common.

The analysis in this study shows that the cost reduction side of the equation offers tremendous value potential: about $500 billion in aggregate for the eight industries for which we quantified value. Cost reduction should be easier for companies to pursue because it involves change within their control. It doesn't require shifts in cultural expectations or in consumer behavior. That said, capturing this value is not a simple matter and may entail significant investments in process and technology.

INDUSTRY	DESCRIPTION	CIRCULAR VALUE THEME
Metals & Mining	Minerals and metals are used in everything from consumer electronics to high-strength steel for industrial applications, jewelry and renewable energy generation.	Circular inputs
O&G	Oil and gas (O&G) includes upstream activities (exploration and production), midstream activities (transportation, storage and processing), and downstream activities (purification, refining, logistics/transport and retail).	Energy transition
Chemical	The chemical industry produces intermediary and end products used by almost all other industries, including basic chemicals and its products, petrochemicals, fertilizers, paints, gases, pharmaceuticals, dyes, etc.	Circular inputs
Electricity	The electricity industry includes power generation, transmission, distribution and retail to commercial or residential customers.	Shift to renewable and efficient distribution and transmission
M&IE	Machinery & industrial equipment (M&IE) includes heavy-duty and off-road equipment for lifting and moving goods and materials.	End-of-use potentials: reuse and recycle
ICT	The information & communication technology (ICT) industry includes devices and equipment for information and communication such as smartphones, computers, routers, etc.	Reverse infrastructure: refurbish and recycle
Personal Mobility	Personal mobility is the use of private or public vehicles by individuals for transportation.	Shift to electric and circular operations
Household	The household industry provides products such as furniture, white goods and appliances.	Repair and reuse
FMCG	Fast-moving consumer goods (FMCG) products are primarily categorized into packaged food, beverages, toiletries, personal and home care, characterized by high frequency of purchases and large volumes.	Circular packaging
Fashion	The fashion industry produces, sells and markets clothing and accessories.	Circular material use

Fig. 4.1 Industries and circular value themes

Types of Value (cross-industry), by 2030
USD Billion

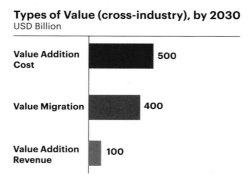

Value Addition Cost — 500

Value Migration — 400

Value Addition Revenue — 100

Fig. 4.2 Cost initiatives and value migration are the largest drivers of value across industries (*Source* Accenture Research)

Generating net new value in terms of revenue is a heavier lift; for example, reducing operating costs around water and energy requires less effort than building a new renewable energy offering. Our analysis estimates that value addition for new revenue generation equates to around 10% of the total value at stake, roughly $100 billion. The difficulty in new revenue generation could be due to a number of factors, for example: (a) circularity as a theme on its own may not generate additional demand for products and services; (b) consumers in most industries may be unwilling to pay a price premium for circular products; and (c) competition from new players in adjacent industries can erode growth opportunities, e.g., automotive companies offering on-demand mobility services must compete against pure-play on-demand mobility providers such as Uber.

Nevertheless, the value at stake in terms of migration between industry players can be much larger, as much as $400 billion. A couple of factors are at play here. Consumer and regulatory shifts are triggering change in industries like automotive (toward EV) or utilities (toward renewables). We also see less extreme but significant shifts in consumer preferences for circular products in other industries. In FMCG, circular packaging is becoming a foundational factor/license-to-compete while in fashion, niche segments are pushing demand for responsible products. Maintaining and gaining market share depend on having the right circular value propositions.

These three fundamental types of value can be split further so that the opportunities can be categorized into seven main themes (see Fig. 4.3).

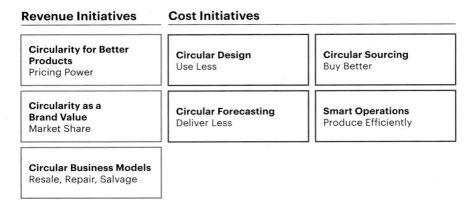

Fig. 4.3 Seven themes for value creation

These value categories demonstrate the potential to improve a company's profitability in different ways. Three of the initiatives help increase a company's revenues:

- **Pricing**: Using circular principles as a way of making better products and charging consumers or customers more for them. This is called premiumization.
- **Branding**: Using a strong circular economy strategy to differentiate a brand from competitors, thereby attracting new customers. This should result in improved market share.
- **Business models**: Using our five circular business models as a way of finding entirely new sources of income.

The four other **cost initiatives** help to reduce a company's cost base.

Each value category approach enables more intelligent and efficient use of resources:

- **Design**: Rethinking the way products are designed to reduce the cost of the raw materials required to make them—for example, reducing the amount of packaging needed.
- **Sourcing**: Understanding the resource flows of a business to help ensure that it sources only what it precisely needs and that, as much possible, those resources come from recycling or reuse.

- **Forecasting**: Deploying advances in analytics and logistics technology to reduce waste in three areas: products made and never sold, overstock in inventories, or items delivered to the wrong locations.
- **Production**: Reducing the production costs of energy, water, and other basic resources, which are becoming increasingly expensive.

The relative contribution of each of these seven value categories differs across industries, as shown in Fig. 4.4.

Each industry has a different level of impact per initiative

	Circular Initiatives	M&M	O&G	Chem.	Elec.	M&IE	ICT	P.Mob.	House.	FMCG	Fash.
REVENUES	Circularity for Better Products – Pricing Power										
	Circularity as Brand Value – Market Share										
	Circular Business Models – Resale, Repair, Salvage										
COSTS	Circular Design – Use Less										
	Circular Forecasting – Deliver Less										
	Circular Sourcing – Buy Better										
	Smart Operations – Produce Efficiently										

Value not quantified (M&M and Chem. columns)

Legend:
- ☐ Insignificant
- ▨ Low: < 10% of total impact
- ▨ Medium: 10-20% of total impact
- ■ High: >20% of total impact

Key:

M&M:	Metals & Mining	**P.Mob.:**	Personal Mobility
O&G:	Oil & Gas	**House.:**	Household
Chem.:	Chemicals	**FMCG:**	Fast-moving Consumer Goods
Elec.:	Electricity	**Fash.:**	Fashion
M&IE:	Machinery & Industrial Equipment		
ICT:	Information & Communications Technology		

Fig. 4.4   Heatmap for value by industry and theme

In the FMCG industry, for example, circular design has the greatest impact (>20% of the total impact). Companies that design products and packaging with fewer raw materials should be able to realize significant value. By contrast, the FMCG industry might see limited opportunity for premiumization, given the price sensitivity of most markets. In other industries like fashion, though, opportunities are more heavily concentrated in revenue-generating initiatives, making it critical for brands to differentiate themselves and establish new business models. Specific differences among these industries will be explored in the following industry profiles.

We present the industry profiles in order (roughly) from those industries closest to the extraction point of resources to those closest to the end consumer. For each industry, we discuss the circular landscape, highlighting key sources of waste and untapped value in their value chains and explore the opportunities with greatest value potential. Finally, we reflect on the barriers each industry faces and key enablers to unlock true circularity at scale.

Chapter Takeaways

- In general, consumer-facing industries such as FMCG and fashion have seen the most circular activity, but B2B companies are starting to experience a push from customers (or from the customers of customers).
- In certain industries like machinery and industrial equipment, and mobility, circular principles naturally align with the way that companies have long managed their businesses (e.g., an emphasis on after-sales maintenance and services).
- Circular opportunities can blur industry lines—for example, oil and gas companies migrating into the electricity and e-mobility sectors.
- Different industries may need to focus on different types of waste. Metals and mining companies should concentrate on reducing wasted resources and wasted capacity (machine downtime), whereas the ICT industry should focus on wasted lifecycles (premature product disposal) and wasted embedded values.
- Companies can generate circular value in three ways: value addition through cost reduction, revenue migration, and value addition through revenue generation. The first two areas of opportunity are currently more substantial than the third.
- There are seven main themes for value creation: pricing, branding, business models, design, sourcing, forecasting, and production. The first three enable companies to generate revenue, while the remaining four help them to reduce their cost base. All seven types of opportunities are spread unevenly across the different industries.

Notes

1. Australian Retailers Association, "Survey Shows More Than Half of Consumers Would Pay More for Sustainable Products," July 12, 2019, https://blog.retail.org.au/newsandinsights/survey-shows-more-than-half-of-consumers-would-pay-more-for-sustainable-products (accessed August 19, 2019).
2. United States Environmental Protection Agency, "Stationary Refrigeration Service Practice Requirements," 2017, https://www.epa.gov/section608/stationary-refrigeration-service-practice-requirements (accessed August 8, 2019).
3. Eastman, "Eastman Offers Innovative Recycling Technology for Polyesters," March 5, 2019, https://www.eastman.com/Company/News_Center/2019/Pages/Eastman-offers-innovative-recycling-technology-for-polyesters.aspx (accessed August 8, 2019).
4. Tom Szaky—CEO and founder of TerraCycle, Interview by Jessica Long, Mikayla Hart and Jenna Trescott, Telephone Call, London, May 24, 2019.
5. Operating profit is defined at earnings before interest, tax, depreciation, and amortization (EBITDA).

5

 Metals & Mining Industry Profile

Table 5.1 Industry summary

 Metals & Mining industry today: Noticeable progress with respect to energy, carbon, and water, with some organizations targeting waste initiatives. "Circular economy" terminology is gaining traction throughout the value chain and starting to catalyze innovation

Case for change	Today	Looking ahead
Industry size	~$2.3 trillion	~$3.6 trillion (projection for 2030)
Illustrative waste volumes	• In 2015, four billion gallons of water were used for mining operations in the United States, accounting for 1% of the country's total water withdrawals[1] • The metals and mining sector is among the world's largest generators of waste, accounting for ~10 billion tons a year[2] • The production of one ton of copper generates ~110 tons of waste ore and ~200 tons of overburden[3,4] • In a single year, the worldwide mining industry generates ~6.5 million tons of tailings[4]	• A surge in metal demand will drive increased extraction and waste generation: – The amount of e-waste that contains precious metals is expected to grow to 27 million tons by 2030[5] – According to the International Energy Agency (IEA), by 2030 the amount of installed wind power globally will nearly double, requiring an additional 2 million tons of copper[6] – By 2030, the number of electric vehicles (EV) on the road is expected to reach 125 million, up from 3.1 million vehicles in 2017, according to IEA.[7] EVs require a larger array of minerals and metals
Value at stake	–	Levels of penetration in the circular space are highly variable by metal, and the recycling industry is fragmented with a lack of penetration of large mining players. Therefore, an accurate value projection cannot be generalized for the industry

© The Author(s) 2020
P. Lacy et al., *The Circular Economy Handbook*,
https://doi.org/10.1057/978-1-349-95968-6_5

🔋 Industry Status

Minerals and metals are used in everything from consumer electronics to high-strength steel for industrial applications, jewelry, and renewable energy generation. Demand for primary materials will continue to escalate, driven by rising global population, rapid urbanization, spread of digital technologies, and economic growth. According to the international financial institution the World Bank, the transition to a low-carbon economy will result in increased primary demand for aluminum, cobalt, lithium, silver, nickel, lead, zinc, and other metals. Glencore, a British-Swiss commodity trading and mining company, has found that meeting the Clean Energy Ministerial target of 30 million EV sales by 2030 would require 314 kilotons of cobalt per year by 2030—more than triple the demand in 2017.[8] However, current cobalt reserves are only predicted to last for 23 years, so innovative alternatives are needed to satisfy demand.[9] While some resources, such as cobalt, are scarce, others are still abundant. Iron, for instance, is plentiful with 5.6% of earth's crust made of iron.[10] Where the supply-side risks are low, demand-driven commodity price fluctuations tend to sway the balance between secondary and primary metal usage. As the price of primary feedstock rises on the back of strong demand,[11] the industry will experience higher recycling rates, the supply and use of secondary raw materials, investments in recycling, and more sophisticated purification technologies.

To date, circular economy innovation has focused on operational improvements. Mining leaders have started to connect efficiency initiatives and the circular economy more explicitly, especially in the domains of energy, water use, and carbon-neutral operations. Downstream circularity is also evolving, driven by two major factors: supply risk and visibility throughout the value chain, and customer pull by manufacturers that have embedded increasing levels of material sustainability in their products. For example, an original equipment manufacturer (OEM)-led shift in the automotive industry toward greater circularity in both design and use of secondary materials is already having an impact on mining companies. The automobile maker Renault is collaborating with large players in the metals recycling value chain (e.g., Suez) to enhance recycling capabilities and develop mutually beneficial programs. Using its experience as a manufacturer, Renault provides valuable insights about end-of-use resources for car dismantling.[12]

? Waste to Wealth Challenges

The mining industry must address three major areas of waste (see Fig. 5.1). The first is wasted resources with respect to the inputs used. In the United States alone, more than 15 million cubic meters of water were withdrawn for mining operations in 2015, accounting for 1% of the country's total water withdrawals (or about 6000 Olympic-size swimming

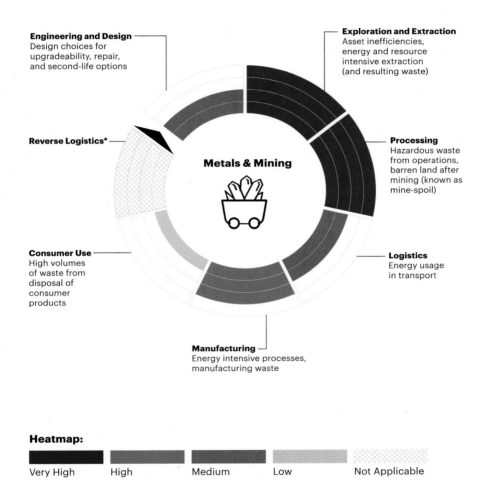

Fig. 5.1 Waste analysis diagram

pools).[1] Enormous amounts of energy are also required. Mining and metal production operations consume about 7.5% of the global energy supply (IEA 2016) and account for about a tenth of global energy consumption today.[13,14]

The second is wasted embedded value. The most relevant waste category here is waste from operations, both mineral (tailings) and non-mineral waste (overburden or waste rock). Production of one ton of copper, for example, generates about 110 tons of tailings and roughly 200 tons of overburden.[4] The average ore grade has declined by about 25% in a span of 10 years, resulting in higher levels of overburden.[15] Non-hazardous mineral and non-mineral waste, as well as slag from smelting, are valuable resources that can have multiple applications, such as landscaping material, aggregate in construction, or feedstock for cement and concrete.[16]

The third major area of waste comes from sub-optimal management and procurement of equipment. According to recent research, equipment utilization rates for mine operators are around 30–50%, suggesting that mining organizations could benefit from more flexible ownership models for machinery, including as-a-service agreements.[17]

 ## Waste to Wealth Opportunities

The mining industry has three broad areas of opportunity (see Table 5.2). The first has to do with renewable inputs. In general, the uptake of renewable energy by the mining industry has been relatively slow, but the improved economics of solar and wind, together with the threat of potential carbon pricing, are now driving organizations to actively strike deals with local utility companies for the supply of renewable energy.[18] Chile, where mining energy requirements are typically higher because of the challenging topography, has been a global leader with as many as nine different mining companies having installed renewable capacity to date.[19]

The second area involves upstream waste. Industry leaders are already rolling out zero-waste-to-landfill initiatives and innovative solutions, such as the recycling of quartz from iron-ore mining waste for producing synthetic quartz, used in kitchen and bathroom countertops.[24] Best practice indicates that a successful waste strategy starts with a detailed mapping and quantification of all waste streams. Waste management partners then identify, or develop, optimal waste solutions and applications for by-products. Mine closure and land rehabilitation present a new frontier for circularity, as companies begin to extend the lifecycle of mines. This could be based on top-soil

Table 5.2 Waste to wealth opportunity summary.

Circular economy opportunity	Scaling the use of renewable inputs	Capitalizing circular opportunities upstream	Implementing innovative business models in the marketplace
Type of opportunity	Scaling the use of renewable inputs	Operational/upstream circularity	Downstream circular models
Value at stake		Not quantified[20]	
Value levers	• Reduced cost of energy	• New revenue sources • Reduced cost of goods	• New revenue sources • Market share gain
Target waste	• Energy consumption • Carbon footprint	• Operational waste • Wastewater	• End-of-use waste
Value chain focus	• Extraction, exploration, and processing	• Extraction, exploration, and processing	• Manufacturing and industrial use
Technology amplifiers	• Breakthroughs in renewable energy technologies	• IoT, advanced analytics, predictive algorithms, sensors, and technologies to turn by-products into goods	• Platforms, IoT, blockchain for traceability, robotics, machine learning, AI, advanced analytics, and advanced material technologies
Case study	To help curb diesel consumption and mitigate fuel-price risks, the steel recycling company Cronimet has built a one-megawatt solar PV plant as part of a solar-diesel hybrid system at its "Zimbi" mine in South Africa. The company shifts its flexible load from peak periods during the evening to the daytime when solar resources are abundant, resulting in a reduction in annual diesel consumption by about 24%[21]	The American mining company Newmont Goldcorp's waste-to-ore demonstration plant uses sensor technology to determine which rocks have a higher probability of mineralization. An air knife then separates those rocks, which helps eliminate 20–30% of the waste that had previously come from the mill processes, while also reducing energy use. The company has also increased its reuse of oil and grinding balls, and it recycles its scrap metal, paper, pallets, glass, and aluminum. In addition, some sites have implemented composting programs for organic waste[22]	In 2018, VRB Energy, the battery manufacturer, signed a Strategic Cooperation Framework Agreement with Pangang Group Vanadium and Titanium Resources, the world's largest vanadium-oxide producer. The agreement includes long-term supply and leasing of vanadium electrolyte and joint development of the global vanadium flow battery industry. Pangang V&T will join with VRB Energy to establish commercial leasing of vanadium electrolyte[23]

rehabilitation or the re-purposing and reuse of sites, as with the Kidston Mine Project in north Queensland, Australia.[25]

The third opportunity area is in the downstream business. This typically focuses on material stewardship practices and materials recovery. One study has estimated that recovering gold, copper, and other metals from discarded electronics is 13 times cheaper than mining for virgin equivalents.[26] Companies could also develop and maintain a marketplace platform for trading secondary metals, waste by-products, idle equipment, or end-of-use assets. Advocating a circular business model, Umicore's product offering is centered on closing the loop on material flows for clients. Umicore buys sustainably mined cobalt raw materials to manufacture materials for rechargeable batteries that power EVs. When the batteries are no longer useful, they recycle them to recover the cobalt.[27] The cobalt is then used to make new battery materials, and the same happens with nickel. Another nascent option is to deploy a Product as a Service business model—multinational steel and mining company ArcelorMittal has introduced a rental business model for its steel sheet piles.[28]

Technology Amplifiers

With advances in IoT, data science, ore extracting and processing technology, robotics, sensors, and other technologies, companies are seizing many of the opportunities described above. Examples include:

- Anglo American's FutureSmart Mining initiative is exploring the use of modular swarm robotics—fleets of low-cost, modular mining robots that go directly into the orebody without touching the surrounding overburden.[29]
- The steel manufacturer Tata Steel is deploying a low-carbon smelter technology that is able to utilize raw materials of lower quality and produces highly concentrated CO_2 ideally suited for carbon capture and utilization technologies.[30]
- Waste, water, and energy management company Veolia is pioneering the extraction of precious materials from various healthcare sources, including cancer treatment drugs (platinum), pacemakers and insulin pumps (gold), and burn dressings (silver).[31]

- Mitsubishi Materials, the Japanese cement and metals manufacturer, has invested >$100 million in urban mining, including testing ways to transport and disassemble lithium-ion batteries to mine rare metals from them.[32]
- Diamond company De Beers Group has tested a carbon-sequestration technology in kimberlite rock, capturing carbon in the rock from which diamonds are extracted to offset GHG emissions. The technology has potential application beyond diamonds.[33]

Obstacles to Overcome

The most significant challenge in the metals and mining industry is that the primary demand for minerals and metals will continue to rise in the near term; therefore, the total resource demand is unlikely to be fulfilled by secondary supplies, as there simply isn't enough accessible scrap or used material. Moreover, complex alloys and engineered metals require very high purity and quality, and the current ability of secondary market systems to provide product to such standards is limited.

To overcome the barriers to the circular transition, a number of factors are key. Technology innovation to improve accessibility and purity of recycled metals is vital. In addition, traditional mining companies must explore new business models and capabilities that support circularity within upstream operations, and downstream with cutting-edge customer offerings. As Mark Cutifani, CEO of Anglo American emphasizes, "A shift toward a more circular economy presents a significant opportunity for mining companies that are willing to embrace it by re-imagining their business and partnering with the intermediate and end users of the essential metals and minerals they produce; for Anglo American, as a leading producer of many of the materials critical to a cleaner, more electrified and consumer-driven world, this goes to the heart of our purpose and is a challenge we are addressing directly through our FutureSmart Mining approach - coupling step change innovations in technology and sustainability to change the future footprint of mining across the entire value chain."

Chapter Takeaways

The adoption of circular business models in upstream and downstream businesses can address major waste pools while unlocking significant value for the industry. Increased adoption requires supportive regulations and stakeholder collaboration.

Opportunities
- Scaling the use of renewable inputs, e.g., solar or wind energy and zero abstraction of water for operations or closed water loops
- Capturing circular opportunities upstream, e.g., zero waste to landfill, operational waste and waste by-products opportunities, equipment and consumables, chemicals and land rehabilitation
- Implementation of innovative business models to "trade" valuable waste

Technology amplifiers
- Breakthroughs in renewable energy technologies
- Platforms, IoT, blockchain for traceability, advanced analytics and predictive algorithms, robotics, machine learning, and AI
- Advanced material technologies

Obstacles to overcome
- Primary product demand is rising and unlikely to slow in the near to mid-term
- New policy instruments that extend far beyond existing waste legislation are required
- Decarbonization poses risks of "imposed" circular models for businesses

Notes

1. Fluence, "Water Use in the Mining Industry," August 1, 2018, https://www.fluencecorp.com/mining-industry-water-use/ (accessed August 12, 2019).
2. Brian D. Colwell, "Sustainability & The Circular Economy Finally Break into The Mining Industry," November 2, 2017, https://briandcolwell.com/sustainability-the-circular-economy-finally-break-into-the-mining-industry/ (accessed August 12, 2019).
3. Overburden is material overlaying a deposit of useful geological materials or bedrock.
4. Rajdeep Das & Ipseet Choudhury, "Waste Management in Mining industry," *Indian Journal of Scientific Research*, 2013, https://www.ijsr.in/upload/1080184324CHAPTER_24.pdf (accessed August 12, 2019).
5. C.P Baldé et al., "Global e-waste Monitor 2017," United Nations University, 2017, https://www.itu.int/en/ITU-D/Climate-Change/Documents/GEM%202017/Global-E-waste%20Monitor%202017%20.pdf (accessed August 9, 2019).

6. Nelson Bennett, "Global Energy Transition Powers Surge in Demand for Metals," Mining.com, 2019, http://www.mining.com/global-energy-transition-powers-surge-demand-metals/ (accessed August 9, 2019).

7. Tom DiChristopher, "Electric Vehicles Will Grow from 3 Million to 125 Million by 2030, International Energy Agency forecasts," CNBC Markets, 2018, https://www.cnbc.com/2018/05/30/electric-vehicles-will-grow-from-3-million-to-125-million-by-2030-iea.html (accessed August 9, 2019).

8. Jocelyn Timperley, "Explainer: These Six Metals Are Key to a Low-Carbon Future," Renew Economy, April 16, 2018, https://reneweconomy.com.au/explainer-six-metals-key-low-carbon-future-95544/ (accessed August 09, 2019).

9. Accenture, "Mining New Value from the Circular Economy," 2019, https://www.accenture.com/_acnmedia/PDF-98/Accenture-Circular-Economy-in-Mining.pdf#zoom=50 (accessed August 9, 2019).

10. Anne Marie Helmenstine, "Interesting and Useful Facts about Iron," ThoughtCo, 2019, https://www.thoughtco.com/interesting-iron-facts-606469 (accessed August 9, 2019).

11. Because global output is not immediately responsive, e.g., mines need to increase production, new mines need to be permitted, etc.

12. United States Environmental Protection Agency, "U.S.-Hosted Workshop on the Use of Life Cycle Concepts in Supply Chain Management to Achieve Resource Efficiency," March 22–23, 2016, https://www.epa.gov/sites/production/files/2016-09/documents/g7_us_workshop_summary_proceedings_final.pdf (accessed August 12, 2019).

13. Organization for Economic Co-operation and Development, "Working Party on Resource Productivity and Waste," November 9, 2017, http://www.oecd.org/officialdocuments/publicdisplaydocumentpdf/?cote=ENV/EPOC/WPRPW(2016)2/FINAL&docLanguage=En (accessed August 12, 2019).

14. Marija Maisch, "Mining Sector to Rely Increasingly on Renewables, Report Finds," *PV Magazine*, 2018, https://www.pv-magazine.com/2018/09/11/mining-sector-to-rely-increasingly-on-renewables-report-finds/ (accessed August 12, 2019).

15. Guiomar Calvo, Gavin Mudd, Alicia Valero, and Antonio Valero, "Decreasing Ore Grades in Global Metallic Mining: A Theoretical Issue or a Global Reality?" *Resources* 5 (4): 36, https://www.mdpi.com/2079-9276/5/4/36/htm (accessed August 12, 2019).

16. Bernd G. Lottermoser, "Recycling, Reuse and Rehabilitation of Mine Wastes," *Elements*, 2011, https://www.researchgate.net/publication/277387306_Recycling_Reuse_and_Rehabilitation_of_Mine_Wastes (accessed August 12, 2019).

17. Purple Window, "Asset Management and the Future of the Mining Industry," 2017, http://purple-window.com/asset-management-future-mining-industry/ (accessed August 12, 2019).

18. Henry Sanderson, "Miners Turn to Green Power Options," *Financial Times*, 2018, https://www.ft.com/content/b3b7fe4a-a5fc-11e8-a1b6-f368d365bf0e (accessed August 12, 2019).

19. IEEFA, "Energy-Intensive Mining Companies Look to Renewables for Cost Savings," September 11, 2018, http://ieefa.org/energy-intensive-mining-companies-look-to-renewables-for-cost-savings/ (accessed August 12, 2019).

20. Levels of penetration in the circular space are highly variable by metal, and the recycling industry is fragmented with a lack of penetration of large mining players. Therefore, an accurate value projection cannot be generalized for the industry.

21. Deloitte, "Renewables in Mining: Rethink, Reconsider and Replay," 2017, https://www2.deloitte.com/content/dam/Deloitte/global/Documents/Energy-and-Resources/gx-renewables-in-mining-final-report-for-web.pdf (accessed August 12, 2019).

22. Goldcorp, "2017 Sustainability Report," 2017 http://csr.goldcorp.com/2017/_img/docs/2017-Sustainability-Report.pdf (accessed August 12, 2019).

23. Global News Wire, "VRB Energy Signs Strategic Cooperation Framework Agreement with Pangang Group Vanadium and Titanium Resources, the World's Largest Vanadium Oxide Producer," June 7, 2018, https://www.globenewswire.com/news-release/2018/06/27/1530483/0/en/VRB-Energy-signs-Strategic-Cooperation-Framework-Agreement-with-Pangang-Group-Vanadium-and-Titanium-Resources-the-world-s-largest-vanadium-oxide-producer-Agreement-includes-long-te.html (accessed August 12, 2019).

24. Nathalie Jollien, "Recycling Quartz from Mining Waste," Phys.org, 2018, https://phys.org/news/2018-06-recycling-quartz.html (accessed August 12, 2019).

25. *The Guardian*, "Pumped Hydro Project That Reuses Old Goldmine Expected to Win Federal Funding," 2017, https://www.theguardian.com/australia-news/2017/sep/21/pumped-hydro-project-that-reuses-old-goldmine-expected-to-win-federal-funding (accessed August 12, 2019).

26. Kirstin Linnenkoper, "Forget About Metal Ores, 'Urban Mining' Is 13 Times Cheaper," Recycling International, 2018, https://recyclinginternational.com/business/forget-about-metal-ores-urban-mining-is-13-times-cheaper/ (accessed August 12, 2019).

27. Umicore, "Sustainable Procurement Framework for Cobalt," https://www.umicore.com/storage/main/sustainablecobaltsupplybrochurefinal.pdf (accessed August 9, 2019).

28. Arcelor Mittal, "ArcelorMittal's Rental Business Model for Steel Sheet Piles," 2017, https://europe.arcelormittal.com/newsandmedia/europenews/3170/Rental-business-model-for-steel-sheet-piles (accessed August 16, 2019).

29. Paul Moore, "Anglo Sees a Future with Swarms of Underground Modular Mining Robots Operating in Deep Mines," *International Mining*, January 4, 2018, https://im-mining.com/2018/01/04/anglo-sees-future-swarms-underground-modular-mining-robots-operating-deep-mines/ (accessed August 12, 2019).

30. Tata Steel, "Low Carbon and Circular Economy," https://www.tatasteeleurope.com/en/innovation/hisarna/circular-economy (accessed August 16, 2019).

31. Accenture, "Sustainability in Mining: Q&A With Sonia Thimmiah," https://www.accenture.com/in-en/insight-perspectives-natural-resources-sustainability-sonia (accessed August 12, 2019).

32. *Nikkei Asian Review*, "Japanese Companies Digging for Gold in Urban Waste" October 3, 2017, https://asia.nikkei.com/Business/Japanese-companies-digging-for-gold-in-urban-waste (accessed August 12, 2019).

33. De Beers Groups, "Climate Change," https://www.debeersgroup.com/building-forever/our-impact/environment/climate-change (accessed August 12, 2019).

6

Oil & Gas (O&G) Industry Profile

Table 6.1 Industry summary

O&G industry today: O&G is one of the most energy- and emissions-intensive industries. Growing de-carbonization pressure from investors and consumers, accelerated technology learning, and increased regulation are driving many companies to improve their energy footprint, increase circularity of resources, and pursue new forms of greener energy

Case for change	Today	Looking ahead
Industry size	~$5 trillion	~$7.7 trillion (projection for 2030)
Illustrative waste volumes	• Energy production is the second largest consumer of freshwater worldwide, and O&G companies produce approximately 900 billion gallons of wastewater a year from operations[1] • Nearly three-quarters (72%) of methane emission leakages occur during production, with the remaining during processing, transmission, storage, and distribution[2] • From 2010 to 2018, there were 59 large spills (7 tons or more), resulting in an immense impact on the environment and 163 kilotons of lost oil[3]	Various world energy scenarios depict average annual growth as follows: • Global primary energy demand for oil from 2020 to 2040 will fall in the range of -24–19%[4] • Global primary energy demand for gas from 2020 to 2040 will fall in the range of 25–54%[4] • Global CO_2 emissions from 2020 to 2040 will fall in the range of -27–6%[4]
Value at stake	–	~$20–$160 billion (0.3–2% of EBITDA) by 2030

© The Author(s) 2020
P. Lacy et al., *The Circular Economy Handbook*,
https://doi.org/10.1057/978-1-349-95968-6_6

🔋 Industry Status

The O&G sector is one of the world's largest industries. It includes upstream activities (exploration and production), midstream (transportation, storage, and processing), and downstream (purification, refining, logistics/transport, and retail). Companies face significant price volatility, as shifting geopolitical, market, and technology dynamics affect the balance between supply and demand. The industry has already started to move away from oil and toward less carbon-intensive natural gas, commonly positioned as a "bridge fuel," due in large part to the shale gas/oil revolution enabled by horizontal drilling technology.

For the larger energy transition, with increasing environmental regulations and investor pressures, companies are shifting their portfolios in favor of low-carbon businesses. Industry leaders have diversified, investing in alternative energies and the associated technological infrastructure (solar, wind, hydrogen, battery storage) and in new segments of the energy value chains (EV charging, retail energy, utilities). In addition, the industry has also invested in partnerships and acquisitions to drive efficiency and reduce the environmental footprint of the current hydrocarbon value chain. Such a move is critical, given that the share of fossil fuels in the total primary energy supply has remained stable at about 81% for the past three decades.[5] Indeed, petrochemicals are expected to be the largest growing demand segment for the O&G industry. According to the International Energy Association (IEA), petrochemicals are set to account for more than a third of the growth in world oil demand up to 2030 and nearly 50% of the growth to 2050.[6]

❓ Waste to Wealth Challenges

O&G companies have some of the largest energy and carbon footprints in the world, with production and use accounting for over 50% of global GHG emissions associated with energy consumption.[7] Companies can begin to tackle this challenge by addressing three key areas of waste (see Fig. 6.1).

The first is waste from energy-intensive activities up- and midstream in the value chain. Extraction is becoming more energy intensive as fields mature. This expands use of secondary and enhanced recovery methods that require water and gas injection, and chemical or thermal (steam) flooding to boost production. Further downstream, refining is still the most energy- and emissions-intensive stage of production, using significant amounts of

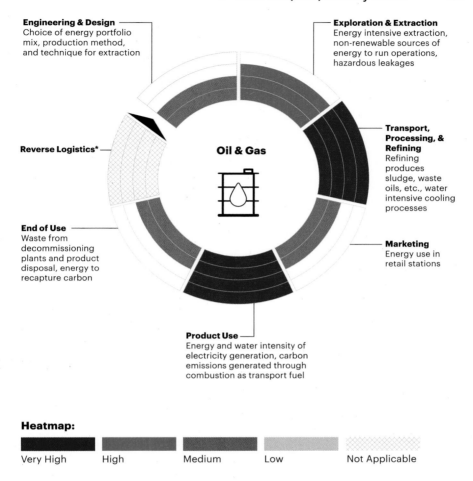

Engineering & Design
Choice of energy portfolio
mix, production method,
and technique for extraction

Exploration & Extraction
Energy intensive extraction,
non-renewable sources of
energy to run operations,
hazardous leakages

Reverse Logistics*

Oil & Gas

**Transport,
Processing, &
Refining**
Refining
produces
sludge, waste
oils, etc., water
intensive cooling
processes

End of Use
Waste from
decommissioning
plants and product
disposal, energy to
recapture carbon

Marketing
Energy use in
retail stations

Product Use
Energy and water intensity of
electricity generation, carbon
emissions generated through
combustion as transport fuel

Heatmap:

| Very High | High | Medium | Low | Not Applicable |

*While the 'Reverse Logistics' stage does not produce unique waste streams per se,
it is included in the diagram as it is a key part of a circular value chain.

Fig. 6.1   Waste analysis diagram

water for cooling and processing. Given the vast amounts of heat required
for multiple refining stages, refining accounts for about half of all the energy
consumed by the industry.

The second area is waste from operations (methane leakages alone cost
the industry about $30 billion a year) and unrealized value from potential
by-products across the value chain.[8] There is potential, for example, to capture carbon for use in CO_2 enhanced oil recovery (EOR), in which the CO_2
reduces the oil's viscosity and increase its flow to the well.

The third major area is waste that results from underutilized equipment. With extended use of renewable energy and electrification, utilization rates of O&G equipment could decline, and equipment could be retired early. Companies have been exploring options to maximize the end-of-use value from these assets, for example, by creating an offshore pipeline for carbon capture.

Waste to Wealth Opportunities

Our research has identified three areas of opportunity (see Table 6.2). The first involves improving the utilization, efficiency, and performance of assets and plants in operation today. The Malaysian O&G company Petronas, for example, has gone so far as to create a platform for other companies to use its idle tankers.[9]

The second area of opportunity lies with reducing operational waste and leakages. Some energy companies are seizing opportunities to reuse and recycle energy, solid waste, and water in their operations and beyond. Shell's gas-to-liquids plant in Qatar, for example, runs on reused water.[13] In oil-field services, Halliburton is working with Nuverra, an environmental solutions provider to handle drilling solids and treat and recycle frac water.[14] The Italian oil and gas company Eni, for instance, reutilizes flare gas for power generation to benefit local populations in the Congo and Nigeria.[15] In addition, key opportunities downstream are enabling circularity by maximizing utility in the end use (e.g., increased petrochemical plastics quality and durability) and the increased use of molecule-circulating loops.[16]

The third opportunity focuses on sustainable energy and fuels. In 2018, the top O&G companies jointly spent around 1% of their budgets on clean energy, with many investments going into business acquisitions.[17] While not a high percentage, it indicates that leaders in the industry are shifting their strategies. Consider the petroleum refining company Total S.A., which has been expanding into electricity through a number of acquisitions over the past five years, including acquiring Direct Energie (the French electric utility company) for more than $1.7 billion in 2018. The company has also been growing its stake in the EV charging business through deals with ChargePoint, G2mobility, and others.[18] Other major players, such as Chevron, BP, and Shell, are also starting to enter or scale presence in these spaces (e.g., Shell has already bought First Utility in the UK and is the main candidate to acquire the Netherlands-based Eneco Holding N.V.).[19,20,21,22]

Table 6.2 Waste to wealth opportunity summary

Circular economy opportunity	Become more effective and efficient with assets in place today	Reduce waste and introduce circularity into the hydrocarbon value chain	Grow via diversification into new energy
Type of opportunity	Smart operations—produce efficiently	Circular operations—use circular inputs	Circularity as brand value—market share
Value at stake (by 2030)	~$10–$35 billion	~$2.5–$5 billion	~$20–$125 billion
Value levers	• Reduce decommissioning costs • Decrease operational expenditures • Increase asset utilization	• Reduce cost of goods sold • Reduce procurement costs • Pursue new revenue sources	• Increase market share • Pursue new revenue sources
Target waste	• Asset inefficiencies • End-user waste • End-of-use waste	• Operational waste • Leakages	• Non-renewable feedstock • Large energy and carbon footprint
Value chain focus	• Upstream, midstream, downstream, and retail • End of use	• Upstream, midstream, and downstream • End of use	• Upstream, downstream and retail
Technology amplifiers	• AI, platforms, big data and analytics, wearables, mobility, and robotics	• AI, cloud systems, data analytics, robotics, drones, advanced technologies, and IoT	• Breakthroughs and advances in technologies in renewable energy, fuel space and platforms
Case study	Robotic Drilling Systems has developed a fully electric and robotic drill floor for fast and fully unmanned operation of pipes and tools. Studies indicate potential annual savings of up to 40 rig days per rig. The drilling system also has the potential to decrease the drilling waste generated; reduce energy consumption and CO_2 emissions; and lower the operational costs with less downtime, low noise, and faster installation[10]	BP is leveraging San Francisco-based Kelvin Inc.'s sensor and AI-enabled solution to monitor and remotely manage production operations in Wyoming. Thanks to the system, BP estimates that methane-emissions events from venting have declined 74% (and overall costs have dropped 22%), all while production volumes have increased by 20%[8]	Shell, the global group of energy and petrochemical companies, has created a "New Energies" business to pursue low-carbon technologies, including hydrogen stations, fast-charging stations for EVs, bio-fuels (joint venture with Raizen), and wind and solar projects.[11] The company is reportedly investing $2 billion annually into the new energies division and expects its expansion into cleaner power generation to yield returns of between 8 and 12%[12]

Technology Amplifiers

A number of emerging innovations could play a substantial role in capturing the value of these opportunities.

- Carbon capture, utilization, and storage (CCUS) is a fast-emerging technology that allows large carbon emitters to convert their waste stream (captured CO and CO_2) into a new source of income as an industrial component for applications ranging from materials production (cement, plastics, and polymers) and sustainable aviation fuels, to carbonating beverages, algae cultivation, and EOR. One company scaling CCUS is LanzaTech, which has innovated a biological catalyst (a bacteria) that converts a variety of waste carbon pollution (such as industrial emissions and unsorted, unrecyclable plastic waste) into fuels and other products. Freya Burton, LanzaTech's Chief Sustainability and People Officer, describes their approach as, "giving carbon a new lease on life by locking it into a material cycle."
- Schlumberger, one of the world's largest oilfield services company, is piloting the use of customized smart glasses that provide real-time information, including live gauge readings, inspection and safety checklists, inventory checks, and step-by-step procedure videos. The glasses could help workers save time on routine tasks and improve equipment maintenance.[23]
- Oil and gas exploration and production company Apache Corporation has gone a step further, using predictive analytics to *anticipate* the failure of critical pumping equipment.[24]
- Researchers from Penn State University have found that industrial and domestic waste could become a viable alternative source for engineering high-performance ceramic proppants for use in hydraulic fracturing.[25]

 Obstacles to Overcome

The O&G industry is balancing the need to continue investments in optimizing the hydrocarbon value chain, while also simultaneously investing in a low-carbon transition for a more sustainable, circular future. As Ahmad A. Al Sa'adi, Senior Vice President of Technical Services at Saudi Aramco, the national petroleum and natural gas company of Saudi Arabia, explained, "Climate change presents a grand challenge for the oil and gas industry in addressing the ambitious targets set by the 2015 Paris Agreement, by delivering energy to satisfy global economic growth while reducing greenhouse gas emissions and mitigating the climate change impact."[26] Decisions will be informed by a number of factors, including the maturity of certain technologies. In the case of carbon capture, the global capacity for CO_2 capture is currently the equivalent of taking more than eight million motor vehicles off the road but, according to the IEA, nearly $4 trillion would be needed for CCUS projects to meet the world's two-degree target by 2050.[27] Externally, crucial factors include the growing market demand for CO_2, policies that embrace low-carbon and carbon recycling solutions, and industry collaborations to accelerate innovation. According to J. Jon Imaz, CEO of the Spanish energy company Repsol, industry collaboration will be critical across opportunity areas: "Collaboration is a key concern because we need it. We need to work together to have a multiplying effect."

Ultimately, industry leaders must also prove that these broader strategies are commercially viable relative to O&G margins. Referring to his company's diversification into low-carbon energy and electrification, Imaz says, "We are trying to get the returns because we want to be a player and an actor in this business."

 Chapter Takeaways

Emerging technologies are enabling companies to deploy circular initiatives across the value chain, allowing businesses to pivot to new models for carbon recycling and renewable portfolio diversification.

Opportunities

- Reduce resource intensity and become more effective and efficient with current assets
- Reduce waste and introduce circularity into the hydrocarbon value chain
- Grow via diversification into low-carbon energies

Technology amplifiers

- Mobility, augmented reality, drones, autonomous robots, AI, platforms, big data and analytics, and IoT
- Continued advancements in renewable energy, storage, and renewables
- Breakthroughs in energy harvesting and CCUS technologies

Obstacles to overcome

- Capital investment required to scale low-carbon technologies and infrastructure
- Downstream industry demand for low-carbon energy and carbon-based (circular) products
- Policy and collaboration

Notes

1. Nichole Saunders, "Getting Dangerously Creative with Oil and Gas Wastewater," Environmental Defense Fund, October 12, 2017, http://blogs.edf.org/energyexchange/2017/10/12/getting-dangerously-creative-with-oil-and-gas-wastewater/ (accessed August 12, 2019).
2. EPA, "Estimates of Methane Emissions by Sector in the United States," May 22, 2019, https://www.epa.gov/natural-gas-star-program/estimates-methane-emissions-sector-united-states (accessed August 9, 2019).
3. ITOPF, "Oil Tanker Spill Statistics 2018," 2018, https://www.itopf.org/fileadmin/data/Documents/Company_Lit/Oil_Spill_Stats_2019.pdf.
4. World Energy Council in collaboration with Accenture Strategy and Paul Scherrer Institute, "World Energy Scenarios, 2019".
5. IEA, "Global Energy Demand Grew by 2.1% in 2017, and Carbon Emissions Rose for the First Time Since 2014," March 22, 2018, https://www.iea.org/newsroom/news/2018/march/global-energy-demand-grew-by-21-in-2017-and-carbon-emissions-rose-for-the-firs.html (accessed August 9, 2019).
6. IEA, "Petrochemicals Set to Be the Largest Driver of World Oil Demand, Latest IEA Analysis Finds," October 5, 2018, https://www.iea.org/newsroom/news/2018/october/petrochemicals-set-to-be-the-largest-driver-of-world-oil-demand-latest-iea-analy.html (accessed August 9, 2019).
7. CDP, "Executive Summary: Beyond the Cycle," November 2018, https://www.cdp.net/en/investor/sector-research/oil-and-gas-report (accessed August 9, 2019).
8. Environmental Defense Fund in Collaboration with Accenture Strategy, "Fueling a Digital Methane Future," 2019, https://www.edf.org/sites/default/files/documents/Fueling%20a%20Digital%20Methane%20Future_FINAL.pdf (accessed August 9, 2019).
9. Oil & Gas Portal, "Innovation R&D," http://www.oil-gasportal.com/innovation-rd/robotic-drilling-system/? (accessed August 9, 2019).
10. Shell, "New Energies," https://www.shell.com/energy-and-innovation/new-energies.html (accessed August 9, 2019).
11. Kelly Gilblom, "Can Big Oil Reinvent Itself? One Giant Will Soon Find Out," Bloomberg, February 26, 2019, https://www.bloomberg.com/news/articles/2019-02-26/can-oil-reinvent-itself-shell-s-power-push-divides-investors (accessed September 2, 2019).
12. Elaine Maslin, "Getting Lean and Mean in Malaysia," Hart Energy, June 26, 2018, https://www.hartenergy.com/exclusives/getting-lean-and-mean-malaysia-31177 (accessed August 30, 2019).
13. Shell, "Producing Water in the Desert," https://www.shell.com/about-us/major-projects/pearl-gtl/producing-water-in-the-desert.html (accessed August 16, 2019).

14. Halliburton, "CleanWave® Frac Flowback and ProducedWater Treatment," https://www.halliburton.com/en-US/ps/stimulation/stimulation/water-solutions/cleanwave.html?pageid=4975&navid=2427?node-id=h8cyv98a (accessed August 16, 2019).

15. Eni, "Eni for Development," https://www.eni.com/docs/en_IT/enicom/publications-archive/sustainability/ENI-FOR-DEVELOPMENT-eng.pdf (accessed August 16, 2019).

16. Accenture, "Taking the European Chemical Industry Into the Circular Economy—Executive Summary," 2017, https://www.accenture.com/_acn-media/pdf-45/accenture-cefic-report-exec-summary.pdf (accessed August 9, 2019).

17. Ron Bousso, "Big Oil Spent 1 Percent on Green Energy in 2018," *Reuters*, November 12, 2018, https://in.reuters.com/article/us-oil-renewables/big-oil-spent-1-percent-on-green-energy-in-2018-idINKCN1NH004 (accessed August 9, 2019).

18. Bate Felix, "France's Total Completes Direct Energie Deal and Buys Electric Vehicles Charging Firm," September 20, 2018, https://uk.reuters.com/article/us-total-deals/frances-total-completes-direct-energie-deal-and-buys-electric-vehicles-charging-firm-idUKKCN1M016W (accessed August 16, 2019).

19. Chevron, "Renewable Energy," https://www.chevron.com/corporate-responsibility/climate-change/renewable-energy (accessed August 16, 2019).

20. BP, "Alternative Energy," https://www.bp.com/en/global/corporate/what-we-do/alternative-energy.html (accessed August 16, 2019).

21. Ron Bousso and Susanna Twidale, "Shell Goes Green as It Rebrands UK Household Power Supplier," *Reuters*, March 24, 2019, https://uk.reuters.com/article/uk-shell-power/shell-goes-green-as-it-rebrands-uk-household-power-supplier-idUKKCN1R50OL (accessed August 16, 2019).

22. Clara Denina, Stephen Jewkes, and Toby Sterling, "Shell's Lead in Bidding for Dutch Eneco Increases as Enel, Total Drop Out: Sources," *Reuters*, June 24, 2019, https://www.reuters.com/article/us-eneco-m-a-bidders/shells-lead-in-bidding-for-dutch-eneco-increases-as-enel-total-drop-out-sources-idUSKCN1TP20Q (accessed August 16, 2019).

23. Tractica, "Enterprise Wearable Technology Case Studies," 2015, https://www.tractica.com/wp-content/uploads/2015/08/WP-EWCS-15-Tractica.pdf (accessed August 9, 2019).

24. World Economic Forum in collaboration with Accenture, "Digital Transformation Initiative Oil and Gas Industry," 2017, http://reports.weforum.org/digital-transformation/wp-content/blogs.dir/94/mp/files/pages/files/dti-oil-and-gas-industry-white-paper.pdf (accessed August 9, 2019).

25. Patricia L. Craig, "Industrial Waste Can Be Engineered into Proppants for Shale Gas and Oil Recovery," Penn State News, February 12, 2014, https://news.psu.edu/story/303833/2014/02/12/research/industrial-waste-can-be-engineered-proppants-shale-gas-and-oil (accessed August 16, 2019).

26. Al-Khobar, "Petro Environment 2019: Balancing Energy Sustainability with Environmental Protection," WebWire, March 14, 2019, https://www.webwire.com/ViewPressRel.asp?aId=237408 (accessed September 2, 2019).

27. Global CCS Institute, "The Global Status of CCS: 2017," 2017, https://www.globalccsinstitute.com/wp-content/uploads/2018/12/2017-Global-Status-Report.pdf (accessed August 9, 2019).

7

 Chemical Industry Profile

Table 7.1 Industry summary

Chemical industry today: The circular economy is gaining traction in the industry due to diminishing non-renewable resources and tightening environmental regulation, with companies identifying ways to eliminate toxic products and by-products

Case for change	Today	Looking ahead
Industry size	~$4 trillion	~$6.9 trillion (projection for 2030)
Illustrative waste volumes	• In the last 70 years, 8.3 billion tons of plastic have been produced, out of which 6.3 billion tons have been discarded[1] • A typical car today contains ~250 kg of chemical content[2] • ~95% of the value of plastic packaging material (or $80–$120 billion in economic value) is lost annually because of a short first use[3] • The United States recycles just 9% of its plastic trash[4]	• ~20% of the world's oil production is projected to manufacture plastics by 2050[4] • Without action, the volume of plastic in the ocean will double by 2030[5] • More than 400 million tons of hazardous wastes are produced annually[6]
Value at stake	–	Studies on cost efficiency are highly specific to a particular chemical/waste stream and, therefore, cannot be generalized to the entire industry

© The Author(s) 2020
P. Lacy et al., *The Circular Economy Handbook*,
https://doi.org/10.1057/978-1-349-95968-6_7

Industry Status

The chemical industry is one of the largest and most diversified manufacturing industries, producing intermediary and end products that are used by almost all other industries. Spurred to action by dwindling non-renewable resources and stringent environmental regulations, the industry has started making progress toward circularity. This includes creating products with renewable/sustainable inputs, making the transition from single use to multiple uses (thus reducing total polymer demand), and minimizing hazardous content leaking into the environment. "When it comes to business growth, the last decade was about volumes, but this decade is about a more inclusive definition of value and resource efficiency and effectiveness," says Saori Dubourg, Board of Executive Directors, BASF, a German chemical company. "Across our entire portfolio, it was clear that circularity could help us minimize risks and capitalize on opportunities by changing our business models."

Waste to Wealth Challenges

Chemical companies must address three major waste streams (see Fig. 7.1). The first is the use of non-renewable resources as feedstock and as sources of energy. About 8% of the world's oil production is used to manufacture plastic, a number projected to rise to about 20% by 2050.[7] Moreover, the chemical industry is the world's largest industrial energy consumer.[8]

The second major stream involves waste generated from the manufacturing of chemicals, including process residues, spent catalysts or solvents, spilled oil, sludge, and contaminated chemical containers. The industry is responsible for close to 200 of the world's most polluted sites, potentially putting approximately three million people at the risk of exposure.[9]

The third large stream consists of waste generated from consumer products. Chemicals are the building blocks for many consumer goods—a typical car today contains approximately 250 kilograms of chemical content.[2] Polymers, principally used to make plastic goods, constitute about 80% of the chemical industry's production output.[10] According to a 2016 report by the World Economic Forum (WEF), about 95% of the value of plastic packaging material ($80 billion to $120 billion in economic value) is lost annually.[11]

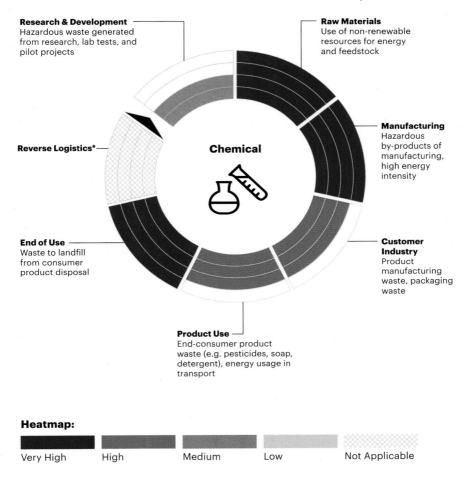

Research & Development
Hazardous waste generated from research, lab tests, and pilot projects

Raw Materials
Use of non-renewable resources for energy and feedstock

Reverse Logistics*

Chemical

Manufacturing
Hazardous by-products of manufacturing, high energy intensity

End of Use
Waste to landfill from consumer product disposal

Customer Industry
Product manufacturing waste, packaging waste

Product Use
End-consumer product waste (e.g. pesticides, soap, detergent), energy usage in transport

Heatmap:

Very High | High | Medium | Low | Not Applicable

*While the 'Reverse Logistics' stage does not produce unique waste streams per se, it is included in the diagram as it is a key part of a circular value chain.

Fig. 7.1 Waste analysis diagram

 # Waste to Wealth Opportunities

The rise of the circular economy has created a number of opportunities for the chemical industry (see Table 7.2). One such opportunity could be driven by "circulating molecules." As the term suggests, circulating molecules

Table 7.2 Waste to wealth opportunity summary

Circular economy opportunity	Developing technology to circulate molecules through renewable feedstock and to reduce environmental footprint in supply chains	Developing technology and business models to circulate molecules through reuse and recycling	Enabling the circular economy and digitization in downstream industries
Type of opportunity	Circular sourcing—buying better	Circular business models—reuse and recycling	Circularity as a brand value—market share
Value at stake		Not quantified[12]	
Value levers	• Reduced cost of energy • Price premium • Reduced cost of goods	• Reduced cost of energy • Price premium • Reduced cost of goods	• Increased market share • Reduced cost of goods
Target waste	• Wasted non-renewable resources • Waste generated from manufacturing chemicals (wasted lifecycles)	• Waste generated from manufacturing chemicals (wasted lifecycles)	• Waste generated from end consumer products (wasted embedded value)
Value chain focus	• Raw materials • Chemicals manufacturing	• Raw materials • Chemicals manufacturing	• Customer industry • End use
Technology amplifiers	• Breakthroughs in bio-based materials technology and materials science innovation	• Advancements in the mechanical and chemical recycling of products at scale	• Advanced materials technologies, smart products, digital connectivity, IoT, big data, and predictive algorithms

(continued)

Circular economy opportunity	Developing technology to circulate molecules through renewable feedstock and to reduce environmental footprint in supply chains	Developing technology and business models to circulate molecules through reuse and recycling	Enabling the circular economy and digitization in downstream industries
Case study	In BASF's Verbund system, the by-products of one plant are used as raw materials of another. Overall, the chemical processes consume less energy, create less waste, and therefore conserve resources. Based on the "biomass balance (BMB) method," BASF partly replaces finite fossil feedstock in the Verbund with certified renewable resources. One example of a BMB product is the bioplastic Ultramid® used as a packaging solution[13]	ExxonMobil Chemical, one of the world's largest chemical companies, has created Vistamaxx performance polymers, which reduces the need for (and costs of) separating incompatible plastics. These new polymers are a proven, cost-effective solution that allows low-cost recycling and are targeted at high-value applications[14]	The Dutch paints and performance coatings company AkzoNobel has developed a tool that uses data analytics to accurately predict how much ship owners can save by using different coatings on their cargo tankers. Proprietary algorithms analyze billions of data points to generate a full cost-benefit analysis that details the impact (estimated fuel consumption, fuel cost, and CO_2 emissions) of different coating options before they are applied to the hull of a ship[15]

means reusing existing molecules, either in the form of hydrocarbons contained in biomass or in the chemical materials contained in consumer products.[2] Our research points to the following potential approaches for accomplishing that.

Companies could consider developing technology to increase the use of molecule-circulating loops in their supply chains. A number of technologies are available today for producing chemicals out of renewable or diversified feedstock, and the renewable chemicals market alone is estimated to reach around \$84.3 billion by 2020.[16] DSM's Decovery®, a plant-based, eco-friendly resin, is one example of a recent innovation in this space. "We are scaling this innovation by engaging our value chain partners, from suppliers to customers and beyond, in order to accelerate the transition to bio/plant-based paints & coatings," says Feike Sijbesma, CEO of DSM.

Another significant opportunity is through reuse and recycling. In terms of reuse, technologically proven solutions for polyethylene terephthalate (PET) bottles and plastic shopping bags have been available for some time. Those approaches could conceivably be extended to other products like automotive parts, components of electronic products, and white goods. In terms of recycling, the process can be either mechanical (collecting and processing used end products and then reinserting their intact molecules back into the value chain further upstream without modifying their chemical bonds) or chemical (breaking up long-chain hydrocarbons into precursors). An example of a mechanical recycling process is VinyLoop, a patented process developed by the Solvay Group, the Belgian chemicals company. The process separates PVC from other materials through the process of dissolution filtration and separation of contaminants.[17]

Lastly, companies can enable the circular economy and digitization in downstream industries—for example, more fuel-efficient cars require lighter materials, and more energy-efficient houses depend on better insulation. For chemical companies, the opportunity lies in creating new ways to retain a stake in the value of the molecule, with substantial potential payback. Successfully enabling circularity downstream is projected to drive additional and new demand for more sustainable chemicals, resulting in a potential increase of 26% (from 2015 levels to 2030).[18]

⚙ Technology Amplifiers

A range of advances in materials science, digital technologies, and other fields have unlocked various areas of opportunity:

- Big data technology and machine-learning techniques are helping the molecular manufacturing technology start-up Zymergen to quickly design custom microbes for producing plastics and other basic industrial materials. The platform has enabled the firm to increase net margin by more than 50% and to halve the time to bring new products to market.[19]
- BASF is deploying IoT and blockchain technology to better manage its supply chain with "smart pallets" that monitor their location, temperature, and load state.[20]
- The petrochemical manufacturing company SABIC's renewable polyethylene (PE) and polypropylene (PP) require 84% less fossil fuel for manufacturing (compared with fossil-based equivalents) and are both fully recyclable.[21]
- Specialty chemicals producer Covestro uses innovative manufacturing processes that, between 2005 and 2016, cut CO_2 emissions by 43.8% even as the production volume increased.[22]

Obstacles to Overcome

The transformation of the chemical industry is fundamentally complex and will take considerable time and effort, especially given the highly technical nature of modification of molecular bonds. This modification inherently changes the nature of the product itself and is therefore challenging and energy intensive to pursue. Several circulating molecule technologies, such as chemical recycling and carbon utilization loops, are not yet feasible at industrial scale.

The necessary capital expenditures cannot be borne by the private sector alone. Even if 20% of the European chemical industry's capital spending were channeled into circular economy projects, it would still take 35–60 years to build the necessary circulating loops.[2] Governments will need to support research and investments in this arena and implement the necessary regulatory and policy frameworks, focusing on crucial issues like consumer safety (see Part III: "Policy—The Role of Policymakers").

Chapter Takeaways

The chemical industry produces the building blocks for many consumer goods and thus holds immense potential for circularity through innovation, advances in biotechnologies, and digital interventions across the value chain.

Opportunities

- Developing technology to circulate molecules through renewable feedstock and reduce negative environmental footprint across supply chains
- Developing technology and business models to circulate molecules through reuse and recycling
- Enabling the circular economy and digitization in downstream industries

Technology amplifiers

- Breakthroughs in bio-based and degradable materials technology, chemical recycling, mechanical recycling, and advanced materials science innovation
- Digital connectivity, IoT, big data, and predictive algorithms
- Smart products

Obstacles to overcome

- Although the circular economy holds tremendous potential, the transformation is fundamentally complex and will take time
- Significant and continuous long-term investments are needed in infrastructure and innovations
- Supportive regulatory and policy frameworks must be implemented to drive the circular economy transformation and address consumer safety risks

Notes

1. University of Georgia, "More Than 8.3 Billion Tons of Plastics Made: Most Has Now Been Discarded," July 19, 2017, https://www.sciencedaily.com/releases/2017/07/170719140939.htm (accessed August 9, 2019).
2. Accenture, "Taking the European Chemical Industry Into the Circular Economy," 2017, https://cefic.org/app/uploads/2019/02/Accenture-Cefic-circular-economy-brochure.pdf (accessed August 9, 2019).
3. Ellen MacArthur Foundation, "The New Plastics Economy Rethinking the Future of Plastics," 2016, https://www.ellenmacarthurfoundation.org/assets/downloads/EllenMacArthurFoundation_TheNewPlasticsEconomy_Pages.pdf (accessed August 9, 2019).
4. Laura Parker, "Fast Facts About Plastic Pollution," National Geographic, 2018, https://news.nationalgeographic.com/2018/05/plastics-facts-infographics-ocean-pollution/ (accessed August 9, 2019).

5. The Maritime Executive, "IEA: Ocean Plastic Waste May Double by 2030," October 5, 2018, https://www.maritime-executive.com/article/iea-ocean-plastic-waste-may-double-by-2030 (accessed August 12, 2019).

6. The World Counts, "Hazardous Waste Statistics," https://www.theworld-counts.com/counters/waste_pollution_facts/hazardous_waste_statistics (accessed August 12, 2019).

7. Laura Parker, "Fast Facts About Plastic Pollution," National Geographic, 2018, https://news.nationalgeographic.com/2018/05/plastics-facts-info-graphics-ocean-pollution/ (accessed August 9, 2019).

8. Peter G. Levi and Jonathan M. Cullen, "Mapping Global Flows of Chemicals: From Fossil Fuel Feedstocks to Chemical Products," Environ. Sci. Technol. 2018, 52, 1725 – 1734, https://pubs.acs.org/doi/pdf/10.1021/acs.est.7b04573 (accessed August 9, 2019).

9. Pure Earth, "2016 World's Worst Pollution Problems," 2016, https://www.worstpolluted.org/docs/WorldsWorst2016Spreads.pdf (accessed August 9, 2019).

10. Techofunc, "Business Model & Value Chain of Chemicals Industry," 2012, http://www.technofunc.com/index.php/domain-knowledge/chemicals-in-dustry/item/business-model-value-chain-of-chemicals-industry (accessed August 9, 2019).

11. World Economic Forum, "The New Plastics Economy—Rethinking the Future of Plastics," 2016, http://www3.weforum.org/docs/WEF_The_New_Plastics_Economy.pdf (accessed August 9, 2019).

12. Studies on cost efficiency are highly specific to a particular chemical/waste stream and, therefore, cannot be generalized to the entire industry.

13. BASF, "K 2019—New Products from Plastic Waste: BASF Customers Showcase Prototypes Made from Chemically Recycled Material," July 9, 2019, https://www.basf.com/global/en/media/news-releas-es/2019/07/p-19-254.html (accessed August 16, 2019).

14. ExxonMobil, "Rethink Recycle with Vistamaxx™ Performance Polymers," https://www.exxonmobilchemical.com/en/products/polymer-modifiers/vis-tamaxx-performance-polymers/rethink-recycle (accessed August 16, 2019).

15 Tessella, "Tessella Helps AkzoNobel Launch Shipping Industry's First Predictive Coating Efficiency App Using Big Data Analytics," https://www.tessella.com/news/tessella-helps-akzonobel (accessed August 16, 2019).

16. MarketsandMarkets, "Renewable Chemicals Market worth 84.3 Billion USD by 2020," 2015, https://www.marketsandmarkets.com/PressReleases/renewable-chemical.asp (accessed August 9, 2019).

17. VinylPlus, "PVC recycling technologies," April 2015, https://vinylplus.eu/uploads/Modules/Documents/2015-04-20-pvc-recycling-brochure---english.pdf (accessed November 26, 2019).

18. Accenture Proprietary Research.

19. World Economic Forum in collaboration with Accenture, "Digital Transformation Initiative: Chemistry and Advanced Materials Industry," January 2017, http://reports.weforum.org/digital-transformation/wp-content/blogs.dir/94/mp/files/pages/files/dti-chemistry-and-advanced-materials-industry-white-paper.pdf (accessed August 9, 2019).

20. BASF, "BASF Invests in Smart Supply Chain Start-Up Ahrma," 2017, https://www.basf.com/global/en/media/news-releases/2017/12/p-17-374.html (accessed August 9, 2019).

21. SABIC, "Innovations By SABIC to Minimize Food Wastage, Reduce Weight, and Lower Carbon Footprint of Packaging Materials," June, 21, 2016, https://www.sabic.com/en/news/4327-innovations-by-sabic-to-minimize-food-wastage-reduce-weight-and-lower-carbon-footprint-of-packaging-materials (accessed August 16, 2019).

22. Covestro, "Using Intelligent Processes to Achieve Greater Sustainability," 2019, https://www.covestro.com/en/sustainability/how-we-operate/modern-processes (accessed August 9, 2019).

8

⳨⳨ Electricity Industry Profile

© The Author(s) 2020
P. Lacy et al., *The Circular Economy Handbook*,
https://doi.org/10.1057/978-1-349-95968-6_8

Table 8.1 Industry summary

Electricity industry today: Electricity generation is still largely sourced from fossil fuels, but the industry is currently being disrupted by decarbonization, decentralization, and digitalization trends, with opportunities for reducing losses and maximizing plant and equipment utilization

Case for change	Today	Looking ahead
Industry size	$2.7 trillion	$3.5 trillion (projection for 2030)
Illustrative waste volumes	• In the United States, coal combustion waste (CCW) is the second most abundant waste material after household waste[1] • Global electricity demand rose by 4% in 2018, nearly twice as fast as overall energy demand, and at its fastest pace since 2010[2] • Generation from coal- and gas-fired power plants increased considerably, driving up CO_2 emissions from the sector by 2.5%[2]	• ~400,000 tons of used fuel is expected to be generated from nuclear power plants worldwide from 2010 to 2030[3] • By 2040, electricity use is forecasted to increase by 70%[4] • By 2040, electricity generation is expected to account for 40% of all the energy used in the world[4]
Value at stake	–	$160–$510 billion (5–15% of EBITDA) by 2030

🔋 Industry Status

The electricity industry includes power generation and transmission and distribution, serving customers from retail to commercial or residential. Heavily reliant on fossil fuels, the industry has been undergoing significant disruption with the emergence of clean fuels across its value chain. The global renewable energy market, which was valued at approximately $928 billion in 2017, is projected to reach over $1.5 trillion by 2025.[5] This is being driven by the rapid reduction in the cost of clean generation technology, the digitization and decentralization of all aspects of the grid, and government policies aimed at promoting private-sector investments.

In 2017, global energy-related emissions reached a historic high and many European countries have since begun to experience declines. This is driven by a combination of factors, including the development of increasingly cost-effective methods for capturing and sequestering carbon.[6] According to one estimate, the global CCS market is expected to grow from $2.2 billion in 2016 to about $4.2 billion by 2022.[7]

❓ Waste to Wealth Challenges

The industry has four major waste areas (see Fig. 8.1). The first is the use of non-renewable resources with large carbon footprints for power generation. Despite industry attempts to decarbonize, coal consumption for electricity generation is growing almost at the same rate as that of electricity consumption: about 3% annually between 2000 and 2017.[8]

The second area is waste generated from plant operations. All fossil fuel power plants produce operational waste along with the significant quantities of GHG and air pollutants. In the United States, the electricity sector is responsible for roughly 27.5% of the total GHG emissions, and coal combustion residues are the second most abundant waste material after household waste.[9,10]

The third major area of waste is from energy losses. For electricity generation through steam turbines, 65% of the energy is wasted as heat.[11] Additional losses of about 8% occur through transmission and distribution because of technical inefficiencies and pilferage.[12]

Finally, there is waste generated from the premature retirement of equipment and components. Plant lifetimes typically range from 30 to 45 years for natural gas plants to 30–60 years for coal and nuclear plants.[10]

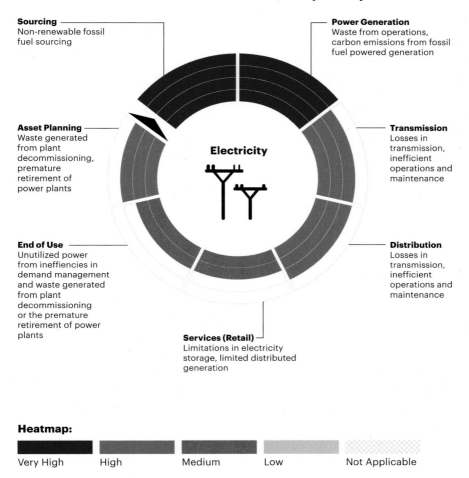

Sourcing
Non-renewable fossil
fuel sourcing

Power Generation
Waste from operations,
carbon emissions from fossil
fuel powered generation

Asset Planning
Waste generated
from plant
decommissioning,
premature
retirement of
power plants

Electricity

Transmission
Losses in
transmission,
inefficient
operations and
maintenance

End of Use
Unutilized power
from ineffiencies in
demand management
and waste generated
from plant
decommissioning
or the premature
retirement of power
plants

Distribution
Losses in
transmission,
inefficient
operations and
maintenance

Services (Retail)
Limitations in electricity
storage, limited distributed
generation

Heatmap:

| Very High | High | Medium | Low | Not Applicable |

Fig. 8.1 Waste analysis diagram

In addition, the decommissioning of power plants can produce large quantities of construction, demolition, and equipment waste; metal scrap; and chemical or radioactive waste, depending on the type of energy source used.

Waste to Wealth Opportunities

For companies in the electricity industry, there are three large areas of opportunity (see Table 8.2). Renewable or circular resources, including solar,

Table 8.2 Waste to wealth opportunity summary

Circular economy opportunity	Electricity generation using renewable or circular resources such as solar, wind, waste to energy, geothermal, etc.	Improved resource utilization across the electricity value chain	Intelligent electricity generation, transmission, distribution, and consumption
Type of opportunity	Circular sources of power—use renewables and waste	Smart operations—produce efficiently	Intelligent networks—manage networks
Value at stake (by 2030)	$70–$165 billion	*Calculated as a part of other two opportunities*	$85–$290 billion
Value levers	• Gain of market share • Reduced cost of goods	• New revenue sources • Reduced cost of operation and end of use	• New revenue sources • Reduced cost of distribution and transmission
Target waste	• Wasted materials (non-renewable resources)	• Wasted materials (operations) • Wasted embedded value (end of use) • Wasted capacity (underutilization)	• Wasted lifecycles (losses across the supply chain) • Wasted capacity (energy end use)
Value chain focus	• Electricity generation	• Electricity generation • Electricity transmission and distribution • End-of-use recovery	• Electricity generation, transmission, distribution, and consumption
Technology amplifiers	• Improvements in renewable energy technologies	• Advanced equipment/infrastructure technologies that enable higher efficiencies • Breakthroughs in recycling and upcycling technologies	• Intelligent networks • Smart metering and consumption • IoT and analytics for maximizing asset utilization, real-time maintenance, accurate forecasting, etc.

	Circular economy opportunity	Electricity generation using renewable or circular resources such as solar, wind, waste to energy, geothermal, etc.	Improved resource utilization across the electricity value chain	Intelligent electricity generation, transmission, distribution, and consumption
Case study		By switching from gas to sustainably generated steam, the paints and coatings company Nouryon (formerly AkzoNobel) has increased the share of renewables for its Dutch operations by 10%. This constitutes a CO_2 reduction of around 100,000 tons per year. In addition, Nouryon is working with Google, Philips, and DSM to source power from a new wind park in the Netherlands. An annual total of 350 million kilowatt-hours could be generated from the park once it becomes operational in 2019[13,14]	When Canada's largest clean power company TransAlta decommissioned Canada's oldest wind farm, the company recycled 90% of the turbines. Overall, a total of 1252 tons of metal from blades, towers, wiring, and pad-mount transformers was recycled. In addition, TransAlta also recycled 44,600 liters of oil[15]	In a product as service model envisioned by CIRCUSOL (funded by the Horizon 2020 program of the European Commission), a supplier would provide solar power generation and storage to a user as a service. Specifically, the PV system and batteries would be installed at the user's site, but the supplier would remain the owner and be responsible for their optimal functioning. At the end of the equipment's useful life, the supplier would take back the system and either give it a second use or recycle it[16]

wind, waste to energy, biomass, and geothermal, comprise the first area. Maturing technologies, decreasing costs, favorable policies, and increasing customer demand should ease the transition from use of fossil fuels. Renewable energy now has an existing global capacity of over 2100 gigawatts, equivalent to the power of 19 million Nissan Leafs, and in 2018, 26% of global electricity was generated from renewables.[17,18]

Improved resource utilization across the value chain presents the second area of opportunity. Companies could, for example, work with industrial equipment partners to offload end-of-use equipment and infrastructure to be repurposed, reutilized, or recycled. The value of scrap metal in used equipment can, in some cases, be high enough to fully offset the cost of demolition.[10] "We are using eco-design principles to collaborate with suppliers in order to increase our use of easy-to-recover materials," says Jean-Pascal Tricoire, Chairman and CEO, Schneider Electric, a French multinational corporation.

Intelligent operations for electricity generation, transmission, distribution, and consumption illustrate the third area of opportunity. This includes demand-supply forecasting, intelligent grids, smart meters, decentralized energy generation, and smart network management and consumption. With increased use of analytics, for example, companies could more accurately forecast demand and supply to minimize waste and maximize asset utility. Furthermore, electrical grids could be enabled for bidirectional power flows for "prosumers," consumers who would sell excess energy from their rooftop solar or mini-wind systems. In total, these types of intelligent systems across the supply chain have the potential to add about 5% of sales in EBITDA.[19]

 ## Technology Amplifiers

In the future, a number of emerging innovations could play a prominent role in helping companies to close the circular loop:

- The city of Helsinki's fully owned energy company "Helen" provides solar technology for different properties that are then able to feed their excessive solar power to a grid. The company is also developing solutions to recover waste heat from properties, as well as new geothermal energy technologies.[20]

- In 2018, NextEra, an energy company, generated nearly 100% of its total power from a mix of clean energy sources: solar, wind, natural gas, and nuclear, and the company has announced plans to invest $40 billion in further expanding its renewable energy portfolio, including a "30 by 30" strategy to install more than 30 million solar panels by 2030.[21,22]
- The multinational energy company Enel has installed two vehicle-to-grid (V2G) EV charging stations both at the Genoa headquarters of the Italian Institute of Technology and at the Milan headquarters of the RSE, a public research institute.[23] The zero-emission solution supports bidirectional charge management: When EVs are stationary, their batteries transmit power into the grid, helping to balance and stabilize the network in return for remuneration. "Creating a circular mindset has been one of our biggest success factors," says Luca Meini, Head of Circular Economy at Enel.

Obstacles to Overcome

Companies face several significant barriers. First, they must address the lack of policy support and government incentives that has inhibited the shift to circular opportunities. Even in countries where power production and supply are completely privatized, government commitments to renewable energy, tax structures, financial incentives, and trade policies will strongly determine the pace of the shift toward renewables and the level of customer participation. This is especially true in emerging markets where consumer awareness of (and thus demand for) cleaner alternative energy sources is lower.

Another major challenge is access to financing. Electric power generation and distribution are among the most capital-intensive industries, and considerable funding is needed for any major initiative. For example, intelligent grids equipped with smart meters and sensors have immense potential that could be implemented at scale. Unfortunately, though, many regions lack the last-mile connectivity, data security protocols, and operational capabilities necessary, and building that infrastructure will require sizable investments.

Chapter Takeaways

The electricity industry holds strong potential for shifting to renewable sources, smart infrastructure, and new circular business models to amplify resource use across the value chain.

Opportunities

- Electricity generation using renewable or circular resources such as solar, wind, waste to energy, geothermal, etc.
- Improved resource utilization across the electricity value chain (recovery from scrap/demolition materials, water recycling, reusing ash as an input for the construction industry, etc.)
- Intelligent electricity generation, transmission, distribution, and consumption (demand-supply forecasting, intelligent grids, smart meters, decentralized energy generation, smart network management, and smart consumption)

Technology amplifiers

- Maturing renewable energy technology; digital infrastructures with IoT-enabled smart sensors and meters; predictive analytics for accurate forecasting of maintenance, lifetimes, and demand; and dynamic and flexible grid infrastructures

Obstacles to overcome

- Need for policy support and incentives for renewable energy and flexible power supply and consumption models
- Access to financing for new projects, such as the digital augmentation of grids and production facilities
- A communication infrastructure across regions that can serve intelligent grid networks

Notes

1. Linda Luther, "CRS Report for Congress: Managing Coal Combustion Waste (CCW)—Issues with Disposal and Use," Congressional Research Service, January 12, 2010, https://fas.org/sgp/crs/misc/R40544.pdf (accessed August 16, 2019).
2. IEA, "Global Energy & CO_2 Status Report," https://www.iea.org/geco/electricity/ (accessed August 9, 2019).
3. World-nuclear.org, "Processing of Used Nuclear Fuel," https://www.world-nuclear.org/information-library/nuclear-fuel-cycle/fuel-recycling/processing-of-used-nuclear-fuel.aspx (accessed August 16, 2019).
4. ExxonMobil, "2018 Outlook for Energy: A View to 2040," https://corporate.exxonmobil.com/en/~/media/Global/Files/outlook-for-energy/2018-Outlook-for-Energy.pdf (accessed August 16, 2019).

5. Amit Narune and Eswara Prasad, "Global Renewable Energy Market Opportunities and Forecasts 2018–2015," Allied Market Research, 2019, https://www.alliedmarketresearch.com/renewable-energy-market (accessed August 9, 2019).

6. International Energy Agency, "Global Energy & CO_2 Status Report 2018," 2019, https://www.iea.org/geco/emissions/ (accessed August 9, 2019).

7. Stratistics Market Research Consulting, "Carbon Capture and Storage (CCS)—Global Market Outlook (2016–2022)," 2017, https://www.strategymrc.com/report/carbon-capture-and-storage-ccs-market (accessed August 9, 2019).

8. Carine Sebi, "Explaining the Increase in Coal Consumption Worldwide," Phys.org, 2019, https://phys.org/news/2019-02-coal-consumption-worldwide.html (accessed August 9, 2019).

9. EPA, "Sources of Greenhouse Gas Emissions," 2019, https://www.epa.gov/ghgemissions/sources-greenhouse-gas-emissions (accessed August 9, 2019).

10. Marilyn A. Brown et al., "Solid Waste from the Operation and Decommissioning of Power Plants," US Department of Energy, 2017, https://www.energy.gov/sites/prod/files/2017/01/f34/Environment%20Baseline%20vol.%203–Solid%20Waste%20from%20the%20Operation%20and%20Decommissioning%20of%20Power%20Plants.pdf (accessed August 9, 2019).

11. Electropaedia, "Battery and Energy Technologies," 2005, https://www.mpoweruk.com/energy_efficiency.htm (accessed August 9, 2019).

12. The World Bank, "Electric Power Transmission and Distribution Losses," 2018, https://data.worldbank.org/indicator/EG.ELC.LOSS.ZS?end=2014&start=1960 (accessed August 9, 2019).

13. Philips, "Opening of New Dutch Wind Farm Puts Philips on course to Becoming Carbon Neutral by 2020," May 16, 2019, https://www.philips.com/a-w/about/news/archive/standard/news/press/2019/20190516-opening-of-new-dutch-wind-farm-puts-philips-on-course-to-becoming-carbon-neutral-by-2020.html (accessed August 21, 2019).

14. AkzoNobel, "Sustainability Fact Sheet," 2019, https://www.akzonobel.com/en/for-media/media-releases-and-features/sustainability-fact-sheet (accessed August 9, 2019).

15. Michelle Froese, "Decommissioning Canada's Oldest Wind Farm," Windpower Engineering & Development, 2017, https://www.windpowerengineering.com/business-news-projects/decommissioning-canadas-oldest-wind-farm/ (accessed August 9, 2019).

16. Circusol, "Service-Based Business Models for Circular Economy in the Solar Power Sector," https://www.circusol.eu/files/brand%20resources/Circusol-Brochure-21x21cm.pdf (accessed August 16, 2019).

17. IRENA, "Renewable Energy Statistics 2018," 2018, https://irena.org/-/media/Files/IRENA/Agency/Publication/2018/Jul/IRENA_Renewable_Energy_Statistics_2018.pdf (accessed August 9, 2019).

18. IEA, "Tracking Clean Energy Progress," https://www.iea.org/tcep/power/renewables/ (accessed August 9, 2019).

19. Accenture Analysis.

20. Helen.fi, "Helen Katri Vala Heating and Cooling Plant," 2018, https://www.helen.fi/en/company/energy/energy-production/power-plants/katri-va-la-heating-and-cooling-plant/ (accessed August 9, 2019).

21. NextEra Energy, "Renewable Energy," 2019, http://www.nexteraenergy.com/sustainability/environment/renewable-energy.html (accessed August 9, 2019).

22. Mathew DiLallo, "Why NextEra Energy Continues to Bet Big on Renewables," The Motley Fool, 2019, https://www.fool.com/investing/2019/02/02/why-nextera-energy-continues-to-bet-big-on-renewab.aspx (accessed August 9, 2019).

23. Enel, "Electric Mobility: Enel X, Nissan and RSE Launch Italy's First Test of Vehicle-to-Grid Technology Applied to Innovative Services," May 24, 2019, https://www.enel.com/media/press/d/2019/05/electric-mobility-enel-x-nissan-and-rse-launch-italys-first-test-of-vehicle-to-grid-technology-applied-to-innovative-services (accessed August 30, 2019).

9

Machinery & Industrial Equipment (M&IE) Industry Profile

Table 9.1 Industry summary

	M&IE industry today: Products are conventionally built to last, but the M&IE industry has only scratched the surface of capturing value through circular models that extend product use and reuse valuable parts	
Case for change	**Today**	**Looking ahead**
Industry size	$0.7 trillion	$1.5 trillion (projection for 2030)
Illustrative waste volumes	• Nearly all of the 1.7 billion ton iron ore market is used to make steel[1] • Machinery is idle 40–60% of running time[2,3]	• Approximately 3 billion tons of iron ore will be needed by 2030 (+75%)[1] • Availability of key virgin resources is a risk for the industry
Value at stake	–	$70–$220 billion (5–14% of EBITDA) by 2030

🔋 Industry Status

M&IE includes heavy-duty and off-road equipment for lifting and moving goods and materials. Thus, products and solutions are generally not personalized and are based on established technologies (motors, hydraulic drives, and so on) that allow for long lifecycles of up to 30 years.[4]

In many respects, M&IE already has well-integrated circular principles. Most of the machinery requires extensive maintenance over the course of its useful life. Consequently, after-sales services often account for a significant amount of revenue, and these opportunities can be enhanced through business models that eliminate ownership altogether. Moreover, the use of

© The Author(s) 2020
P. Lacy et al., *The Circular Economy Handbook*,
https://doi.org/10.1057/978-1-349-95968-6_9

recycled materials is common.[5] In addition, companies like Caterpillar, the American construction equipment manufacturer, and Hitachi, the Japanese conglomerate, have been offering buy-back programs through which customers can return their used equipment, meaning reverse infrastructures are already in place.[6,7] To date, however, only minor attention has been paid to end-of-use potential in terms of conserving and maintaining product value. The M&IE industry is strongly positioned for scaling circular business models, and companies need to build on existing momentum toward increased circularity.

Waste to Wealth Challenges

The M&IE industry has three major areas of waste (see Fig. 9.1). The first occurs in manufacturing, which contributes large amounts of pollution through processes like casting, forging, machining, and welding.

The second major area of waste is with respect to capacity. It has been estimated that idle times in construction machinery can be attributed to 40–60% of total running times.[2]

The third area is wasted valuable metals. Although metal recycling has been a success story when compared to other materials, there is still much that can be done. Despite being the world's most recycled material, only 40% of global steel is produced using recycled input.[8] Moreover, along with metallic ores, virgin materials such as coal are still widely used across the industry.

Waste to Wealth Opportunities

Across industries, M&IE has one of the largest opportunities in the circular economy (see Table 9.2). M&IE customers find value in purchasing energy- and material-efficient products that last longer, and they are willing to pay an upfront premium for longer-term savings. Major manufacturers like Caterpillar, Toyota, and Okuma currently offer premium models, which they could grow by incorporating a circular value proposition. In total, we expect 5% of sales to be transferred from other products to premium circular brands.

Another huge area of opportunity is circular business models that capitalize on long and costly product development times, combined with the value of materials used and relatively long lifecycles. As shown in Table 9.2, there

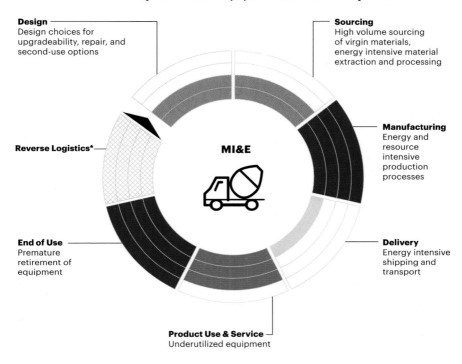

Design
Design choices for
upgradeability, repair, and
second-use options

Sourcing
High volume sourcing
of virgin materials,
energy intensive material
extraction and processing

Manufacturing
Energy and
resource
intensive
production
processes

Reverse Logistics*

MI&E

End of Use
Premature
retirement of
equipment

Delivery
Energy intensive
shipping and
transport

Product Use & Service
Underutilized equipment

Heatmap:

Very High   High   Medium   Low   Not Applicable

*While the 'Reverse Logistics' stage does not produce unique waste streams per se,
 it is included in the diagram as it is a key part of a circular value chain.

Fig. 9.1 Waste analysis diagram

are three ways to capture the opportunity. First, companies could extend
equipment lifecycles and increase their utilization with service-oriented
(as opposed to ownership) models that focus on repair, maintenance, and
upgrades. To that end, designing for repairability/modularity and embedding sensors in equipment can help enable cost-efficient maintenance,
repair, and upgrades. Various add-on services and alternative circular models like pay-per-use leasing that generate more revenue per equipment also
extend product use. Second, firms can take advantage of multiple lifecycles

Table 9.2 Waste to wealth opportunity summary

Circular economy opportunity	Increase equipment utilization and prolong lifecycles through service models	Enable multiple lifecycles through resale to second-use markets	Recover valuable parts and metals into circular manufacturing
Type of opportunity	Circular business models—service based	Circular business models—resale and reuse	Circular sourcing—buying better
Value at stake (by 2030)	$5–40 billion through circular consumption models		$50–110 billion
Value levers	• Increased revenue per equipment • Price premium	• Revenue from market share gain (loss avoidance), as this market cuts into demand for lower-priced equipment	• Reduced cost of goods sold
Target waste	• Wasted capacity of equipment not fully utilized for its useful life	• Wasted lifecycles due to lack of second-use options	• Wasted embedded value of unrecovered components and metals from waste streams
Value chain focus	• Design (e.g., for longer lifecycles and repairability) • Product usage and services (new consumption models)	• Design for longer lifecycles • End-of-use recovery for resale	• Design for end of use can increase ease of recovery • End-of-use recovery • Reverse logistics • Sourcing • Manufacturing
Technology amplifiers	• Embedding IoT technologies into equipment can enable cost-efficient service models	• Digital technologies can track equipment for recovery, evaluation, and value estimation so that it can be directed to the market of highest value	• Digital technologies can track equipment for recovery and evaluation, and robotics can be used for disassembly

Circular economy opportunity	Increase equipment utilization and prolong lifecycles through service models	Enable multiple lifecycles through resale to second-use markets	Recover valuable parts and metals into circular manufacturing
Case study	Volvo Construction Equipment (Volvo CE), the construction and industries equipment manufacturer, allows customers to return their equipment for refurbishment to ensure optimal working conditions. Three separate packages are available. The first restores the technology back to optimal fuel consumption levels and increased uptimes. The second restores the hydraulic system of the equipment to ensure higher productivity, durability, reliability, uptime, and overall performance. And the third package offers a complete rebuild of the equipment to a near-new condition. Rebuilding and retro-fitting old equipment to the working conditions of a new counterpart is approximately half the cost of a new machine, and customers are provided with financing and extended warranty options[9]	Komatsu has a used-equipment retrofitting and resale program for both mining and construction machinery. Through the program, distributors conduct a 100-point inspection of used equipment for both interior and exterior standards, after which they make the required retrofits and repairs to reach optimal performance levels. The equipment then receives certification and is sold at a fraction of the price of a new product[10]	Caterpillar focuses on the entire product lifecycle, with product design and development as a central part of repair, refurbishment, and remanu-facturing at the end of use to a "same as when new" condition. To increase the recovery of end-of-use equipment, product return is built into the company's exchange business model, with customers charged a deposit that is later refunded when they return their used components. The firm also uses a proprietary system to globally manage returns from dealers and inspection facilities and to determine the refund credit amounts. The result is that Caterpillar can salvage 70% of its newly designed machinery. The company currently recycles more than 150 million pounds of end-of-use iron annually[11,12]

through resale to second-use markets. We expect this market to grow in the cost-conscious segments, cutting into demand for mass-market and lower-priced equipment. And third, companies could also recover and reuse valuable parts and metals at end of use, when repair and resale are no longer economically feasible.

 ## Technology Amplifiers

Intensifying global competition and increasing commoditization are shifting value pools from machinery products to software and services. Since hardware-driven growth is limited, M&IE companies are starting to move toward digital solutions. These technologies have enabled companies to tap into new opportunities and develop platforms for implementation, for example:

- AMP Robotics is using AI and robotics to fundamentally change the cost of recycling. AMP has successfully developed a new kind of sorting technology for recycling facilities: the Cortex robot. It is capable of automating the separation of commodities with practically no retrofit or change to existing operations.[13] Cortex robots are powered by Neuron—AI that perceives material in the dirty, commingled conditions found in facilities today.[13]
- The tire company Michelin Solutions is focused on digital solutions for their customers, such as EFFIFUEL™—an ecosystem that uses sensors inside vehicles to collect data, like fuel consumption, tire pressure, temperature, speed, and location. This offering serves Michelin's strong circular vision and ambitions, so that customers can reduce carbon emissions while improving performance.[14]
- Researchers at the Swedish Chalmers University of Technology developed a new optimization algorithm for industrial equipment. By tweaking the acceleration in the movement of industrial robots, energy consumption can be sliced by 40% while retaining the given production time.[15]

 ## Obstacles to Overcome

The M&IE industry faces a number of challenges in moving toward circularity. Although the corporate functions of design and manufacturing are mostly planned and carried out with a global perspective, sales and after-sales activities have local autonomy (in order to be close to customers and to deal with local competitors). That calls for strategic changes to better integrate those functions, with the growing importance of sales and after-sales. Moreover, new sales strategies and operational changes would help scale customer interest and participation in new business models. This might include improving the infrastructure to handle remanufactured products, integrating recovery into the sales model, and also scaling reverse logistics for remanufacturing, which can be a significant barrier given the widespread global nature of delivery networks.

Policy and regulation changes will also be crucial to drive the market acceptance and pricing parity of remanufactured products (see Part III, "Policy—The Role of Policymakers"). Currently, remanufactured components are regarded as "used" products and cannot be sold or used in some countries, despite having "as good as new" warranties by the OEM.[16] With the appropriate changes, reused/remanufactured components and products will be considered equivalent to those made from virgin material, paving the way for their general acceptance.

 Chapter Takeaways

Circular business models can significantly address waste pools and unlock value but will rely on changes to the current operating model.

Opportunities

- Rental, sharing, repair, and other models that increase equipment utilization and prolong lifecycles
- Models that enable multiple product lifecycles via resale to second-use markets
- Recovery models that enable valuable parts and metals to be reused

Technology amplifiers

- Existing technologies like GPS and robotic systems can enable better monitoring and maintenance of equipment, which can then enable circular models for machine in-use and parts recovery

Obstacles to overcome

- Separation of sales and service (after-sales) teams limits customer interest and participation in new models for use and return
- Due to the global spread of manufacturing, localized models are needed to enable reverse flows
- Policies and regulations hinder market acceptance and pricing parity for remanufactured products

Notes

1. Rio Tinto, "Iron Ore Seminar," 2015, https://www.riotinto.com/documents/150903_Presentation_Iron_Ore_Seminar_Sydney.pdf (accessed August 9, 2019).
2. Caterpillar, "Engine Idle Reduction System: Less Idle, More Profit With Eirs," 2019, https://www.cat.com/en_US/by-industry/oil-and-gas/well-service-technology/engine-idle-reduction-system/less-idle-more-profit-with-eirs.html (accessed August 9, 2019).
3. Chrys Kefalas, "Forty Percent of Manufacturing Machines Are Under-Utilized, so This Company Came Up with a Way to Share Them," National Association of Manufacturers, 2017, https://www.shopfloor.org/2017/10/40-manufacturing-machines-utilized-company-came-way-share/ (accessed August 9, 2019).
4. UNFCCC, "Tool to Determine the Remaining Lifetime of Equipment," 2009, https://cdm.unfccc.int/methodologies/PAmethodologies/tools/am-tool-10-v1.pdf (accessed August 9, 2019).
5. Global Market Insights, "Recycling Equipment & Machinery Market Size by Machine, by Processed Material, Industry Analysis Report, Regional Outlook, Growth Potential, Price Trends, Competitive Market Share & Forecast, 2018–2025," 2018, https://www.gminsights.com/industry-analysis/recycling-equipment-and-machinery-market (accessed August 9, 2019).
6. Cat Financial, "Used Equipment," https://www.catfinancial.com/en_US/solutions/used-equipment.html (accessed August 30, 2019).
7. Hitachi Construction Machinery, "Let Us Buy Back Your Hitachi Wheel Loader," https://www.hitachicm.eu/buy-back-hitachi-wheel-loader/ (accessed August 30, 2019).
8. Rick LeBlanc, "An Introduction to Metal Recycling," Small Business, 2019, https://www.thebalancesmb.com/an-introduction-to-metal-recycling-4057470 (accessed August 9, 2019).
9. Curt Bennick, "Rebuilt Loaders Cut Production Costs," Construction PROS.com, 2019, https://www.forconstructionpros.com/equipment/earthmoving/article/10819127/use-remanufacturing-to-cut-wheel-loader-costs (accessed August 9, 2019).
10. Komatsu Used, "Welcome to the New Standard of Excellence," https://www.komatsuused.com/construction (accessed August 16, 2019).
11. Caterpillar, "Sustainability in China," Caterpillar, 2015, http://s7d2.scene7.com/is/content/Caterpillar/CM20161026-85160-30817 (accessed August 9, 2019).
12. Caterpillar, "The Benefits of Remanufacturing," 2019, https://www.caterpillar.com/en/company/sustainability/remanufacturing/benefits.html (accessed August 9, 2019).

13. AMP Robotics, "AMP Robotics Launches New AI Guided Dual-Robot System for the Recycling Industry," May 9, 2019, https://www.amprobotics.com/newsroom (accessed August 30, 2019).
14. Michelin Solutions, "EFFIFUEL™ From MICHELIN® solutions Progress Report and Outlook," 2014, https://www.michelin.com/en/press-releases/effifuel-from-michelin-solutions-delivers-fuel-savings/ (accessed August 19, 2019).
15. Evan Ackerman, "Robots With Smooth Moves Are Up to 40% More Efficient," IEEE Spectrum, August 27, 2015, https://spectrum.ieee.org/automaton/robotics/industrial-robots/robots-with-smooth-moves-are-more-efficient (accessed August 9, 2019).
16. Caterpillar, "Caterpillar's Remanufacturing of End-of-Life Components," Business Europe, 2017, http://www.circulary.eu/project/caterpillar-remanufacturing/ (accessed August 9, 2019).

10

 Information & Communications
Technology (ICT) Industry Profile

Table 10.1 Industry summary

ICT industry today: Rapid innovation and high replacement rates have inundated the market with devices. While efforts for Product Use Extension and collection at end of use are beginning to take hold, they have not scaled to capture the value potential of ICT hardware

Case for change	Today	Looking ahead
Industry size	$0.6 trillion	$1.3 trillion (projection for 2030)
Illustrative waste volumes	• The world generates around 50 million tons of e-waste annually[1] • E-waste makes up 70% of the hazardous waste deposited in landfills[2] • Only 20% of e-waste is collected and formally recycled[1]	• 2030: The ICT industry is responsible for 1.25 gigatons of carbon dioxide-equivalent (CO_2e) emissions (1.97% of global emissions)[3] • 2025: 64 million tons e-waste[4]
Value at stake	–	$20–$50 billion (1–3% of EBITDA) by 2030

Industry Status

During the last decade, the market has been flooded with devices that support every aspect of work and daily life. The result is a market prone to falling prices and short innovation cycles. The emergence of the cloud and big data has also led to an expanding technological infrastructure, namely large-scale datacenters. Infrastructure needs will mount as advancements, such as artificial intelligence (AI), demand greater computational power, storage, and Internet speeds. In parallel, next-generation 5G wireless networks require hardware and software upgrades in global network infrastructure. Moreover, the transition to a low-carbon economy coupled with trends for enhanced user experience will drive the growing volume of electronics, such as those in smart appliances, vehicles, and wind- and solar-power generation systems. This will lead to higher demand and price for key raw materials such as cobalt, copper, and rare earth metals.

Value chains in this industry tend to stretch across the globe and, therefore, are complex to disrupt from a circular perspective. This presents end-of-use challenges as the points of production and resource recovery are geographically dispersed. Geopolitical changes and uncertainties like China's National Sword policy to stop accepting foreign e-waste add further complexity.[5] Strategic capital investments, such as the recently opened e-waste processing facility in Dubai, the largest of its kind in the world, are aimed at pursuing the global opportunities presented by the circular paradigm.[6]

Waste to Wealth Challenges

ICT devices have relatively short lives, as consumers seek easy access to the latest technologies at the lowest possible costs. On the enterprise technology side, servers are replaced every three to five years, on average.[7] This tendency to prematurely replace existing products with newer models leads to two major pools of waste (see Fig. 10.1).

The first is wasted lifecycles. Because of soaring demand for the latest technologies, perfectly functioning devices and hardware are often replaced. On average, people use their smartphones for only 22 months, even though potential use of those devices is much longer (around 4.7 years, as of 2015).[8]

The second large waste pool is embedded value. Most ICT devices, enterprise technology equipment, and network infrastructure hardware contain valuable materials currently not being recovered. In 2016, 44.7 million tons of e-waste were generated globally (of which only about 20% is currently documented to be collected and recycled).[9] For that year, the value of raw materials alone in global e-waste streams was estimated at 55 billion euros.[9]

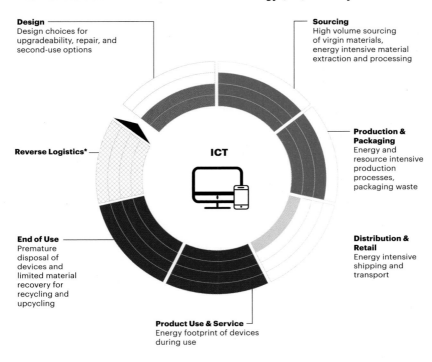

Design
Design choices for upgradeability, repair, and second-use options

Sourcing
High volume sourcing of virgin materials, energy intensive material extraction and processing

Reverse Logistics*

ICT

Production & Packaging
Energy and resource intensive production processes, packaging waste

End of Use
Premature disposal of devices and limited material recovery for recycling and upcycling

Distribution & Retail
Energy intensive shipping and transport

Product Use & Service
Energy footprint of devices during use

Heatmap:

Very High   High   Medium   Low   Not Applicable

*While the 'Reverse Logistics' stage does not produce unique waste streams per se, it is included in the diagram as it is a key part of a circular value chain.

Fig. 10.1 Waste analysis diagram

 ## Waste to Wealth Opportunities

The ICT industry has multiple opportunity areas to embrace (see Table 10.2). Refurbishment and reuse of existing ICT devices illustrate the first area of opportunity. Over the years, recovery businesses like Amazon Renewed, Inrego, and Laptops Direct have begun to collect or buy back previously owned devices to resell (or re-lease) them. Refurbished electronic devices can

Table 10.2 Waste to wealth opportunity summary

Circular economy opportunity	Refurbishment and reuse of ICT devices	Recovery of valuable materials from ICT devices at end of use	Redesign of products and packaging to use less materials
Type of opportunity	Circular business models—refurbishment and reuse	Circular business models—resale of waste	Circular design—use less
Value at stake (by 2030)	$10–20 billion	$2.5–5 billion	$10–20 billion
Value levers	• Additional revenue	• Additional revenue • Reduced cost of materials	• Reduced cost of materials
Target waste	• Wasted lifecycles due to lack of second-use options	• Wasted embedded value of materials not recovered • Wasted resources	• Reduction in material use
Value chain focus	• Design (for longer lifecycles and modularity) • Product usage • End of use • Reverse logistics	• End of use • Reverse logistics • Sourcing	• Design (to minimize material inputs) • Production and packaging
Technology amplifiers	• Digital platforms to buy/sell products	• Robotics for disassembly and intelligent sorting systems	• Cloud, AI/machine learning, virtual reality, IoT
Case study	Inrego buys used professional IT equipment from organizations. Around 90% of all received equipment is reusable; the remaining is recycled downstream. Inrego enables municipalities, businesses, and consumers to buy professional IT equipment at half the price of new products. In 2014, the company reconditioned 260,000 units that saved 2800 tons CO_2e emissions[10]	Technology company Apple's newest disassembly robot, Daisy, can take apart up to 200 iPhone devices per hour, removing and sorting components to enable the company to recover valuable materials[11]	In late 2014, technology company Dell implemented the industry's first certified closed-loop process for manufacturing a computer—taking plastics from the e-waste recovered and then melting, mixing, and molding that into new parts for new products. This led to an estimated $2 million in savings, in new material use in production[12]

perform as good as new when loaded with updated software and drivers, doubling (or even tripling) their useful lives.[13] In 2017, refurbished smartphone sales grew by 13%, for instance, compared with just a 3% growth in new smartphone sales.[14] New consumption models, such as leasing or rental, can help facilitate product returns to enable refurbishment and reuse.

A case study on network routers offered by telecom service providers in Germany demonstrates the benefits of new business models for other types of hardware as well. Accenture analysis concluded that shifting to a rental model of routers led to an 80% reduction in material losses and 45% reduction in CO_2 emissions compared to the linear model due to superior recovery and collection rates. Furthermore, reusing recovered routers led to a 35% cost savings, demonstrating the multi-tiered value opportunities of new business models.[15]

Recovery of valuable materials from ICT devices at end of use presents the second area of opportunity. A typical iPhone contains an estimated 25 grams of aluminum and 15 grams of copper, as well as much smaller but significant amounts of valuable metals like gold, silver, and platinum.[16] Recycling end-of-use consumer devices and reselling embedded materials such as glass, plastics, and metal can deliver an estimated \$2.5–5 billion of incremental revenue.[17]

Redesigning for less material use is the third area of opportunity. Smarter designs could reduce material use in parts like casings for consumer devices and product packaging, enabling the industry to realize an estimated \$10–20 billion value opportunity through reduced cost of materials and packaging. Circular design principles can also cost-effectively extend use of a product. The abovementioned Accenture analysis on routers found that certain design choices (e.g., using scratch-resistant materials) can reduce refurbishment costs by about 50%. At Cisco, the goal is to enable product designers to consider different ways to extend a product's use, to make disassembly easier, and to incorporate other circular principles. "We want to get to a place where a Circular Design decision is the default choice, as long as it has equivalent cost and performance," says John Kern, Cisco's Senior Vice President of Supply Chain Operations.

Technology Amplifiers

Companies are developing innovative ways to create cost efficiencies throughout the ICT value chain, leveraging technology to enable circular solutions. Here are a few examples:

- The asset lifecycle management company Apto Solutions recovers value from unwanted assets and protects customers from costly data breaches using an integrated process that prolongs use of their technology before finally recycling it back into the economy. In 2014, Apto Solutions saved over 14,800 metric tons of fossil fuels and 19 million gallons of water and prevented 1315 metric tons of hazardous waste from ending up in landfill.[18]
- Using modular architecture, the sustainable smartphone startup Fairphone designed the Fairphone 2 to last longer than the average smartphone. The device boasts easy repairs, customization, and upgrades for long-lasting use. A lifecycle assessment study estimated a 30% reduction in CO_2 emissions across the entire lifecycle of the Fairphone 2.[19]
- Digital solutions can also enhance traceability and transparency throughout the ICT value chain. The Dutch startup Circularise is developing a blockchain-based communication protocol called "smart questioning" to promote value chain transparency without the public disclosure of datasets or supply chain partners. This pre-validation guarantees data accuracy without the need to disclose sensitive company or product information.[20]

Obstacles to Overcome

The demand for ICT devices will only grow, further squeezing resources and creating larger e-waste streams. In response, companies must address two key challenges.

The first is collection at end of use. Consumers often do not return their unwanted ICT devices after upgrading to a newer model. One solution would be new business models that allow companies to provide access to products while retaining ownership, thus facilitating controlled takeback at end of use. Another solution is to offer customers product takeback incentives. According to an Accenture consumer survey, 74% of consumers are most encouraged to participate in a product takeback program that provides convenient returns or incentives, like discounts or reward points.[21] Apple's trade-in program, for example, offers customers credit for eligible devices, regardless of the model or condition, along with convenient return options via prepaid return shipping or at any store location.[22]

The other challenge is e-waste. The cost of compliance in recycling e-waste is relatively high in developed countries, raising the risk of ICT devices ending up in less-developed countries with little or no governance on appropriate end-of-use handling. Technology can enable favorable economics in the recycling industry. In particular, increased deployment of robotics to disassemble products can help improve not just the efficiency but also the quality of material that comes out of the recycling process. "There's also the potential of using machine vision to recognize waste even per brand," notes Matanya Horowitz, founder of AMP Robotics, an AI and robotics company. And that's just the beginning. "With AI, it's possible to create new metrics for the sorting industry," says Horowitz. "We'll be able to gain insights that will enable us to make our takeback programs more effective."

E-waste that ends up in landfills or is recycled using basic methods through the informal sector—as is the case in less-developed countries—is extremely harmful to the surrounding communities. As such, global policy standards such as Extended Producer Responsibility laws would bolster visibility and traceability throughout the value chain and support the development of responsible end-of-use practices around the world (see Part III, "Policy—The Role of Policymakers").

 Chapter Takeaways

A significant value opportunity can be captured from circular initiatives in the ICT industry with the establishment of an efficient reverse-logistics infrastructure to enable reuse, refurbishment, and recycling.

Opportunities

- Refurbishment and reuse of ICT devices
- Recovery of valuable materials through recycling
- Redesign of products and packaging to decrease material usage

Technology amplifiers

- Digital platforms to facilitate resale of ICT devices
- Intelligent sorting systems to cost-effectively identify and separate e-waste
- Robotics for disassembly to facilitate refurbishment, remanufacture, and recycling practices

Obstacles to overcome

- Lack of efficient reverse flows for product takeback
- E-waste streams that lack regulation for safe and appropriate end-of-use handling

Notes

1. UN Environment, "UN Report: Time to Seize Opportunity, Tackle Challenge of E-Waste," 2019, http://www.unenvironment.org/news-and-stories/press-release/un-report-time-seize-opportunity-tackle-challenge-e-waste (accessed August 9, 2019).
2. Kevin N. Perkins, Marie-Noel Brune Drisse, Tapiwa Nxele, and Peter D. Sly, "E-Waste: A Global Hazard," *Annals of Global Health*, 2014, https://www.sciencedirect.com/science/article/pii/S2214999614003208 (accessed August 9, 2019).
3. GeSI and Accenture Strategy, "SMARTer 2030: ICT Solutions for 21st Century Challenges," 2015, https://unfccc.int/sites/default/files/smarter2030_executive_summary.pdf (accessed August 9, 2019).
4. Research and Markets, "E-Waste Management Market Size, Share & Trends Analysis Report By Processed Material, By Source, By Application And Segment Forecasts, 2018–2025," 2018, https://www.researchandmarkets.com/reports/4613411/e-waste-management-market-size-share-and-trends (accessed August 9, 2019).
5. Cheryl Katz, "Piling Up: How China's Ban on Importing Waste Has Stalled Global Recycling," Yale Environment 360, March 7, 2019, https://e360.yale.edu/features/piling-up-how-chinas-ban-on-importing-waste-has-stalled-global-recycling (accessed August 27, 2019).
6. Gulf News UAE, "World's LARGEst E-Waste Recycling Facility Opens in Dubai," 2019, https://gulfnews.com/uae/worlds-largest-e-waste-recycling-facility-opens-in-dubai-1.62884040 (accessed August 9, 2019).
7. SherWeb Blog, "Cost of Server Ownership: On-Premise vs. IaaS," April 21, 2019, https://www.sherweb.com/blog/cloud-server/total-cost-of-ownership-of-servers-iaas-vs-on-premise/ (accessed August 30, 2019).
8. Torro Cases, "How to Extend the Lifespan of Your Smartphone," CEO Today, 2018, https://www.ceotodaymagazine.com/2018/02/how-to-extend-the-lifespan-of-your-smartphone/ (accessed August 9, 2019).
9. United Nations University, "The Global E-Waste Monitor 2017," 2017, https://collections.unu.edu/eserv/UNU:6341/Global-E-waste_Monitor_2017__electronic_single_pages_.pdf (accessed August 9, 2019).
10. Inrego, "Computers & Smart Phones," https://www.remanufacturing.eu/studies/f6a18b15473d6fa8400e.pdf (accessed August 9, 2019).
11. Apple, "Apple Adds Earth Day Donations to Trade-In and Recycling Program," 2018, https://www.apple.com/newsroom/2018/04/apple-adds-earth-day-donations-to-trade-in-and-recycling-program (accessed August 9, 2019).
12. Bryony Collins, "Dell Eyes $63 Billion E-Waste Recycling Opportunity: Q&A," BloombergNEF, July 29, 2019, https://about.bnef.com/blog/dell-eyes-63-billion-e-waste-recycling-opportunity-qa/ (accessed August 30, 2019).

13. Patty Osterberg, "Electronics and the Growing Trend Towards Reuse and the Circular Economy," SERI, 2017, https://sustainableelectronics.org/news/2017/06/22/electronics-and-growing-trend-towards-reuse-and-circular-economy (accessed August 9, 2019).
14. TAdviser, "Smartphones (World Market)," 2019, http://tadviser.com/index.php/Article:Smartphones_(world_market) (accessed August 9, 2019).
15. Rat Fur Nachhaltige Entwicklung in Collaboration with Accenture Strategy, "Opportunities of the Circular Economy in Germany," 2017, https://www.nachhaltigkeitsrat.de/wp-content/uploads/migration/documents/RNE-Accenture_Studie_Chancen_der_Kreislaufwirtschaft_04-07-2017.pdf (accessed August 9, 2019).
16. Bianca Nogrady, "Your Old Phone Is Full of Untapped Precious Metals," BBC, http://www.bbc.com/future/story/20161017-your-old-phone-is-full-of-precious-metals (accessed August 9, 2019).
17. Accenture Analysis.
18. The Forum of Young Global Leaders in Collaboration with Accenture Strategy, "The Circulars 2016 Yearbook," https://thecirculars.org/content/resources/The_Circulars_Yearbook_2016_Final.pdf (accessed August 9, 2019).
19. Fairphone, "Impact Report Vol. 1," https://www.fairphone.com/wp-content/uploads/2018/11/Fairphone_Report_DEF_WEB.pdf (accessed August 9, 2019).
20. World Economic Forum in Collaboration with Accenture Strategy, "Harnessing the Fourth Industrial Revolution for the Circular Economy Consumer Electronics and Plastics Packaging," 2019, http://www3.weforum.org/docs/WEF_Harnessing_4IR_Circular_Economy_report_2018.pdf (accessed August 9, 2019).
21. Accenture 2019 Consumer Survey.
22. Apple, "Apple Trade In: Turn the Device You Have into the One You Want," 2019, https://www.apple.com/uk/shop/trade-in (accessed August 9, 2019).

11

Personal Mobility Industry Profile

Table 11.1 Industry summary

 Personal Mobility industry today: While a shift to EVs and car-sharing economy models is disrupting the automotive industry, manufacturing is still extremely resource intensive and end-of-use vehicles generate millions of tons of waste every year

Case for change	Today	Looking ahead
Industry size	$2 trillion	$5 trillion (projection for 2030)
Illustrative waste volumes	• Cars on average have a low utilization rate of only 5–10% maximum[1] • The average lifecycle of private vehicles in the United States is 13–17 years, but the average age is only 11.5 years[2] • Road transport accounts for 17% of global greenhouse gas emissions[3] • Some 13% of end-of-use vehicle waste generated in the EU is not recycled or reused[4] • Around 240 pounds of waste is generated in manufacturing a vehicle, and over 39,000 gallons of water is used[5,6]	• 100 million cars are estimated to be produced in 2030 (from 70.5 million in 2018)[7,8] • End-of-use vehicle waste will increase by 45% between 2005 and 2030[9] • Road transportation will spike by 30% by 2030[10] • The number of EVs on the road is expected to reach 125 million (from 3.1 million vehicles in 2017) by 2030 (IEA)[11]
Value at stake	–	$240–$610 billion (5–12% of EBITDA) by 2030

© The Author(s) 2020
P. Lacy et al., *The Circular Economy Handbook*,
https://doi.org/10.1057/978-1-349-95968-6_11

Industry Status

Personal mobility is the use of private or public vehicles by individuals for transportation. It is important to distinguish between indirect and direct circularity in this industry. Specifically, macrotrends such as vehicle sharing, alternative drivetrains (moving away from internal combustion engines), and autonomous vehicles are separate from the "pure play" (or direct) circular economy transformations. With these macrotrends, inefficiencies such as indirect emissions remain unaddressed, with an unintended net negative impact on the environment—if car travel becomes more convenient, then the total distance traveled by vehicles will likely increase, resulting in more vehicles being manufactured and energy being consumed.[12] Direct circular uptake, on the other hand, targets resource utilization inefficiencies head-on, i.e., decreasing energy and material intensity in manufacturing.

Given this distinction, the industry has taken significant but "indirect" steps toward circularity, with the greatest progress in fuel efficiency and tailpipe emissions reduction. Jaguar Land Rover, Mercedes-Benz, Volvo, and other automakers have already committed to partial or full-fleet electrification in the next five to ten years. Vehicle sharing and pooling highlight another disruption, illustrated by the popularity of DriveNow and ZipCar. By 2030, one in 10 cars is expected to be a shared vehicle.[13] Despite these areas of notable progress, manufacturing remains heavily resource intensive, and end-of-use vehicles generate millions of tons of waste every year.

 Waste to Wealth Challenges

The personal mobility industry incurs four major areas of waste (see Fig. 11.1). The first lies in manufacturing: 20% of total GHG emissions for internal combustion engine vehicles and as much as 47% for battery EVs are generated during the production phase.[14] In addition, around 110 kilograms of waste is generated in manufacturing a vehicle.[5] The second area is wasted capacity. On average, automobiles have low utilization rates—typically 5 to 10%—leaving $7 trillion worth of passenger cars unused at any one time.[1,15] The "use phase" also has a high waste footprint. This includes carbon (road transport accounting for 17% of global GHG emissions), in addition to other wastes such as microplastics shed from tires, precious metals particles emitted by catalytic converters, wasted embedded value

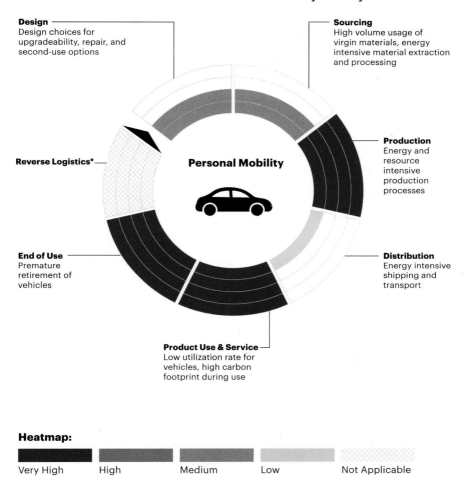

Design
Design choices for upgradeability, repair, and second-use options

Sourcing
High volume usage of virgin materials, energy intensive material extraction and processing

Personal Mobility

Reverse Logistics*

Production
Energy and resource intensive production processes

End of Use
Premature retirement of vehicles

Distribution
Energy intensive shipping and transport

Product Use & Service
Low utilization rate for vehicles, high carbon footprint during use

Heatmap:

Very High   High   Medium   Low   Not Applicable

*While the 'Reverse Logistics' stage does not produce unique waste streams per se, it is included in the diagram as it is a key part of a circular value chain.

Fig. 11.1   Waste analysis diagram

not retrieved from parts, and consumables (such as filters, fluids, and wiper blades) changed during the vehicle's life.[16,17,18] Lastly, a wide range of high- and low-value waste occurs at the product's end of use. In Europe, privately owned cars have an estimated average age of 9.7 years with 12 million vehicles being taken off the road every year.[19,20] This equates to millions of tons of potentially valuable waste from end-of-use vehicles.[21]

Waste to Wealth Opportunities

There are three big areas of opportunity in this industry (see Table 11.2). The first comes from the large shift to alternative drivetrains. EVs alone had a global share of 4.6% of new sales in 2018, nearly doubling since 2017.[22] This shift highlights an opportunity to greatly reduce mobility emissions in the use phase.

Vehicle and ride sharing present another intriguing area of opportunity. Through 2030, we expect 11% of car sales to migrate to the sharing economy (as a new consumption model), putting automakers on notice to innovate their business models to stay competitive.[28] The IT products and services company Fujitsu America expects use of shared cars to increase over 50% by 2030.[29] Sale and reuse of remanufactured components via after-markets is the third area of opportunity. Currently, remanufactured parts are sold at 50–70% of their original price, with hefty environmental savings (up to 80% less energy, 88% less water, 92% fewer chemical products, and 70% less waste production).[20]

Reducing the resource intensity of manufacturing vehicles and waste resulting from production processes opens another window of opportunity. Smart manufacturing and technologies such as Industrial IoT, data analytics, and robotics can make production more efficient, resulting in leaner operations while also reducing recall rates from faulty parts. According to the European Automobile Manufacturers' Association (ACEA) in 2018, the CO_2 emissions from vehicle manufacturing in Europe have fallen by more than a fifth since 2008.[31]

 ## Technology Amplifiers

Advances in materials science, AI, big data analytics, and other technologies have meant that companies can seize some of the circular value of EVs and ride sharing. In the future, emerging innovations could stimulate further advances. Among the more interesting examples:

- AI-based generative design technology: The American automotive company General Motors, for instance, has partnered with software company Autodesk to rapidly explore multiple permutations of a part's design, potentially resulting in cars with smaller environmental footprints.[32]

Table 11.2 Waste to wealth opportunity summary

Circular economy opportunity	Shift to EVs	Car-sharing and rental business models	Reuse and remanufacturing of components	Reducing the resource intensity of manufacturing
Type of opportunity	Circularity as a brand value—market share	Circular business models—car sharing and rental	Circular business models—reuse and remanufacture	Smarter operations—less defects
Value at stake (by 2030)	$160–225 billion	$10–85 billion	$5–20 billion	$50–135 billion
Value levers	• Market-share gain (loss avoidance)	• New sources of revenue	• Reduced cost of goods sold	• Reduced cost of goods sold
Target waste	• Fossil-fuel emissions during use phase	• Wasted capacity of cars that are not fully utilized over their use	• Wasted embedded value of components and metals not recovered from waste streams	• Energy and resource-intensive production processes
Value chain focus	• Design • Sourcing • Production • Use and service	• Use and service	• Design for disassembly • End-of-use recovery for reuse • Reverse logistics • Sourcing • Manufacturing	• Production
Technology amplifiers	• Improving battery technology to lower costs and extend driving range	• Digital platforms to enable car-sharing and rental business models	• Robotics for disassembly to drive recovery and remanufacturing	• Industrial IoT, data analytics, and robotics to increase the efficiency of production

(continued)

Table 11.2 (continued)

Circular economy opportunity	Shift to EVs	Car-sharing and rental business models	Reuse and remanufacturing of components	Reducing the resource intensity of manufacturing
Case study	Tesla is a leading producer and seller of EVs worldwide. By the end of 2018, the company had sold more than 530,000 EVs worldwide[23] Based on that figure, Tesla claims to have saved more than four million tons of CO_2 to date, equivalent to emissions from 9.7 billion miles driven by an average passenger vehicle[24]	Through its car2go service, German automaker Daimler rents its fleet of Smart Cars and Mercedes-Benzes for one-way usage. Consumers simply park a vehicle near their destination when they're done, and car2go handles the rest. Already 2.5 million people have registered for the service.[24] The global car fleet could be reduced by one-third if sharing schemes are widely adopted[25]	Ancillary remanufacturing at the German automobile company Audi's Ingolstadt plant gives old, disused, and broken starter motors and alternators a second life as original spare parts. This enables the automaker to save around 240 tons of steel, 100 tons of copper, and 80 tons of aluminum[26]	American multinational automaker Ford has placed IoT sensors on virtually every piece of production equipment at its River Rouge facility outside of Detroit. Downstream machines can detect if parts they receive from an upstream machine deviate in even the minutest dimension from specifications, thereby indicating possible problems in upstream machines that can be immediately identified and fixed[27]

- Industrial use of 3D printing could cut waste as well as decrease material needs and costs in manufacturing processes by up to 90%.[33] Set to hit both the Asian and European markets in 2019, a design-led 3D-printed low speed electric vehicle (LSEV), is priced as low as $7500, the result of the collaboration of a Shanghai-based 3D printing materials company, Polymer, and an Italy based electric car start-up, XEV.[34]
- The Technical University of Eindhoven in the Netherlands has developed the world's first bio-based circular car, with its chassis and all bodywork consisting of natural and bio-based materials. No metal or traditional plastics were used for the structural parts of the vehicle.[35]
- The combination of hardware and software technologies has led to the development of autonomous driving, with better fuel efficiency and energy utilization. The start of 2018 heralded a wave of hype for autonomous vehicles, with Alphabet's Waymo well on its way to launching a driverless taxi service in Phoenix, Arizona, and Uber's efforts to log millions of test miles with its fleet of self-driving vehicles.[36]
- Telematics allows vehicles to share data with the outside world. Predictive maintenance based on telematics data and forward-looking projections is becoming more intelligent.[37] The ability to predict a service event could potentially result in considerable material and energy savings, especially for cargo vehicles and larger fleet operators.

Obstacles to Overcome

At the current rate of adoption, an estimated 11 million tons of spent lithium-ion batteries from EVs will need to be recycled by 2030.[38] Many of those "spent" batteries still have up to 70% capacity left, and automakers like Tesla, Nissan, and BMW have been working on second-use options, such as using the batteries as stationary power sources.[38,39] Tesla, a leader in this area, introduced stationary energy storage products in 2015.[40] In 2018, Nissan used 148 Leaf batteries (both new and used) to power Amsterdam's soccer stadium.[39,41]

Second-use options would also mitigate increased supply risks, as electrification and digitization of vehicles have created a surge in demand for metals and minerals. Demand for lithium chemicals, most of which are destined for batteries, rose by nearly a third in 2018 from the previous year.[42] Similarly, the global demand for refined cobalt, another key input in batteries, almost tripled from 2000 to 2016.[43]

Another obstacle has been end-of-use management. In developing countries, the required infrastructure for managed vehicle end-of-use processing is largely non-existent, with fragmented and largely informal recycling industries.[44] In developed economies, in contrast, most cars are retired before the end of their full use potential. Although vehicle recycling rates are high in these geographies, most of the resultant material streams are generally of low quality and therefore find application in lower-value goods and industries, such as construction. There are, however, technical opportunities for innovation to address this and convert today's downcycling to future upcycling, particularly for metals and some plastics.[45] In Europe, the End of Life Vehicles Directive stipulates that the industry must ensure that 95% of a vehicle by weight is reused, recycled, or recovered; future regulations could address the need for upcycling. European-based manufacturers seized the opportunity to demonstrate that such high recovery levels can be achieved profitably.[9] Renault, for example, set up its ICARRE95 project collaboration to increase the recycling rate of end-of-use vehicles by developing technological and economic structures for the recycling of their materials.[46] Today, more than a third of the total mass of Renault vehicles manufactured in Europe comes from recycled materials.[47]

 Chapter Takeaways

Circular economy initiatives can address waste pools and unlock significant value. A key focus area is increasing visibility into material flows across the complex global supply chain.

Opportunities
- Shift toward EVs, reducing the environmental impact of cars during the use phase
- Car-sharing and rental business models, increasing the utilization of vehicles
- Reuse and remanufacturing of components, recovering valuable resources from vehicles
- Increasing efficiency and reducing waste during manufacturing, allowing for leaner operations and reducing recall rates from faulty parts

Technology amplifiers
- Robotics for disassembly, which can enable recovery and remanufacturing
- Digital platforms for car-sharing models
- Predictive maintenance

Obstacles to overcome
- Lack of adequate infrastructure for end-of-use management
- Increased supply risk due to surging demand for metals such as lithium for batteries
- E-waste from lithium batteries

Notes

1. David Z. Morris, "Today's Cars Are Parked 95% of the Time," Fortune, March 13, 2016, http://fortune.com/2016/03/13/cars-parked-95-percent-of-time/ (accessed August 16, 2019).
2. Scott Vaughan, "Average Lifespan for U.S. Vehicles," BERLA, November 16, 2016, https://berla.co/average-us-vehicle-lifespan/ (accessed August 9, 2019).
3. United Nations Climate Change, "Global Car Industry Must Shift to Low Carbon to Survive—CDP," UNFCCC, 2018, https://unfccc.int/news/global-car-industry-must-shift-to-low-carbon-to-survive-cdp (accessed August 9, 2019).
4. Eurostat Statistics Explained, "End of Life Vehicle Statistics," 2018, https://ec.europa.eu/eurostat/statistics-explained/index.php/End-of-life_vehicle_statistics (accessed August 9, 2019).
5. Sharon Guynup, "The Zero-Waste Factory," *Scientific American*, 2017, https://www.scientificamerican.com/custom-media/scjohnson-transparent-by-design/zerowastefactory/ (accessed August 9, 2019).
6. United States Environmental Protection Agency, "Water Trivia Facts," 2016, https://www3.epa.gov/safewater/kids/water_trivia_facts.html (accessed August 9, 2019).
7. Accenture analysis (Extrapolation of Car Production Up to 2030) based on data from International Organization of Motor Vehicle Manufacturers, "2018 Production Statistics," 2018, http://www.oica.net/category/production-statistics/2018-statistics/ (accessed August 9, 2019).
8. I. Wagner, "Estimated worldwide Automobile Production from 2000 to 2018 (in million vehicles)," Statista, 2019, https://www.statista.com/statistics/262747/worldwide-automobile-production-since-2000/ (accessed August 9, 2019).
9. J. Heiskanen et al., "A Look at the European Union's End-of-Life Vehicle Directive—Challenges of Treatment and Disposal in Finland," May 2013, https://www.resource-recovery.net/sites/default/files/heiskanenjetal2013fullpaper.pdf (accessed August 9, 2019).
10. Epure, "On the Road to 2030—Decarbonising Europe's Road Transport Sector," 2016, https://www.epure.org/media/1350/briefing-on-the-road-to-2030-decarbonising-europes-road-transport-sector.pdf (accessed August 9, 2019).
11. Tom DiChristopher, "Electric Vehicles Will Grow from 3 Million to 125 Million by 2030, International Energy Agency forecasts," CNBC Markets, 2018, https://www.cnbc.com/2018/05/30/electric-vehicles-will-grow-from-3-million-to-125-million-by-2030-iea.html (accessed August 9, 2019).
12. Payton Chang, "Self-Driving Cars and Their Environmental Impact," Stanford University, 2017, http://large.stanford.edu/courses/2017/ph240/chang-p2/ (accessed August 9, 2019).

13. McKinsey & Company, "Automotive Revolution—Perspective Towards 2030," 2016, https://www.mckinsey.com/~/media/mckinsey/industries/high%20tech/our%20insights/disruptive%20trends%20that.%20will%20transform%20the%20auto%20industry/auto%202030%20report%20jan%202016.ashx (accessed August 9, 2019).

14. Steel Market Development Institute, "The Importance of the Production Phase in Vehicle Life Cycle GHG Emissions," https://www.steelsustainability.org/-/media/files/autosteel/programs/lca/the-importance-of-the-production-phase-in-vehicle-life-cycle-ghg-emissions---final.ashx?la=en&hash=9B008DB7D45B3DB69962A2DF-C47DEA8EC5AF9649 (accessed August 9, 2019).

15. Peter Lacy, Andreas Gissler, and Mark Pearson, "Automotive's Latest Model: Redefining Competitiveness Though the Circular Economy," Accenture Strategy, 2016, https://eu-smartcities.eu/sites/default/files/2017-12/Accenture-POV-CE-Automotive.pdf (accessed August 9, 2019).

16. Sandra Laville, "Tyres and Synthetic Clothes 'Big Cause of Microplastic Pollution'," *The Guardian*, November 22, 2018, https://www.theguardian.com/environment/2018/nov/22/tyres-and-synthetic-clothes-big-cause-of-microplastic-pollution (accessed August 9, 2019).

17. Geert De Clercq, "Platinum from Road Dust, Veolia Cleans Up on British Streets," Reuters, December 2, 2014, https://www.reuters.com/article/britain-environment-dust/platinum-from-road-dust-veolia-cleans-up-on-british-streets-idUSL6N0TM38A20141202 (accessed August 9, 2019).

18. CDP, "Which Automotive Companies Will Seize the Opportunities in a Low-Carbon Economy? Executive Summary," 2018, https://b8f65cb373b1b7b15feb-c70d8ead6ced550b4d987d7c03fcdd1d.ssl.cf3.rackcdn.com/cms/reports/documents/000/002/953/original/CDP-autos-exec-summary-2018.pdf?1516266755 (accessed August 9, 2019).

19. Circle Economy & ABN AMRO, "On the Road to the Circular Car," August 2016, http://www.t2ge.eu/sites/www.t2ge.eu/files/attachments/abn-amro-the-circular-car-report.pdf (accessed August 9, 2019).

20. Ellen MacArthur Foundation, "The Circular Economy Applied to the Automotive Industry," 2013, https://www.ellenmacarthurfoundation.org/news/the-circular-economy-applied-to-the-automotive-industry (accessed August 9, 2019).

21. European Commission, "End of Life Vehicles," http://extranet.novacomm-europa.eu/environment/waste/elv/index.htm (accessed August 9, 2019).

22. Electrive.com, "All-Electric Car Market Share on the Rise Worldwide," 2018, https://www.electrive.com/2018/12/13/all-electric-car-market-share-on-the-rise-worldwide/ (accessed August 9, 2019).

23. Mark Kane, "Tesla Production and Deliveries Graphed Through Q4 2018," Inside EVs, 2019, https://insideevs.com/tesla-production-deliveries-graphed-q4-2018/ (accessed August 9, 2019).

24. Fred Lambert, "Tesla Releases Fascinating New 'Impact Report', Claims It Helped Prevent 4 Million Tons of CO_2," Electrek, 2019, https://electrek.co/2019/04/15/tesla-impact-report/ (accessed August 9, 2019).

25. Andrew J. Hawkins, "BMW and Daimler Are Putting Their Differences Aside to Beat Uber," The Verge, 2018, https://www.theverge.com/2018/4/2/17188374/bmw-daimler-merger-car2go-reachnow-mobility (accessed August 9, 2019).

26. Transport & Environment, "Does Sharing Cars Really Reduce Car Use?" 2017, https://www.transportenvironment.org/sites/te/files/publications/Does-sharing-cars-really-reduce-car-use-June%202017.pdf (accessed August 9, 2019).

27. Automotive Manufacturing Solutions, "War on Waste," 2014, https://www.automotivemanufacturingsolutions.com/33728.article (accessed August 9, 2019).

28. Stephen Ezell, "Why Manufacturing Digitalization Matters and How Countries Are Supporting It," ITIF, April 2018, www2.itif.org/2018-manufacturing-digitalization.pdf (accessed August 12, 2019).

29. McKinsey & Company, "Automotive Revolution—Perspective Towards 2030," January 2016, https://www.mckinsey.com/~/media/mckinsey/industries/high%20tech/our%20insights/disruptive%20trends%20that.%20will%20transform%20the%20auto%20industry/auto%202030%20report%20jan%202016.ashx (accessed August 9, 2019).

30. PR Newswire, "Fujitsu Forecasts Utilization Rates of Shared Cars to Surpass 50 Percent by 2030," November 15, 2017, https://www.prnewswire.com/news-releases/fujitsu-forecasts-utilization-rates-of-shared-cars-to-surpass-50-percent-by-2030-300556496.html (accessed August 9, 2019).

31. ACEA, "Environmental Impact of Car Production Strongly Reduced Over Last Decade," July, 12, 2018, https://www.acea.be/press-releases/article/environmental-impact-of-car-production-strongly-reduced-over-last-decade (accessed August 9, 2019).

32. General Motors Green, "GM Lightens Up One Gram at a Time," November 8, 2018, https://www.generalmotors.green/product/public/us/en/GMGreen/home.detail.html/content/Pages/news/us/en/gm_green/2018/1108-lightweighting.html (accessed August 12, 2019).

33. US Department of Energy, "Additive Manufacturing: Pursuing the Promise," 2012, https://www1.eere.energy.gov/manufacturing/pdfs/additive_manufacturing.pdf (accessed August 9, 2019).

34. Green Car Congress, "Report Suggests Low-Speed Electric Vehicles Could Affect Chinese Demand for Gasoline and Disrupt Oil Prices Worldwide," 2019, https://www.greencarcongress.com/2019/05/2019022-collins.html (accessed August 9, 2019).

35. Total- Corbion, "World's First Biobased, Circular Car Created Using Luminy from Total Corbion PLA," 2018, https://www.total-corbion.com/news/worlds-first-biobased-circular-car-created-using-luminy-from-total-corbion-pla/?q= (accessed August 9, 2019).

36. Meghan Brown, "Tech Trends 2019: Driverless Cars, Artificial Intelligence & Augmented Reality," Engineering.com, 2019, https://www.engineering.com/DesignerEdge/DesignerEdgeArticles/ArticleID/18283/Tech-Trends-2019-Driverless-Cars-Artificial-Intelligence-Augmented-Reality.aspx (accessed August 9, 2019).

37. Telematics Talk, "Predictive Maintenance: The 'Holy Grail' of Truck Telematics," 2017, https://www.telematicstalk.com/predictive-maintenance-holy-grail-truck-telematics/ (accessed August 9, 2019).

38. Joey Gardiner, "The Rise of Electric Cars Could Leave Us with a Big Battery Waste Problem," *The Guardian*, 2017, https://www.theguardian.com/sustainable-business/2017/aug/10/electric-cars-big-battery-waste-problem-lithium-recycling (accessed August 9, 2019).

39. Electrive, "EVgo & BMW Launching 2nd-Life Battery Project," 2018, https://www.electrive.com/2018/07/11/evgo-bmw-launching-2nd-life-battery-project/ (accessed August 9, 2019).

40. Nichola Groom and Paul Lienert, "Tesla Moves into Batteries That Store Energy for Homes, Businesses," Reuters, May 1, 2015, https://www.reuters.com/article/us-tesla-motors-batteries/tesla-moves-into-batteries-that-store-energy-for-homes-businesses-idUSKBN0NM34020150501 (accessed September 2, 2019).

41. Stephen Edelstein, "Leaf Electric-Car Batteries Can Outlast Vehicles by Up to 12 Years, Nissan Claims," Digital Trends, 2019, https://www.digitaltrends.com/cars/nissan-leaf-batteries-can-outlast-cars-by-10-years-automaker-claims/ (accessed August 9, 2019).

42. Henrique Ribeiro, "SQM Expects Lithium Demand to Grow 20% This Year, Prices to Fall," S&P Global, April 22, 2019, https://www.spglobal.com/platts/en/market-insights/latest-news/metals/042219-sqm-expects-lithium-demand-to-grow-20-this-year-prices-to-fall (accessed August 9, 2019).

43. P. Alves Dias, D. Blagoeva, C. Pavel, and N. Arvanitidis, "Cobalt: Demand-Supply Balances in the Transition to Electric Mobility," European Commission JRC Science for Policy Report, 2018, http://publications.jrc.ec.europa.eu/repository/bitstream/JRC112285/jrc112285_cobalt.pdf (accessed August 9, 2019).

44. *Economic Times*, "The Enormous Test That Awaits India as the Date with Mandatory Vehicle Scrapping Nears," 2018, https://economictimes.indiatimes.com/industry/auto/auto-news/the-enormous-test-that-awaits-india-as-the-date-with-mandatory-vehicle-scrapping-nears/articleshow/66897364.cms?from=mdr (accessed August 9, 2019).

45. Julian M. Allwood, "A Bright Future for UK Steel," The University of Cambridge, 2016, https://www.cam.ac.uk/system/files/a_bright_future_for_uk_steel_2.pdf (accessed August 9, 2019).

46. Business Europe, "RENAULT's Closed-Loop Material Recycling Strategy," August 9, 2017, http://www.circulary.eu/project/renault-closed-loop/ (accessed August 27, 2019).

47. Ellen MacArthur Foundation, "Short-Loop Recycling of Plastics in Vehicle Manufacturing," https://www.ellenmacarthurfoundation.org/case-studies/short-loop-recycling-of-plastics-in-vehicle-manufacturing (accessed September 2, 2019).

12

Household Industry Profile

Table 12.1 Industry summary

Household industry today: White-goods companies that provide large electrical goods such as refrigerators and washing machines have long focused on product efficiency, while furniture companies have focused on cost and aesthetics, but the overall household industry lags on sustainability. Due to low reuse and recycling rates, most products end up in landfills today

Case for change	Today	Looking ahead
Industry size	$220 billion	$310 billion (projection for 2030)
Illustrative waste volumes	White goods/appliances • Appliances account for ~40% of average household energy and 15–40% of water consumption[1,2] • ~99% of refrigerant chemicals are released into the atmosphere[3] • Large and small kitchen, bathroom, and laundry appliances account for 60% of e-waste weight—~40 million tons of e-waste are discarded each year[4] Furniture • About 35% of the wood that is cut for making products like tables, chairs, flooring, and stairs is wasted every year, according to the Forest History Society[5] • In the United States, 264 million tons of municipal solid waste was generated in 2015, including furniture and furnishings (4.6%), white goods (1.8%), and carpets and rugs (1.5%)[6]	• Global e-waste generation is expected to reach 63.7 million tons by 2025, up 30% from 2016 levels[7]
Value at stake	–	$5–$10 billion EBITDA (1–3% of EBITDA) by 2030

© The Author(s) 2020
P. Lacy et al., *The Circular Economy Handbook*,
https://doi.org/10.1057/978-1-349-95968-6_12

Industry Status

Household products such as furniture, white goods, and appliances typically have long-term use and tend to be relatively expensive purchases. But increasing demand for cheaper, more accessible items—associated with the growing middle-class population and product innovation—has led to use of low-quality materials and poor design standards that don't consider reuse and use extension.

With a few notable exceptions, the industry has been slow to adopt circular principles, and recycling remains a challenge. In the EU, more than 80% of furniture is either incinerated or sent to landfill.[8] On the appliance side, more than 80% of all e-waste isn't properly recycled, and about 60% (by weight) comes from large and small kitchen, bathroom, and laundry appliances.[9] In the United States, 38% of the white goods or major appliances were landfilled in 2015 (EPA).[10]

That said, various drivers are pushing the boundaries of the industry's linear economics. The supply of raw inputs is now becoming volatile, sparking price increases in several markets.[11] Demand has also shifted toward "sustainable modern living," with eco-conscious and technology-savvy consumers buying products that are energy efficient, environmentally friendly, ergonomic, digitally enabled, high quality, and durable. A 2013 study found that 71% of households say energy efficiency is very important to them, with a more recent survey revealing that 76% are planning to increase their home's energy efficiency.[12]

 Waste to Wealth Challenges

There are three major areas of waste (see Fig. 12.1). The first occurs during the resource-intensive manufacturing process. In the EU, nearly one billion small and large home appliances are purchased every year, requiring about six million tons of raw materials.[13] Additionally, the manufacturing process uses toxic chemicals including flame retardants, mercury, lead, hydrofluorocarbons (HFCs), and phthalates.

The second major waste area occurs during product usage. For the average household in the United States, home appliances account for 40% of total energy consumption and laundry accounts for 40% of water consumption.[14,15] Microwave ovens alone have been estimated to emit 7.7 million tons of CO_2 per year in the EU, an amount equivalent to auto emissions.[16]

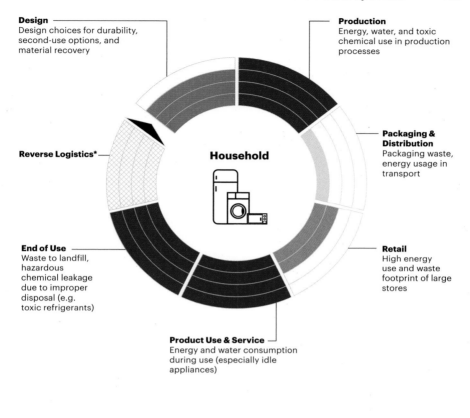

Design — Design choices for durability, second-use options, and material recovery

Production — Energy, water, and toxic chemical use in production processes

Reverse Logistics* —

Household

Packaging & Distribution — Packaging waste, energy usage in transport

End of Use — Waste to landfill, hazardous chemical leakage due to improper disposal (e.g. toxic refrigerants)

Retail — High energy use and waste footprint of large stores

Product Use & Service — Energy and water consumption during use (especially idle appliances)

Heatmap:

| Very High | High | Medium | Low | Not Applicable |

*While the 'Reverse Logistics' stage does not produce unique waste streams per se, it is included in the diagram as it is a key part of a circular value chain.

Fig. 12.1 Waste analysis diagram

The third area of waste is related to the lost embedded value of materials from premature disposal (wasted embedded value) and end-of-use disposal to landfills (wasted lifecycles). On average, home appliances have a useful life of 8–10 years yet they are often replaced sooner, presenting companies with a potentially lucrative area of opportunity.[17] "At Philips, we are already investing in sustainable products which do no harm to the environment. However, when these products come to the end of their use cycle you need to think about how to 'close the loop' for those products that you have sold transactionally to customers. Therefore, we work with our suppliers to avoid toxic materials in the first place and are developing a reverse-supply-chain collaboration to recapture components at the highest possible level," says Frans van Houten, CEO of Philips, a Dutch multinational conglomerate.

 ## Waste to Wealth Opportunities

We estimate the total value at stake for the household industry at $5–$10 billion (EBITDA addition) or 1–3% of sales in 2030 (market size: $310 billion).[18] There are three main areas of opportunity (see Table 12.2).

Circular materials as inputs in manufacturing showcase the first opportunity. Circular materials in furniture production can slice resource consumption by 50% and environmental impact by 30% versus linear models.[22] To that end, Steelcase, the world's leading manufacturer of office furniture and a circular economy industry pioneer, has 50+ Cradle to Cradle Certified™ products and a continuous focus on improvement in design.[23] The company works with its suppliers to optimize the chemical profiles of the materials used, to increase the reuse of its products, among other innovations.

The second area of opportunity is charging premium prices for products that feature increased efficiency, greater durability, and reduced environmental footprint. Unlike other industries, circular household products can command a premium because consumers find value in purchasing efficient, longer-lasting appliances, and other items.[24] The German automation company Siemens' energy-efficient appliances command a 27% price premium, according to Accenture analysis. In addition, advanced circular products can generate new revenue streams through enhanced customer experiences for brands with experience-based consumption models.

New business models for repair, reuse, recovery, and product as a service represent the third area of opportunity. In 2018, IKEA, the world's biggest producer of affordable design furniture, received more than one million orders for spare parts from customers who were able to perform do-it-yourself repairs, thanks to the company's modular product designs.[25] In Northern Europe, the Swedish home appliance manufacturer Electrolux is installing its high-quality washing machines in customer homes, with the appliances connected to a dedicated measuring device that enables the company to track not only the number of washing cycles but also the settings used (e.g., cold versus hot wash). Through this smart metering system, Electrolux is able to offer customers a "pay per-wash" service.[26]

Table 12.2 Waste to wealth opportunity summary

Circular economy opportunity	Reduced material waste and toxicity in production	Design for increased efficiency and reduced footprints	Reuse, repair, and resale models for second-hand products
Type of opportunity	Circular manufacturing—use circular or sustainable inputs	Circularity for better products—pricing power	Circular business models—resale and recycle
Value at stake (by 2030)	*Not quantified*	$10 billion	$0.5 billion
Value levers	• Reduced cost of materials	• Price premium	• Increased revenue per product
Target waste	• Wasted use of material resources that are not recycled • Wasted embedded value of materials not recovered	• Material resources that are not recycled • Energy and chemical inputs • Embedded value of materials not recovered	• Unused capacity across useful life • Untapped additional lifecycles because of lack of second-use options
Value chain focus	• Material choice and design for recyclability • End-of-use recovery • Reverse logistics and recycling of metal, plastic, glass, and textile	• Design (e.g., for improved energy consumption and reduced emissions and toxicity) • Material choice and design for recyclability • End-of-use recovery • Reverse logistics and recycling of metal, plastic, glass, and textile	• Design (e.g., for longer lifecycles and repairability) • Use and services (new consumption models) • End-of-use recovery for resale
Technology amplifiers	• Breakthroughs in material extraction and recycling technologies and innovation in materials science (bio-based, non-toxic, upcycling, etc.)	• Advanced technologies that allow for higher efficiencies in energy consumption, lower emissions, and decreased usage of toxic chemicals	• Digital direct-to-consumer, sharing platforms, crowdsourcing, etc.

(continued)

Table 12.2 (continued)

Circular economy opportunity	Reduced material waste and toxicity in production	Design for increased efficiency and reduced footprints	Reuse, repair, and resale models for second-hand products
Case study	Pennsylvania-based furniture company Emeco builds chairs made from 80% recycled aluminum. The chairs are 100% recyclable and the company's unique manufacturing process is 17 times less energy intense than using virgin aluminum, delivering furniture products three times stronger than steel.[19] Emeco also collaborated with The Coca-Cola Company to introduce a chair made from 111 recycled plastic bottles. Since 2010, this innovative effort has diverted more than 30 million plastic bottles from landfill[19]	The home appliances company Whirlpool dishwashers have intelligent sensors in the 6th sense technology that determines a dish's soil level and are intuitive, smart, and highly efficient. Once it determines the soil level and load size, it automatically selects the correct washing cycle to clean the dishes. These washers use half the water and energy of the average dishwasher[20]	Kaiyo, an online marketplace is committed to great design, exceptional customer care, and a more sustainable planet. Headquartered in New York City, Kaiyo makes the process of buying and selling used furniture easier than ever by handling pickup, storage, inspection, cleaning, and delivery. The company offers savings of up to 90% on top furniture brands diverting over 800,000 pounds of furniture from landfill[21]

Technology Amplifiers

Technologies are enabling companies in the household industry to seize various areas of opportunity. For example:

- In China, Haier Group, the manufacturing owner of GE Appliances, uses IoT to remotely monitor water quality in its washing machines. The data is then fed into a software that adapts the washing program to ensure optimal results.[27]
- Modular designs have allowed IKEA to implement a Product Use Extension model, and 3D printing has given rise to the possibility of faster prototyping and production on demand, shortening the design and development cycle of furniture pieces.[28]
- Oak Ridge National Laboratory and General Electric are developing a new type of dryer that uses a heat pump cycle to generate hot air for drying. The resulting, more efficient dryer has the potential to reduce energy consumption by 60% compared to conventional models.[29]
- Bundles, a Netherlands-based company, designs technology to offer appliances on a pay-per-use basis. The company uses IoT technology to monitor products and reduce energy, water, and detergent use and provides maintenance and refurbishment service to prolong product use.[30]

 # Obstacles to Overcome

A huge challenge for the household industry is the need for a more established reverse logistics, collection, and recycling infrastructure. Producers currently lack incentives to make the necessary investments, and the costs would offset any benefits to be gained from material recovery or recycling of household appliances. Today, only about 10% of furniture and roughly 20% of e-waste are being recycled.[8,31]

Another considerable barrier is limited customer awareness and demand. Despite burgeoning interest in circular household products, widespread awareness is still lacking. Instead, the furniture market has been experiencing the growth of a fast-moving, low-cost, and low-quality segment. Furthermore, customers are rarely given proper guidance on how to maintain, repair, or responsibly recycle home goods. Companies can do a great deal to help consumers overcome this obstacle.

Chapter Takeaways

The household industry is linked to large waste pools with respect to the use of virgin raw materials, high disposal rates, and large usage footprints. At the same time, the industry has strong potential for material recovery and remanufacturing, improved footprints with smart power and resource consumption, and development of rental and secondary marketplaces.

Opportunities
- Reduced material waste and toxicity in production
- Design for increased efficiency and reduced footprints
- Models for fractional ownership, repair, and resale that increase the useful life of products

Technology amplifiers
- Breakthroughs in material extraction and recycling technologies, and innovation in materials science
- Advanced technologies that enable higher efficiencies in energy consumption, lower emissions, and decreased usage of toxic chemicals
- Digital direct-to-consumer, sharing platforms, crowdsourcing, etc.

Obstacles to overcome
- Inadequate reverse-logistics and recycling infrastructure
- Limited material recovery for furniture and home appliances
- Insufficient customer awareness and enablement for Product Use Extension

Notes

1. Jeff Desjardins, "What Uses the Most Energy in Your Home?" Visual Capitalist, November 14, 2016, https://www.visualcapitalist.com/what-uses-the-most-energy-home/ (accessed August 30, 2019).
2. Alliance for Water Efficiency, "Residential Clothes Washer Introduction," http://www.allianceforwaterefficiency.org/Residential_Clothes_Washer_Introduction.aspx (accessed August 30, 2019).
3. Green America, "Climate Friendly Fridges Are Truly Cool," Medium, 2018, https://medium.com/@GreenAmerica/climate-friendly-fridges-are-truly-cool-6b1092148861 (accessed August 12, 2019).
4. The World Counts, "Electronic Waste Facts," 2019, http://www.theworld-counts.com/counters/waste_pollution_facts/electronic_waste_facts (accessed August 12, 2019).
5. Emily Monaco, "Reclaimed Wood Furniture: From Wood Waste Comes Beautiful, Sustainable Designs," Eco Salon, 2016, http://ecosalon.com/reclaimed-wood-furniture-wood-waste/ (accessed August 12, 2019).

6. EPA, "Guide to the Facts and Figures Report about Materials, Waste and Recycling," 2019, https://www.epa.gov/facts-and-figures-about-materials-waste-and-recycling/guide-facts-and-figures-report-about-materials (accessed August 12, 2019).

7. Cision PR Newswire, "The Global E-waste Market Generated Is Expected to Reach 63.705 Million Metric Tons by 2025," August 27, 2018, https://www.prnewswire.com/news-releases/the-global-e-waste-market-generated-is-expected-to-reach-63-705-million-metric-tons-by-2025–300702656.html (accessed August 27, 2019).

8. European Environmental Bureau, "Circular Economy Opportunities in the Furniture Sector," 2017, https://mk0eeborgicuypctuf7e.kinstacdn.com/wp-content/uploads/2019/05/Report-on-the-Circular-Economy-in-the-Furniture-Sector.pdf (accessed August 12, 2019).

9. UN University, "The Global E-waste Monitor 2014," https://i.unu.edu/media/unu.edu/news/52624/UNU-1stGlobal-E-Waste-Monitor-2014-small.pdf (accessed August 12, 2019).

10. EPA, "Durable Goods: Product-Specific Data," https://www.epa.gov/facts-and-figures-about-materials-waste-and-recycling/durable-goods-product-specific-data (accessed August 12, 2019).

11. Janine Wolf, "Whirlpool Sinks with Raw Material Costs Climbing Around the World," Bloomberg, 2018, https://www.bloomberg.com/news/articles/2018-07-23/whirlpool-sinks-as-raw-material-costs-climb-around-the-world (accessed August 12, 2019).

12. Nielsen, "Consumers Want Energy Efficiency, But What Will They Do About It?" 2015, https://www.nielsen.com/us/en/insights/article/2015/consumers-want-energy-efficiency-but-what-will-they-do-about-it/ (accessed August 12, 2019).

13. Redazione, "Home Appliance: Focus on Circular Economy," Home Appliances World, January 26, 2018, http://www.homeappliancesworld.com/2018/01/26/home-appliance-focus-on-circular-economy/ (accessed August 30, 2019).

14. Jeff Desjardins, "What Uses the Most Energy in Your Home?" Visual Capitalist, 2016, https://www.visualcapitalist.com/what-uses-the-most-energy-home/ (accessed August 12, 2019).

15. Alliance for Water Efficiency, "Residential Clothes Washer Introduction," http://www.allianceforwaterefficiency.org/Residential_Clothes_Washer_Introduction.aspx (accessed August 12, 2019).

16. University of Manchester, "Microwaves Could Be as Bad for the Environment as Millions of Cars Suggests New Research," 2018, https://www.manchester.ac.uk/discover/news/microwaves-could-be-as-bad-for-the-environment-as-cars-suggests-new-research/ (accessed August 12, 2019).

17. InterNACHI, "InterNACHI's Standard Estimated Life Expectancy Chart for Homes," https://www.nachi.org/life-expectancy.htm (accessed August 12, 2019).

18. Accenture Analysis.
19. Emeco, "Make More with Less," https://www.emeco.net/materials (accessed August 12, 2019).
20. Whirlpool, "Freestanding Appliances Collection 2016," https://www.whirlpool.co.uk/assets/pdf/WH_FS_UK_2016.pdf (accessed August 16, 2019).
21. Kaiyo, "Mission Statement," https://kaiyo.com/mission-statement/ (accessed August 12, 2019).
22. RISE Research Institutes of Sweden, "The Furniture Industry Is Converting to the Circular Economy," 2017, http://www.mynewsdesk.com/press-releases/the-furniture-industry-is-converting-to-the-circular-economy-2345704 (accessed August 12, 2019).
23. Steelcase, "The Future Is a Circle," https://www.steelcase.com/research/articles/topics/sustainability/steelcase-named-circulars-finalist/ (accessed August 16, 2019).
24. U.S. Energy Information Administration, "Incremental Costs of Higher Efficiency Can Vary by Appliance," 2013 https://www.eia.gov/todayinenergy/detail.php?id=11431 (accessed August 12, 2019).
25. Augusta Pownall, "IKEA to Begin Renting Furniture as Part of Wider Sustainable Push," Dezeen, 2019, https://www.dezeen.com/2019/02/20/ikea-rental-furniture-circular-economy-design/ (accessed August 12, 2019).
26. Ellen Macarthur Foundation, "In-depth—Washing Machines," October 9, 2012, https://www.ellenmacarthurfoundation.org/news/in-depth-washing-machines (accessed August 16, 2019).
27. Cision PR Newswire, "Haier Unveils World's First Smart Laundry Room at AWE 2019," March 14, 2019, https://www.prnewswire.co.uk/news-releases/haier-unveils-world-s-first-smart-laundry-room-at-awe-2019-868633021.html (accessed August 12, 2019).
28. Mark Yong, "Why Furniture Design Faces a Digital Disruption," SPH Magazines, 2017, https://thepeakmagazine.com.sg/design-news/why-furniture-design-faces-a-digital-disruption/ (accessed August 12, 2019).
29. Energy.gov, "Heat Pump Clothes Dryer," https://www.energy.gov/eere/buildings/downloads/heat-pump-clothes-dryer (accessed August 12, 2019).
30. Ellen Macarthur Foundation, "Bundles—A Model Offering Multiple Benefits for Multiple Electronic Products," https://www.ellenmacarthurfoundation.org/case-studies/internet-enabled-pay-per-wash-a-model-offering-multiple-benefits (accessed August 12, 2019).
31. C. P. Baldé et al., "The Global E-waste Monitor 2017," United Nations University, 2017, https://www.itu.int/en/ITU-D/Climate-Change/Documents/GEM%202017/Global-E-waste%20Monitor%202017%20.pdf (accessed August 12, 2019).

13

 Fast-Moving Consumer Goods (FMCG) Industry Profile

Table 13.1 Industry summary

 FMCG industry today: FMCG companies are at the forefront of recognizing the need to shift toward a circular economy, but the industry remains highly resource intensive with significant waste upstream and across the value chain

Case for change	Today	Looking ahead
Industry size	$2.4 trillion	$3.2 trillion (projection for 2030)
Illustrative waste volumes	• Agriculture (crop and livestock production for food), forestry, and land use accounts for approximately 24% of GHG emissions[1] • One-third of global food production is lost or wasted across the value chain[2] • Despite recycling efforts, only 14% of plastic packaging is currently recycled[3]	• Global food demand will double, and we will need a 69% increase in food calories to feed 9.6 billion people by 2050[4,5] • Plastic production is set to be the largest driver of increasing demand for oil to 2050 (IEA)[6]
Value at stake	–	$30–$110 billion (1–4% of EBITDA) by 2030

Industry Status

In many ways, the FMCG industry is leading the shift to a circular economy, already implementing circular initiatives, for example, to minimize water and waste usage. Typical production processes, however, are still

© The Author(s) 2020
P. Lacy et al., *The Circular Economy Handbook*,
https://doi.org/10.1057/978-1-349-95968-6_13

resource intensive. "With a truly circular product or process, there will be absolutely no waste, just like in nature," notes Virginie Helias, Chief Sustainability Officer at Procter & Gamble (P&G), US multinational consumer goods company.

Potential areas for improvement are considerable but consumer-facing opportunities are often embraced first. Driven by rising concern for reducing plastic consumption, companies have launched initiatives to use less packaging or design packaging for easier reuse, recycling, or composting. FMCG companies like Unilever, Nestlé, and Danone have all set targets for 100% of their plastic packaging to be fully reusable, recyclable, or compostable by 2025.[7]

❓ Waste to Wealth Challenges

The industry faces three major areas of waste (see Fig. 13.1). The first is raw materials. The choice of ingredients or input materials has a big impact on a product's footprint, from the caloric efficiency and resource use of food and beverages to the chemical toxicity in beauty and skincare items. With food products, for example, meat and dairy require significant inputs for relatively little caloric gain due to their high feed conversion ratios—for instance, producing one kilogram of beef requires over 15,000 liters of water.[8] Globally, agriculture uses 70% of the planet's freshwater supply.[9]

The second area of waste occurs in production and handling. The industry relies heavily on agriculture, which accounts for most freshwater consumption and tropical/subtropical deforestation, erosion, and pesticide use. Current agricultural practices generate a range of pollutants that often runoff into water environments with a range of associated risks to human and ecosystem health.[10] Moreover, food systems account for 20–30% of all human-caused greenhouse gas emissions globally.[11] Studies have shown that everyday consumer products are responsible for over one-third of air pollutants.[12]

The third major area is material and packaging waste across the value chain. Globally, one-third of food ($1 trillion in retail value) is lost or wasted due to overproduction, product and packaging damage, and/or technical malfunctions.[2] Toast Ale brews award-winning craft beer using fresh, surplus bread from bakeries and sandwich makers that would otherwise go to waste.[13] The bread replaces one-third of the virgin malted barley required in brewing, and the company has been aggressively scaling its business through contracting and licensing, from over 11 tons of bread to a 2020

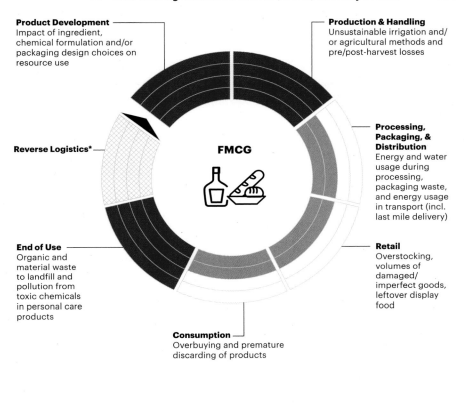

Product Development
Impact of ingredient, chemical formulation and/or packaging design choices on resource use

Production & Handling
Unsustainable irrigation and/or agricultural methods and pre/post-harvest losses

Processing, Packaging, & Distribution
Energy and water usage during processing, packaging waste, and energy usage in transport (incl. last mile delivery)

Reverse Logistics*

FMCG

End of Use
Organic and material waste to landfill and pollution from toxic chemicals in personal care products

Retail
Overstocking, volumes of damaged/imperfect goods, leftover display food

Consumption
Overbuying and premature discarding of products

Heatmap:

| Very High | High | Medium | Low | Not Applicable |

*While the 'Reverse Logistics' stage does not produce unique waste streams per se, it is included in the diagram as it is a key part of a circular value chain.

Fig. 13.1   Waste analysis diagram

goal of at least 100 tons. This is compounded by waste on the consumer side—the average US family throws away half of the food it buys.[14] There is also significant waste in packaging. Of the total volume of plastics used, FMCG packaging represents 26%, of which only 14% is recycled (and just 5% of plastic packaging material value is retained for subsequent use due to poor sorting technology).[3]

Waste to Wealth Opportunities

Enormous opportunities exist for FMCG companies to differentiate, especially by appealing to more selective consumers. Millennial and Gen Z consumers are increasingly expecting companies to be sustainable and are migrating to smaller, more purpose-driven brands. We predict a 4% migration in sales per annum to products with more sustainable packaging.[15] Overall, the total value at stake for the industry from circular packaging opportunities is estimated at $30 billion to $110 billion (EBITDA addition) or 1–4% of sales in 2030 (market size: $3.2 trillion).[15] More broadly across the value chain, companies should pay attention to the following three areas of opportunity (see Table 13.2).

The first is improving efficiency and reducing inputs and waste along the production stages of the value chain, starting with substitute raw material inputs. Consider the plant-based protein movement. Given the massive burden that meat and dairy production places on natural resources, alternative protein sources can alleviate pressure on finite resources, freeing up vast amounts of land currently used for crops and livestock. Plant-based protein is increasingly popular, with pioneering companies such as Impossible Foods offering their signature Impossible Burger at more than 7000 restaurants globally.[20] Companies such as Tyson Foods and Nestlé are also investing heavily in this space.

The second area of opportunity is designing products that require less material, are less toxic, or are made from recycled or recyclable material. "Our responsibility for our product goes beyond the last sip. We are committed to having 100 percent of our product in packaging that is returnable or made from majority recycled content by 2025. Closing the loop and reusing materials is good for the planet and good for our business," says Tony Milikin from AB InBev.

New models to increase recovery and recycling present a third major area of opportunity. Loop, TerraCycle's recently launched "milkman model reimagined," is a circular shopping platform that focuses on the packaging of everyday essentials like shampoos and toothpaste, transforming them from single-use disposables to durable, refillable, and feature-packed designs. "Loop arose to shift single-use goods to multi-use," explains Tom Szaky, CEO of TerraCycle. "We quickly discovered that moving from disposable to durable designs enables new types of relationships between consumers, businesses, and products."

Table 13.2 Waste to wealth opportunity summary

Circular economy opportunity	Production efficiency to reduce and reuse waste	Product and packaging that uses less material	New models to increase recovery and recycling
Type of opportunity	Smart operations—produce efficiently	Circular design—use less	Circular business models—recover and recycle
Value at stake (by 2030)	$5–$10 billion	$15–$50 billion	Early stage—not calculated
Value levers	Reduced cost of goods sold	Reduced cost of materials	Increased revenue per product and/or packaging
Target waste	• Wasted energy, chemical, and water inputs • Wasted material and agricultural by-products	• Wasted use of material resources that cannot be recycled • Wasted embedded value of materials not recovered	• Wasted embedded value of materials not recovered • Wasted lifecycles due to lack of second-use options
Value chain focus	• Production and handling • Processing, packaging, and distribution	• Product development (ingredient choice and packaging/product design for circularity) • End-of-use recovery, sorting, and recycling	• Product development (e.g., design for reusability and recyclability) • Consumption (new direct-to-consumer (D2C) models) • End-of-use recovery, sorting, and recycling
Technology amplifiers	• Digital and physical technologies that improve productivity and help track waste and material flows	• Material innovation; tracking, sorting, and recycling technologies	• Tracking, sorting, and recycling technologies

(continued)

Table 13.2 (continued)

Circular economy opportunity	Production efficiency to reduce and reuse waste	Product and packaging that uses less material	New models to increase recovery and recycling
Case study	Multinational drink and brewing holdings company AB InBev's breweries adhere to zero waste and have achieved recycling rates over 99% around the world[16,17]	The Coca-Cola Company, one of the world's largest beverage companies, has launched 100% recycled PET (rPET) bottles in several countries and is making a strategic investment in Loop Industries to purchase a supply of 100% rPET plastic to accelerate the increased use of recycled materials in the creation of its bottles[18]	US multinational retail corporation Walmart is developing an auto-replenishment application in which IoT tags are added to products. Using Bluetooth, radio frequency, or other technology, the tags would monitor product usage and auto-order replacements or refills, as well as track the expiration dates and product recalls[19]

Technology Amplifiers

Various advances in materials science and digital technologies have enabled companies to grasp these opportunities, thanks in part to emerging technologies. Innovative examples include:

- Product tracking technologies—from blockchain to graphene labels that can be "tattooed" directly on the skins of certain foods—offer new ways to reduce food that gets lost or wasted.[21] Researchers in Genoa, Italy, have discovered a way to add electronic components to temporary tattoos, paving the way for "smart" electronics that could be transferred onto food or pills.[21] This breakthrough technology could monitor food supply and even track what's going on in our bodies.
- A revolution in bio-based technologies offers other promising possibilities. The food tech startup Apeel Sciences is using plant extracts derived from discarded agricultural by-products to create invisible tasteless coatings that extend the shelf life of fresh products by five times for some product varieties.[22]
- Bite Toothpaste has developed tablets that could displace the one billion toothpaste tubes that are thrown away annually.[23] Such technical innovations in packaging have been transforming the industry, with innovative brands reimagining staple products in ways that eliminate the need for packaging altogether.
- Indian conglomerate ITC has launched an initiative that leverages IT to virtually connect value chain participants in agriculture. E-Choupal provides real-time information to farmers allowing them to align farm output with market demand. E-Choupal has empowered millions of farmers, improving productivity, income, and Indian agricultural capacity.[24]

 # Obstacles to Overcome

The lack of a proper collection, sorting, and waste infrastructure is often why so much material ends up in landfills. The FMCG industry consumes massive amounts of energy for logistics and distribution, which will only be exacerbated by the movement toward decentralized distribution models. Companies can mitigate these risks by optimizing their reverse flows (e.g., by utilizing empty trucks post-delivery).

There is huge potential for agri-food chains to change toward circular models of production and consumption. In production, regenerative agriculture, and healthier eating habits are gaining traction, with $5.7 trillion a year spent globally on health, environmental, and economic costs of food production.[25] FMCGs like Danone have been looking at how circular principles can transform the food system from farm to fork, for instance by transitioning toward production models that renew soil health and regenerate natural systems.[26] Eric Soubeiran, VP for Nature and Water Cycles stated: "Agriculture is at the center of many of the challenges we face today, from climate change to biodiversity loss. By transforming farming practices, agriculture can be part of the solution. At Danone, we are working with a range of partners to develop and promote regenerative agriculture practices that reduce GHG emissions and sequestrate more carbon in the soil, preserve water resources and enhance biodiversity. All of this while empowering farmers and protecting animal welfare."

On the other side of the supply chain, current consumption patterns face multiple challenges. In cities, for example, less than 2% of nutrients in food and organic wastes (excluding manure) are re-inserted back into nutrient cycles, losing potential value, and adding to future environmental costs.[27] Some companies are approaching the food waste challenge in novel ways. Oddbox, a social enterprise tackling food waste, for example, is changing the perception of edible fruits and vegetable that do not make it onto supermarkets' shelves due to aesthetic standards and sells boxes of "wonky veg and freaky fruit," reducing food waste and providing customers with a local, seasonal, and cheaper food source. To date the company has given value to nearly 1 m kgs of food produce that would have otherwise gone to waste and saved nearly 1.5 m kgs of CO_2e.[28]

Consumer awareness is another challenge. Companies can harness the power of advertising to shape a new consumer culture that embraces circularity instead of promoting excessive consumption. By engaging consumers, companies can be more agile in testing concepts while reducing waste. P&G, for example, turned to crowdfunding platform Indiegogo to test a prototype of their recent razor innovation for the Gillette brand before reaching the production phase. This enabled them to raise awareness, gauge interest, and solicit direct consumer feedback.[29]

Finally, policymakers have an important role to play. Government support will be critical to building out the needed infrastructure. Tightening regulations on materials and products, such as laws that incentivize returns and bans on use of specific materials, will help fuel an industry-wide transition. In California, which is leading the United States on environmental policies, regulations on labeling (e.g., a ban on the term "biodegradable" for plastics) are aimed at preventing companies from misleading consumers and rewarding those with more stringent requirements. The European Parliament has voted to ban common single-use plastic items by 2021 and EU member states will have to achieve a 90% collection target for plastic bottles by 2029 (see Part III, "Policy—The Role of Policymakers").[30]

 Chapter Takeaways

To address waste leakage across the value chain, the industry must innovate and engage consumers, regulators, and partners to shift behaviors and establish a much-needed infrastructure for circular economy.

Opportunities
- Production efficiency to reduce inputs and waste, and recycle/revalorize (give new value to) by-products
- Products and packaging that use less (and more circular) materials
- New models to increase recovery and recycling

Technology amplifiers
- Breakthroughs in textile recycling technologies and innovation in materials science
- Emerging technologies for process innovation and efficiency
- Digital platforms that enable D2C (direct-to-consumer) models

Obstacles to overcome
- Lack of infrastructure for sorting, recycling, and composting
- Low consumer awareness and understanding of how to reduce waste
- Inadequate government regulations, especially for products/packaging

---

Notes

1. United States Environmental Protection Agency, "Global Greenhouse Gas Emissions Data," 2017, https://www.epa.gov/ghgemissions/global-greenhouse-gas-emissions-data (accessed August 9, 2019).
2. FAO, "Food Loss and Food Waste," 2019, http://www.fao.org/food-loss-and-food-waste/en/ (accessed August 12, 2019).
3. World Economic Forum, "The New Plastics Economy Rethinking the Future of Plastics," 2016, http://www3.weforum.org/docs/WEF_The_New_Plastics_Economy.pdf (accessed August 9, 2019).
4. FAO, "How to Feed the World 2050," 2009, http://www.fao.org/fileadmin/templates/wsfs/docs/Issues_papers/HLEF2050_Global_Agriculture.pdf (accessed August 9, 2019).

5. Janet Ranganathan, "The Global Food Challenge Explained in 18 Graphics," World Resources Institute, 2013, https://www.wri.org/blog/2013/12/global-food-challenge-explained-18-graphics (accessed August 9, 2019).

6. IEA, "Petrochemicals set to be the largest driver of world oil demand, latest IEA analysis finds," October 5, 2018, https://www.iea.org/newsroom/news/2018/october/petrochemicals-set-to-be-the-largest-driver-of-world-oil-demand-latest-iea-analy.html (accessed August 9, 2019).

7. New Plastics Economy, "Companies Take Major Step Towards a New Plastics Economy," 2018, https://newplasticseconomy.org/news/11-companies-commit-to-100-reusable-recyclable-or-compostable-packaging-by-2025 (accessed August 9, 2019).

8. *The Guardian*, "How Much Water Is Needed to Produce Food and How Much Do We Waste?" 2016, https://www.theguardian.com/news/datablog/2013/jan/10/how-much-water-food-production-waste (accessed August 9, 2019).

9. The World Bank, "Annual Freshwater Withdrawals, Agriculture (% of Total Freshwater Withdrawal)," 2015, https://data.worldbank.org/indicator/er.h2o.fwag.zs (accessed August 9, 2019).

10. A. Davey, et al., "Understanding the Impact of Farming on Aquatic Ecosystems," World Bank Blogs, January 31, 2008, https://blogs.worldbank.org/opendata/chart-globally-70-freshwater-used-agriculture, http://science-search.defra.gov.uk/Document.aspx?Document=WQ0112_7092_FRP.doc (accessed August 9, 2019).

11. FCRN Foodsource, "Food Systems and Greenhouse Gas Emissions," https://foodsource.org.uk/31-what-food-system%E2%80%99s-contribution-global-ghg-emissions-total (accessed August 9, 2019).

12. Varda Burstyn, "Dispatches from the Chemical Edge," Chemical-Edge, 2018, https://chemical-edge.com/2018/03/13/air-fresheners-and-many-other-common-chemicals-cause-smog-are-more-toxic-than-traffic-emissions-the-stunning-new-study-in-science-that-finally-puts-regulation-of-everyday-toxics-on-the-agenda/ (accessed August 9, 2019).

13. Toast, "Toasting Change," https://www.toastale.com/impact/ (accessed August 12, 2019).

14. Suzanne Goldenberg, "Half of All US Food Produce Is Thrown Away, New Research Suggests," *The Guardian*, 2016, https://www.theguardian.com/environment/2016/jul/13/us-food-waste-ugly-fruit-vegetables-perfect (accessed August 9, 2019).

15. Accenture Analysis.

16. Mike Hower, "AB InBev's Environmental Efforts Generate $420 Million in Revenue," Sustainable Brands, 2013, https://sustainablebrands.com/read/waste-not/ab-inbev-s-environmental-efforts-generate-420-million-in-revenue (accessed August 9, 2019).

17. Sean O'Kane, "Anheuser-Busch Orders Hundreds of Hydrogen Trucks from Zero-Emission Startup Nikola," The Verge, 2018, https://www.theverge.com/2018/5/3/17314606/anheuser-busch-budweiser-hydrogen-trucks-zero-emission-startup-nikola (accessed August 9, 2019).

18. CCEP, "CCEP Partners with Loop Industries to Purchase 100% Recycled PET," 2018, https://www.ccep.com/news-and-events/news/ccep-partners-with-loop-industries-to-purchase-100-recycled-pet (accessed August 9, 2019).

19. CB Insights, "Walmart's IoT Patent Application Takes Aim at Amazon Dash," May 4, 2017, https://www.cbinsights.com/research/walmart-iot-patent/ (accessed August 16, 2019).

20. Angela Moon and Joshua Franklin, "Exclusive: Impossible Foods Raises $300 Million with Investors Eager for Bite of Meatless Burgers," Reuters, May 13, 2019, https://www.reuters.com/article/us-impossible-foods-fundraising-exclusiv/exclusive-impossible-foods-raises-300-million-with-investors-eager-for-bite-of-meatless-burgers-idUSKCN1SJ0YK (accessed August 9, 2019).

21. Paula Bolyard, "Edible 'Smart' Tattoos on Food Could Track Health, Monitor Food Supply," PJ Media, 2018, https://pjmedia.com/lifestyle/edible-smart-tattoos-food-track-health-monitor-food-supply/ (accessed August 9, 2019).

22. Pieter Boekhout, "Edible Solution Doubles Shelf Life of Fresh Produce," iGrow, 2017, https://herbert-kliegerman.squarespace.com/news/edible-solution-doubles-shelf-life-of-fresh-produce (accessed August 9, 2019).

23. Bite Toothpaste, "Sustainability," https://bitetoothpastebits.com/pages/sustainability (accessed August 9, 2019).

24. ITC, "E-Choupal—The world's Largest Rural Digital Infrastructure—Empowering 4 Million Farmers," https://www.itcportal.com/businesses/agri-business/e-choupal.aspx (accessed August 12, 2019).

25. Ellen MacArthur and Martin Stuchtey, "Fixing the Food System: How Cities Can Truly Feed the World," The Telegraph, April 4, 2019, https://www.telegraph.co.uk/business/how-to-be-green/cities-feed-world/ (accessed September 2, 2019).

26. Sustainable Brands, "DanoneWave Gives Regenerative Ag Boost with New Soil Health Initiative," https://sustainablebrands.com/read/supply-chain/danonewave-gives-regenerative-ag-boost-with-new-soil-health-initiative (accessed September 2, 2019).

27. "Cities and the Circular Economy for Food", Ellen MacArthur Foundation, May 2019, https://www.ellenmacarthurfoundation.org/assets/downloads/CCEFF_Exec-Sum_May-2019-Pages_Web.pdf (accessed August 9, 2019).

28. Oddbox, "What Is Oddbox?" https://www.oddbox.co.uk/ (accessed August 9, 2019).

29. Sarah Vizard, "How Coca-Cola, Lego and Gillette Tapped into the Wisdom of Crowds," *Marketing Week*, February 13, 2019, https://www.marketing-week.com/coca-cola-lego-gillette-crowdfunding/ (accessed August 9, 2019).

30. European Parliament News, "Parliament Seals Ban on Throwaway Plastics by 2021," March 27, 2019, http://www.europarl.europa.eu/news/en/press-room/20190321IPR32111/parliament-seals-ban-on-throwaway-plastics-by-2021 (accessed August 9, 2019).

14

Fashion Industry Profile

Table 14.1 Industry summary

Fashion industry today: Facing increased social and regulatory pressures (driven by fast retailing), companies have been tackling waste in their direct operations, but introducing circular solutions across the value chain is the next frontier

Case for change	Today	Looking ahead
Industry size	$0.6 trillion	$1.1 trillion (projection for 2030)
Illustrative waste volumes	• 92 million tons of clothing (mostly cotton and polyester) become waste every year[1] • Less than 1% is recycled at the end-of-use[2] • 0.5 million tons of microfibers end up in the ocean every year, equal to over 50 billion plastic bottles[2] • 20% of all industrial water pollution is attributed to textile dyeing and treatment[2] • Industry accounts for ~10% of all CO_2 emissions[3]	• Waste will grow to 148 million tons (+62%) by 2030[4] • 118 billion cubic tons of water will be consumed (+50%) by 2030[4] • 35% more land is projected to be required for fiber production by the industry by 2030[5] • Emissions are projected to more than double by 2025[6]
Value at stake	–	$30–$90 billion (3–8% of EBITDA) by 2030

© The Author(s) 2020
P. Lacy et al., *The Circular Economy Handbook*,
https://doi.org/10.1057/978-1-349-95968-6_14

🔋 Industry Status

The fashion industry—the business of making and selling clothes and accessories—is highly resource-intensive. Moreover, over the last two decades, fast retailing has transformed the market, with many customers now treating clothing as nearly disposable. The typical consumer wears a clothing item only for a fraction of its useful life before disposing it, contributing to a doubling in clothing production over the past 15 years.[6] The current linear operating model is under the microscope as environmental and social stresses continue to mount around the world.[7]

These industry dynamics have led to growing interest in circular solutions. Many companies have had some success in addressing waste in their most direct operations. Some firms have also begun to work with Tier 1 factory suppliers on waste in manufacturing. These efforts, however, represent relatively small parts of the value chain. The bottom line is that closing the loop is going to take a great deal more effort.

❓ Waste to Wealth Challenges

The current linear value chain is heavily reliant on virgin materials from non-renewable sources. This includes fertilizers to grow cotton, oil to manufacture synthetic fibers, various chemicals to produce dye, and so on. That, along with clothing increasingly being treated as disposable, has led to waste challenges across the entire value chain (see Fig. 14.1).

The first thing to consider is the material mix. The choice of materials has a large impact on the overall footprint of clothing from cultivation (land, fertilizer, water use) to processing (energy, chemical and water use) to use (microplastics pollution) and ultimately recyclability at end of use. Conventional cotton, for example, consumes significant amounts of inputs. In fact, it takes 20,000 liters of water to produce a single T-shirt and pair of jeans.[8]

Resource-intensive production is another large waste area. The industry's carbon emissions are expected to more than double by 2025.[6] Moreover, the processing stage consumes considerable energy, and the spinning and rinsing of fibers can also be chemical and water intensive, with water pollution an issue of growing concern.

The third waste area is product disposability. The lack of an infrastructure for collection and recycling means that an excessive amount of clothing ends up in landfills. Globally, just 20% of clothing is reused or recycled.[9]

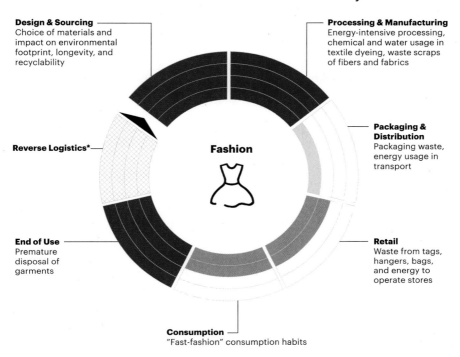

Design & Sourcing
Choice of materials and
impact on environmental
footprint, longevity, and
recyclability

Processing & Manufacturing
Energy-intensive processing,
chemical and water usage in
textile dyeing, waste scraps
of fibers and fabrics

Reverse Logistics*

Fashion

**Packaging &
Distribution**
Packaging waste,
energy usage in
transport

End of Use
Premature
disposal of
garments

Retail
Waste from tags,
hangers, bags,
and energy to
operate stores

Consumption
"Fast-fashion" consumption habits

Heatmap:

Very High   High   Medium   Low   Not Applicable

*While the 'Reverse Logistics' stage does not produce unique waste streams per se,
it is included in the diagram as it is a key part of a circular value chain.

Fig. 14.1 Waste analysis diagram

Waste to Wealth Opportunities

Let's explore the three key areas of opportunity highlighted in Table 14.2.

The first examines "circular materials" that use fashion waste as raw inputs into the value chain, not only reducing material intensity but also lowering costs. The international chain of fast-fashion retail clothing stores, C&A, for example, has launched their first GOLD level Cradle to Cradle Certified™ garment. This is the first time that a fashion brand has developed a circular

Table 14.2 Waste to wealth opportunity summary

Circular economy opportunity	Circular materials that use waste as raw inputs	Intelligent and circular operations that reduce waste in production	Models for fractional ownership, repair, and resale that increase product use and extend clothing use
Type of opportunity	Circular sourcing—buying better	Smart manufacturing—more efficient production	Circular business models—resale and repair
Value at stake (by 2030)	$5–30 billion	$5–15 billion	$10–20 billion
Value levers	Reduced cost of materials	Reduced cost of goods sold	Increased revenue per garment
Target waste	• Material resources that cannot be recycled • Embedded value of materials not recovered	• Non-renewable energy, chemical inputs, and material from scraps and samples	• Lack of utilization across product use • Lack of second-use options
Value chain focus	• Material choice and design for recyclability • End-of-use recovery • Reverse logistics and textile recycling	• Material choice and sourcing • Processing and manufacturing processes and technologies	• Design (e.g., for longer lifecycles and repairability) • Use and services (new consumption models) • End-of-use recovery for resale
Technology amplifiers	• Breakthroughs in textile recycling technologies and innovation in materials science (bio-based, non-toxic, upcycling, etc.)	• Smart planning/forecasting tech and emerging technologies for reducing/eliminating inputs, 3-D printing, etc.	• Digital D2C (direct-to-consumer) models, sharing platforms, crowdsourcing, etc.

Circular economy opportunity	Circular materials that use waste as raw inputs	Intelligent and circular operations that reduce waste in production	Models for fractional ownership, repair, and resale that increase product use and extend clothing use
Case study	After a decade of research, the sportswear manufacturer Adidas has developed a 100% recyclable performance running shoe that is "made to be remade." Each component is made from 100% reusable thermoplastic polyurethane (TPU)—it's spun to yarn, knitted, molded, and cleanfused. Once the shoes come to the end of their first use and are returned to Adidas, they are washed, ground into pellets, and melted into material components for a new pair of shoes, with zero waste[10]	DyeCoo, a supplier of industrial CO_2 dyeing equipment has developed a patented technology that eliminates water and processing chemicals completely from the fabric dyeing process. The technology uses CO_2 (a byproduct from the industry) instead of water as a dyeing medium, in a closed-loop system. Some 95% of the CO_2 is recycled in the machine for reuse. The product quality is the same or better compared to the traditional process, while requiring only half the dyeing time. This cuts both energy and dye consumption by 50%[11]	US outdoor clothing company Patagonia's Worn Wear program provides incentives for the extended use and reuse of garments. Patagonia customers are encouraged to return items that are in good condition and receive a credit for future purchases. Patagonia then cleans the garment and resells it on the Worn Wear website, assigning a premium to vintage or used wears. Patagonia achieved $1 million in sales of used clothes from Worn Wear in the first six months of the campaign, and close to 85,000 items of clothing were traded in[12]

product at scale, incorporating important attributes such as materials that are certified organic, safe and non-toxic, 100% compostable, and made from 100% renewable energy, recycled water, and with social fairness—all offered at value retail prices and offered to the industry in an open source.[13] To date, C&A has produced over 1.3 million GOLD Cradle to Cradle Certified™ garments including new innovations in prints and embroidery.[14] Here, success relies on design for recyclability and the scaling of end-of-use garment collection and textile recycling technologies.

The second area explores intelligent and circular operations—applying advanced analysis and circular principles to demand forecasting, product designs, sourcing, and manufacturing. When done effectively, oversupplies and waste are reduced, ultimately helping to decouple input use from processes.

The third area of opportunity is new business models, including re-commerce, rental, and repair. These can give consumers access to high-quality fashion without the commitment and cost of ownership, while also encouraging companies to design for longevity/multiple uses and to ensure end-of-use garment collection. The successful launch of businesses such as Rent the Runway has shown there is a market for a new type of ownership based on subscription, especially among millennial consumers.[15] A recent Accenture and Fashion for Good research collaboration suggested that these new business models could be economically viable across a range of categories, from mid-market to luxury.[16] But getting these complex models right will require collaboration between disruptive start-ups, traditional retailers, and emerging software-as-a-service (SaaS) providers. As well as subscription rental services, incumbent fashion retailers are also increasingly looking to realize value from the secondary market, based on the success of businesses such as the RealReal in the United States.[17]

 Technology Amplifiers

We see a number of promising innovations on the horizon in the fashion industry, including the following:

- Innovation in materials science is increasing the availability of alternative sustainable materials, including a flood of promising bio-based alternatives and materials derived from waste by-products. PrimaLoft, which makes the microfiber insulation that fills jackets made by brands like L.L. Bean, has spent five years innovating a new insulation made from 100% recycled polyester, which they aim to biodegrade if it ends up in landfill or oceans.[18]

- Emerging technologies are enabling new business models for the constant recirculation of clothing, such as rental, resale, and sharing platforms. Le Tote's clothing subscription service, for instance, provides customers with an "endless wardrobe" of new styles.[19] And crowdsourcing production models are further enabling precision in production planning—Betabrand, a retail clothing company, produces items according to pre-orders, avoiding waste from leftover inventory.[20]

- New technologies, such as waterless dye processes and 3-D garment printing, are improving efficiencies and minimizing waste from production. The textile recycling company Renewcell has developed a new technology for dissolving cotton and other natural substances into new, biodegradable raw materials.[21]

- Intelligent radio-frequency identification (RFID) filaments are being developed that can be integrated into traditional garments, allowing for easy tracking. Digital identity start-up EON is innovating "content thread" that looks and feels much like a normal thread, but through RFID technology it can store digital information and be scanned from a distance.[22]

- WGSN, the world's biggest fashion forecaster, uses AI to reduce forecasting errors by up to 50%. Machine learning, an AI technique, matches supply with demand to limit unnecessary manufacturing and reduce fashion's environmental footprint.[23,24]

Obstacles to Overcome

The fashion industry seems ripe for a major transformation, with digitalization already changing the competitive landscape and consumer interaction. According to a recent study, almost 7000 retail stores across the United States were shut in 2017 alone, while online brands have transitioned to D2C (direct-to-consumer) models to provide end-to-end customer experiences.[25] Such relationships allow companies to sway customers to transform the ways in which they use and relate to clothes by, for example, encouraging rental or resale. Yet, despite a shift in consumer attitudes in certain markets, production continues to rise. "We are still only 'managing harm' and not really environmentally positive," notes Rick Ridgeway, Patagonia's VP of Public Engagement.

Scalable solutions will be essential to address the waste problems in any meaningful way. Today only about 20% of end-of-use clothing in Europe goes to collection and a good portion of that still goes to landfill.[26] To achieve higher recycling rates, the industry needs to develop better solutions, such as partnerships with delivery providers or donation centers for taking back, sorting, and preparing garments for recycling. To date, the industry also lacks the ability to recycle textiles in a way that enables performance and cost parity, and much of the clothing that is spared from landfill goes to "downcycled" applications such as cloth rags. The Spanish clothing company Inditex, for one, plans to invest $3.5 million in textile recycling technologies to upscale post-consumer mechanical fiber recycling. "In an ideal circular world, every piece of fabric and garment produced is being recollected and reused into new fabrics," says Reinier Mommaal, CEO and Co-Founder of DyeCoo.

None of the above will come easily. True circularity in the fashion industry demands greater pull from consumers and an increased push from regulators to incentivize brands to work with suppliers to make fundamental changes to their business models.

 Chapter Takeaways

Despite tremendous opportunity and rising momentum, the industry needs to move beyond small-scale pilots and initiatives and focus on scalable solutions.

Opportunities

- Circular materials that use waste as raw inputs
- Intelligent and circular operations that reduce waste in production
- Models for fractional ownership, rental, subscription, and resale that increase use and extend clothing life

Technology amplifiers

- Breakthroughs in textile recycling technologies and innovations in materials science
- Emerging technologies for process innovation and efficiency (e.g., digital tracking of garments)
- Digital platforms that enable D2C models

Obstacles to overcome

- Lack of systemwide end-of-use garment collection and textile recycling solutions
- Need for greater consumer pull and regulations to accelerate brand action

Notes

1. Kaya Dory, "Why Fast Fashion Needs to Slow Down," UN Environment, 2018, https://www.unenvironment.org/news-and-stories/blog-post/why-fast-fashion-needs-slow-down (accessed August 12, 2019).

2. Ellen MacArthur Foundation, "A New Textiles Economy: Redesigning Fashion's Future," 2017, https://www.ellenmacarthurfoundation.org/assets/downloads/A-New-Textiles-Economy_Full-Report_Updated_1-12-17.pdf (accessed August 12, 2019).

3. UNFCCC, "UN Helps Fashion Industry Shift to Low Carbon," 2018, https://unfccc.int/news/un-helps-fashion-industry-shift-to-low-carbon (accessed August 12, 2019).

4. Global Fashion Agenda and The Boston Consulting Group, "Pulse of the Fashion Industry," 2017, https://globalfashionagenda.com/wp-content/uploads/2017/05/Pulse-of-the-Fashion-Industry_2017.pdf (accessed August 12, 2019).

5. UK Parliament, "Fixing Fashion: Clothing Consumption and Sustainability," 2019, https://publications.parliament.uk/pa/cm201719/cmselect/cmenvaud/1952/full-report.html (accessed August 12, 2019).

6. Nathalie Remy, Eveline Speelman, and Steven Swartz, "Style That's Sustainable: A New Fashion Formula," McKinsey & Company, 2016, https://www.mckinsey.com/business-functions/sustainability/our-insights/style-thats-sustainable-a-new-fast-fashion-formula (accessed August 12, 2019).

7. Elias Janshan, "M&S, Burberry, Topshop, Boohoo, Missguided, Primark & Asos Defend Practices in Parliament," Retail Gazette, 2018, www.retailgazette.co.uk/blog/2018/11/ms-burberry-topshop-boohoo-missguided-primark-asos-defend-practices-parliament/ (accessed August 12, 2019).

8. WWF, "Sustainable Agriculture: Cotton," 2019, https://www.worldwildlife.org/industries/cotton (accessed August 12, 2019).

9. Allison McCarthy, "Are Our Clothes Doomed for the landfill?" Remake, 2018, https://remake.world/stories/news/are-our-clothes-doomed-for-the-landfill/ (accessed August 12, 2019).

10. Tim Newcomb, "Adidas Futurecraft Performance Sneakers 'Made to Be Remade'," Forbes, April 18, 2019, https://www.forbes.com/sites/timnewcomb/2019/04/18/adidas-futurecraft-performance-sneakers-made-to-be-remade/#5ac1fac9258d (accessed August 12, 2019).

11. Lydia Heida, "Can Waterless Dyeing Processes Clean Up the Clothing Industry?" Yale Environment 360, 2014, https://e360.yale.edu/features/can_waterless_dyeing_processes_clean_up_clothing_industry_pollution (accessed August 12, 2019).

12 Patagonia, "2018 Environmental + Social Initiatives Book," 2018, https://issuu.com/thecleanestline/docs/patagonia-enviro-initiatives-2018?e=1043061/67876879 (accessed August 12, 2019).

13. C&A, "Circular Fashion Products," http://sustainability.c-and-a.com/sustainable-products/circular-fashion/circular-fashion-products/ (accessed August 12, 2019).

14. The Forum of Young Global Leaders in collaboration with Accenture Strategy, "The Circulars 2018 Yearbook," 2018, https://thecirculars.org/content/resources/TheCirculars_2018_Yearbook_Final.pdf (accessed August 12, 2019).

15. Sapna Maheshwari, "Rent the Runway Now Valued at $1 Billion With New Funding," *The New York Times*, March 21, 2019, https://www.nytimes.com/2019/03/21/business/rent-the-runway-unicorn.html (accessed August 12, 2019).

16. Accenture Strategy in Collaboration with Fashion for Good, "The Future of Circular Fashion: Assessing the Viability of Circular Business Models," https://d2be5ept72nvlo.cloudfront.net/2019/05/The-Future-of-Circular-Fashion-Report-Fashion-for-Good.pdf (accessed August 12, 2019).

17. Pamela N. Danziger, "Luxury Brands Can't Ignore Fashion Reseller the RealReal Anymore," Forbes, 2018, https://www.forbes.com/sites/pamdanziger/2018/08/22/luxury-brands-cant-ignore-fashion-reseller-the-realreal-anymore/#50c966741a20 (accessed August 12, 2019).

18. Adele Peters, "This Microplastic Biodegrades Instead of Sitting Around for Hundreds of Years," Fast Company, January, 28, 2019, https://www.fastcompany.com/90297349/this-microplastic-biodegrades-instead-of-sitting-around-for-hundreds-of-years (accessed August 12, 2019).

19. Le Tote, "How It Works," https://www.letote.com/how-it-works (accessed August 12, 2019).

20. Betabrand, "What Does Pre-order Mean?" https://support.betabrand.com/hc/en-us/articles/207831213-What-does-Pre-order-mean- (accessed August 12, 2019).

21. European Union, "European Circular Economy Stakeholder Platform," https://circulareconomy.europa.eu/platform/en/good-practices/renewcell-dissolves-natural-fibers-biodegradable-pulp (accessed August 12, 2019).

22. Global Change Award, "Content Thread," 2017, https://globalchangeaward.com/winners/content-thread/ (accessed August 12, 2019).

23. *The Economist*, "The Future of Fashion," Youtube Video, 2:23, Posted November 15, 2018, https://www.youtube.com/watch?v=M-drGOlhDn0 (accessed August 9, 2019).

24. Sagent, "The Future of Fashion," *The Economist*, November 15, 2018, http://sagentlabs.com/resource/future-fashion-economist (accessed August 9, 2019).

25. Neal McNamara, "Big Retailers Will Close 7000 Stores In 2018," Patch, 2017, https://patch.com/washington/bellevue/big-retailers-will-close-7-000-stores-2018 (accessed August 12, 2019).

26. Gustav Sandin and Greg M. Peters, "Environmental Impact of Textile Reuse and Recycling—A Review," *Journal of Cleaner Production*, 2018, https://www.sciencedirect.com/science/article/pii/S0959652618305985 (accessed August 12, 2019).

15

E-Commerce Meets the Circular Economy

In the preceding three profiles, we break "retail" down into three separate industries—household, FMCG, and fashion, due to the diversity of product type and distinctive circular opportunities in these areas. However, what cuts across these three (and arguably, *all* industries) is the role of e-commerce.

The E-Commerce Boom

Over the last two decades, online and mobile technologies have dramatically transformed the retail industry. Today, the world's largest retailers are massive omnichannel conglomerates with complex value chains, making them key figures in any move toward greater circularity. To appreciate the central role these companies can play, we first need to understand the basic dynamics of the industry.

In 1995, when the global e-commerce conglomerate Amazon first began selling books, online shopping was a new phenomenon. By 2019, total online sales were higher than in-store sales of general merchandise in the United States.[1] E-commerce has taken off, thanks to its ability to meet society's growing demand for just-in-time products at the same or even less cost than traditional stores. The combination of reduced transactional costs, the ubiquity of devices, and the growing sophistication of AI and tremendous increases in electronic data has made e-commerce attractive for just about every industry. Online retailers now sell everything from garments and consumer electronics to vehicles, logistics, web services, financial products, home services, and mortgages.

© The Author(s) 2020
P. Lacy et al., *The Circular Economy Handbook*,
https://doi.org/10.1057/978-1-349-95968-6_15

The relatively frictionless, seamless shopping experience of e-commerce has led to exploding consumerism. This has been most visible in China where nearly 400 million people are now considered to be middle class and, therefore, have more spending capacity.[2] The resulting sales figures are staggering: Online shopping makes up one in seven retail purchases worldwide, accounting for about $3.5 trillion in 2019.[3] Accenture research found that online channels, which used to be the least productive conduit to sales, are exhibiting an annual growth rate of 8.8% that far exceeds growth rates of other channels. Sales in traditional large-format stores, for example, are growing by just 2.7%.[4]

The explosion of global connectivity, contract manufacturing, and turn-key pack-and-ship logistics has enabled even individual entrepreneurs to go from an idea to scaling a multimillion-dollar business from anywhere in the world within weeks. Amazon's Fulfilment by Amazon business program, for example, enables small businesses to leverage its platform, infrastructure, and wide distribution network to sell their products. According to the company, more than one million small businesses in the United States (and over two million globally) utilize the online marketplace to sell products. Using this service, the businesses get access to Amazon Prime's free two-day shipping, as well as the company's customer service and returns.[5] Similarly, online marketplaces such as Alibaba, Etsy, eBay, and others have also provided small businesses with the platform and tools to reach millions of customers.

A More Sustainable Option?

There is no clear consensus on whether e-commerce channels or brick and mortar stores have more substantial environmental footprints.[6,7] The ongoing technological transformation of the retail industry has, from a sustainability and circular economy perspective, been both promising and challenging. On the one hand, it offers an unprecedented opportunity for sustainable optimization of the retail value chain through, for example, more efficient sourcing, production, warehousing, and distribution. On the other hand, it has been an engine for fueling unsustainable consumption levels and habits—larger quantities of both higher- and lower-value items, more frequent orders, faster (even same-day) deliveries, with more return options (e.g., allowing consumers to buy multiple sizes of garments in different colors to try at home and then return). Global retail leaders will need to develop better, more sophisticated, strategies for balancing growth with environmental impact.

Applying Circularity

The circular economy provides a lens through which retailers can address this balance. By applying circular principles, companies can increase their competitiveness and develop stronger, longer-lasting connections with customers. Walmart, a US multinational retail corporation, for example, has started to embrace circularity and has committed to achieving zero waste to landfill from operations in the United States, UK, Canada, and Japan by 2025.[8] In 2017, the company published a study on the emissions implications of different retail channels, as part of the conversation about the retail industry and its potential to reduce the carbon emissions associated with the delivery of products.[9]

Faced with growing concerns over product and packaging waste, Amazon invested $10 million in recycling solutions in partnership with the Closed Loop Fund in 2018, making it easier for customers and communities to recycle.[10] The online retailer has also launched Amazon Second Chance: a "one-stop shop for Amazon customers to learn how to minimize their impact on the environment through reuse, refurbishing, and recycling."[11] In China, where the e-commerce retail market transaction size in 2017 exceeded that of France, Germany, the UK, Japan, and the United States combined, Tencent and Alibaba, two major players in China's e-commerce landscape, have made considerable investments in the circular economy.[12] For example, Alibaba, the world's largest online retailer, invested in a second-hand electronics recycling platform, a consumer electronic rental platform, a sharing platform for clothes, as well as a consumer-to-business (C2B) recycling business that offers ATM machines where users can recycle their mobile phones and get paid.[13] One online store has gone a step further to support the circular economy by creating a hub where people can easily find sustainable products—the Cradle to Cradle Marketplace is a UK-based start-up that only sells Cradle to Cradle Certified™ eco-friendly products.[14]

The global retail industry has the opportunity to be a positive force for change, helping to make consumption more circular. Some progress has been made by industry leaders, but to maintain momentum and go further the industry needs to scale its uptake of circularity. It should integrate circular economy principles at the heart of the decision-making process when determining the optimal distribution channel mix. Last-mile delivery models, the final step of the delivery process from a distribution facility to the end user is regarded as a major challenge for e-commerce players and could be leveraged to launch reverse logistics businesses. As consumption escalates

and consumers are given more ways to buy, the imperative will be on businesses to identify and implement the optimal mix of channels that appeal to
customers, drive economic efficiencies and minimize environmental impact.
With a circular economy lens, leaders will be able to reduce or eliminate
waste across their distribution channels, offer products and services that
unlock new revenue streams, optimize their logistics networks, and ultimately increase their competitiveness and profitability.

Notes

1. Matthew Rothstein, "The Internet Has Passed Brick-and-Mortar Retail
   Sales for the First Time Ever," Bisnow, 2019, https://www.bisnow.com/
   national/news/retail/online-retail-sales-pass-brick-and-mortar-first-time-am-
   azon-98347 (accessed August 12, 2019).
2. Charlotte McEleny, "Retail Nirvana: How Consumerism Found a Devoted
   Following in China," The Drum, 2019, https://www.thedrum.com/news/
   2019/01/31/retail-nirvana-how-consumerism-found-devoted-following-
   china (accessed August 12, 2019).
3. Fred Pearce, "In Store or Online—What's the Most Environmentally Friendly
   Way to Shop?" GreenBiz, 2019, https://www.greenbiz.com/article/store-or-
   online-whats-most-environmentally-friendly-way-shop (accessed August 12,
   2019).
4. Accenture, "CPG Sales: Are Your Modern Relationships Ecommerce-ready?"
   2018, https://www.accenture.com/_acnmedia/PDF-79/Accenture-Cpg-
   Sales-Modern-Relationships-Ecommerce.pdf (accessed August 12, 2019).
5. Geoff Williams, "How to Start a Profitable Business on Amazon," US News,
   2018, https://money.usnews.com/money/personal-finance/earning/articles/
   2018-08-22/how-to-start-a-profitable-business-on-amazon (accessed August
   12, 2019).
6. Jamshid Laghaei, Ardeshir Faghri and Mingxin Li, "Impacts of Home Shopping
   on Vehicle Operations and Greenhouse Gas Emissions: Multi-year Regional
   Study," *International Journal of Sustainable Development & World Ecology*, 2015,
   https://www.tandfonline.com/doi/abs/10.1080/13504509.2015.1124471?-
   journalCode=tsdw20#.Vr5M9nt5ius (accessed August 12, 2019).
7. AlterNet, "Online Shopping vs. Brick-and-Mortar: Which Is More Eco-
   Friendly?" EcoWatch, 2017, https://www.ecowatch.com/online-shopping-
   brick-mortar-eco-friendly-2247525362.html (accessed August 12, 2019).
8. Walmart, "2018 Global Responsibility Report Summary," 2018, https://
   corporate.walmart.com/media-library/document/2018-grr-summary/_prox-
   yDocument?id=00000162-e4a5-db25-a97f-f7fd785a0001 (accessed August
   12, 2019).

9. Walmart, "The Emissions Implications of Modern Retailing: Omnichannel vs. Stores and Online Pure-Plays," 2017, https://cdn.corporate.walmart.com/00/5a/3c20743a4f0db2d00c452aebea95/omni-channel-emissions-modeling-whitepaperfinal04182017.pdf (accessed August 12, 2019).

10. Amazon, "Investing in Recycling Solutions to Protect the Planet," 2018, https://blog.aboutamazon.com/sustainability/investing-in-recycling-solutions-to-protect-the-planet (accessed August 12, 2019).

11. Amazon, "5 Easy Ways to Reuse, Repair, and Recycle," 2018, https://blog.aboutamazon.com/sustainability/5-easy-ways-to-reuse-repair-and-recycle (accessed August 12, 2019).

12. Rob Smith, "42% of Global e-Commerce Is Happening in China. Here's Why," World Economic Forum, 2018, https://www.weforum.org/agenda/2018/04/42-of-global-e-commerce-is-happening-in-china-heres-why/ (accessed August 12, 2019).

13. Ecommerce Strategy China, "The Competition Between Tencent and Alibaba Spreads to the Circular Economy," 2018, https://www.ecommerce-strategychina.com/column/the-competition-between-tencent-and-alibaba-spreads-to-the-circular-economy# (accessed August 12, 2019).

14. Hannah Ritchie, "Cradle to Cradle Marketplace First Online Store Dedicated to Circular Economy Products," 2015, https://sustainablebrands.com/read/product-service-design-innovation/cradle-to-cradle-marketplace-first-online-store-dedicated-to-circular-economy-products (accessed August 12, 2019).

Part III

How Do We Get There?—Making the Pivot

16

How to Make the Circular Pivot

At this point, you should have a good understanding of the current state of play for advancing the circular economy. Leading companies across industries show clear progress, but they are just scratching the surface in terms of unlocking the full potential of circular business models and technologies. So, what's needed to accelerate that transition?

Achieving growth and profitability while deploying circular initiatives and technology solutions is no small task. Such undertakings have inherent risks and require substantial investments in resources and capabilities. In our research, we have found that organizations successful in getting such major initiatives underway did three things simultaneously: (1) they transformed the existing value chain to remove waste, reduce value erosion, and drive up investment capacity; (2) they grew the core business organically with circular offerings embedded to sustain fuel for investments; and (3) they invested in disruptive growth opportunities that would take their journey to circularity to the next level.

Jumping feet first into all three actions at once—what Accenture calls a "wise pivot" (see Fig. 16.1)—requires thoughtful and deliberate coordination across and outside the organization.[1] The wise pivot is a pragmatic approach for a company to continuously reinvent itself in an age of disruption, a roadmap that can hasten the transition from a linear to a circular business. Without such an enterprise-wide effort, companies will find it hard to scale their circular efforts and gain competitive advantage.

The need to manage transformation and reinvention is not new, but the business environment has changed. In the past, companies have had to recalibrate in the face of large disruptions in their operating environment, for example, with the IT revolution, the Internet, and, more recently, the rise of social media.

© The Author(s) 2020
P. Lacy et al., *The Circular Economy Handbook*,
https://doi.org/10.1057/978-1-349-95968-6_16

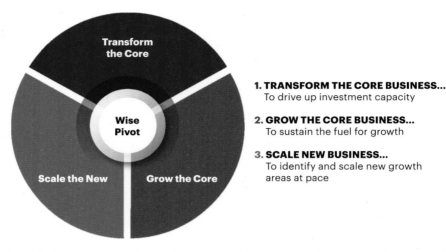

1. TRANSFORM THE CORE BUSINESS...
To drive up investment capacity

2. GROW THE CORE BUSINESS...
To sustain the fuel for growth

3. SCALE NEW BUSINESS...
To identify and scale new growth areas at pace

Fig. 16.1 The wise pivot (*Source* Accenture, "Make Your Wise Pivot to the New," June 14, 2018, https://www.accenture.com/gb-en/insights/consulting/wise-pivot [accessed August 20, 2019])

Typically, specific functions within the organization have responded to these changes, sometimes by automating mostly existing processes. These are different times: Today the landscape in which firms operate is much more dynamic and volatile. It requires quicker responses, cross-functional solutions, and often entirely new business models and processes. Companies must know not just what and where to change but also *how* to pivot to new business models and technologies when implementing a circular strategy. And, as many executives now recognize, participating in the circular economy has become the new imperative for organizations to grow sustainably. So, it's not a matter of "should we go circular?" but "which models make the most sense for my business and how do I get there while remaining competitive?" In other words, transitioning to circular business models is essential for any business to grow and remain competitive in today's environment. "This is imperative for our survival," says Christopher Davis, International Director of Corporate Social Responsibility and Campaigns at The Body Shop International, a cosmetics skincare and perfume company. "If you think about starting a business today, designing a business around a circular economy philosophy, ultimately it's going to give you better returns in the long run."[1]

Four Dimensions of a Successful Transformation

So *how*, exactly, do companies successfully implement a wise pivot to circularity? First, firms must mature across four fundamental dimensions (see Fig. 16.2):

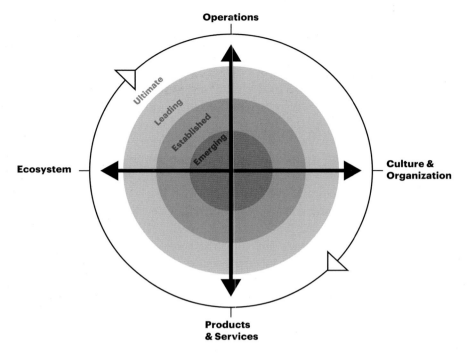

Fig. 16.2 Maturity diagram

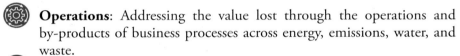

Operations: Addressing the value lost through the operations and by-products of business processes across energy, emissions, water, and waste.

Products & Services: Rethinking the design, lifecycle, and end of use of a product or service to optimize usage, eliminate waste, and close product loops.

Culture & Organization: Embedding circular principles into the fabric of an organization through redefined working practices, policies, and procedures.

Ecosystem: Collaborating and partnering with public- and private-sector actors to create an enabling environment for collective transformation.

Initially, we considered these four dimensions as consecutive step functions, simply because organizations tend to focus first on the areas that are within their purview, that is, to "get their house in order." What has become clear, however, is that all four areas are interdependent and need to be addressed together, though not necessarily with equal emphasis, to gain the greatest traction for circular economy initiatives. For instance, for companies to be circular, they must tackle both their operations (gain control over and contain all waste in their system) and their core products and services portfolio (stop the continuous flow of more materials that turn into waste and reinvent their portfolios to be indefinitely reused and recycled). And to optimize these initiatives for success, well-functioning cultures and ecosystems are essential to embed the right behavior shifts that underly the economics of circular initiatives.

While an "ideal" circular journey might tackle all of these dimensions in parallel, most organizations are at different levels of maturity across these four areas. Consider the technology sector. Many companies in the high-tech industry have been focusing their resources on reducing waste in their *Operations*, especially in energy- and water-intensive data centers. As they gain efficiencies and cut costs in their internal operations, some of these firms have turned their attention to waste in their *Product & Service* portfolios, including some encouraging initiatives focused on design for circularity and product takeback. Other players have been focusing on enhancing their *Culture & Organization* first, as the backbone of their transition, making circularity core to their corporate strategy, mission, and ethos. For those companies, the priority has been transitioning the workforce and creating the policies and procedures to support their circular objectives. Finally, some organizations want to learn from others and support broader industry challenges by engaging with the *Ecosystem*, for example, by joining e-waste consortiums in relevant geographies.

A Holistic View

Circular value chains are complex, and the trick is to take a holistic perspective in identifying the right mix of high-value initiatives across the four dimensions to maximize return on investment. Generally, although a plethora of circularity options exists across each of the areas, leaders need to identify and prioritize initiatives according to their organization's needs, growth appetite, place in the market, and current maturity. Companies typically do a broad scan to identify the potential circular economy opportunities across the four dimensions, and then down-select the highest-value opportunities, i.e., those that will tackle the biggest areas of waste while maximizing economic returns (as described in Part 2).

Step 1—Opportunity identification: After identifying the areas of greatest waste across their value chain, companies should list the range of possible circular economy opportunities open to their industry and business. We typically suggest companies start broad and brainstorm a long list of ideas—drawing from best practice, leading case studies, internal and external interviews, etc.—to identify opportunities to build upon current initiatives with a circular lens and investigate new business models or ventures. The creative free flow of ideas is a useful approach to define the "art of the possible" for how circularity can bring additional value to an existing business, and how it can help shift legacy businesses to new ways of working. For example, German car manufacturer BMW operates a Co-Creation Lab, an open innovation platform where the public can share ideas on the future of cars and co-create products and services. Using this approach, BMW can better understand customers' requirements, while gaining insight into a range of possible concepts at the same time.[2]

Step 2—Value analysis: Once a breadth of ideas has been captured, executives should perform a funneling exercise to focus on the potential opportunities of highest value. As an example, that process might look something like the following:

1. **Initial "pass/fail" filters** are applied first to weed out the ideas and concepts that are not viable for the organization, such as not being a fit with the industry, or pose potential legal or safety risks.
2. Using the shorter list of ideas that made the cut, executives should then go through a **qualitative prioritization exercise** to identify the highest-value opportunities for the near, medium, and longer term. This involves defining a set of assessment criteria, typically measuring the opportunities against internal metrics, i.e., their ability to achieve business goals (e.g., strategic fit with core competencies, ability to create or enable value through growth or differentiation, cost reduction, brand enhancing, etc.), and the ease of implementation (e.g., technical viability, maturity barriers, stakeholders, cost, and time), as well as external drivers, such as the potential to have an impact on the organization's broader ecosystem.
3. The next stage of prioritization should focus on a **quantitative assessment** to develop a business case for the narrowed list of opportunities, looking across the traditional financial value drivers (e.g., revenue generation or cost reduction) as well as the environmental and social costs or opportunities (e.g., carbon saved or jobs gained/lost), see Fig. 16.3 for an overview of the typical value drivers.

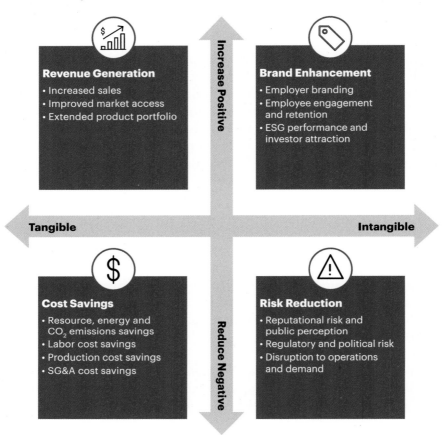

Fig. 16.3 Key value drivers (*Source* Modified from Daniel Esty and Andrew Winston, "Green to Gold," p. 102, Wiley, 2009 and Michael Porter, "The Competitive Advantage: Creating and Sustaining Superior Performance," p. 101, Free Press, 1985)

4. With the business case as a guide, executives can determine which opportunities to pursue right away (i.e., quick wins) versus initiatives they should pilot or invest in over time (e.g., a proposed idea that requires testing with customers).

Step 3—Roadmap: Finally, after identifying a suite of circular economy opportunities, executives can shape a roadmap for the phasing of the initiatives, bundling opportunities into programs with the necessary sponsorship, change management, and governance. At this stage, initiative plans can be further defined, along with value propositions for new business models and partners, and business cases structured to ensure tracking and value delivery.

Step 4—Prototyping/piloting: For companies starting out, there should be several initiatives they can implement right away to deliver immediate results and garner support for longer-term initiatives. Often, companies will start their journey with circular initiatives that have more attractive economics to help build momentum and fund future higher-risk or slower-return programs. When structuring the roadmap, executives should remember that, in building a true circular strategy, the highest-value initiatives (such as unlocking value through service-based models) often rely on initiatives that are "enablers." These might include integrating circular principles in upfront design, redesigning processes, and setting up ecosystem partnerships. Therefore, it's essential to have a more comprehensive, enterprise-wide view when setting up circular programs and strategies. "We take a holistic view of circularity, looking at five areas: usage and choice of materials, production processes, product design, product use, and product end-of-use," says CEO of H&M Group, Karl-Johan Persson. "We are progressing on each of these fronts, noting that the areas are in different stages of maturity."

The Maturity Journey

For organizations to simplify how they can improve each focus dimension and choose the right mix of initiatives for their business, they must understand their current stage of maturity. Each stage has its own considerations and issues, affecting where an organization should focus its efforts, with the goal of becoming a "leading," or ideally "ultimate" circular company.

Emerging companies are just starting out on their circular journey and are likely to have a stronger tie between their growth and use of natural resources. These businesses should first conduct a broad assessment of their internal operations and current ways of working to identify quick wins to reduce waste and support their shift to circularity. Efforts tend to focus on driving internal efficiencies and improvements (e.g., in areas like reducing waste to landfill) or increasing their use of renewable energy.

Established companies are part-way through their circular journey and have realized some substantial wins around operational efficiency and waste, and have likely seen successes within their product portfolio. These companies should take their learnings and focus on the "hard spots" in their organizations to close the loop, pushing the envelope on traditionally challenging parts of the business (i.e., by engaging product design, partners, suppliers, etc.) and transforming circular initiatives into business-as-usual. Once companies have experimented with circular economy initiatives, they also tend to understand the complexity and value potential for industrializing efforts with technology, particularly data analytics, to inform the decision-making for circular practices.

Leading companies in the circular space pivot their entire corporate strategy toward circularity, with a goal toward closing their own loops and decoupling their company's growth from the use of resources. They dedicate more time and attention to their role in the broader ecosystem, operating with both public and private sectors to transform their environment and overcome key obstacles for their industries. This includes playing a role in shaping and influencing policy agendas, sharing learnings, and working with partners, third parties, and competitors. Although a number of entrepreneurial start-ups and SMEs are on the verge of becoming a "leading" company, there are not yet examples of multinational corporations operating in this space in a completely holistic way across all four dimensions.

Ultimate circularity should be the mission of all businesses, given the daunting challenges we face in creating a sustainable future for all. This ultimate state goes beyond eliminating waste to completely transforming value chains so that the company has a net positive environmental impact, with indefinite circulation of resources, materials, products, and services. For example, the ultimate circular company would go beyond carbon neutrality and zero waste to being additive, regenerative, and restorative. While we may not have examples of the ultimate circular company today, we can point to promising successes that demonstrate this possibility, such as the centuries-old principles of regenerative and restorative agriculture that have been more recently embraced by some food companies.

Getting Started

When beginning, refreshing, or enhancing their circular economy strategy, companies can evaluate their maturity across the four dimensions versus their industry and cross-industry peers to identify gaps and potential leadership opportunities. It's important to note that, although we have grouped initiatives by typical progression and maturity levels to provide a starting point for companies, the initiatives do not need to be implemented in a linear way (from emerging to ultimate). In fact, companies can pursue multiple initiatives along the spectrum at once or leapfrog to "leading" and "ultimate" ambitions to increase and accelerate the impact of those efforts.

Our experience has shown that an organization will succeed in driving scalable value from circular strategies by maturing optimally along each of the four dimensions. We will spend the next four chapters diving into each of those dimensions to help organizations understand how to select, implement, and scale the right mix of circular economy initiatives.

 Chapter Takeaways

- To scale circular economy initiatives as a competitive asset, companies must learn to perform a "wise pivot." This requires undertaking simultaneous strategies: transforming the existing value chain to eliminate waste and value erosion, growing the core business with circular offerings, and investing in disruptive growth initiatives, including those that intersect with parallel industries and ecosystems.
- Becoming a leading circular organization requires maturity along four dimensions: Operations, Products & Services, Culture & Organization, and Ecosystem. To progress successfully, companies must look inward and outward across the value chain and external ecosystem.
- While companies may be inclined to focus first on the areas within their immediate control, it is important they consider all four dimensions holistically due to their interdependencies.
- Although a plethora of opportunities exists across the maturity dimensions, leaders must identify and prioritize the right mix of initiatives to unlock maximum value and attain the greatest impact for their organizations.
- There are four stages within the maturity journey: emerging, established, leading, and ultimate. It is important for organizations to understand where they currently fall in the maturity journey and set sights high to work toward ultimate circularity.

Notes

1. Closing the Loop Film, "Quotations," http://www.closingtheloopfilm.com/quotations/ (accessed August 9, 2019).
2. BMW Group, "BMW Group Co-Creation Lab," PressClub Global, July 20, 2010, https://www.press.bmwgroup.com/global/article/detail/T0082655EN/bmw-group-co-creation-lab?language=en (accessed August 12, 2019).

17

 Operations

When companies begin taking their first steps on a circular journey, they typically start by focusing on internal operations. They might look at ways to cut energy consumption and reduce (or altogether eliminate) waste associated with business activities through "zero waste to landfill" initiatives. But that's only the beginning. Eventually, organizations ambitious about circularity must undertake a transition to renewable sources of raw materials and energy, while considering ways to reuse waste within their organizational boundaries or solutions to convert waste into useful by-products for other businesses and industries.

Four Areas of Focus

Operational initiatives are often more straightforward to pursue as a starting point in comparison with the three other maturity dimensions (Products & Services, Culture & Organization, and Ecosystem). In practice, circular operational initiatives can often build upon or act as an umbrella for existing efficiency and sustainability efforts. They also tend to have business cases with relatively short-term paybacks and typically reside within the organization's boundaries. As a result, companies often tend to focus their circular efforts on internal operations initially, first conducting a broad-based assessment to identify "quick wins" before delving into larger transformation initiatives around those areas.

To that end, in our research we have found four main areas in which companies typically focus their circular operational initiatives: energy, emissions, water, and waste (see Table 17.1).

© The Author(s) 2020
P. Lacy et al., *The Circular Economy Handbook*,
https://doi.org/10.1057/978-1-349-95968-6_17

Table 17.1 Four areas of focus

Focus area	The toolbox	Operations in action
Energy	Identifying and implementing measures that reduce energy consumption, increase operational energy efficiency, and start to shift from fossil fuels to renewable sources	The world's largest brewer AB InBev has set a target to obtain 100% purchased electricity from renewable sources by 2025, resulting in a 25% reduction in its carbon footprint across the value chain.[1] The company is also adding a renewable electricity symbol to Budweiser labels to celebrate its commitment to climate change and to engage customers on the issue[2]
Emissions	Identifying emission points within the direct scope of core operations as well as throughout the supply chain and then making suitable interventions to reduce those emissions	Sustainable materials company Newlight Technologies uses carbon captured from greenhouse gases to produce a bioplastic material called AirCarbon that can match the performance of oil-based plastics[3]
Water	Reducing a company's water dependence by minimizing water abstraction, prioritizing water-saving opportunities, and increasing water reuse to improve efficiency and reduce costs	One of Europe's largest food-processing companies, ABP, is tackling how water is managed in its facilities to achieve cost savings through resource efficiency. Water is crucial to ABP's business and, through its *Doing More With Less* program (including implementation of a data monitoring system for real-time water flow readings), the company aims to reduce water usage by 50% by 2020[4]
Waste	Reaching zero waste by eliminating waste leakage throughout company operations and reducing wasted capacity by maximizing asset utilization	In January 2015, consumer goods company Unilever reached a new industry-leading achievement of sending zero non-hazardous waste to landfill across more than 600 sites in 70 countries, including factories, warehouses, distribution centers, and offices.[5] After identifying the different non-hazardous waste streams in its operations, Unilever has found alternative routes for the waste from these sites[5]

Making the Pivot

To get started, executives should first pinpoint the biggest waste pools, leakages, and value erosion in their operations, as outlined in the industry chapters. Companies within the apparel industry, for instance, might choose to focus on water because garment manufacturing consumes vast amounts of that resource (it takes 2700 liters of water to make just one cotton shirt) and up to 20% of industrial water pollution is attributed to textile dyeing and treatment.[6,7] Chemical companies, on the other hand, might decide to channel their efforts on energy consumption, given the industry is the world's largest industrial energy consumer. However, even within the same industry, different firms can have widely differing strategies. Much will depend on whether a company is at the start of its circular journey (emerging), in the middle of it (established) or toward the end (leading to ultimate)—see Table 17.2 for a view of the full spectrum.

A Circular Journey: Water

Let's take the focus area of water as an example. An *emerging* circular economy company (just beginning its efforts toward circularity) might start by conducting a water risk analysis and then implement initiatives to reduce its water consumption and eliminate contamination, whereas a *leading* company (more advanced in its circularity journey) might instead be focusing on significant water reuse, or even water restoration/regeneration across its entire value chain.

Companies could also consider two types of water initiatives as a starting point, with the goal to reduce or eliminate total water consumption. The first is to *reduce water abstraction*, which is the process of taking or extracting water from a natural source (such as a river, lake, or groundwater aquifer) for irrigation, industrial applications, or other operational uses. In an interesting application, the Changi Airport system collects and treats rainwater, which accounts for 28–33% of its total water used, resulting in savings of approximately $280,000 per annum.[8] The second type of initiative is to *reduce water consumption*. In 2015, apparel company Levi Strauss conducted a comprehensive lifecycle assessment of its core products and found that a single pair of the popular 501 jeans used 3781 liters of water over its full cycle. Levi Strauss then developed a new finishing technique that saves up to 96% of water in the denim finishing process.[9]

Ultimately, companies should be making substantial progress across both abstraction and consumption, moving toward water positivity (generating more water than consumed), with the goal of replenishing and returning more water to the environment than they use.[10] A host of emerging technologies will help companies reach such ambitious targets. One steelmaker in India, for example, leveraged Ecolab's IoT technology to reuse and recycle water, saving the equivalent of the annual drinking water needs of Kolkata and Pune

Table 17.2 Illustrative characteristics of increasing company maturity

		Emerging	Established	Leading	Ultimate	The maturity journey: from → to
	Energy	• Limited use of renewables • Heavy grid dependency • Purchase of energy certificates	• Increased use of renewables • Some grid dependency • Clean energy solely from Power Purchase Agreements (PPAs)	• 100% renewably powered • Little grid dependency • Grid balancing • Zero black/gray energy across whole value chain	• 100% renewably powered • No grid dependency • Energy provider/supplier to the grid, markets, and communities	• From limited use of renewable sources to 100% renewable operations and ultimately producing more energy than is used • Actions include: (1) identifying and targeting energy-saving measures at relevant points in the value chain to drive cost reduction and (2) identifying alternative energy sources to shift away from fossil fuels
	Emissions	• Scope 1 targets for direct emissions • Pilot carbon-reduction policies and initiatives • Some carbon offset but limited reduction	• Scopes 1 and 2 targets for direct and indirect emissions • Internal carbon pricing • Emissions reduction scaled across operations	• Carbon neutral • Wholesale reduction to the point of zero emissions • Targets and initiatives scaled across whole value chain	• Carbon positive • Directly supporting the generation of clean energy (beyond value chain)	• From setting targets and piloting initiatives to reducing direct emissions to becoming carbon positive and supporting clean energy generation • Actions include identifying emission points across value chain and making suitable interventions
	Water	• Water targets in place • Water risk analysis conducted • Reduction initiatives in place • Little implementation of wholesale water efficiency	• Focus on water efficiency and in-depth analysis • Implementation of water targets • Supply chain agility to reduce water use	• Water neutral • Water-use reduction/ greater efficiency across whole value chain	• Water positive • Provision of water/ water facilities (beyond value chain)	• From target setting and baselining to becoming water positive and provisioning water or facilities • Actions include: (1) mitigating excessive water abstraction to reduce dependence on a finite natural resource and (2) prioritizing water-saving opportunities to improve efficiency and reduce costs with net-neutral targets

	Emerging	Established	Leading	Ultimate	The maturity journey: from → to
Waste	• Majority of waste to landfill • Some initiatives on waste to energy • Recycling procedures in offices and in parts of operations • Identifying wasted resource capacity hotspots	• Zero waste • Majority waste to energy and recycling • Some initiatives on downcycling operational waste • Zero-based budget approach to resource use	• Closed-loop initiatives scaled across operations • All input is recycled • Various downcycling/upcycling initiatives • Fully maximizing human and physical asset utilization	• Entirely closed-loop model across value chain or within an industry/cross-sector ecosystem for all resources and materials	• From reducing waste to landfill to an entirely closed-loop system for all resources • Actions include: (1) finding hotspots of waste leakage in business operations and targeting zero waste transformation in those areas and (2) assessing the productivity of human and physical assets and targeting maximum utilization of their active time
Overall takeaways	• Initiatives are largely cost-cutting exercises to create the financial capacity to invest in further circular initiatives (e.g., broad-brush activities to cut water waste in the supply chain)	• Initiatives are more targeted, identifying savings opportunities in traditionally challenging parts of the supply chain such as sourcing and logistics (e.g., supporting farmers to improve their agricultural practices to minimize water waste upstream in the supply chain)	• Initiatives are delivered with zero dependency on non-renewable inputs, and benefits are shared and realized through the value chain	• Initiatives go beyond net zero to net positive, to focus on the regeneration of resources	• Resource efficiency and effectiveness can rapidly translate into cost savings and is therefore one of the easier areas of circularity from the four dimensions in which to make progress quickly (i.e., 80% closing of the loop). However, it is one of the harder areas in which to completely close the loop, due to challenges associated with particular supply chain activities like logistics and last-mile delivery

combined.[11] Ecolab monitors 40,000 systems deployed at customer sites for water quality and quantity, sharing insights and learnings across global operations.[12] "This drives better performance and outcomes. It's good for business and for the planet," states Doug Baker, Chairman and CEO, Ecolab.

 Top Tip: Circularity as a Sustainability Accelerator

As mentioned earlier, many companies already have sustainability initiatives underway, such as programs for waste and carbon emissions reductions. Businesses can use those efforts as stepping-stones to make the transition toward true circularity. It's important for executives to understand what the circular economy means for their current sustainability initiatives and goals, which often include energy, emissions, water, and waste targets and how it is additive. The circular economy brings further advantages in two specific ways. First, it is focused on driving waste entirely out of a system, not just reducing or redirecting it. To accomplish that, companies might need to change fundamental ways in which they operate, for instance, by sourcing only renewable inputs or by producing energy through the production process itself. Second, the circular economy is focused on maximizing *business impact* alongside *resource impact*. Solutions for addressing waste streams should both realize environmental benefits and contribute positively to the company's financials, such as through new revenue streams from the sale of waste by-product as feedstock or through reduced operating costs.

The question naturally arises: Should companies manage their sustainability and circular efforts separately? The answer is no. Integration is key. From the start, sustainability has been changing the boundaries of corporate strategy by becoming a source of innovation and competitive advantage for industry leaders.[13] And over time, the whole notion of a responsible, trusted organization, once seemingly disconnected from the value-generation imperative, has evolved away from "do no harm" toward "doing well by doing good." Sustainability strategy is the mechanism to achieve that, playing at both the operational and marketplace levels through practices that are both "common" (what all peers do) and "strategic" (what competitors cannot easily match). Just as the boundaries between industries and sectors blur to give rise to ecosystems enabled by technology advances and free markets, internal organizational functions become increasingly porous and interlinked with strategy, sustainability, and circularity, all nesting within each other. Consequently, certain operations-focused circular practices that target cost efficiencies will be within the purview of operational improvement teams. Other initiatives focused on the adoption of circular business models will likely be spearheaded by strategy, R&D, and marketing departments. To balance these different efforts well, companies must take a holistic enterprise-wide view, with the connective tissue linking the various initiatives to sustainability objectives and the corporate circular strategy. Without that integration, different parts of the organization could not only miss opportunities for synergistic collaboration; they could easily end up working at odds with each other.

The Value Drivers

Just as many companies start their journey to circularity with an operations lens, many circular programs initially focus on cost savings as their primary value driver. Other common objectives include risk mitigation, revenue generation, and sustainability-related brand enhancement. Let's explore each of these value drivers in more detail.

Revenue Generation: Some of the most compelling opportunities for operational circularity are in revenue generation, especially for companies that have found ways to sell their operational waste streams to other industries as inputs. Consider Metsä Group, a Finnish forest-industry cooperative that manufactures products from renewable wood sources. Metsä works with a network of companies to utilize every production side stream at its highest possible value. One tree can be used to produce sawn timber, plywood, paperboard, and pulp, as well as in the food industry for concentrate in juices and ice creams. Currently, 92% of the Metsä Group's production side streams are directed into reuse as materials (e.g. pulp-based textiles or bio-composites) or energy. The cooperative is responsible for 15% of Finland's renewable energy.[14]

Cost Savings: Working toward operational circularity often brings cost savings through increased efficiencies (greater productivity of existing assets and equipment), reduced inputs (lower consumption of energy, water, and material inputs) and reduced disposal costs. Companies can achieve impressive results even by focusing on just one area. Google and DeepMind Technologies, for example, have been using artificial intelligence (AI) to improve the energy efficiency of data centers. In the system, sensors within and outside of a data center track how various environmental factors affect its performance, and AI predicts the impact those variables may have on the site's future energy consumption. When Google deployed the system at a live data center, the company was reportedly able to attain a 40% decrease in the amount of energy needed to cool the facility.[15]

Risk Reduction: As resources become scarcer (and price fluctuations become increasingly commonplace), operational circularity has clear risk-reduction benefits. That's one of the reasons why automotive company Ford developed a closed-loop recycling system to reuse aluminum scrap leftover from the production of the Ford F-150, its best-selling vehicle in the United

States. The system can recover 20 million pounds of aluminum per month, enough for more than 37,000 F-series truck bodies.[16] Ford's closed-loop system helps reduce the company's dependency on virgin materials and lessens its vulnerability to volatile commodity markets. Moreover, reprocessing recycled aluminum requires 90% less energy and a fraction of the water compared with the mining of new aluminum supplies.[17]

 Brand Enhancement: Finally, an often-overlooked benefit of achieving greater circularity in operations is its significant impact on brand building and reputational value. According to a recent global consumer survey, 81% of respondents across generations and genders believe that companies should help the environment.[18] Given such consumer sentiment, companies that make bold commitments to circularity can build their brand value to gain competitive advantage. This is one reason why many corporations have been very publicly proclaiming such plans. Consumer brand Colgate, for instance, launched a social media campaign (#EveryDropCounts) that included a 30-second video clip showing that almost four gallons of water get wasted when people keep the faucet running while brushing.[19] The ad campaign went viral, garnering more than 10 million views on YouTube.[20]

🔍 Case Study: Anheuser-Busch InBev

Anheuser-Busch InBev is an example of a company that is progressing along a maturity journey in operational circularity. Initially, the multinational beverage company focused on cost savings through reductions in energy and water usage. Specifically, from 2013 to 2017, AB InBev saved $60 million through efficiency improvements, largely attributed to on-site water efficiency and risk management as well as energy-efficient LED lighting and energy-saving controllers.[21] Next, the company shifted toward sourcing all purchased electricity from renewable sources by 2025, which would be the equivalent of removing 500,000 cars from the road. To date, AB InBev has contracted 50% of its renewable electricity needs, including 100% contracts that will provide renewable electricity for 100% of operations in North America.[22] And now, AB InBev is not only approaching "grid independent" for brewing beer; the company is, like other circular leaders, also beginning to generate additional revenues by selling excess energy back to the grid. Moreover, AB InBev has also begun to link these initiatives to its products and brand. By 2025, all of the company's Budweiser beer around the world will be brewed using 100% renewable electricity sources, and these products will have a symbol that will enable consumers to make better-informed purchasing decisions.[23]

Technology as an Enabler

Whether a company is just beginning its circular journey or well on the way, technology often plays a crucial role in achieving circularity in operations. Technology is a powerful enabler of operational efficiencies, especially in continuously monitoring and improving daily operations to cut resource consumption. Digital technologies are a case in point. Thanks to the IoT and other digital innovations, Enevo, a US waste management company, has been able to optimize waste pickup and provide "waste technology as a service." The company measures its customers' energy, water, and waste indicators and then feeds the data into machine-learning models to identify solutions for decreasing costs and increasing sustainability over time.[24] In a similar application, SKF, a Swedish bearing and seal manufacturer, has optimized the maintenance of industrial machinery by analyzing IoT data on the equipment's operating conditions to better predict when failures might occur or replacements are needed, reducing equipment downtime.[25] Machine learning can also detect previously unnoticed patterns throughout the supply chain in order to predict demand with better accuracy.

An array of biological and physical technologies—including bio-energy, materials science, 3D printing, and hydroponics—can also help companies use fewer resources, swap in alternative renewable inputs, and enhance productivity, in essence, to do more or better with less. DyeCoo, a textile company, is a good example of that. DyeCoo's technology eliminates water and chemicals completely from the fabric dyeing process and instead uses supercritical carbon dioxide to dye fabrics at the same quality or better. Just one DyeCoo dyeing machine can help save 32 million liters of water and 160,000 kilograms of processing chemicals per year. The technology is extremely efficient and fully circular: The carbon dioxide is a by-product of other industrial processes and is recycled for use in the next batch.[26]

In other applications, technology is playing a critical role in energy harvesting and in capturing and reprocessing waste for alternative uses. Carbon Engineering, a Canadian clean energy company, has developed direct air capture (DAC) technology that converts atmospheric carbon dioxide into low-carbon fuels for transport and for use in enhanced oil recovery. According to the company, the technology can scale up to capture one million tons of carbon dioxide per year with each commercial facility. That quantity is equivalent to the annual emissions of 250,000 average cars.[27]

Leading Practices to Drive Transformation

What accounts for the success of companies like Levi Strauss, Ford, and AB InBev in driving the circular economy in their organizations? In our research, we uncovered several common leading practices.

Move Forward with Renewables at Scale

"Going big" on renewable energy emerged as a common theme. Multinational technology company Microsoft has succeeded in re-prioritizing energy as a C-suite issue and has improved its energy efficiency, while increasing the proportion of renewables in its overall energy mix. In 2011, company leaders commissioned an evaluation into risk exposure regarding Microsoft's current energy position. The report concluded that the firm faced significant risk from carbon regulations, pricing, and availability. To mitigate this risk, Microsoft compiled a team of 14 experts in renewable energy, electricity markets, battery storage, and local energy generation (or "distributed energy") to develop and execute a central energy strategy for the firm.[28] Microsoft's CFO and President played a strong role in devising this comprehensive roadmap. The company then set ambitious targets to source 50% of energy for its data centers from wind, solar, and hydroelectric power by 2018. By the early 2020s, Microsoft seeks to increase this to 60%.[28] To meet those targets, business units are charged internally for carbon emissions, with funds reinvested into renewable energy programs.[28]

Measure Resource Inputs and Outputs to Incentivize Change

Many companies measure their energy consumption. To attain operational circularity, however, they must also quantify their usage of water and other resources, and they need a data-generated view of the waste streams they produce. Only with such detailed information can organizations properly manage and control those quantities in the most efficient ways, and they can also begin to implement programs to incentivize change. "Zero-waste" initiatives are a good place to start. The platinum division of mining company Anglo American is on track to meet its goal of sending zero waste to landfill by 2020, thanks to a partnership with waste specialists to analyze waste streams at each site and explore opportunities to develop cost-effective reuse and recycling business ventures with community members.[29] Internal carbon pricing programs are another metrics-driven approach to spurring change. Mahindra & Mahindra, an Indian automotive and farm equipment company, set an internal carbon price of $10 per ton that was so effective that the firm plans to extend the pricing to its other businesses along its supply chain.[30]

Embed Circularity into Closed-Loop Operational Systems

A circular pivot must be led from the top of the organization, but, critically, it also needs to be embedded into the everyday operational decision-making level, moving beyond the borders of the facilities to include new partners and systems. When global brewer Heineken was planning a new brewery in Mexico, the company designed the facility for circularity throughout its operations.[31] At the site, half of the thermal energy required for brewing will be obtained by recovering waste heat from an adjacent glass factory (which in turn will use in its products the residual glass it receives from Heineken). As the new plant runs, it will produce biogas that will be used for heat in the brewing process. In addition, a water-treatment plant will purify the water used in production so that 30% of it can be reused in other processes; by-product sludge will be used by nearby farms to improve the soil; and spent grains (also a by-product of beer production) will be used as cattle feed. Lastly, on-site solar panels will provide some of the brewery's electricity, with the rest powered by off-site wind and solar power.

Think "Outside the Box" to Maximize Value

Operational leaders in the circular economy shared another commonality: "outside the box" thinking to create additional value from circular initiatives which can provide commercial opportunities for the business, but also benefit consumers and communities. Many of these new business models have ingeniously turned spare capacity into revenue streams. Coyote, a third-party logistics provider acquired by UPS, is helping to fill the spare capacity of empty trucks that are making a return trip. Coyote matches those vehicles with businesses that need their freight transported, thus reducing empty return-truck miles, also known as "deadheading" in the industry.[32] Using Coyote's service, one large US brewing company was able to fill 900,000 empty miles of its fleet of trucks in 2018 alone, generating considerable additional revenues.[33]

Others have stretched their innovative thinking even further. Thanks to an alliance with conservationists, rice farmers in California, a water-stressed region, have been renting their fallow fields as "pop-up wetlands." Over the years, agricultural expansion in California has replaced 90% of wetlands, resulting in a drastic plunge in the numbers of annual visits by waterfowl and shorebirds.[34] In response, The Nature Conservancy (TNC), a charitable environmental organization, used a massive database of crowdsourced information from amateur birdwatchers to predict when and where birds would need a habitat area in California. TNC then contracted with farmers to temporarily rent their fallow agricultural fields in those areas (shorebirds need land only for a few weeks a year).[34] The results have been impressive: a five-fold increase in the number of shorebirds over February into March, with the rented fields averaging 20 times the shorebird density compared with control fields.[34]

Another example is method's factory in Chicago, which fuses circular economy principles with an urban development perspective to maximize benefits to business, society, and the environment. Method established the factory on the south side of Chicago, the first new facility in over 30 years in an area that's experienced major disinvestment. "We decided to invest and develop an area where infrastructure is dated and people need jobs," explains Adam Lowry, Co-Founder of method. "With more urbanization, it is also better from an energy and water standpoint to invest in a city." The factory generates renewable energy on-site and is water neutral. The company also invested $1 million to reinforce the factory's roof. This investment is generating additional revenue and providing fresh produce to the area through a rental agreement with urban farm, Gotham Greens.

 Chapter Takeaways

- Operations can be a good place to start circular economy efforts, given the organizational control, opportunities to build on existing sustainability initiatives, and relatively quick returns and cost savings.
- Companies should use circularity as a way to boost or build upon existing sustainability efforts to address the biggest areas of waste across energy, emissions, water, and material inputs in their operations.
- The value of circular operations is not limited to cost reduction. Companies must get creative in thinking about new ways to eliminate and monetize waste, such as through selling waste streams to parallel industries or through renting out their excess production, storage, or logistics capacity via supply-chain-as-a-service models.

- Ultimately, circularity means driving waste out of processes altogether until operations are zero waste or, ideally, they generate more resources than they consume. This end state will protect companies from resource volatility and will build trust to help preserve market competitiveness.

Before getting their circular operational initiatives off the ground, executives should take a look around the enterprise to assess the factors driving waste and value leakage across the business. In addition, they need to spotlight key areas to focus their efforts with respect to energy consumption, carbon emissions, water usage, and waste management. The following considerations will help in that review.

Sample Questions to Answer

Shaping strategy & programs

☐ What are our objectives and what business models make sense to utilize?

☐ What initiatives are already under way throughout the organization that can be brought together and scaled within a cohesive circular economy strategy?

☐ What are the key additional sources of waste and value erosion in our operations, and how can they be addressed?

☐ What would it mean for our operations to be net positive and regenerative?

Capturing value

☐ What data is needed to understand and pinpoint the biggest opportunities to address resource use and waste and to optimize operations?

☐ To what extent can our operational initiatives drive down costs and make our supply chain more resilient?

☐ Are there opportunities to create new revenue streams through our operational wastes or excess capacity in the supply chain?

☐ Who could our customers and partners be (e.g., an adjacent industry)?

Functions to Engage

☐ **Procurement** to source renewable and recycled inputs and determine future resource strategies (e.g., for scarce or otherwise limited natural resources)

☐ **Operations** to implement initiatives across physical production, distribution, and retail sites

☐ **Environmental Management & Sustainability** to provide best practices, guidance, and alignment across the organization

☐ **Marketing** to communicate the initiatives and their impact to broader stakeholders

☐ **Finance** to build business cases with multi-year returns and cross-departmental benefits

---

Dependencies/Intersection Points

☐ **Products & Services**: Designing products with circular principles is synergistic with circular operations, meaning that for a product to be "circular" the processes and conditions to produce it must also be circular, and likewise, circular operations help make circular products.

☐ **Culture & Organization**: Making holistic operational changes requires embedding circularity into decisions and behaviors, such as by incorporating renewable and circularity principles into the procurement criteria and processes.

☐ **Ecosystem**: Sourcing renewable and circular inputs and selling excess waste to other industries require ecosystem development to ensure there are enough suppliers and cost-effective options and buyers to scale circular models across operations.

Notes

1. ABInBev, "Sustainability Is Our Business," https://www.ab-inbev.com/sustainability/2025-sustainability-goals.html (accessed August 9, 2019).
2. ABInBev, "We're Pushing Towards 100% Renewable Electricity with the Largest Unsubsidized Renewable Solar Deal in UK History," December 19, 2018, https://www.ab-inbev.com/news-media/news-stories/we-re-pushing-towards-100--renewable-electricity-with-the-larges.html (accessed August 9, 2019).
3. Newlight Technologies, "From Greenhouse Gas to Plastic," https://www.newlight.com/ (accessed August 9, 2019).
4. Carbon Trust, "Top Environmental Impact Reduction Performers Recognised at Carbon Trust Corporate Sustainability Summit," October 17, 2017, https://www.carbontrust.com/news/2017/10/carbon-trust-corporate-sustainability-summit-awards/ (accessed August 9, 2019).
5. Unilever, "Unilever Announces New Global Zero Waste to Landfill Achievement," February 9, 2016, https://www.unilever.com/news/press-releases/2016/Unilever-announces-new-global-zero-waste-to-landfill-achievement.html (accessed August 9, 2019).
6. Deborah Drew, "The Apparel Industry's Environmental Impact in 6 Graphics," World Resources Institute, 2017, https://www.wri.org/blog/2017/07/apparel-industrys-environmental-impact-6-graphics (accessed August 9, 2019).
7. Pamela Ravasio, "How Can We Stop Water from Becoming a Fashion Victim?" *The Guardian*, 2012, https://www.theguardian.com/sustainable-business/water-scarcity-fashion-industry (accessed August 9, 2019).

8. Rainwaterharvesting.org, "Rainwater Harvesting in Singapore," www.rainwaterharvesting.org/international/singapore.htm (accessed August 16, 2019).

9. Adele Peters, "In Its Quest to Decrease Water Use, Levi's Is Open Sourcing Production Methods," Fast Company, March 22, 2016, https://www.fastcompany.com/3057970/in-its-quest-to-decrease-water-use-levis-is-open-sourcing-production-methods (accessed August 16, 2019).

10. Unilever, "Sustainable Living," https://www.hul.co.in/sustainable-living/ (accessed August 16, 2019).

11. Ecolab "Indian Steel Producer Forges Ahead with Water Savings," https://en-uk.ecolab.com/stories/indian-steel-producer-forges-ahead-with-water-savings (accessed August 30, 2019).

12. Ecolab, "Supporting Asia's Data Centre Growth with Sustainable Water Use," https://en-nz.ecolab.com/stories/ap-data-center (accessed August 30, 2019).

13. Ioannis Ioannou and George Serafeim, "Yes, Sustainability Can Be a Strategy," Harvard Business Review, 2019, https://hbr.org/2019/02/yes-sustainability-can-be-a-strategy (accessed August 9, 2019).

14. Metsä Group, "Sustainable and Resource-Efficient Bioeconomy Enables Circular Economy," 2019, https://www.metsagroup.com/en/Sustainability/bioeconomy/Sivut/default.aspx (accessed August 9, 2019).

15. Caroline Donnelly, "Google Deepmind Doubles Down on AI-led Efforts to Improve Datacentre Energy Efficiency," Computer Weekly, 2018, https://www.computerweekly.com/news/252447126/Google-Deepmind-doubles-down-on-AI-led-efforts-to-improve-datacentre-energy-efficiency (accessed August 9, 2019).

16. Mich Dearborn, "One Chip at a Time: How One Engineer's Innovation Has Ford Now Recycling 20 Million Pounds of Aluminum a Month," Ford Media Center, April 21, 2017, https://media.ford.com/content/fordmedia/fna/us/en/news/2017/04/21/ford-recycling-20-million-pounds-of-aluminum-monthly.html (accessed August 16, 2019).

17. Edwin Lopez and Jennifer McKevitt, "Ford's New Closed-Loop Systems Help It Recycle 23% More Aluminum into Its Trucks," Supply Chain Dive, April 26, 2017, https://www.supplychaindive.com/news/fords-new-closed-loop-systems-help-it-recycle-23-more-aluminum-into-its-t/441124/ (accessed August 16, 2019).

18. Nielsen, "Global Consumers Seek Companies That Care About Environmental Issues," 2018, https://www.nielsen.com/eu/en/insights/article/2018/global-consumers-seek-companies-that-care-about-environmental-issues/ (accessed August 9, 2019).

19. Sydney Ember, "Super Bowl 50, Analyzing the Ads," The New York Times, https://www.nytimes.com/interactive/projects/cp/media/super-bowl-50-commercials (accessed August 16, 2019).

20. Colgate US, "Colgate #EveryDropCounts," Youtube Video, 0:30, Posted January 22, 2016, https://www.youtube.com/watch?v=z5Ar0eCp6uE (accessed August 16, 2019).

21. Edie Newsroom, "World's Largest Brewer Saves £50m Through Sustainability Strategy," 2017, www.edie.net/news/7/World-s-largest-brewer-saves--60m-through-sustainability-strategy-/ (accessed August 9, 2019).

22. PR newswire, "Anheuser-Busch and Enel Green Power Announce Renewable Energy Partnership," 2017, www.prnewswire.com/news-releases/anheuser-busch-and-enel-green-power-announce-renewable-energy-partnership-300518935.html (accessed August 9, 2019).

23. RE100, "AB InBev Takes Step Forward on Renewables as Budweiser Announces Renewable Electricity Label," 2018, http://there100.org/news/14270244 (accessed August 9, 2019).

24. Enevo, "Welcome to a New Era of Waste Solutions," https://www.enevo.com/ (accessed August 16, 2019).

25. SKF, "Optimizing Rotating Equipment," https://www.skf.com/group/services/services-and-solutions/internet-of-things/2025-outlook-optimizing-maintenance-with-iot.html (accessed August 16, 2019).

26. Business Europe, "DyeCoo's Water-Free and Process-Chemical Free-Dyeing Technology for Textiles," February 15, 2019, http://www.circulary.eu/project/dyecoo/ (accessed August 9, 2019).

27. Carbon Engineering, "Direct Air Capture," https://carbonengineering.com/about-dac/ (accessed August 30, 2019).

28. Andrew Winston, George Favaloro and Tim Healy, "Energy Strategy for the C-Suite," *Harvard Business Review*, 2017, https://hbr.org/2017/01/energy-strategy-for-the-c-suite (accessed August 30, 2019).

29. Anglo American," 2018 Sustainability Report," 2018, https://www.angloamerican.com/~/media/Files/A/Anglo-American-PLC-V2/documents/annual-updates-2019/aa-sustainability-report-2018.pdf (accessed August 9, 2019).

30. Kevin Moss, "3 Ways Businesses Can Lead the Transition to a Low-Carbon Economy," World Resources Institute, 2019, https://www.wri.org/blog/2019/05/3-ways-businesses-can-lead-transition-low-carbon-economy (accessed August 9, 2019).

31. Adele Peters, "This Brewery Is Designed as a Model for the Circular Economy," Fast Company, 2018, https://www.fastcompany.com/40536868/this-brewery-is-designed-as-a-model-for-the-circular-economy (accessed August 9, 2019).

32. Harry Hotze, "ITA Spotlight: Coyote Logistics," Illinois Technology Association, 2017, https://www.illinoistech.org/news/379146/ITA-Spotlight-Coyote-Logistics.htm (accessed August 9, 2019).

33. Coyote, "Cheers to 900,000 Empty Miles Eliminated in 2018," 2019, https://resources.coyote.com/case-studies/900k-empty-miles-eliminated-in-2018 (accessed August 9, 2019).
34. Anne Canright, "Pop-Up Wetlands: A Success Story," Breakthroughs, 2014, https://nature.berkeley.edu/breakthroughs/fa14/pop-up-wetlands (accessed August 9, 2019).

18

 **Products & Services**

Companies are largely defined by their products and services. It's how they are best known by consumers, employees, and investors; it's often how businesses are organized internally; and it's how corporate performance is usually measured. As a result, transforming those offerings, especially legacy products, to incorporate circularity can be quite complex.

What does it actually mean to bring circularity into an organization's portfolio of offerings? It requires companies to design and develop products and services with no waste. Ideally, a circular product would be (1) designed for indefinite reuse, (2) created only with circular or sustainable materials, (3) kept in useful life for as long as possible, and (4) able to be disassembled into materials or components that could be brought back into a value chain (either its own or another's) at the end of use at the highest possible value (e.g., returned to feedstock instead of used for energy). Simply put, in true circularity, products and materials are indefinitely used and recirculated in a closed-loop system. While simple in concept, though, accomplishing true circularity is an enormous undertaking, requiring a complete shift away from the current linear consumption model.

Four Areas of Focus

Taking the steps to create circular products and services can, at first, seem like an overwhelming task. But we can break the process down into more manageable pieces by considering the four key stages of a product's lifecycle: design, use, use extension, and end of use (see Table 18.1).

© The Author(s) 2020
P. Lacy et al., *The Circular Economy Handbook*,
https://doi.org/10.1057/978-1-349-95968-6_18

P. Lacy et al.

Table 18.1 Four areas of focus

Focus area	The toolbox	Products & Services in action
Design	The conception, planning, and building of a circular product or service. The aim is to redesign products to use less resource-intensive, single-use materials, and to extend their use. The process can also enable the repurposing of products at end of use to deliver value beyond their first usage	Furniture company Steelcase is incorporating recycled content into products like their new Think desk chair, which also has improved durability, versatility and "timeless appeal" to encourage a longer life. The product also has fewer parts so that it can more easily be re-purposed or taken apart at end of use[1]
Use	Maximizing the value delivered through the *single use* of a circular product or service in its *original form*. The aim is to leverage a Product as a Service or Sharing Platforms model to maximize product utilization	Tire manufacturer Michelin has more than 500,000 commercial fleet vehicles enrolled in its tire leasing program, which optimizes the management and fuel efficiency of tires in use via real-time traceability of vehicle data[2]
Use extension	Maximizing the value delivered through *multiple uses* of a circular product or service in its *original form*. Initiatives in this area include extending the use of products through the Product Use Extension business model, i.e., maintenance or repair services, or through reselling them on a secondary market	In 2018, outdoor clothing company The North Face launched a "Renewed" collection of refurbished products sourced from returned, defective, or damaged apparel[3]
End of use	Maximizing the value delivered through *multiple uses* of a circular product or service in *any form*. This might include identifying circular uses for waste at end of use and repurposing it by recycling (or upcycling) as well as by creating or supporting a secondary materials market	British multinational retailer Marks & Spencer is using its own waste from wine production to create and commercialize a new skincare product line[4]

It's important to note that all four stages are closely interlinked, and mature companies should address all aspects of the product lifecycle in this way. For example, a shift to a sharing or leasing business model may affect the *use* of a product, which then has implications for *design,* such that the product must be made more durable and be easily maintained and repaired. Oftentimes, sensors or other devices will be needed to track the product's use or condition to allow for predictive maintenance and repair. Similarly, to recover products and materials at *end of use* for repurposing or remanufacturing, companies must consider the *design* of those products so that they can be easily disassembled or made with materials that can be effectively recycled or reused. Further, increasing the recoverability of *end of use* might be achieved through a Product as a Service business model that will affect the *use* and ownership of those products.

Thinking holistically across these four stages will enable companies to move beyond "products with circular attributes" to truly "circular products" and that transformation will involve either an open- or closed-loop system (see "Open Versus Closed Loop"). In addition, leaders need to think about their products relative to the other three circular dimensions (Operations, Culture & Organization, and Ecosystem) that are described in this book. For example, once companies have tackled operations, they tend to shift their focus toward their product portfolios. But products and services could also be a starting point for multi-category and consumer-facing firms, such as general retailers, that are looking to engage consumers and test the demand for and business value of circular concepts.

 Open Versus Closed Loops

Circular pathways for products and materials can either be "closed loop" (in which the waste from one product is collected and recycled into the same new product, e.g., aluminum cans that are recycled directly back into new cans, over and over again) or "open loop" (in which one industry's waste becomes the raw input to another, e.g., US coffee company Starbucks' spent coffee being used as fertilizer).[5] We are often asked whether closed-loop applications are inherently better than open-loop ones. The answer is, it depends.

Closed-loop applications are perceived as inherently better than open-loop ones. If materials or components are indefinitely brought back into a value chain, then it should reduce product costs, reduce or eliminate non-renewable resource use, and protect against potential supply shortages. However, with a closed loop, companies might be more limited with respect to the products, parts, or materials that can actually be fed back into the same product. Bringing products and materials back into systems at scale requires the right economics, collection infrastructure, consumer incentives, and technical capability. As we saw in the industry profiles, most industries are still working to overcome these barriers, and as a result, there are few examples of closed-loop products or materials today. For instance, not one product currently meets the Cradle to Cradle™ Platinum certification requirement—a system that evaluates products across five quality categories (material health, materials reutilization, renewable energy and carbon management, water stewardship, and social fairness).[6]

With an open loop, companies might be able to find feasible applications of their "waste," as it becomes a valuable feedstock for another system. However, the downside is that most open-loop applications today involve downgrading of the product or material into less-valuable solutions, and therefore, they are not *truly* circular. That said, we believe that open-loop applications could be "as good" and potentially even more impactful than closed-loop applications, but the *entire* system has to be made "closed." This would require suppliers of circular inputs as well as customers to have circular ecosystems also designed to collect and reuse products in a circular way. In this respect, creating an effective open-loop ecosystem is much more complex, but can be more rewarding in its spillover impact to other companies and industries.

Consider waste-to-resource company Continuus Materials, for example, which has developed a proprietary system to process municipal and post-industrial waste streams into a fully recyclable product. EVERBOARD™ is an extremely durable, moisture, and mold-resistant building panel that is superior in performance compared to conventional building materials, yet is priced at parity. By utilizing end-of-use materials and producing the upcycled board in the same location, the company created a truly circular ecosystem that converts locally collected waste into locally distributed, high-performance building materials. Continuus Materials' CEO, Chris Riley, speaks to the potential for ecosystem-level impact: "Our solutions bring together two of the largest material industries out there, waste and building materials. The building materials industry is one of the few that has the capacity to absorb a significant portion of the waste being generated" (Fig. 18.1).

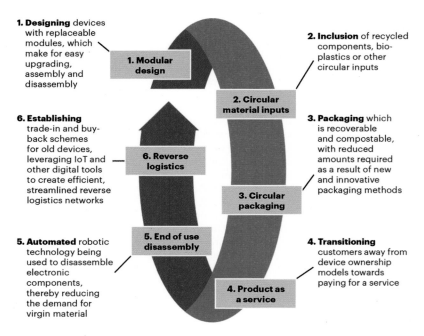

1. Designing devices with replaceable modules, which make for easy upgrading, assembly and disassembly

1. Modular design

2. Inclusion of recycled components, bioplastics or other circular inputs

2. Circular material inputs

6. Establishing trade-in and buy-back schemes for old devices, leveraging IoT and other digital tools to create efficient, streamlined reverse logistics networks

6. Reverse logistics

3. Packaging which is recoverable and compostable, with reduced amounts required as a result of new and innovative packaging methods

3. Circular packaging

5. Automated robotic technology being used to disassemble electronic components, thereby reducing the demand for virgin material

5. End of use disassembly

4. Transitioning customers away from device ownership models towards paying for a service

4. Product as a service

Fig. 18.1 An illustrative closed-loop product

Making the Pivot

To get started, companies should select initiatives by focusing on the products and materials in their portfolio with the greatest potential for driving value through circularity. Numerous factors must be considered, including market trends, customer readiness, and broader strategic priorities. A company facing increased competition and heightened consumer scrutiny, for example, may choose to prioritize initiatives that will enhance the value proposition for customer acquisition and retention, such as through circular products or models that link to loyalty programs. Take, for example, the heightened public focus on single-use plastics. Companies in the FMCG, retail, or food services industries may put at the top of the list initiatives with the greatest exposure to a downstream consumer audience, such as pivoting to plastics-free or circular packaging. To that end, German chemical and consumer goods company Henkel is aiming for 100% of its packaging to be recyclable, reusable, or compostable by 2025.[7] On the other hand, a firm that is focused on cost reduction may prioritize circular initiatives that reduce the costs of goods sold, such as through minimizing the amount of material in a product.

Two other crucial factors are the available technologies and infrastructure maturity essential to circularity, and both affect the phasing of near-term initiatives versus longer-term, strategic investments. Some opportunities, such as substituting a recycled or alternative input into a product, may be relatively easy to scale across the existing value chain. Contrast that with larger transitions to entirely new business models and product portfolios. Those approaches may demand substantial investments in technology and infrastructure, but they can also open doors to considerable future growth. Essity, a global hygiene and health company that is one of the world's largest tissue manufacturers, is investing approximately $40 million in the technology to produce pulp from alternative fiber that comes from plant-based agricultural by-products instead of conventional wood-based pulp. The process will enable a reduction in the use of water, energy, and chemicals, while the by-product of the integrated pulping process can be further refined to serve as a substitute for oil-based chemicals.[8]

The scale and size of an organization will further affect how it can (and should) roll out circular initiatives. A large organization may choose to start with a particular region, product line, or brand to pilot initiatives, targeting segments that are most likely to value circular models. For example, automakers have typically focused on the appeal of their EV models to already sustainability-minded customers. But organizations shouldn't stop there. Once they have successfully "proven" their circular products and services, they can then focus on value chain efficiencies to enable broader portfolio transition.

A Circular Journey: Use Extension

In general, companies tend to advance through several steps of maturity when building circular portfolios: first taking stock of their existing products and services (see "Taking Stock"), then identifying and piloting opportunities, and eventually transforming the entire business and portfolio to be circular. The journey may involve a dramatic change in how a company operates. "We are transforming our business model, for example in switching technology, from 'we sell you a box, then we come back in three years and try to sell you an upgrade' to 'we sell you technology in a subscription model and enable you to maximize the value to your business'. In this model, the physical product will have a significantly longer lifecycle," explains John Kern, Senior Vice President of Supply Chain Operations at Cisco.

Products & Services initiatives get to the heart of circularity, cutting across the value chain—from rethinking design and material development, to reuse, and finally to recycling back into the system at end of use (see Table 18.2). And they also depend on whether a company is beginning its journey or is well along the path toward circularity. As just one example, consider the focus area of use extension, which has two major types of initiatives that companies can pursue. The first is to *extend product use through repair or maintenance activities*. This can be accomplished by raising awareness and by providing product support services that will increase customer value and loyalty, improve the brand, and generate additional sources of revenue. Patagonia, for instance, through its "anti-growth" approach and efforts like the "Don't Buy This Jacket" campaign, informs consumers on the effects of their purchases. The US clothing company designs products specifically using high-quality materials, which in turn enable effective repair and reuse. And this ultimately has helped Patagonia gain deeper knowledge of its customer needs. "Our focus on repairability has helped us understand the hidden challenges in fixing an issue, which we have shared with the design team to ensure new garments are designed with repairability in mind, hence closing the feedback loop," says Rick Ridgeway, Patagonia's VP of Public Engagement.

Table 18.2 Illustrative characteristics of increasing company maturity

🌿	Emerging	Established	Leading	Ultimate	Maturity journey: from → to
Design	• Conducting assessment of the current lifecycles of materials and their resource footprints • Identifying recycling opportunities with current product/service components	• Using innovative designs of products/ services aimed to enhance circularity • Leveraging locally sourced recyclable/ biodegradable materials where possible • Targeting waste leakages for redesign	• Using large-scale modularity in product offerings • Achieving 100% material reutilization (e.g., Cradle to Cradle™ platinum certified) • Deploying technologies to scale new offerings	• Making the transition to Product as a Service for a circular customer relationship • Designing entire portfolio of services with circularity at the forefront • Achieving a portfolio of 100% modular products from 100% circular materials	• xFrom conducting lifecycle assessments on current offerings to an entire portfolio designed with circularity at the forefront • Actions include: (1) identifying resource-intensive materials/ products and redesigning using circular inputs, (2) re-evaluating product design process to deliver value beyond single use, (3) designing components that extend value delivery within the current lifespan
Use	• Offering largely single-use products/ services • Identifying the scope for reuse of products possible through sharing initiatives • Having negative externalities still occurring through use (e.g., carbon emissions)	• Implementing some initiatives to reuse existing products (e.g., via sharing/ leasing model) • Mitigating against negative externalities	• Aiming for 100% utilization of offering • Extending lifecycle to facilitate rotation to Product as a Service offerings • Using technology to enable scale-up across the business • Reducing negative externalities to little or none	• Leveraging the Sharing Platforms or Product as a Service models to maximize product utilization in the *full* product portfolio • Closing the loop across all business lines • Achieving zero negative externalities	• From identifying reuse opportunities within a portfolio consisting of mostly single-use products to maximizing product utilization and closing the loop across all business lines • Actions include: (1) leveraging a sharing network/subscription/ leasing model for product use, (2) leveraging technology to improve current service offering

(continued)

Table 18.2 (continued)

	Emerging	Established	Leading	Ultimate	Maturity journey: from → to
Use extension	• Offering largely single-use products/services • Providing little/no repair maintenance services	• Extending lifecycle through the collection and resell market • Providing repair/maintenance services (e.g., large-scale corporate repair services)	• Making technologically enabled repair services available to all consumers • Engaging with consumers at a high level to encourage circular behaviors	• Designing all products for use by multiple users • Reinforcing durability branding with lifetime guarantee for all products/services	• From lack of repair or maintenance services to durable products with a lifetime guarantee • Actions include: (1) optimizing product use and performance through awareness raising and support services, (2) selling products through a resale distribution and retail platform
End of use	• Identifying opportunities for material recyclability • Tracking material flow to landfill disposal	• Extending waste collection/capture across the supply chain • Leveraging an existing platform/secondary material market	• Capturing and allocating all internal waste back into the supply chain or into revenue generation from the material market • Using technology and sharing platforms to scale up the secondary materials market	• Eliminating all net material leakages across the value chain • Capturing and recycling all waste materials continuously	• From monitoring waste to landfill to eliminating leakage across the value chain in a closed material loop • Actions include: (1) identifying circular uses of waste at the end of the product/service lifecycle and adapting for remanufacture/recycling/upcycling, (2) creating or supporting a secondary market for materials model

	Emerging	Established	Leading	Ultimate	Maturity journey: from → to
Overall takeaways	• Can be tackled on an ad hoc basis with specific budget allocated to business units/supply chain hotspots • Good for companies looking to grow their core business through innovative and improved product/service offerings	• Investment capacity (grown through cost reductions in supply chain hotspots—see Chapter 17) can be leveraged to venture into new business areas/models such as Product as a Service	• True product circularity requires design rethinking and significant budget allocation, fostered by innovative ways of working that are encouraged and rewarded (see Chapter 19)—key for companies to scale new growth areas and business	• In ultimate circularity, the full portfolio of products and materials are indefinitely used and recirculated in a closed-loop system, requiring meaningful integration of initiatives across design, use, use extension, and end of use	• Circular products and services start with designs embedding circular principles and ways of working but are ultimately realized with the use of technology (particularly digital innovations like cloud computing, big data, and mobile devices) to bring and scale those designs to market

The second type of initiative is to *extend product use through resale*, often in secondary markets. An example would be equipment manufacturer Komatsu's program for retrofitting and reselling used mining and construction machinery (see Chapter 9 for more detail).[9] In another example, JCB India Ltd., a manufacturer and supplier of heavy construction machines, extends product uses through its "Recon Care" engine recovery and recycling program.[10]

Using either approach, the goal is to ultimately extend use across all products and services. In doing so, companies need to facilitate the extended use of products and collection for reselling via technology enablement, collection programs, and resale platforms.

 Top Tip: Taking Stock

To better manage the circular transformation of a product portfolio, most companies start off with a prioritization exercise that zeroes in on the offerings and business models to focus on first. This process could be embedded within the broader circular opportunity assessment and strategy (discussed in Part III, "How to Make a Circular Pivot"), or it could be conducted as a separate analysis that specifically looks closely at Products & Services. The exercise may contain the following four basic steps:

1. **Conduct a product inventory**: Assess your current portfolio and truly understand all of the materials being used in its creation and service, including water, energy, feedstock, etc. The goal is to identify where there are areas of greatest resource intensity and waste leakage and to be aware of the lifecycles of the materials used. A baseline analysis can help determine where your biggest needs and opportunities are—for example, products that have significant water footprints, that rely on single-use plastics, that are highly underutilized, that tend to be discarded prematurely, or that have valuable materials that have ended up in a landfill. The analysis can lead to the redesign, re-formulation, or discarding of a product altogether. When Unilever conducted a full portfolio assessment in 2017, the company found that its "Sustainable Living Brands" grew 50% faster than the rest of the business and that some of its least sustainable products were actually performing the worst financially. Insights like these drive portfolio growth and rationalization decisions, not only identifying items to discontinue but also uncovering opportunities to double down on products and processes that may unknowingly already be sustainable. Just a year later, Unilever's Sustainable Living Brands were delivering 75% of the company's growth.[11]

2. **Map products and models to circular opportunities**: Once the initial inventory is completed, you can then begin identifying and mapping circular materials, business models, and services against the current portfolio. IKEA, for instance, took products like a sofa as a starting point, identified wasted

lifecycles as an opportunity and then figured out how circular models (e.g., second sale, replacing the slipcover, or refurbishing services) can be applied over the product's age to create value from increased lifecycle revenues. Some products might be great candidates for recycled plastics, alternative materials, or the use of renewable energy options. EkoPlaza, a Dutch supermarket chain, has been able to use alternative biodegradable packaging to help eliminate the use of plastics in more than 700 items, including yogurts, snacks, fresh fruit, and vegetables.[12] Other products might be better suited for service models. Case in point: automobiles, which have a long useful life but low utilization rate.

3. **Assess and prioritize opportunities**: After the portfolio mapping has been completed, you should assess your opportunities against a set of criteria. These will typically be some mix of strategic, organizational, and market factors, such as:

   - Urgency—How important is it to change the consumption model for this product and what are the impacts of its material and/or resource inputs?
   - Strategic fit—Does the opportunity align with your strategic direction and competitive differentiators?
   - Capability fit—Do you have the required skills, systems, and processes necessary to pursue the opportunity?
   - Technical feasibility—Do the technologies and infrastructure exist that will enable you to pursue the opportunity at scale and cost-effectively?
   - Customer demand—Do customers' value owning the product or do they value the utility of the product?

Some opportunities might be prioritized as quick wins if they are technically feasible and on trend with customer preferences and interests (e.g., subscription services for fashion). Other opportunities might currently be less feasible but could warrant strategic long-term investments in new supply chains and ecosystems (e.g., the mining of returned appliances and electronics).

4. **Develop the business case**: You now need to develop a viable business case, which should include specifics of the customer value proposition and targeted customer segments. You should develop your concept for the new product, service, or business model in detail in order to calculate the investment needs (e.g., for people, R&D, etc.), operational costs (added costs or savings), and expected revenues (e.g., from recurring service revenue, resale, or premium potential). A valuation of the circular initiatives will inform their sequencing and prioritization and enable the tracking of financial, social, and environmental benefits (e.g., landfill diversion, emissions reduction, or job creation). Ecolab, which provides water, hygiene and energy solutions to the food, energy, healthcare, industrial and hospitality markets, has worked with paper clients to reuse recycled fiber without compromising strength and quality for the papermaker. Ecolab Chairman and CEO Doug Baker speaks to financial return as a driver: "The best results have the lowest total operating costs, and must have high returns for the business as well as the environment."

The Value Drivers

Transforming your product and service portfolio to circularity is crucial to remain competitive in a consumer-conscious and resource-constrained world. As we discussed in the previous chapter, circularity will help a business effectively manage and utilize the materials and resources it needs within its operations. But circular products and services go one step further: Building a circular portfolio will ultimately reduce a company's exposure to risk and drive long-term growth and profitability. Simply put, circular products and services allow nearly limitless consumption, as growth is no longer constrained by resource availability or environmental impact.

Revenue Generation: Shifting to circular products and services can offer tremendous opportunities for revenue growth. For instance, the Dutch multinational Philips has been able to create value from moving toward a circular portfolio for revenue growth. In 2018, green and circular revenues amounted to 64 and 12% of the company's sales, respectively.[13] Philips' initiatives included the following: SmartPath, an economical way to upgrade existing Philips systems to current standards while enhancing capacities; the Diamond Select portfolio of refurbished healthcare systems, which provides customers with state-of-the-art technology at more affordable prices; and Lumify, a flexible subscription service that provides access to ultrasound transducers, apps, and an online ecosystem, all at reduced upfront costs to customers. Philips believes a shift to circular business models has the potential to generate significant value, both for customers and for the company itself. Long-term partnership with customers creates win-win situations in which the customers get better service and outcomes, while the company has a longer-lasting and thus more predictable revenue stream.

Cost Savings: Circularity can also drive waste out of the product design and production stages to make leaner products, reducing raw material costs. And some companies have obtained additional savings by using their own recycled materials as raw input. Over half of the recycled plastic that Dell is using in its products is coming from the company's own closed-loop supply chain, which amounts to 13.7 million pounds of recycled plastics. John Pflueger, Principal Environmental Strategist at Dell, explains: "We decided to close the loop on plastics versus selling it back to the market and that resulted in $2 million in cost savings so far. It also boosted our brand recognition, enabled a dialogue with our customers, and allowed us to innovate with partners as more people started to realize the possibilities of the circular economy."

⚠️ **Risk Reduction:** Circularity can help shield a company against forthcoming government regulations on materials and products. Under Waste Electrical and Electronic Equipment (WEEE) regulations in the UK, retailers must now provide a free method for customers to dispose of their old household electronic equipment whenever they sell a new version of that product. If a company doesn't have its own takeback service, it must join the Distributor Takeback Scheme.[14] And it's not just electronics products that are being regulated. EPR policies, which we'll explore more in the "Role of Policymakers" section, are also being introduced for lower-value items like plastic bottles, potentially holding manufacturers responsible for preventing plastic waste from entering landfills and the natural environment. Industries across the board are feeling the pressure toward circularity. For instance, the EU has banned more than 1300 chemicals from cosmetic products that are known or suspected to be hazardous to health.[15] In addition, the EU Cosmetics Directive requires the pre-market safety assessments of cosmetics, mandatory registration of cosmetic products, and government authorization for the use of nanomaterials. It has also prohibited animal testing for cosmetic purposes.[15] We expect these types of regulations to become more widespread in the future, given recent trends.

Another huge concern is the availability of resources. As discussed in Chapter 1, we are already using more resources than the earth is able to regenerate. Because circularity can potentially help a company establish an indefinite supply of raw inputs, it can safeguard against the risk of a resource "running out" and protect against commodity price volatility (most commodity prices spiked in the first quarter of 2019).

🏷️ **Brand Enhancement:** Circularity will also protect against market loss as consumers continue to care more about the environment and change their purchasing behaviors accordingly. Across the board, we are seeing an increased customer preference not only for greater sustainability, but also for circular products and materials, which will drive brand value and protect market share. In fact, a recent Accenture survey indicated that 75% of consumers *want* to buy more environmentally friendly products.[16] And the same survey found that 83% believe it's important or extremely important for companies to design products that are meant to be reused or recycled.[12]

Case Study: IKEA

IKEA is trialling strategies to fundamentally transition its model to be more circular and shift the consumption model for how consumers buy and use furniture. IKEA has progressed from designing for recyclability to enabling a circular flow of materials to fostering a culture of recycling among its customers. Throughout this ongoing journey, the company has evolved from an emerging circular company to a leading organization. Early on that journey, IKEA developed an approach for identifying and prioritizing materials that were of the most value for recycling from an environmental perspective and that effort resulted in the selection of a total of over 25 materials as suitable for circular resource chains.[17]

Next, the company incentivized customers to return old IKEA furniture and textiles via reward mechanisms and set up the collection infrastructure to enable the reverse flow of its products. For instance, customers can email photos of their old IKEA furniture so that it can be assessed for recyclability. They can then drop off their used or broken damaged IKEA furniture at the store and receive a voucher for the value of the old furniture in return. IKEA then re-sells these used products at a fraction of the original price. In 2018, dedicated "Recovery" teams at IKEA franchisee Ingka Group repaired and repacked 8.7 million damaged products to be re-sold instead of going to waste.[18] Given IKEA's scale, if concepts such as these are extended across the business, they could have an enormous impact via reducing end-of-use waste.

More recently, IKEA announced it will begin leasing furniture-as-a-service, representing a significant shift from the traditional model, which could prolong the product lifespan. This year, the company also launched a new circular store, which includes learning dedicated space for customers to learn about product use extension, upcycling and reducing waste. Through such efforts, IKEA is bringing customers on their journey to becoming a circular and climate positive business.

Technology as an Enabler

Technological innovations have been a linchpin in the circular economy, and perhaps nowhere is that more evident than in the products and services they've enabled. The examples are as varied as they are numerous.

In the design stage, circular inputs are made possible by breakthroughs in physical and biological technologies, such as via material innovation (e.g., plant-based coatings that extend product use or bio-based materials that are compostable at end-of-life) and process innovation (e.g., 3D printing technologies that can create modular products, use fewer materials, and result in less waste, or biological technologies that enable waterless dying). Tarkett, a flooring solutions company, for instance, has developed a modular carpet tile that uses recycled material from waste windshields and safety glass.[19] Advances in materials science have also opened up new possibilities to design for recyclability. Henkel is working with its supplier Ampacet Corporation to develop an innovative solution for black plastic packaging that is fully recyclable. While black plastic has long been unrecyclable (due to the carbon black pigment), the new packaging material will use an alternative carbon-free black color, enabling used bottles to be integrated back into the value chain.[20]

IoT, advanced analytics, and various other digital technologies can also help companies optimize product lifetime performance, reduce negative environmental externalities, and enable new business models for product use extension. For example, digital direct-to-consumer technologies are extending the life of products by enabling rental models, sharing platforms, and marketplaces. For example, Stuffstr offers a platform for people to instantly sell back any item purchased from participating retailers. Using the retailer's app or website, the customer is presented with an instant buy-back price on every item and can sell items back simply by tapping a button. When the customer is ready, Stuffstr provides free, same-day pickup and pays the customer using store credit the moment the items are received. An important element of the model is Stuffstr's algorithm for calculating the offer prices, which uses artificial intelligence to project the items' resale value and then estimates the costs of collecting and processing the items.[21]

To further capture product end-of-use opportunities, companies have embraced a host of digital, physical, and biological technologies. For example, robotics can automate the sorting and disassembly of products, while advanced analytics and backbone data engines can help track and optimize the valuation and direction of reverse product and material flows. IoT can also be deployed to increase product recovery and recycling. Information company Hewlett-Packard Inc. (HP), for example, has deployed a Product as a Service business model with connected printers that automatically requests replacement ink cartridges before customers need them. The used cartridges are then mailed to HP for refilling as part of a closed-loop system of recycling, and the subscription service charges a monthly fee for performance (number of pages printed) rather than for the amount of ink used.[22]

Leading Practices to Drive Transformation

In our research, we encountered a number of companies that have made significant progress in their journey toward creating and growing circular product portfolios. We collated our learnings from those leading firms to glean insights into how they achieved their success.

Reinvent Supply Chains

Scaling circular Products & Services initiatives often requires setting up entirely new supply chains. Supplier engagement is a key starting point, and leading companies tend to collaborate closely with their suppliers to develop and source ideas that will enable the reengineering of circular products.

It's not just an issue of selecting the right partners. It's also a matter of establishing the right dependencies and enabling more open communication among them. As John Kern from Cisco explains, "We need to have enough suppliers that can reprocess and find renewable inputs. Industry marketplaces can be game-changing for taking one industry's waste and putting it into another's material flow." A case in point is GemChina, which focuses on the large amounts of battery and e-waste being created by the electronics and electric vehicle (EV) markets. The company's technology enables the recycling of scrapped lithium batteries from EVs, extracting the nickel, cobalt, and other important resources, transforming them into materials that can then be fed back into the supply chains of battery producers like Samsung SDI and Ecopro Co Ltd.[23] To date, GemChina has the highest used-battery recycling capacity in China, processing more than 10% of the total waste battery, or about 300,000 tons, per year.[24]

Establishing a new supply chain is one thing; getting it to scale is more daunting. The use of a shared infrastructure can help. Loop, a new zero-waste platform for consumer products launched by TerraCycle, enables circular flows between brands and consumers. The recently launched initiative already offers about 300 items—from Tide detergent to Pantene shampoo and Häagen-Dazs ice cream to Crest mouthwash—all in reusable packaging. After using the products, customers put the empty containers in a Loop tote on their doorstep. The tote is then picked up by a delivery service and sent back to Loop where the containers are cleaned, sent to the manufacturer to be refilled, and shipped out to consumers again. "Loop echoes the convenience of disposability while solving for the negatives: waste disposal and degrading packaging quality," says Tom Szaky, CEO of TerraCycle. Loop is providing the infrastructure to enable the ambitions of major brands, such as Unilever. "We believe Loop will complement our existing efforts to create a plastic system that works and a packaging system that is truly circular by design," says David Blanchard, Unilever's Chief R&D Officer.[25]

Set Product Targets

Companies need to set long-term, ambitious targets related to Product and Service portfolios and then build a roadmap and plan for how to get there. Even the mere presence of the targets will help signal positive change to employees, suppliers, and the market. Establishing targets for circular portfolios and materials can take a number of different forms. Some goals, for example, may pertain to the use of circular materials. H&M Group set the target to use 100% recycled or other sustainably sourced materials for all its products by 2030, as part of its mission to become a fully circular and climate positive business.[26] Other goals are specific to a firm's product portfolio. As part of its commitments to reach zero waste in operations and use sustainable materials in core products and packaging by 2030, Danish toymaker Lego is focusing on developing fully bio-based materials. Another approach is to set goals for revenue growth through circular products and portfolios. Veolia has a 2020 target to generate more than €3.8 billion in revenue in the circular economy.[27] A number of companies have gone a step further by setting goals at the product level. According to James Quincey, Chairman and CEO of The Coca-Cola Company, "It goes up and down the chain. When we set targets, we don't set them just for the company, we set them for the products that are an ecosystem of many companies."

While setting any type of product target, companies should consider the following: (a) potential barriers and requirements to achieving those goals, e.g., the required collection infrastructure or recycling technologies, and (b) potential unintended consequences and considerations of solution-specific goals. For instance, if a company intends to double down on the use of bio-plastics, it needs to ensure that the appropriate infrastructure and processes are in place to avoid contamination of recycling streams.

Focus on Customer Centricity

Leading circular companies are adept at engaging the consumer in the circular experience and value proposition. The public has a heightened sensitivity toward sustainability, climate change, and general social awareness that provides brands with an opportunity to differentiate on environmental and social performance. However, that may not always be the case, as customers are not yet broadly basing purchasing decisions on circular economy ideals, so it is important to shape circular propositions that appeal to conventional value drivers, such as affordability, convenience, or product performance. Therefore, leaders are catering circular offers to different customer segments and communicating the value proposition so that customers understand what makes circular products and models better *for them*.

Adam Lowry, co-founder of method and Ripple Foods, created two brands that highly resonate with consumers for both their sustainability *and* their product attribute values. "The reason method is the largest green cleaning brand is that it created mainstream demand for sustainably designed products," explains Lowry. "A lot of people liked how it looked in their homes." With Ripple Foods, which we'll explore more in the next section, Lowry's goal was to win on taste and nutrition, in addition to its environmental benefit.

Brands are also differentiating the consumer experience at the end of the product's use, such as by enabling their used products to "go to good" rather than landfill. For instance, US women's clothing retailer Ascena Retail Group has partnered with Give Back Box to allow customers to print a free shipping label from its website to donate clothing and accessories. As of 2017, customers and associates have donated more than 6000 boxes to charities such as Goodwill and the Salvation Army.[28]

Design Innovatively

Leading companies agree that one of the most important—and challenging—tasks is to integrate circular economy principles into portfolio planning and design from the outset. Indeed, from material and ingredient choice to design specifications that extend product use and enhance recoverability, circular thinking must be incorporated way upstream to achieve the best outcomes. International Flavors & Fragrances (IFF), for example, has been innovating to build a circular fragrance in accordance withCradle to Cradle™ certification criteria (which can be a useful framework to structure design principles and aspire toward external certification). These criteria apply to fragrance properties (e.g., no eco-toxins), manufacturing processes (e.g., the use of renewable feedstock), and design for end of use (e.g., biodegradable). To develop a circular fragrance, IFF went through its entire catalog of ingredients and screened them against the criteria to facilitate the design process.[29]

Oftentimes, small- and medium-size firms that have incorporated circularity as part of their core ethos are better positioned for circular innovation. Ripple Foods, for instance, has innovated a portfolio of nondairy milk substitutes made from peas, which are high in nutritional value, require significantly less water, and produce fewer GHG emissions than dairy or nut milks. According to founder and CEO, Adam Lowry, Ripple's goal from the start was to "design a non-dairy product with the best environmental and nutritional benefit." While many nut-based milk substitutes require large amounts of imported water and come in formats that lack protein, at its outset Ripple sought to solve the question: How do you create a nutritious product with a better environmental impact? They chose legumes since they don't require any nitrogen fertilizer (they are actually nitrogen fixers), and they are rotational crops (they grow where it rains). To top it off, the Ripple product has eight times the protein of almond milk.

Another example is feminine hygiene disruptor THINX, which has created "period-proof," absorbent and washable underwear and reusable tampons. By innovating the functionality of the product itself, THINX offers a solution that could virtually eliminate the need for single-use sanitary products, all of which go to landfill today (the company estimates that an individual uses nearly 20 sanitary products on average per cycle, equating to approximately 250–300 pounds of waste in a lifetime).[30]

Develop a Robust Reverse Logistics Capability

To close their loops, leading companies have either set up their own reverse logistics infrastructure or have collaborated with partners to provide that capability. H&M chose the first approach and introduced a full-scale garment-collection initiative across all its stores around the world. Thanks to that effort, the retailer was able to collect over 20,000 tons of textiles for reuse and recycling in 2018—the equivalent of 103 million T-shirts.[31] An example of the second approach (working with partners) is the "Collective Recycling Project," which has established a recycling network in Chile that aims to reduce waste and boost responsible disposal. The project started as a joint collaboration between Walmart Chile, Coca-Cola Chile, PepsiCo, Nestlé, and Unilever, with a goal to recycle 1200 metric tons of waste annually through five recycling centers in Santiago. That operation has now scaled to 15 centers managed by TriCiclos, which provides the companies with a monthly report with data on the waste collected. The companies, in turn, can use the information to redesign and improve their products and packaging.[32]

Collecting end-of-use products is a good first step, but it's also important to optimize the value of that return flow. This requires processes and systems to track and analyze return volumes, product types, flow paths, customer demand, and other important data to determine the right channels, to enable efficient product flows, and to maximize revenues. "We need information about which materials are available and their performance to enable a frictionless flow of materials, and we need the right technology infrastructure to connect buyers and sellers," explains Erika Chan, Director of Sustainability Services from Dell. It's important to note that, while waste strategies typically focus on a waste hierarchy (see Part I, "The Circular Business Models"), the highest value disposition may vary given internal (e.g., inventory levels) and external (e.g., market demand) conditions. Robust and dynamic return logistics systems can help optimize the flows of returned product to the right channels.

 Chapter Takeaways

- Companies can build circular product and service portfolios by focusing on initiatives across four key areas: design, use, use extension, and end of use.
- The initiative areas are closely interlinked and require holistic strategies across all four in order to ultimately create truly circular products that are used indefinitely with a zero (or ideally a net positive) impact.
- The journey to true circularity of products and services is complex. It may require setting up entirely new supply chains and completely new approaches to upfront product design and development.
- It also offers the greatest potential rewards as a driver of strategic growth, brand value, and customer engagement, as well as long-term competitiveness by lowering costs and ensuring an indefinite supply of raw inputs.
- Companies can take a stepped approach to prioritizing their circular product and services initiatives, focusing first on the opportunities with greatest strategic fit, market demand, and technical readiness.
- Achieving product circularity is enormously challenging and complex. It requires leadership, innovation, strong cross-functional alignment, and the creation of supporting ecosystems of suppliers and partners (discussed in detail in the next two chapters).

Transforming a company's product portfolio toward circularity is a massive undertaking. To increase the odds of success, executives need to conduct an honest assessment to gauge important factors in the organization's readiness for that transformation. The enterprise-wide survey should help identify the key areas of focus and determine the important technologies that will be required. The following checklist can help in that assessment.

Sample Questions to Answer

Identifying circular opportunities

☐ What materials are in my current products?

☐ Where are the areas of greatest resource intensity and waste leakage in my product and service portfolio (e.g., resource-intensive materials or processes)?

☐ Which required resources will face the most volatility, shortage risk, or future regulation?

☐ Which circular initiatives are most relevant for each product in my portfolio (given the product attributes, customers, and markets)?

☐ Where are there dependencies (e.g., design for repairability to enable as-a-service use models)?

Shaping your circular portfolio

☐ What circular initiatives align most with my company's strategy, strengths, and differentiators?

☐ Which of my customer segments will most value circular products and business models?

☐ Does our organization have the required skills, systems, and processes to pursue the opportunities?

☐ Does the technology and supply chain infrastructure exist to cost-effectively scale?

☐ What mix of initiatives will create the most value for my company today and in the future?

Realizing circular growth

☐ How can I shape meaningful and relevant value propositions for my customers?

☐ What is the business case and how will I measure and track both financial and broader societal and environmental benefits?

☐ How can I set up new supply chains to grow the circular portfolio?

☐ Where should I partner with pre-competitively or with adjacent industries?

☐ How can I integrate circular principles into upfront strategy, design, and product development?

☐ What targets should I set to drive action in my company, suppliers, and ecosystem partners?

☐ How can I build an efficient, effective returns process?

Functions to Engage

- ☐ **Design and Product Development** to implement design initiatives aimed at using less resource-intensive material, designing for life extensions, and repurposing at end of use
- ☐ **Sourcing and Procurement** to shift to alternative materials and inputs, including innovations in materials and circular inputs
- ☐ **Product and Brand Marketing** to shape relevant and impactful value propositions and drive circular portfolio growth
- ☐ **Sales** to engage customers and markets in circular offerings, including transitioning to as-a-service and takeback models
- ☐ **Reverse Logistics** to set up and optimize return flows for products coming back into the organization and value chain at end of use
- ☐ **(Re)Manufacturing** to set up and manage new forward flows for returned products and parts to enter into resale or remanufacture

Dependencies/Intersection Points

- ☐ **Operations:** Circular internal operations and processes are foundational to creating circular products and services. If sourcing and manufacturing are resource-intensive and wasteful, then that will extend to the lifecycle profile of the product.
- ☐ **Culture & Organization:** Cross-functional alignment (e.g., with sales, marketing, finance, R&D, etc.) throughout the organization is a critical requirement to successful circular offerings. For instance, if sales teams are not marketing services or communicating takeback programs to customers, Product as a Service and end-of-use recovery initiatives will not be widely adopted.
- ☐ **Ecosystem:** Commercial partners and suppliers play a key role in bringing circular products and services to market. They are absolutely critical to the supply and collection-side infrastructure to enable circular flows.

Notes

1. Steelcase, "Rethinking Think," 2019, https://www.steelcase.com/research/articles/topics/innovation/rethinking-think-2/ (accessed August 12, 2019).
2. Michelin Solutions, "With the Creation of Michelin Solutions, Michelin Is Partnering Trucking Companies to Help Them to Reduce Their Fuel Bill with an Initial Innovative Solution Called EFFIFUEL™," July 11, 2013, https://www.michelin.com/en/documents/with-the-creation-of-michelin-solutions-michelin-is-partnering-trucking-companies-to-help-them-to-reduce-their-fuel-bill-with-an-initial-innovative/ (accessed August 16, 2019).

3. Cision PR Newswire, "The North Face Launches 'Renewed' to Keep Apparel in Use Longer," June 6, 2018, https://www.prnewswire.com/news-releases/the-north-face-launches-renewed-to-keep-apparel-in-use-longer-300660594.html (accessed August 16, 2019).
4. Andrew McDougall, "Marks & Spencer Is Using Its Own Waste from Wine Production to Create and Commercialize a New Skincare Product Line," Cosmetics Design-Europe, July 23, 2014, https://www.cosmeticsdesign-europe.com/Article/2014/07/24/Marks-Spencer-skin-care-range-from-grape-waste-product (accessed August 16, 2019).
5. Pulse, "Starbucks Korea Recycles 97% of Coffee Grounds This Year," November 20, 2018, https://pulsenews.co.kr/view.php?year=2018&no=725855 (accessed August 16, 2019).
6. C2C Certified, "Get Cradle to Cradle Certified™," https://www.c2ccertified.org/get-certified/levels/platinum/v3_0 (accessed August 27, 2019).
7. Henkel, "Henkel Announces Ambitious Targets for Sustainable Packaging," September 3, 2018, https://www.henkel.com/press-and-media/press-releases-and-kits/2018-09-03-henkel-announces-ambitious-targets-for-sustainable-packaging-873418 (accessed August 16, 2019).
8. Essity, "Essity Invests in Sustainable Alternative Fiber Technology," 2019, https://www.essity.fr/media/press-release/essity-invests-in-sustainable-alternative-fiber-technology/21e1f75622ad642b/ (accessed August 12, 2019).
9. Komatsu Used, "A Brand New Way of Thinking About Used Equipment," https://www.komatsuused.com/construction (accessed August 30, 2019).
10. The Forum of Young Global Leaders in Collaboration with Accenture Strategy, "The Circulars 2017 Yearbook," https://thecirculars.org/content/resources/TheCirculars_2017_Yearbook_Final.pdf (accessed August 16, 2019).
11. Unilever, "Unilever's Purpose-Led Brands Outperform," 2019, https://www.unilever.com/news/press-releases/2019/unilevers-purpose-led-brands-outperform.html (accessed August 12, 2019).
12. Matthew Taylor, "World's First Plastic-Free Aisle Opens in Netherlands Supermarket," The Guardian, https://www.theguardian.com/environment/2018/feb/28/worlds-first-plastic-free-aisle-opens-in-netherlands-supermarket (accessed August 16, 2019).
13. Thomas Fleming and Markus Zils, "Toward a Circular Economy: Philips CEO Frans van Houten," McKinsey 2014, https://www.mckinsey.com/business-functions/sustainability/our-insights/toward-a-circular-economy-philips-ceo-frans-van-houten (accessed August 29, 2019).
14. Gov.uk, "Electrical Waste: Retailer and Distributor Responsibilities," 2019, https://www.gov.uk/electricalwaste-producer-supplier-responsibilities (accessed August 12, 2019).
15. Safe Cosmetics, "International Laws," http://www.safecosmetics.org/get-the-facts/regulations/international-laws/ (accessed August 30, 2019).
16. Accenture 2019 Consumer Survey.

17. Accenture Analysis.
18. IKEA, "IKEA Sustainability Report FY18," 2018, https://www.ikea.com/ms/hu_HU/pdf/sustainability_report/IKEA_Sustainability_Report_FY18.pdf (accessed August 12, 2019).
19. Tarkett, "Tarkett Releases Its 2018 Corporate Social & Environmental Responsibility Report," March 25, 2019, https://www.tarkett.com/en/content/tarkett-releases-its-2018-corporate-social-environmental-responsibility-report (accessed August 16, 2019).
20. Plastics Today, "Henkel, Ampacet Make Black Plastic Packaging Easier to Recycle," 2019, https://www.plasticstoday.com/content/henkel-ampacet-make-black-plastic-packaging-easier-recycle/149419921761096 (accessed August 12, 2019).
21. Rebecca Smithers, "Money for Old Socks: John Lewis to Buy Back Clothes to Cut Waste," *The Guardian*, June 18, 2018, https://www.theguardian.com/business/2018/jun/18/money-for-old-socks-john-lewis-to-buy-back-clothes-to-cut-waste (accessed August 27, 2019).
22. Ellen MacArthur Foundation, "Bringing Printing as a Service to the Home," 2017, https://www.ellenmacarthurfoundation.org/case-studies/bringing-printing-as-a-service-to-the-home (accessed August 12, 2019).
23. Ellen MacArthur Foundation, "GEM China: Conserving Materials for the Next Mobility Revolution," 2017, https://www.ellenmacarthurfoundation.org/case-studies/avoiding-3-million-tonnes-of-waste (accessed August 12, 2019).
24. Ellen MacArthur Foundation, "Conserving Materials for the Next Mobility Revolution," https://www.ellenmacarthurfoundation.org/case-studies/avoiding-3-million-tonnes-of-waste (accessed August 29, 2019).
25. Sara Weinreb, "Loop's Zero Waste Platform Is Changing the Culture of Disposability One Pint of Ice Cream at a Time," Forbes, March 7, 2019, https://www.forbes.com/sites/saraweinreb/2019/03/07/loops-zero-waste-platform-is-changing-the-culture-of-disposability-one-pint-of-ice-cream-at-a-time/#478341f42122 (accessed August 20, 2019).
26. H&M Group, "Sustainability Report 2018," https://sustainability.hm.com/content/dam/hm/about/documents/masterlanguage/CSR/2018_sustainability_report/HM_Group_SustainabilityReport_2018_Chapter4_100%25Circular%26Renewable.pdf (accessed August 29, 2019).
27. Veolia, "The Essentials 2018," https://www.veolia.com/sites/g/files/dvc2491/files/document/2019/04/Veolia-2018-The-Essentials.pdf (accessed August 12, 2019).
28. Ascena Retail Group, "Responsibility Report Fiscal 2018," https://www.ascenaretail.com/wp-content/uploads/2018/10/ascena-Responsibility-Report-2018.pdf (accessed August 16, 2019).

29. Business Wire, "IFF Debuts First-Ever Cradle to Cradle Certified™ Fragrance: PuraVita™," https://www.businesswire.com/news/home/20160512006588/en/IFF-Debuts-First-Ever-Cradle-Cradle-Certified%E2%84%A2-Fragrance (accessed August 16, 2019).

30. Alexandra Wee, "6 Easy Ways to Reduce Your Period Waste," THINX, 2019, https://www.shethinx.com/blogs/womens-health/how-to-reduce-period-waste-reusable-products (accessed August 12, 2019).

31. H&M Group, "Recycling," 2019, https://hmgroup.com/sustainability/Planet/recycling.html (accessed August 12, 2019).

32. Jennifer Elks, "Nestle, Coke, Pepsi and Unilever Join Forces to Combat Waste in Chile," Sustainable Brands, 2014, https://sustainablebrands.com/read/collaboration-cocreation/nestle-coke-pepsi-unilever-join-forces-to-combat-waste-in-chile (accessed August 12, 2019).

19

👥 Culture & Organization

A company's culture may be difficult to define, but it nonetheless has an enormous impact on the way employees behave and go about their daily work. As such, businesses will struggle to transition to circularity unless they succeed in embedding it into their DNA. This means weaving circular principles into the core vision and corporate mission, while providing the right organizational incentives to: encourage people to innovate for circularity, implement circular operations, deliver circular products and services, and actively seek partnerships and engage with the company's external ecosystem. It also means making circularity central to all functions and business units across the enterprise, with policies, processes, and work practices in place to actively engage people at *all* levels in the circular ways of working. Accenture research has concluded that driving change initiatives solely from the top can be highly counterproductive. When examining change programs involving nearly one million employees at more than 150 organizations, the lowest performing 25% had high involvement of top leadership to implement change, with a disconnect lower in the organization. In contrast, the top 25% of performers had succeeded in engaging leaders at all levels throughout the organization in the change initiative.[1] The results are evident: employees need to participate and feel fully involved in planning an organization's change journey to facilitate the acceptance of new cultural values.

© The Author(s) 2020
P. Lacy et al., *The Circular Economy Handbook*,
https://doi.org/10.1057/978-1-349-95968-6_19

Four Areas of Focus

For many companies, organizational change is neither a simple nor straight-forward task, but the process is critical to the success of any holistic circular strategy. In our research, we have found that, to establish a circular culture and organization, companies first need to recognize and accept that the current model is unsustainable, then focus on the following four areas: vision, innovation, people, and governance (see Table 19.1).

Table 19.1 Four areas of focus

Focus area	The toolbox	Culture & Organization in action
Vision	Setting a long-term goal with milestones and supporting targets for becoming a circular organization over time. Initiatives in this area are aimed at developing time-bound objectives to support the circular vision and mobilize the required resources that can help business units prioritize and implement circular initiatives	Oil refining company Neste aims to become a global leader in renewable and circular solutions, with a vision of "Creating responsible choices every day." The company has designed a strategy to realize its sustainability aspirations, including lowering its carbon footprint in production, becoming a solution provider for chemical recycling, and increasing its use of renewable raw materials[2]
Innovation	Breaking down research and development (R&D) silos to encourage innovation across the organization, instilling a "laboratory" mindset to drive innovative circular thinking, sharing best practices and relevant use cases, conducting learning expeditions to embed circular principles and design in organizational centers of innovation, and encouraging the operational and product/service pivot to circularity	Swedish home furnishings company IKEA has created the innovation lab Space10 in Copenhagen to research and design solutions that create more sustainable living. Space10's projects span a wide range of topics, including clean energy, autonomous vehicles, and urban farming[3]
People	Engaging employees with circular projects sponsored from the top of the organization, providing training and internal support systems for those workers by identifying and empowering the people who can drive the change journey, and incentivizing circular performance at all levels against clear KPIs	Innocent Drinks, the juice and smoothie company owned largely by The Coca-Cola Company, built an engagement plan for their workforce as part of its 2020 sustainability strategy. The company has asked each member of its workforce to add a sustainability role to his or her job description[4]

(continued)

Table 19.1 (continued)

Focus area	The toolbox	Culture & Organization in action
Governance	Recognizing that the established internal ways of doing business are likely to impede circular decision-making at speed and be a barrier for further uptake; making the circular economy a core element in the company's ways of working and structure by embedding circularity in policies, processes, and procedures; and focusing on accountability and agile decision-making enablement from the "shop floor to the corporate headquarters"	General Mills, the consumer food company, has committed to 100% sustainable sourcing of 10 prioritized commodities, including oats, wheat, and corn by 2020. To accomplish this, the company launched a sustainability governance committee, to set targets, policy, and strategy, and to decide on key investments. The company has also embedded a broader team within different functions, focused on executing those strategies and policies[5]

Making the Pivot

When prioritizing circular initiatives, executives should remember that Culture & Organization is a key enabler, and that any transformation efforts should be managed in conjunction with other ongoing work. That is, efforts to embed circular principles in the organizational culture should be managed in coordination with the company's ongoing circular initiatives in the three other dimensions (Operations, Products & Services, and the Ecosystem). A shared language and common goals toward circularity help avoid confusion. Once qualifying initiatives have been selected, pilot projects should take place across various parts of the organization, encompassing different business units and functions over time to create a strong foundation for more inclusive enterprise-wide change.

When prioritizing circular projects, leaders must assess which business functions are critical for success (and which are complementary), and they must identify where changes to the traditional ways of working may be most needed. Consider a company that's implementing a new initiative for product circularity. Their plan is to increase product takeback and redirect those returns to the highest value of second use by sending them to functions that handle refurbished resale, services delivery, or parts recovery. Although this initiative may be driven by logistics teams, it requires the engagement of sales teams in communicating and enforcing takeback policies and incentives, such as discounts to encourage customers to return products at end of use. This can be a big challenge in a company where sales teams are used to longstanding legacy incentives that must then be modified to accommodate the new business model.

Similarly, when integrating circularity into product designs, it can be a significant shift for teams of engineers, designers, and technicians that have traditionally been focused on cost or performance and that now need to adopt a new way of thinking to incorporate new, and often disruptive, principles. Questions arise, such as, what kind of materials should they select? How can they avoid designing single-use products? In what ways can they increase product durability? For operational initiatives, the challenge is usually not as great as with product initiatives because an organization's sustainability targets are typically tied to operations, such as energy efficiency, water reduction, and waste elimination. Teams within operational functions will likely be familiar with circular principles since they tend to have more experience with sustainability projects.

But, regardless of familiarity and comfort, executives should not rest until the *entire* organization is aligned to circularity. Circularity should not feel like something "extracurricular" for the workforce, it should be embedded into employees' tasks and functions just as any other facets of their roles. Moreover, companies need to have comprehensive and pervasive communication and engagement activities as they progress along their circular journey. The goal is to promote awareness and to remove any tension between those teams championing change and those that might be resistant. This enterprise-wide effort should be conducted in addition to more targeted efforts that bring together certain groups and functions that are key to implementing specific initiatives (e.g., bringing together devices, sales, and logistics in the example above).

A Circular Journey: Vision and People

Different companies will have different goals depending on their level of maturity. Table 19.2 summarizes the various characteristics of companies as they advance in their circular journey. Initiatives across the four areas of focus—vision, innovation, people, and governance—can range widely, depending on the maturity of an organization. It's important to note that the initiatives across the four focus areas are closely interrelated. Consequently, companies must take a holistic approach to transforming their organizational culture, as the success of one initiative will hinge on the others. Therefore, let's examine the vision and people focus areas in parallel.

A company can start by setting a circular goal for a specific business unit, perhaps the facilities or operations team. As the organization becomes more mature in its circular journey, it would look to set an *ambitious, long-term goal* that puts circularity at the heart of its mission statement to lead a circular revolution in the wider value chain and ecosystem. IKEA, for example, has stated its goal of becoming "people and planet positive" by 2030. Commitments include increasing the portion of plant-based choices in IKEA food offerings, such as the veggie hotdog launched in 2018; removing all single-use plastic products by 2020; and achieving zero emissions on home deliveries by 2025.[6] Those goals cannot be achieved without validating targets with internal teams and other stakeholders, including shorter-term milestones to hold people accountable.

After setting corporate goals, executives need to make circularity real and relevant. Specifically, they must *raise awareness* and *educate* internal stakeholders on what the circular economy is, what it means for the company and strategy, and how it will affect people's roles and responsibilities. "It is important to be humble when we talk about circularity as it is a new concept that needs explaining," says Virginie Helias, Chief Sustainability Officer at global consumer goods company, P&G. This is echoed by Marc Delaye, Senior Executive Vice President of Development, Innovation and Markets at water, waste, and energy management solutions company Veolia, "The cultural transformation towards the circular economy requires real commitment from leadership to take action and raise awareness of what the circular economy means for us."

For one thing, the circular economy could have different interpretations. BASF, the German chemical company, did a detailed analysis of more than 9000 interviews with consumers, subject-matter experts, politicians, and technologists to understand industry trends across regions. The study uncovered that "circular doesn't equal circular"—that is, the term could mean different things within and across industries. In addition, people are often confused as to how circularity differs from broader sustainability initiatives and how it might help drive business value.

According to Lisa Brady, Director of Supply Chain Sustainability and Circular Economy at technology conglomerate Cisco, it's hard to make circularity "real" for people. "They understand it's the right thing to do, but that doesn't create behavioral change," Brady explains. "It's not intuitive that the circular economy is a business imperative." Therefore, in addition to broad education, it often helps to socialize successful, circular "lighthouse" projects within the company that bring the concept to life. As John Pflueger, Principle Environmental Strategist at Dell puts it, "With every pilot we complete and every successful use of recovered materials, we learn a little more about what it takes to find success. A big piece of the transformation is in these learning cycles and communicating both what we've learned and what we know about existing opportunities within our business."

In addition, a core set of tangible *circular economy principles* underpinning the circular goal can help business units or brands prioritize and track their performance to deliver against the broader circular strategy. One effective approach is to select a team or business unit that's already closely aligned to circular principles and then designate that group to drive the implementation of the circular vision and strategies throughout the organization. Another approach to creating organizational principles that resonate with the workforce is to involve people in the process. For example, in 2017, transportation network company Uber's newly appointed CEO had employees submit and vote on cultural values for the workplace. This refresh was meant to address issues that led to an investigation into Uber's corporate culture. The results: 1200 submissions, 22,000 votes, and a set of eight new cultural norms.[7]

Another key aspect for success is to provide internal stakeholders with *resources* that allow for upskilling the workforce on circular economy practices and principles. A company could start by delivering introductory "Circular Economy 101" training to targeted areas of the business, after which it can launch an expanded program to a wider pool of participants. Ultimately, executives can scale a comprehensive company-wide training program, leveraging e-learning solutions for wider engagement. Educating the workforce can be a challenging task—here, a company can partner with an organization that can provide such expertise. Google's partnership with the Ellen MacArthur Foundation, for example, has helped embed circular economy principles into the fabric of Google's organization and culture.[8]

Finally, to transform the corporate culture and enable a vision of circularity across the board, an organization needs to establish the *appropriate incentives* that encourage circular thinking among its people. After setting a long-term vision, executives might start by launching a circular incentive program within the sustainability team, outlining the right behaviors, principles, and criteria to be rewarded. The company can then expand the program across a wider range of business units, adapting it to the needs of each unit and ultimately scaling it across the entire organization and leadership hierarchy. Recognizing the importance of incentives, global food and beverage company Danone implemented an incentive program for its top management whereby a portion of long-term incentives is based on the climate performance score attributed to the company by the CDP, a global nonprofit which ranks companies on their environmental progress. The CDP score provides a way to encourage and reward progress toward Danone's commitment to achieve carbon neutrality on its full value chain by 2050.[9]

Table 19.2 Illustrative characteristics of increasing company maturity

	Emerging	Established	Leading	Ultimate	The maturity journey: from → to
Vision	• Circular goals that are quantified and relatable to sustainability strategy are set • Circularity is integrated in the existing set of principles for doing business	• Circular goals are integrated into business strategy • Efforts to drive circularity across the organization take place: Circular principles are explicit in company values, and best practices are shared	• Circular goals are linked to the organizational innovation strategy • Circularity is embedded in the purpose of the organization • Circularity is prioritized in leadership communication	• Circular goals exist at all organizational levels and are linked to business performance metrics • Vision accelerates circularity both within and beyond operational boundaries	• From outlining circular goals and principles for the sustainability function to setting an ambitious vision for circularity at the core of business strategy • Actions include: (1) setting a long-term circular goal with a long delivery time and ROI, (2) setting circular principles that underpin the goals/strategy

(continued)

Table 19.2 (continued)

	Emerging	Established	Leading	Ultimate	The maturity journey: from → to
Innovation	• Employees are aware of circular innovation taking place in the industry • Company commits to develop the organizational capability for circular innovation	• Circularity is implicitly linked to the business innovation agenda • Investment is made in internal innovation sharing and learning under a common "circular" narrative	• Circularity is explicitly linked to the business innovation strategy and the Chief Technology Officer role • Company invests in scaling circular innovation upstream • Circular innovation and R&D are sourced internally and externally	• A substantial circular innovation budget is set across all levels and business units • Company focuses on advanced, market-leading enabling technologies and on disruptive business model innovations	• From a small budget allocation for internal circular innovation to leveraging emerging technology to drive circular innovation at all levels and functions and throughout the wider ecosystem • Actions include: (1) mandating a portion of business unit/function budget for circular innovation purposes, (2) encouraging a "fail-fast" mindset both internally and externally to drive innovative circular thinking

	Emerging	Established	Leading	Ultimate	The maturity journey: from → to
People	• Non-financial incentives and encouragement to adopt behaviors in line with circular ethos • Basic circular awareness employee training is made available	• Circular accountability is introduced at the senior levels and linked to rewards • Circular awareness training is made available, augmented by detailed case study repositories and learning expeditions	• The circular economy is a key component of employee performance at all levels and measured accordingly • Circular training is embedded into core business training curriculum and considered "business as usual"	• Organization plays a prominent role in engaging and upskilling people beyond the direct scope of the business—this includes supply chain partners, consumers, and/or other key stakeholders	• From early-stage circular incentives and trainings in place to full circular engagement across and beyond the business • Actions include: (1) creating incentive programs to encourage circular thinking and culture, (2) providing upskilling resources/opportunities to employees on the circular economy

(continued)

Table 19.2 (continued)

	Emerging	Established	Leading	Ultimate	The maturity journey: from → to
Governance	• The circular economy is a key component/pillar of the company's sustainability policy • The sustainability team features circular economy champions for the business	• Circular performance is reported on internally • The strategy team features circular economy champions for the business	• Circular performance is reported on internally and externally • Circularity is championed by individuals in each business unit and across all functions	• Full visibility of circular KPIs helps drive standards in industry and marketplace • C-level leadership champions circular leadership externally	• From including circularity in company sustainability policy to industry-leading circular governance structure • Actions include: centering the circular economy as a key principle in the company's ways of working and structure
Overall takeaways	• Circular initiatives can be piloted in targeted parts of the business • Communication is launched broadly to promote the transition to a circular business, with training made available	• The circular economy is woven into the company vision and principles • Circularity is a key consideration on the company's growth agenda, encouraged by incentives	• The circular economy is integrated into the business and innovation strategy • A circular culture and values underpin the way people work to become the "new normal" and ensure a successful pivot to circularity	• Circularity is at the heart of the company's purpose and is driving the external ecosystem forward and championing systemic change	• The company adopts a longer timeline to support truly successful delivery of its circular ambitions • Company structures and policies are flexible and adapt continuously to support investment in innovation and training to enable new business models at scale

The Value Drivers

We have found that companies that are most successful at creating circular value through their Operations, Products & Services, and/or Ecosystem have also been leaders at embedding circularity into their Culture & Organization. Although circular-driven change won't happen overnight, it does have potential to generate substantial value over time. Let's explore how Culture & Organization drives value across our four levers:

Revenue Generation: By fostering a culture of innovation, organizations can create new products and services and unlock new revenue streams. In the previous chapter, Products & Services, we discussed the dramatic transformation that Philips is undergoing, as the multinational corporation shifts toward circular business models. In 2018, green and circular revenues amounted to 64 and 12% of the company's sales, respectively.[10] That type of transformation would not have been possible without a focus on corporate culture. "It's a mindset change," explains Frans van Houten, CEO of Philips. "The challenge is now to scale up and embed circular in all processes, and make circular thinking the new normal."

Cost Savings: A circular organizational culture can help generate significant employee value by increasing a company's ability to attract and retain top talent, as purpose-driven business practices, sustainability, and circular themes are increasingly important to the current workforce, as well as to job seekers. This is key in reducing recruitment costs, given the average cost-per-hire for a company is over $4000, according to a report by the Society for Human Resource Management.[11] A recent Cone Communications study revealed the following about millennial job seekers: 76% consider a company's social and environmental commitments before deciding where to work; 64% won't take a job if a potential employer doesn't have strong corporate responsibility practices; and 75% would take a pay cut to work for a socially responsible company.[12] As David Rosenberg, CEO and Co-Founder of urban agriculture company AeroFarms states, "We receive over 2000 applications every month from job seekers. For a company with less than 100 employees, our ability to attract top talent is largely due to our circular ethos. We see this as a real competitive advantage."

Risk Reduction: A circular culture not only supports a company's employee recruitment and retention efforts, but it also helps keep workers engaged. An analysis by Gallup found that companies in the top quartile for engaged employees also had 22% higher profitability, 10% higher customer ratings, 28% less theft, and 48% fewer safety incidents than those in the bottom quartile.[13]

 Brand Enhancement: When a company's culture is projected to consumers through its stated vision, principles, and strategy, it raises brand awareness and drives customer loyalty. As such, it holds the potential to open new markets and customer segments. That's one reason why many companies have actively touted their circular initiatives and organizational culture to the outside world. "We are a purpose-driven company. 'Brewing for a better today and tomorrow' is used both internally and externally to remind ourselves about our unique purpose and to share it with the world," says Flemming Besenbacher, Chairman of Carlsberg Group and the Carlsberg Foundation.

Case Study: Danone

Danone provides a good example of a global corporation that has taken a holistic approach to developing a circular culture.[14] The company's journey illustrates the different stages of cultural maturity depicted in our table.

In the emerging stage, Danone decided to embed circular principles in its operations and organizational design. Specifically, Danone organized its procurement function around three key strategic resource "cycles"—water, milk, and plastic. This was intended to break up traditional linear silos by regrouping procurement, research and innovation, and sustainability under the same leadership. To lead its strategic resources unit, Danone created the position of Chief Cycles and Procurement Officer, currently held by Katharina Stenholm. Katharina described the impact of the cycles organization: "The cycles are ensuring that circularity is embedded within Danone's procurement strategy. It has been a catalyst in transforming how we work, allowing us to leverage capabilities cross-functionally and anchor change in the way Danone operates."

Building on this momentum, Danone took a series of defining decisions. The company launched a new company vision—"One Planet. One Health"—to reflect the company's belief that the planet's health and people's health are interconnected. It became a global leader in plant-based and organic food and beverages through a strategic acquisition. And the company set carbon reduction targets approved by the Science Based Targets initiative, as part of its journey toward zero net emissions across its entire value chain by 2050.

As Danone advanced to the leading stage of maturity, Danone committed to becoming one of the first multi-nationals to be certified as a B Corp. As of 2019, more than 30% of Danone's sales are now covered by B Corp certification, and Danone North America is the largest B Corp in the world. In addition, the company announced nine long-term goals, aligned with the UN Sustainable

Development Goals (SDGs), which outline its vision for sustainable business growth from now until 2030. Responding to environmental challenges by "pre-serving and renewing the planet's resources" is a key component of this vision. It signals Danone's ambition to have a positive impact on the planet (rather than a "do no harm" approach), in line with circular economy principles.

Technology as an Enabler: *Deep Dive on the Chief Technology and Information Officer's Role in a Circular Journey*

Technology is a critical enabler of the circular economy. It helps drive the adoption of sustainable innovations, embed circular processes, provide traceability, perform advanced analytics, and scale solutions, among many other benefits. As we have discussed in Chapter 2 and elsewhere, lead-ing companies have been applying technology in previously unimaginable ways to drive circular value and revamp entire businesses. All this, of course, requires the right leadership from and mindset of the Chief Technology and Information Officer (CTIO).

The CTIO is in a unique position to see horizontally across the com-pany and understand the overall technological needs of the organization, especially across functions that are often siloed. In a 4IR-enabled circu-lar world, the role of the CTIO becomes even more important. Not only must the CTIO position span across the IT department, engineering, R&D, and product development, it must also possess a broad understanding of technologies across the digital, physical, and biological domains, as well as knowledge of how to integrate these rapidly changing technologies across legacy functions. In a circular economy, the role of CTIO evolves to be even more of a corporate change agent, responsible for driving automation, insights, and circular innovations across the organization. In other words, the CTIO office is where the proverbial rubber hits the road as a company implements circular initiatives. So, then, how should CTIOs get started to assume that role?

The Circular CTIO Imperatives

The circular CTIO's first imperative is often to **address resource efficiency**. This means examining the various waste pools generated by the company in order to identify the biggest (and easiest to address) areas of waste creation and handling. The analysis should take into account a number of variables such as energy/water/waste management, inventory management, facilities operational efficiency, data center efficiency, fleet management, and logistics efficiency. CTIOs should be on the lookout for any potential "quick wins": opportunities for minimizing existing waste streams or for generating value out of waste and by-products that can be pursued within an existing business without requiring considerable investments. For example, a CTIO might work in collaboration with the operations function to drive out wasted energy and resources used to power manufacturing plants, leveraging a combination of analytics, automation, and process optimization.

To be effective in implementing circular applications, CTIOs must develop the ability to **identify, assess, and monitor resource usage and efficiency** across the core business value chain. This requires tools for providing visibility across the supply chain, sensors for testing the performance (including resource use) of production facilities and data centers, and systems for gathering performance data to build an analytics capability that can provide insights into efficiency gains, including predictive maintenance. With these capabilities, CTIOs will be able to obtain an in-depth, data-informed understanding of the technology and process changes needed to shift their company from linear to circular. A notable example of a technology that can deliver both circular and economic "quick wins" is cloud computing. The technology delivers multiple efficiencies and economies of scale that can help an organization's operations run in a more cost-effective and flexible manner, as well as contribute to energy and emissions savings. A study by Microsoft and professional services firm WSP found that the Microsoft cloud is up to 93% more energy efficient (and up to 98% more carbon-efficient) than on-site solutions. By 2030, the electricity consumption of data centers in the United States is expected to grow to 73 billion kilowatt-hours annually, the equivalent of the energy consumed by six million homes. This figure would be much higher without the efficiencies realized in commercial cloud data centers.[15]

With an understanding of resource usage and waste pools across the organization, CTIOs can better **identify opportunities to reuse, refurbish, remanufacture, or recycle non-virgin resources** back into the value chain. For many industries, this first involves closing the loop within operations and manufacturing: putting wasted materials on-site (e.g., production by-products, unprocessed water, etc.) back into the company's own internal value chain, often as raw inputs or energy. For some industries, this may also involve taking materials back from the end consumer—both products with remaining useful life as well as those at end of life—requiring a more complex product takeback and reverse logistics capability. By harnessing 4IR technologies, such as artificial intelligence to provide logistics insights for product retrieval or mobile devices to enable consumer returns, reverse logistics can be made more cost-effective and companies can engage customers in their wider circular journey.

CTIOs are also responsible for **developing and testing technological solutions** that could enable the company's journey from linear to circular models of production and consumption. As mentioned earlier, this could involve solutions across the wider range of 4IR digital, physical, and biological technologies. AMP Robotics, for example, developed a solution that leverages digital and physical innovations to revolutionize recycling. The company uses AI (machine vision and deep learning) and robotics to create an intelligent, extremely efficient sorting system. AMP Robotics also uses the cloud to digitize the material stream and optimize operations. This type of solution could be widely applicable for any organization looking to tackle waste recovery.

To identify which 4IR solutions are most appropriate to drive circularity, the CTIO will need to understand the value behind the product that is being sold and identify alternative ways to deliver that same value with less resource use, for example, automakers delivering personal mobility through car sharing versus ownership.

The final imperative for CTIOs is to **regenerate and restore**. Specifically, CTIOs must work closely with R&D and product design teams to help find alternative materials, processes, and technologies to regenerate resources in perpetuity with no (or minimal) loss of energy and resources. The goal is a fully closed-loop system that can upcycle resources infinitely.

In summary, CTIOs need to shape their organization's circular agenda by:

- **Leading the way**: CTIOs will be central in the circular economy transition and, in most cases, will need to drive those initiatives themselves, including staying up to date with trends and working to understand the circular potential of their organizations.
- **Embedding circular innovation**: CTIOs must help foster an innovation culture targeted at circular value by raising internal awareness, by setting up innovation hubs, and/or by assigning specific roles for the discovery and assessment of technologies of circular value.
- **Enabling agility**: CTIOs need to build the foundations for a flexible operating model to enable the testing and pivoting of new technologies and/or business models.

- **Collaborating across functions**: CTIOs should work with teams in R&D, design and development, production, logistics, etc. to understand each business unit's needs, challenges, and readiness and to integrate new technologies that facilitate a circular journey.

Leading Practices to Drive Transformation

Transforming any organizational culture is a massive undertaking, and many companies have stumbled in their attempts to implement the right approach for disrupting their business-as-usual culture and organization. But a number of firms have made significant progress toward achieving a circular culture. Our study of those organizations has revealed a number of leading practices.

Lead from the Top-Down with Flexibility

One thing that leading companies all agree on is that cultural change must have sponsorship and active participation from the top of the organization. According to Flemming Besenbacher, Chairman of Carlsberg Group and the Carlsberg Foundation, "Senior leaders need to drive the process, with a full commitment from the management and board. At Carlsberg, the company's leadership team co-created its sustainability program and 2030 ambitions, which are strongly supported by the CEO and board." To help that trickle flow down through the organizational hierarchy, reporting lines and accountability are crucial. At Nike, management collaborates with teams to determine the appropriate goals, and senior executives are given regular updates of the company's progress toward those goals.

While reporting lines and accountability are important, executives must also lead with flexibility. The circular economy fundamentally changes the way that companies have traditionally done business, which can lead to considerable uncertainty and anxiety among employees. "Driving circularity is about leadership: you need to have the vision and courage to work in a totally unchartered territory, and you sometimes need to take a leap of faith," remarks Virginie Helias, Chief Sustainability Officer at P&G. Because of that uncertainty, executives need to maintain open communications with their teams to figure out what's working (or what's not) and then to adapt accordingly. "It can be challenging to bring different functions together to align on circular economy when they each have their own objectives and goals," says Lisa Brady of Cisco. To address those issues, Cisco set up an Executive Change Network that helped to break down functional silos and get everyone aligned to tackle circularity as a business imperative. "You have to look holistically to tie the parts together," says Brady. Because circular initiatives generally require companies to go outside their comfort zones, such flexibility can often be the difference between failure and success.

Bring Innovation to the Core

For large multinational corporations, transforming an existing culture to encompass circularity can be a daunting task. In contrast, start-ups and SMEs that are founded on a circular and sustainable ethos have an advantage in that they build their cultures from the ground up. Can anything be learned from these smaller, purpose-driven firms? We believe that an important lesson is for companies to avoid "half-measures" and to embrace circularity wholeheartedly. Consider cleaning products company method, which has a very straightforward, ambitious vision ("to create a new sector of the economy that uses the power of business to solve social and environmental problems") and Seventh Generation, a Vermont startup acquired by Unilever that took its name and guiding principle ("in our every deliberation, we must consider the impact of our decisions on the next seven generations") from The Great Law of the Iroquois philosophy that the decisions we make today should result in a sustainable world seven generations into the future.

To move from such lofty corporate visions to concrete actions, management should consider establishing guiding principles and metrics, such as by mandating that a certain percentage of the product development team's budget be applied to a pilot project for circular innovation. In addition, executives should encourage a "test and learn" entrepreneurial mindset by implementing incentives that reward innovative thinking, and by allocating sufficient financial and human resources to circular R&D. At P&G, management had purposefully targeted a low success rate in order to boost overall innovation, all in line with the "fail faster to succeed sooner" approach to R&D. According to A. G. Lafley, former CEO at P&G, "About half of our new products succeed. That's as high as we want the success rate to be. If we try to make it any higher, we'll be tempted to err on the side of caution, playing it safe by focusing on innovations with little game-changing potential."[16] Ultimately, circular thinking needs to be woven into the organizational fabric, becoming the "new normal" in how employees go about their jobs in designing, manufacturing, marketing, selling, and supporting the firm's products and services.

Finally, companies can generate a steady pipeline of innovation by creating distinct business units, or new businesses entirely, that focus solely on capturing the "latest and greatest" innovations in the market. Consider ZX Ventures, a global growth and innovation group within AB InBev. ZX Ventures invests in and develops new products and businesses that meet emerging consumer needs. In addition, AB InBev has also established its Global Innovation and Technology Center, which brings together diverse teams from packaging, product, and process development.[17] "We are continually innovating to bring the best possible products to consumers with the lowest impact on the planet. We know we cannot accomplish our ambitious sustainability goals alone. As a global brewer operating in more than 50 countries, we are supporting entrepreneurs from around the world who have the bold ideas to deliver a sustainable future," states Tony Milikin, Chief Sustainability and Procurement Officer at AB InBev.

Build the Necessary Structures and Capabilities

As companies advance toward greater maturity, they will need to build foundational structures to operationalize their circular initiatives and entrench circular principles within the organizational culture. Developing the right mechanisms to support circular initiatives is key to realizing the potential of circular initiatives in terms of potential revenues, customer engagement, cost savings, and so on.

As part of that infrastructure, companies need to invest in their data architectures to optimize the flows of circular information and to embed the circular economy across functions. "We are digitizing a lot of the interaction between supply chain and engineering, which helps embed the right materials and circular design into their work process," says Lisa Brady of Cisco. In setting up that infrastructure, companies have to think holistically in creating new linkages across the organization. If, for instance, the firm is planning to implement a business model for product use extension, then it needs to connect all the necessary functions to accomplish that. Doing so would require blueprints for digitizing the interactions between those functions in order to establish common workflows and to make the right tools accessible to those who need them.

The adoption of advanced technologies would not only equip people to do their jobs better, but also move them to adopt a circular mindset. Such was the case with Winnow Solutions, which offers an AI tool that helps commercial kitchens reduce their waste. The company's application uses cameras and digital scales to automatically track food that's thrown out, and AI technology helps pinpoint the areas of greatest waste (e.g., dishes with too-large portions). According to Winnow founder Marc Zornes, any technology won't by itself necessarily result in the desired change, but it can empower employees to drive that change from the front lines of the organization. "All chefs abhor food waste," says Zornes. "Winnow brings everybody together around this problem, gives people a sense of purpose in the kitchen, and builds a teamwork mentality. People who see the waste are not always the people who make decisions. Winnow can make that connection to empower the staff to make suggestions and drive change."

Foster a Mindset Shift

Changing the organizational culture typically requires a big shift in mindset, and management needs to impress that on associates across the entire company. American clothing company Patagonia has long been a trailblazer in establishing a culture of corporate responsibility, as evidenced by its current mission statement: "We're in business to save our home planet." And the company doesn't just talk the talk; it walks the walk by actively taking a stand on issues that are central to its core values. Founder Yvon Chouinard has said that, all things being equal, Patagonia always looks to fill a job opening with the person who's committed to save the planet, regardless of the position.[18] At Philips, the electronics multinational, the required transformation in mindset is also being actively pursued with customers. The Dutch corporation is increasingly getting questions from hospitals on how Philips offerings can contribute to the sustainability ambitions of those customers. "Obviously, this often requires a mindset change for customers well," says Frans van Houten, CEO of Philips. "Especially in procurement departments, where people are used to purchase new equipment (and get rid of old machinery) over typical cycles of five to 10 years, rather than upgrade them or move over to different ownership models in which the customer pays for access rather than ownership. We can help them with our expertise."

Another aspect of the shift in mindset involves the recognition that ambitious circular targets and successful delivery require a longer-term time horizon. People need to have enough of a runway to ideate, redesign products and processes, learn, iterate, and ultimately reap the benefits. Moreover, circularity is an evolving field and taking a long-term perspective is key to having a holistic view of the company that can then encourage innovation to flourish across the organization in various business units. As Philips CEO Frans van Houten states: "Our mindset needs to be 15 years out – not just 'now.'"[10]

 Chapter Takeaways

- Culture unlocks the value potential of the circular economy. It is one of the most critical enabling levers to creating a circular economy within a company's operations, across its products and services, and throughout its ecosystem.
- A circular pivot needs ambition (big targets), prioritization (embedded in corporate strategy), scale across the business (employee buy-in), and a longer time horizon to support successful delivery.
- Companies should establish what the circular economy means for them early on and educate people on the case for change by demonstrating how the transition will impact their roles and day-to-day responsibilities. It is crucial to get everyone in the company engaged and to encourage people to contribute to building a circular company.
- A circular journey involves weaving circular principles into the core vision, mission, and culture of a company, such that the organizational structure incentivizes people to embrace innovation around circular operations and deliver circular products and services.

To implement a shift in a company's culture and organization, leaders should first conduct an assessment to understand their company's readiness for a cultural transformation. The assessment should help identify key areas of focus and determine the best strategies to launch a circular journey. The following considerations can help in that assessment.

Sample Questions to Answer

Shaping a circular vision

☐ What does our company wish to be in the future, and how can it drive circular impact?

☐ What circular principles can become central to our company's way of doing business?

☐ How do we create a circular vision that resonates with people across the value chain, and drives the entire industry forward?

☐ How does a circular vision align with our existing business and innovation strategies?

Realizing the vision

☐ How will we instill circular values and principles of working throughout the organization?

☐ What policies and initiatives do we need to put in place to support our circular journey?

☐ Do we need to partner with an external organization to train and upskill employees?

☐ How will we integrate circularity into the broader business innovation strategy?

Bringing people onboard the circular journey

☐ Who are the key internal stakeholders we need to engage to mobilize our organization's circular journey?

☐ How do we implement the appropriate training and incentives across our organization to shift to a circular mindset?

☐ Which teams/business units/functions will be most impacted by the circular transformation?

☐ How do we communicate change effectively and solicit feedback to address uncertainty and manage resistance?

Functions to Engage

☐ **Finance** to enable investment in innovation across the business by designating a portion of the company budget specifically to fund circular initiatives

☐ **Human Resources** to build incentive structures and reward systems that encourage circular behaviors and to develop change management programs and communication

☐ **Marketing** to communicate company vision and strategy to external stakeholders, repositioning the company in the market and promoting (new) circular strategies/offerings

☐ **Design and Development** to adapt processes and include circularity as a key criterion in methodology in order to bring circular vision and principles to fruition in company offerings

Dependencies/Intersection Points

☐ **Operations**: Circular internal operations tend to be the starting point for a company commencing its circular journey. Teams within operational functions usually have experience with sustainability efforts and can be leveraged to catalyze change throughout the organization.

☐ **Products & Services**: Circular innovation could manifest in new products and services. The company needs to maintain open communication and collaboration between relevant teams to deliver innovative offerings.

☐ **Ecosystem**: A company's external ecosystem provides a massive support system as it makes the transition to circularity. In areas where the company lacks necessary internal expertise, partners can provide the tools and capabilities critical for success.

Notes

1. Diana Barea and Yaarit Silverstone, "New Rules for Cultural Change," Accenture, 2016, https://www.accenture.com/t20161216T040430__w__/us-en/_acnmedia/PDF-24/Accenture-Strategy-Workforce-Culture-Change-New.pdf (accessed August 9, 2019).
2. Neste, "Creating a Healthier Planet for Our Children," https://www.neste.com/corporate-info/who-we-are/purpose (accessed August 16, 2019).
3. Joanna Le Pluart, "Secret Innovation Lab Revealed," IKEA, 2016, https://www.ikea.com/ms/en_US/this-is-ikea/ikea-highlights/IKEA-secret-innovation-lab/index.html (accessed August 16, 2019).
4. edie, "Heroes of Change: How Innocent Drinks Is Empowering Its Staff to Drive Sustainability," January 10, 2018, https://www.edie.net/library/Heroes-of-change-How-Innocent-Drinks-is-linking-staff-and-sustainability/6804 (accessed August 16, 2019).
5. Anya Khalamayzer, "More Dirt on General Mills' Sustainable Agriculture Goals," GreenBiz, 2017, https://www.greenbiz.com/article/more-dirt-general-mills-sustainable-agriculture-goals (accessed August 9, 2019).
6. IKEA, "IKEA Takes Sustainable Living to a New Level, with New Commitments to Become People and Planet Positive by 2030," 2018, https://www.ikea.com/us/en/about_ikea/newsitem/060718-IKEA-commits-to-become-people-planet-positive-2030 (accessed August 9, 2019).
7. Anita Balakrishnan, "Uber Employees Voted on New Company Culture—And It Looks a Lot Like Google and Amazon," *USA Today*, 2017, https://www.usatoday.com/story/tech/news/2017/11/07/uber-employees-voted-new-company-culture-and-looks-lot-like-google-and-amazon/842234001/ (accessed August 9, 2019).
8. Ellen MacArthur Foundation, "Circular Economy at Work in Google Data Centers," https://www.ellenmacarthurfoundation.org/case-studies/circular-economy-at-work-in-google-data-centers (accessed August 16, 2019).
9. Danone, "Danone Reaffirms Climate Commitment with Official Recognition from the Science-Based Targets Initiative and Steps up Focus on Regenerative Agriculture," November 15, 2017, https://danone-danonecom-prod.s3.amazonaws.com/COP_press_release_Final.pdf (accessed September 2, 2019).

10. Thomas Fleming and Markus Zils, "Toward a Circular Economy: Philips CEO Frans van Houten," McKinsey, 2014, https://www.mckinsey.com/business-functions/sustainability/our-insights/toward-a-circular-economy-philips-ceo-frans-van-houten (accessed August 29, 2019).

11. Society for Human Resource Management, "Average Cost-Per-Hire for Companies Is $4,129, SHRM Survey Finds," 2016, https://www.shrm.org/about-shrm/press-room/press-releases/pages/human-capital-benchmarking-report.aspx (accessed August 9, 2019).

12. Chuck Beeler, "Young Job Seekers Value Corporate Social Responsibility," Mower, 2019, www.mower.com/insights/young-job-seekers-value-csr/ (accessed August 9, 2019).

13. Tony Schwartz and Christine Porath, "Why You Hate Work," *The New York Times*, 2014, https://www.nytimes.com/2014/06/01/opinion/sunday/why-you-hate-work.html?_r=1 (accessed August 9, 2019).

14. McKinsey Quarterly, "Toward a Circular Economy in Food," 2016, https://www.mckinsey.com/business-functions/sustainability/our-insights/toward-a-circular-economy-in-food (accessed September 2, 2019).

15. Microsoft, "The Carbon Benefits of Cloud Computing: A Study of the Microsoft Cloud," 2018, https://www.microsoft.com/en-us/download/details.aspx?id=56950&WT.mc_id=DX_MVP4025064 (accessed August 9, 2019).

16. A. G. Lafley, "P&G's Innovation Culture," Strategy + Business, 2008, https://www.strategy-business.com/article/08304?gko=b5105 (accessed August 9, 2019).

17. Anheuser-Busch InBev, "Leveraging Technology to Better Engage with Consumers," 2019, https://www.ab-inbev.com/what-we-do/innovation.html (accessed August 9, 2019).

18. Jeff Beer, "Patagonia Is in Business to Save Our Home Planet," Fast Company, December 13, 2018, https://www.fastcompany.com/90280950/exclusive-patagonia-is-in-business-to-save-our-home-planet (accessed August 16, 2019).

20

 **Ecosystem**

No company is an island. When it comes to the circular economy, connecting with your broader ecosystem is especially important. This means working with stakeholders in the same market (including pre-competitively with peers), throughout the value chain, in adjacent industries, and across different regions. And it also means working with investment bodies, governments, NGOs, academia, and so on. The task for executives, then, is to adopt a holistic, systems-wide mindset so that they can build a strong foundation that fosters collaboration for scaling circular initiatives, for leveraging unique capabilities, and for supporting investments in the circular economy. "In order to transition to a circular economy, we need to think holistically about the entire ecosystem and value chain. This means a shift of the traditional models of trade. At DSM, we work with partners across our supply chain to create different patterns of production and consumption. We collaborate with innovators to identify and scale disruptive technologies. We are in a unique position to enable circularity across downstream industries globally, while also contributing to job creation and positive social impact on a local level," says Feike Sijbesma, CEO of DSM, a global purpose-led science company.

Four Areas of Focus

What do we mean by "ecosystem"? In this context, we define a circular ecosystem as the network of organizations collaborating and partnering to create an enabling environment for collective transformation—making it

© The Author(s) 2020
P. Lacy et al., *The Circular Economy Handbook*,
https://doi.org/10.1057/978-1-349-95968-6_20

possible for entire value chains (or for particular regions, e.g., a city or an operational zone) to shift from linear to circular ways of doing business. We view ecosystem engagement as a key stepping stone for companies to not only contribute to circularity in the wider business environment, but also to build the foundation for an effective wise pivot. The ultimate goal is a fully connected organization with suppliers, logistics partners, and technologies enabling material circularity, underpinned by engaged consumers, and supporting policies. According to Jean-Pascal Tricoire, Chairman and CEO of Schneider Electric, a French multinational energy management company, "The biggest impact for us has been making sure we rethink everything we do in a more circular way – within Schneider Electric and the ecosystem around us, including a full-lifecycle relationship with our customers, our suppliers, partners, and integrators of our technology. There is tangible business value from circularity, especially when you bring the right stakeholders together to create system-level change."

Generally speaking, ecosystem leadership has often been viewed as a "final" step once the other dimensions of the circular pivot (Operations, Products & Services, and Culture & Organization) have been tackled. Companies have tended to focus first on "getting their own house in order," that is, they often want to demonstrate their proven circular capabilities before actively participating in broader movements. That's because ecosystems are typically more removed from the direct supply chain of an organization and, in many cases, they require an additional level of trust and openness, especially when working with new partners and peers.

Unfortunately, though, companies can no longer treat their ecosystems as a "backburner" issue. Today, ecosystems must be considered as a *precursor* to achieving scale and impact, especially given the massive challenges that many industries and regions face. Consider, for example, building the collection infrastructure for product takeback or setting up robust alternative supply chains to support an industry transition to circular business models. Such tasks would be a huge undertaking for any single company. Plus, the economic case for change might not be attractive without the support of the full spectrum of partners crucial to success. That's why we believe it's nearly impossible to unlock the circular economy's full potential without considering a company or industry's broader ecosystem. The Coca-Cola Company, for instance, recognized that in order to achieve its own circular economy targets, it needed to work within both its direct value chain and with competitors to move the entire industry forward. The company announced that, by 2030, it would collect a bottle or can for each one that it put in the market. To reach that ambitious goal, The Coca-Cola Company knew that it wasn't going to be enough for the company to concentrate only on its own operations; it also had to work on achieving broad circularity throughout the value chain. "It wasn't just a Coke system; it was a system for all companies," explains Bea Perez, Chief Public Affairs, Communications, Sustainability and Marketing Assets Officer at The Coca-Cola Company.

Companies like The Coca-Cola Company have recognized the importance of proactively shaping their ecosystem, rather than remaining reactive. And they are helping to move their entire sector or industry forward to create an enabling environment for circularity. "You have to be committed in the industry, including your competitors and peers. You need to drive for alignment within your business ecosystem and then broader across the industry," adds Perez.

For leading firms, capturing the potential of the ecosystem has meant a focus on four key areas: sharing, collaboration, investment, and policy (see Table 20.1). Working across these areas will help companies leap past policy and market barriers to achieve the necessary scale and commitment to make circular initiatives financially attractive.

Table 20.1 Four areas of focus

Focus area	The toolbox	Ecosystem in action
Sharing	Non-competitive, transparent sharing of knowledge, information, and learning to support circular thinking and performance. Initiatives in this area center around sharing insight and expertise with peers to address shared challenges. Such exchanges with industry-relevant local or regional partners can fast-forward the uptake of the circular economy at scale	Levi Strauss & Co., a US clothing company, shared its manufacturing trade secrets for a highly efficient process that allows up to 96% of water to be saved in denim garment finishing. The company chose to open up its intellectual property for the greater good of the industry, helping competitors improve their environmental performance and lower their production costs[1]
Collaboration	Bilateral and multilateral partnerships to deliver practical circular solutions. Initiatives in this area focus on establishing bilateral partnerships and working with multilateral public–private stakeholders to bring to market circular solutions that benefit all	Danone has forged an innovative multilateral alliance bringing together leaders from the full agricultural value chain, including animal health and welfare companies, crop nutrition specialists, and an artificial intelligence agri-food start-up. This alliance is exploring how to apply regenerative agriculture practices to dairy farms, from growing animal feed, and rearing animals to producing milk, working closely with farmers in the United States, Europe, and Russia[2]

Table 20.1   (continued)

Focus area	The toolbox	Ecosystem in action
Investment	Financial support to drive circular innovation. Initiatives in this area aim to fuel circular innovation (and, ultimately, disruptive circular solutions) in the market. The investments can be in innovative start-ups, product and business-model development, thought leadership, R&D, and non-commercial third parties such as NGOs or academia	The Global Change Awards, an award program hosted and funded by H&M Foundation, sources early-stage ideas in the circular fashion space, from design, and production to material innovation and recycling. The program has received over 14,000 entries since 2015 and each year the five winners share a €1 million grant and access to an Innovation Accelerator Program[3]
Policy	Support of an enabling regulatory environment for circularity. Initiatives in this area include engaging in local and national discussions as well as international forums to inform and/or influence relevant policy measures and regulations that would foster a regional and global circular economy	The Oceans Plastic Charter adopted in June 2018 lays the groundwork to ensure plastics are designed for reuse and recycling by bringing together leading governments, businesses and civil society organizations[4]

Making the Pivot

Ecosystem initiatives across the four areas of focus (sharing, collaboration, investment, and policy) can vary widely, from investing in start-ups and sharing learnings with peers to creating partnerships to help shape national and international government policies. Companies may pursue a range of projects, depending on their maturity level: emerging, established, leading, or ultimate (see Table 20.2).

A Circular Journey: Collaboration and Sharing

When it comes to collaboration, there are two major types of initiatives that companies can implement. The first is to create *bilateral* partnership solutions. One illustrative case is Veolia's long-term strategic alliance with Danone, to deploy Veolia's expertise in water, waste, and energy management across Danone's processes. This bilateral initiative is part of Danone's overall climate policy, which has targeted zero net carbon emissions by 2050 for operations within the company's direct and shared scope of responsibility.[5]

Table 20.2 Illustrative characteristics of increasing company maturity

	Emerging	Established	Leading	Ultimate	Maturity journey: from → to
Sharing	• Gaining awareness of peers involved and driving positive social impact through circular practices and external engagements • Participating at events to share lessons learned, etc.	• Founding a pre-competitive consortium/platform to share circular insights • Leading bilateral engagements with peers to share circular learnings	• Establishing a global network of non-competitive hubs/consortiums/platforms • Substantially participating to share circular insights for industry solutions	• Regularly convening a forum enabling peers to share circular information non-competitively • Creating large-scale circular employment opportunities in the wider external ecosystem • Sharing intellectual property, which could include manufacturing or other trade secrets, for the benefit of the wider industry	• From initiating information sharing with industry peers to leading multiple knowledge sharing forums • Actions include: (1) sharing insights and expertise to address common challenges with peers, (2) sharing lessons learned with industry-relevant local/ regional partners to address common challenges
Collaboration	• Affiliating with a network of peers and influencers • Assessing the scope for collaborative ways of working to deliver circular solutions	• Deploying targeted initiatives to drive new solutions • Leading conversations to drive further collaboration with peers	• Driving large-scale circular solution(s) through innovative bilateral partnerships • Galvanizing change by fostering cross-industry ways of working with multilateral stakeholders • Setting major circular goals that drive the sector/ value chain forward	• Leveraging circular thought leadership to enhance market-wide circular collaboration • Hosting events/leading solutions (shared working spaces/events/consortiums) to invite collaboration on global issues	• From conducting early conversations for pilots with other peers to enabling and steering industry-wide circular collaboration • Actions include: (1) delivering circular solutions through bilateral partnerships, (2) collaborating with multilateral public–private stakeholders to deliver circular solutions

Table 20.2 (continued)

	Emerging	Established	Leading	Ultimate	Maturity journey: from → to
Investment	• Donating to small-scale research-driven circular initiatives to facilitate their scalability • Making ad hoc, short-term investments	• Impact investing/investing with purpose over time, e.g., structured institutional support • Making longer-term investments targeted to specific research/innovation efforts	• Accelerating the reach of selected circular initiatives with a dedicated circular investment capability • Making long-term investments that scale initiatives up to the pilot and deploy phase	• Providing large-scale financial investment to fund external circular accelerators to scale circular initiatives and research • Making long-term, multi-industry investments	• From small, targeted investments in circular initiatives to leading strategies for long-term, cross-industry investments • Actions include: (1) providing investments to companies, including start-ups, SMEs, etc., (2) providing investments to support circular research, and (3) providing investments to non-commercial third parties
Policy	• Monitoring relevant local, national, and international policies • Engaging in and supporting changes that occur	• Socializing support for circular economy agenda with local and international stakeholders • Lobbying government on key circular issues	• Shaping national and international government policies through direct engagement in those discussions, e.g., advocating for waste tax structures	• Shaping international circular policy as a deciding stakeholder, e.g., participating at the supranational committee level	• From complying with policies and regulations to influencing international circular policies • Actions include: (1) engaging in local and national policy and regulation discussion, (2) engaging in international policy and regulation forums
Overall takeaways	• Participation in an external ecosystem is mainly related to scoping and light touch engagement with a limited number of outside organizations	• Initiatives are more targeted and have greater depth, including some engagement and shaping of partnerships/collaboration efforts with different types of actors within the ecosystem	• A driving position is taken in engaging across most of the ecosystem, including devising solutions to specific circular challenges that will have significant impact across an industry/geography/theme	• Ultimately, a "shaper" role is taken in all areas, focusing on regular collaborations with long-term investments and involvement in international policies	• From passive participant to proactive ecosystem driver, with heavy influence and a leadership position helping others on the journey

Initially, the partnership focused on pilot projects to foster shared learning, including developing "zero liquid discharge" plants and production units for recycled plastic.[5] A couple years later, the two companies worked together to co-design Danone's Nutricia Cuijk production facility in the Netherlands, implementing resource efficiency initiatives that helped Danone move toward its goal of becoming carbon neutral by 2050. Moreover, the two parties have agreed on an ongoing contract that guarantees and incentivizes Veolia to commit to performance improvements.[6] According to Marc Delaye, Senior Executive Vice President, Development, Innovation, and Markets at Veolia, "Both the form and the goals of this alliance make it a truly unique initiative in creating economic, social and environmental value."[5]

The second type of collaboration initiative is to create *multilateral* solutions by convening with multiple stakeholders to address a shared circular challenge. Consider the Platform for Accelerating the Circular Economy (PACE), hosted by the World Economic Forum (WEF) and the World Resources Institute, which includes more than 50 members ranging from leading CEOs to government ministers to heads of international organizations. PACE acts as a project accelerator for business models and markets in various areas. The goal is to develop blended financing models for circular economy projects, to support enabling policy frameworks, to address specific barriers to advancing the circular economy, and to encourage public-private collaborations to scale impact around circular initiatives. One specific PACE initiative, the "New Vision for Electronics," brought together all relevant UN bodies with the support of the WEF and the World Business Council for Sustainable Development to co-create a new shared vision of a circular electronics industry.[7]

To be effective, collaborations within and between organizations should rely heavily on the sharing of unique knowledge and capabilities. A prime example was the successful collaboration between global confectionary manufacturer Mars, multinational IT company IBM, and the US Department of Agriculture (USDA), which worked together to map the cocoa genome for the benefit of the wider industry. Mars contributed its scientific leadership and knowledge of the cocoa supply chain; IBM shared its expertise in computational biology as well as the Blue Gene supercomputer; and the USDA offered its knowledge of the agricultural sector and policy. Pooling these unique capabilities and expertise allowed the collaboration to research and map the cocoa genome to improve crop quality and sustain the supply of cocoa.[8]

Ultimately, the goal across both types of collaborations (bilateral and multilateral) is to foster effective knowledge sharing, while propelling action to tackle industry (and global) issues. Through such initiatives, companies can also seize new collaborative opportunities and gather partners to pilot solutions. Take, for example, H&M, which entered a five-year partnership with the World Wildlife Fund (WWF) in 2011. The primary aim was to improve responsible water use throughout H&M's entire supply chain, going beyond factory lines. The partnership has led to a number of concrete outcomes for H&M, such as water training for 70,000 employees, as well as higher standards for better water and chemical management at more than 500 suppliers. The positive results have inspired further collective action, bringing together other companies, policymakers, and the public to contribute to sustainable water management in targeted areas. In China, for example, the first water stewardship guidelines for the textile industry were introduced. Based on such successes, the partnership was further expanded in 2016 to encompass climate action and a dialogue on strategic issues related to the fashion industry, including the co-creation of tools that would help H&M teams move toward a circular approach when creating new products.[9,10]

The Value Drivers

In the previous chapters, we discussed the various ways that value can be generated within an organization. While Operations, Products & Services, and Culture & Organization mobilize the circular value a company can capture *within* their own enterprise-wide boundaries, a circular ecosystem is critical in supporting and scaling initiatives *outside* the organization, which can, in turn, have a positive impact on the internal operations of a company in the following ways:

Revenue Generation: Sometimes a collaboration is needed to commercialize a unique circular product offering. One example is Southwest Airlines, a US airline that is using circular economy principles to grow revenues and enhance its brand reputation. Rather than dispose of 80,000 leather aircraft seats it removed during a fleet refit earlier this year, for example, the airline gave the leather to US "upcycler" Looptworks, that identifies marketing opportunities for waste materials by converting them into fashionable leather items.[11]

Cost Savings: Collaborations can also be particularly effective for reducing costs. When British automotive company Jaguar Land Rover wanted to decrease the use of virgin aluminum in the production process, it collaborated with Novelis, its material supplier, as well as with Innovate UK, an innovation agency in the UK. The partnership led to REALCAR, an auto developed with a new aluminum alloy that can accommodate recycled content, resulting in reduced costs and a lower environmental impact. Compared with its virgin equivalent, recycled aluminum requires much less energy in production (up to 95% less) and the material has contributed to reducing the global warming potential of a Range Rover TDV6 by 13.8% over its lifetime.[12]

⚠ **Risk Reduction:** To reduce their exposure to future regulatory changes, organizations can proactively engage with policymakers to address potential risks within an industry before they become major problems. Patagonia, for example, has continually worked with policymakers to create the right incentives for favorable business practices. "Regulatory direction setting is important to create an economic environment that favors the use of secondary materials rather than incentivizing the continuous prioritization of virgin materials," says Rick Ridgeway, VP of Public Engagement for Patagonia.

🏷 **Brand Enhancement:** Organizations that are active participants in an external ecosystem also gain value through brand leadership. This can help differentiate a company from its competitors in the industry, not just among customers but also with shareholders, investors, the media, and prospective employees. Many of the world's leading brands are members of major circular ecosystem enablers, such as the Ellen MacArthur Foundation, the Alliance to End Plastic Waste, and the Platform for Accelerating the Circular Economy initiative. By collaborating with such ecosystem-building organizations, companies can link their brand to the wider circular economy mission, signaling that commitment to customers, employees, investors, and other stakeholders.

⚙ Technology as a Key Enabler

In several ways, technology can play a central role in enabling ecosystems. For one thing, digital platforms allow companies and industries to more easily share resources. These platforms drive resource efficiency by helping to extend the use of products and by providing marketplaces for waste. The aim is that the excess capacity or waste of one business (or industry) can become the input for another business (or industry). That was the thinking behind Austin Materials Marketplace, an online platform for businesses and organizations in Texas to connect and find reuse and recycling solutions for waste and by-product materials. Since its launch in 2014, the platform has diverted over 55,000 cubic feet from landfill, generated over $600,000 in cost savings and value creation, and avoided 900 metric tons of carbon emissions.[13]

Online platforms are also a powerful tool for enabling knowledge sharing and open innovation, as participants can easily exchange ideas, share insights, and co-create solutions for overcoming circular challenges. The open access innovation platform Circle Lab acts as a "Wikipedia for circularity": an online space for individuals, businesses, organizations, and cities to discover, discuss, and share circular business practices and strategies to tackle both local and global challenges. During a "Circular Economy Mapping Week," an event organized by a partnership between the Circular Economy Club and Circle Economy, 3000 circular initiatives were documented.[14]

In addition to digital platforms, other innovations can enable companies to more easily share the same value chain or connect different ones. Specifically, advanced analytics and tracking technologies can allow different businesses to use the same logistics infrastructure for route optimization. In Belgium, Nestlé and PepsiCo have partnered to combine their truck fleets and routes for delivering fresh, chilled products to stores. According to the World Economic Forum, the partnership has cut transportation costs by 44% and reduced carbon emissions by 55%. To maintain proprietary information between the two companies (and to avoid any antitrust complaints), a third party handles the intricate logistics of the operation.

Leading Practices to Drive Transformation

A number of companies have had considerable success through participation in circular ecosystems. How were they able to achieve that? Studying those businesses, we can highlight the following key lessons and best practices.

Re-define Value Chain Engagement

In the circular economy, no single company can do it alone. Although businesses can make significant strides to improve their own operations and provide circular products and services, they will eventually need a systems approach to expand and unlock the full potential of circularity. This applies even to large multinationals like Procter & Gamble. Having exhausted the "low-hanging fruit" of its earlier efforts, P&G now realizes that it needs eco-system support to take its circular initiatives to the next level. "We've done all that we can do alone," states Virginie Helias, P&G's Chief Sustainability Officer. Indeed, even a subset of the overall problem might be too enormous for any one company to tackle alone. Consider food waste. "We are try-ing to solve a trillion-dollar problem and we can't do it alone," notes Marc Zornes from Winnow. "We need a plethora of organizations to solve it in different ways."

As industry lines become more blurred and value chains compressed, the circular economy opens up a multitude of possibilities for companies to rethink how they interact up and down their entire value chains with cus-tomers, suppliers, communities, and partners. Many of those possibilities will include invaluable opportunities for collaborations. Cisco has always tried to foster an open and collaborative environment with their suppliers and partners. From those partnerships, Cisco is constantly receiving valuable ideas for how to re-engineer its products. "We're not just dictating policy to our suppliers about what materials they can and can't use," says John Kern, Senior Vice President of Supply Chain Operations at Cisco. "We want them to be part of a collaborative process. We need their ideas."

That said, significant challenges remain in evolving ecosystems to full circularity. A supply chain that is more forward-flow focused, for instance, inherently creates barriers for moving into recycled content, presenting pro-cess challenges for remanufacturing. To overcome those obstacles, compa-nies will need to collaborate closely with their suppliers and other ecosystem actors to optimize reverse flows. This means putting functions in place that can reprocess materials and match supply with demand so that the waste from one flow can become the raw input to another, leading to substantial business value.

The effort required to set up a holistic circular ecosystem should not be underestimated, but it is achievable even for a complex, large-scale network of different parties. A good example of that is the Port of Amsterdam, intent on harnessing systems in a common aim to connect and monetize opera-tional waste streams across industries. The port has become a hub for cir-cular and bio-based growth, surrounded by a cluster of circular companies that include bioplastics and biodiesel producers. The goal is to replace fos-sil fuel cargo with biomass and to convert organic waste, all while creating jobs and spurring economic growth. "The Port of Amsterdam has ambi-tious goals when it comes to the circular economy," notes Micha Hes, the Port of Amsterdam's Business Development Manager, Circular Economy.

To accomplish those objectives, the port has assembled one of the largest bio-based ecosystems within Europe, where organic waste is converted into renewable energy, fuels, fertilizers, and chemical compounds. Already, 6% of its turnover is circular based, and the goal is to grow that number to 10% by 2021.[15]

Leverage (Disruptive) Partners to Develop and Deploy New Solutions

As discussed throughout this book, technology is a key enabler for circular initiatives, especially as companies begin to scale their circular solutions beyond their boundaries. Consequently, executives need to be on the constant lookout for new innovations, and ways in which their ecosystems can help develop those emerging technologies and accelerate their broad adoption to achieve scale. That was the strategy behind Procter & Gamble's collaboration with PureCycle Technologies to speed the adoption of P&G's innovative plastic-recycling method, in which plastics are separated from other waste, delivering an ultrapure recycled polypropylene. P&G has licensed the patented technology to PureCycle, which recently partnered with Nestlé and other companies to help spread adoption of the technology.[16,17] In the fashion industry, Ferragamo, an Italian luxury goods company, has joined with Orange Fiber, a company that manufactures the first fabric made from by-products of citrus juice production. The collaboration has led to a new collection of goods, enhanced by prints by an award-winning designer.[18,19]

For such partnerships to succeed, an organization must forge the capability to understand the value delivered, analyze the scalability of projects, funnel and prioritize partners, and determine compatibility with its existing operating model and processes. Large corporations can offer tremendous resources and capabilities as a partner, but they are often limited in how much risk the core business can take on. From that perspective, partnerships with innovative smaller firms are often necessary.

Invest for the Long Term (and Get "Buy In" from Shareholders and Investors)

Executives and policymakers should be committed to supporting circular ecosystems as long-term investments, and finance departments and financial institutions need to play a key role in providing the necessary resources for circular economy initiatives to take shape (see "Investment—The Role of Financial Services"). Indeed, investment in organizations, business models, products, technologies, or non-commercial third parties is the crucial stepping stone for practical circular solutions to unfold within an industry or region. The Danish government learned that long-term investments in innovations like wind farms were critical to allow such technologies to mature, eventually enabling them to become commercialized without the need for additional subsidies. According to BASF, the German chemical company, large shareholders are starting to adopt long-term thinking, but investment managers need to catch up with that mindset. "There is still uncertainty and lack of cohesiveness on how you measure circular solutions – they don't know what to look for yet," notes Saori Dubourg, Member of the Executive Board at BASF. As such, organizations must help educate shareholders and investors on the value of circularity (and demonstrate it with strong business cases), so that new systems for measurement and management that support a circular economy can be adopted. According to Dubourg, "We need to reframe how we measure success in business and move away from focusing solely on profits to creating profit, human capital, and environmental good. It is key to report on all three elements and link decision-making and incentives to the triple bottom line."

Work Proactively with Policymakers

As a company becomes increasingly engaged with its ecosystem, the regulatory environment can be a key enabler—or a major obstacle (see "Policy—The Role of Policymakers"). Executives are therefore encouraged to work with the public sector and cross-industry peers to co-create smarter policies that will allow a systemic step change in the circular economy. As Luca Meini, Head of Circular Economy at Enel, an Italian energy company, points out, "Legislation can represent a limiting factor in some countries – one of the biggest barriers to success. Legislative silos between sectors should be overcome to enable circular solutions." In many cases, policymakers are willing to support the circular economy, but they often lack a more comprehensive view of what is needed to foster that transition. That is one of the situations where companies can step in, engaging with the public policy community to help shape policy that curbs irresponsible competitors, raises collective standards, and enables innovation. Recognizing a need to keep governments and regulators up to date with circular economy trends and likely business models, companies have been increasingly willing to share their ideas and expertise to support the wider transition.

This is the strategy deployed by Carlsberg and the Danish government. Flemming Besenbacher, Chairman of Carlsberg Group and the Carlsberg Foundation, drafted a report for the Danish government to inspire its work toward the circular economy, suggesting 27 initiatives that might promote circular economy in Danish society and the business world. The issue is of crucial importance to society and to Carlsberg Group because it operates in 98 Danish municipalities that all treat waste differently today. "We are trying to adjust regulation to achieve collective impact, but it takes time and patience to get there," says Besenbacher. "We cannot expect governments to act alone. Partnering with business is key to move the needle and Carlsberg Group is already leading this development."

And sometimes, not only should a company collaborate with governments to enact the appropriate regulations to encourage circularity, it needs to be one step ahead and assume the reins in that effort. That is, before being required to do so, a business could move ahead of the curve by adopting new standards for circular practices, such as a minimum level of recycled content in its products. In Denmark in 2013, multiple associations and companies in the electronics industry entered the "Voluntary Agreement on WEEE (Waste and Electronic Equipment)" jointly with the Ministry for the Environment. The aim was to promote the eco-design of electrical and electronic equipment and to create incentives for better and more separation, reuse, and recycling of used electronics. The results of the agreement, which ran from 2014 to 2016, confirmed the large potential for circular solutions through eco-design.[20] Recently, companies and industry associations have taken a similar approach in addressing the plastics waste problem, which offers the dual benefit of tackling a serious environmental problem and capturing considerable business benefits. The European Strategy for Plastics called on stakeholders to make voluntary pledges to use or produce more recycled plastics and, by the end of 2018, 70 companies and business associations had done so.[21]

When companies do this together with industry peers or partners along the supply chain, it raises the playing field for all, paving the way to engage with policymakers to turn voluntary arrangements into policy. "When industry takes the lead, it is easier to have a productive dialogue and act in concert with government," explains Michael Goltzman from The Coca-Cola Company. "The bigger challenge is when industry does not take the lead and when public opinion and other pressures drive the need for government to act first."

Chapter Takeaways

- Companies can no longer treat their ecosystems as a "backburner" issue. Ecosystems must now be considered as a *precursor* to achieving scale and impact.
- It's crucial that executives proactively shape their ecosystems, rather than remaining reactive and compliant.
- Ecosystem development requires a focus on four key areas: sharing, collaboration, investment, and policy.
- A circular ecosystem is critical in supporting and scaling initiatives *outside* the organization, which can, in turn, have a positive impact on the internal operations of a company in terms of revenue generation, cost reduction, risk reduction, and brand enhancement.
- Digital platforms can connect companies and industries to facilitate the sharing of resources, knowledge, and ideas. This can lead to the co-creation of solutions for overcoming circular challenges and reaping of substantial business value as well.
- As industry boundaries become blurred and value chains compressed, the circular economy opens up myriad possibilities for companies to rethink how they interact up and down their entire value chains with customers, suppliers, communities, and partners. Many of those possibilities will include invaluable opportunities for innovation, collaboration, new business models, and new markets.
- Sometimes, not only must a company collaborate with governments to enact the appropriate regulations to encourage circularity; it needs to be one step ahead of the game and assume the reins in that effort.

Ecosystems are complex "spiderwebs" of interactions and integrations. They are the launchpad for companies to scale the impact of their circular efforts across the wider economy and society. Without these interlinkages, system-level change is hard to achieve. However, how to navigate that journey within an organization requires some guidance. The following considerations will help organizations decide how they can best tailor the right actions to support the ecosystem transition.

Sample Questions to Answer

Collaborating within and outside the value chain

- ☐ What are key bilateral and multilateral partnership opportunities to learn from, contribute to, and help scale circular initiatives for our business?
- ☐ How can we collaborate with our suppliers to bring circular solutions to the market?
- ☐ How can we engage actors within and outside of our industry to share circular challenges and ambitions and encourage co-creation?

Raising awareness and sharing

- ☐ How can we find low-cost ways to raise awareness of our industry's circular challenges (e.g., through sharing case studies online)?

☐ How can we kickstart conversations and ideas around our circular challenges across a diverse pool of actors (e.g., through events, online participation, challenge-focused "hackathons," etc.)?

☐ What capabilities (including technology, processes, and culture) can we offer that may be useful for circularity outside of our value chain? Similarly, what capabilities in other industries may be useful for our business's circularity?

Investing for impact

☐ Where can we invest to fuel circular innovation and accelerate the transition toward a circular economy in our industry?

☐ Who can we partner with to help find and scope opportunities for investment to drive circular value for our business?

☐ How can we work together with our financial providers to influence the reshaping of the financial services sector toward circularity?

Influencing policy

☐ How can we work with peers in our industry to influence circular economy policy?

☐ What information/experience can we share with policymakers to help drive regulation that favors circularity?

☐ Which current regulations may hamper circular progress in our industry?

Functions to Engage

☐ **Finance** to leverage investment for joint innovation projects or Merger & Acquisition (M&A) activity

☐ **Procurement** to develop relationships and initiatives across the supply base

☐ **R&D** to steer strategy and innovation focus toward circularity

☐ **Corporate Affairs** to craft effective relationships within the industry and with policymakers

☐ **Marketing** to communicate partnerships, initiatives, and the impact to broader stakeholders

☐ **Human Resources** to foster a culture open to collaboration and learning

Dependencies/Intersection Points

☐ **Operations**: Innovative projects with external organizations may affect initiatives and processes within different operational functions. Management needs to assess the impact of those changes, as well as consider how to leverage the knowledge and expertise of these individuals.

☐ **Products & Services**: Wider ecosystem engagement and joint innovation projects may have an impact on the design and delivery of products and services, opening doors to new models, channels, and opportunities for growth.

☐ **Culture & Organization**: Effective ecosystem engagement requires embedding a collaborative and open approach into internal values, decision-making, and innovation efforts across all functions of the organization.

Notes

1. Stout, "Creating Value by Sharing Intellectual Property," September 1, 2016, https://www.stout.com/en/insights/article/creating-value-sharing-intellectual-property/ (accessed August 9, 2019).
2. Danone, "Supporting Dairy Farmers On Their Journey Towards Regenerative Agriculture," June 26, 2019, https://www.danone.com/stories/articles-list/supporting-dairy-farmers.html (accessed August 29, 2019).
3. H&M Foundation, "Global Change Award," https://hmfoundation.com/global-change-award/ (accessed August 12, 2019).
4. Government of Canada, "Ocean Plastics Charter," https://www.canada.ca/en/environment-climate-change/services/managing-reducing-waste/international-commitments/ocean-plastics-charter.html (accessed August 12, 2019).
5. Veolia, "Danone and Veolia Announce Unique Global Alliance to Meet the Challenge of Climate Change," 2015, https://www.veolia.com/en/veolia-group/media/press-releases/danone-and-veolia-announce-unique-global-alliance-meet-challenge-climate-change (accessed August 9, 2019).
6. Veolia, "Veolia Supports New State-of-the-Art Danone Nutricia Plant in The Netherlands," 2019, https://www.veolia.com/en/newsroom/communiques-de-presse/veolia-supports-new-state-art-danone-nutricia-plant-netherlands (accessed August 9, 2019).
7. World Economic Forum in Collaboration with the United Nations E-waste Coalition, "A New Circular Vision for Electronics," 2019, https://static1.squarespace.com/static/5c3f456fa2772cd16721224a/t/5c48930b0e2e728d-fff44df3/1548260175610/New+Vision+for+Electronics-+Final.pdf (accessed August 9, 2019).
8. Chris Kelly, "Mars Inc, IBM and USDA Map Genome for Cocoa Plant," Reuters, 2010, https://www.reuters.com/article/us-cocoa-genome/mars-inc-ibm-and-usda-map-genome-for-cocoa-plant-idUSTRE68E0TO20100915 (accessed August 9, 2019).
9. H&M, "Making a Change Together: Midterm Result Report H&M WWF Partnership (January 2016–July 2018)," https://about.hm.com/content/dam/hmgroup/groupsite/documents/masterlanguage/Newsroom/2019/WWF_report/Midterm%20result%20report%20H&M%20WWF%20partnership%202016-2018.pdf (accessed August 9, 2019).
10. World Wildlife Fund, "WWF Global Partnerships Report: Overview of WWF's Largest Corporate Partnerships, Fiscal Year 2016," 2016, http://awsassets.panda.org/downloads/WWF_Global_Partnerships_FY16_FINAL.pdf (accessed August 9, 2019).
11. Elisabeth Braw, "Southwest Airlines Upcycles 80,000 Leather Seats into Bags, Shoes and Balls," *The Guardian*, July 15, 2014, https://www.theguardian.com/sustainable-business/southwest-airlines-upcycle-leather-seats-aeroplane-bags-shoes-balls (accessed August 12, 2019).

12. Paul Cassell, Ian Ellison, Alexandra Pearson, Jamie Shaw, Adrian Tautscher, Steve Betts, Andy Doran, and Milan Felberbaum, "Collaboration for a Closed-Loop Value Chain," University of Cambridge Institute for Sustainability Leadership, 2016, http://www.multivu.com/players/English/7755351-novelis-jaguar-rc5754-recycled-aluminum-alloy/docs/case-study-845192244.pdf (accessed August 9, 2019).
13. Austin Materials Marketplace, "Current Program Metrics," https://austin-materialsmarketplace.org/success-stories (accessed August 9, 2019).
14. Circle Economy, "Circle Lab, Biggest Global Open Access Innovation Platform for the Circular Economy, Launches 1.000 New Case Studies," 2018, https://www.circle-economy.com/circle-lab-biggest-global-open-access-innovation-platform-for-the-circular-economy-launches-1-000-new-case-studies/#.XSz5xZNKiAs (accessed August 9, 2019).
15. John Bensalhia, "Full Circle," Port Strategy, August, 22, 2017, https://www.portstrategy.com/news101/environment/full-circular2 (accessed August 16, 2019).
16. P&G, "P&G Researchers Invent Breakthrough Technology That Will Revolutionize the Recycling Industry," August 22, 2017, https://news.pg.com/blog/PG-Innventure (accessed August 27, 2019).
17. Global Newswire, "PureCycle Technologies Partners with Milliken, Nestlé to Accelerate Revolutionary Plastics Recycling," 2019, https://www.globenewswire.com/news-release/2019/03/13/1752436/0/en/PureCycle-Technologies-Partners-with-Milliken-Nestl%C3%A9-to-Accelerate-Revolutionary-Plastics-Recycling.html (accessed August 9, 2019).
18. Ferragamo, "Orange Fiber Green Fashion Inspiration," 2019, https://www.ferragamo.com/shop/eu/en/sf/collections/orange-fiber--37542 (accessed August 9, 2019).
19. Orange Fiber, "Sustainable Fabrics from Citrus Juice By-Products," 2019, http://orangefiber.it/en/ (accessed August 9, 2019).
20. Dansk Industri, "WEEE Goes Circular. Results from the Voluntary Agreement on WEEE," http://di.dk/SiteCollectionDocuments/Milj%C3%B8/Nyheder/Sarahs%20mappe%20-%20nyheder/WEEE/UK_WEEE%20goes%20circular%202017_publikation_A4_WEB.pdf (accessed August 9, 2019).
21. European Commission, "European Strategy for Plastics—Voluntary Pledges," 2019, https://ec.europa.eu/growth/content/european-strategy-plastics-voluntary-pledges_en (accessed August 9, 2019).

21

💲 Ecosystem Deep Dive #1:
Investment—The Role of Financial Services

The circular economy requires substantial investments in a range of areas, from supporting start-ups experimenting with new circular business models to developing large-scale recycling infrastructure. Currently, the capital that will underpin the shift to new circular business models far outweighs what is readily available and accessible. Through 2050, an estimated $3.5 trillion per year in investments is needed just to build required clean energy infrastructure.[1] That clearly won't be enough. UNCTAD, a UN body dealing with trade, investment, and development, estimates that $3.9 trillion a year is needed in developing countries alone from 2015 to 2030 to fully meet the 17 UN Sustainable Development Goals.[2] Consequently, it's incumbent on financial institutions to recognize their role in a circular economy ecosystem and provide the necessary investments and tools to drive the move from linear to circular. In doing so, they can gain competitive advantage in three important ways:

- **Growth**: During the last decade, the financial industry has begun to appreciate the potential of long-term sustainable business practices and, as that mindset has evolved, more investments have begun to flow. Green bonds, which cover several key elements of the circular economy, for instance, increased over three-hundredfold, from less than $500 million in 2008 to $163 billion in 2017, with a cumulative figure of $580 billion of green bonds sold up to 2018.[3,4] In addition, companies can now issue "transition bonds" to finance technologies or new business models that support the transition to low-carbon intensive alternatives.[1] Growth

© The Author(s) 2020
P. Lacy et al., *The Circular Economy Handbook*,
https://doi.org/10.1057/978-1-349-95968-6_21

opportunities for investors in the circular economy are fast developing, as Leon Wijnands, Global Head of Sustainability from ING confirms: "Within the circular economy, we are seeing new business models and markets opening up. We have seen an increase in appetite within ING to finance circular propositions and clients."

- **Differentiation**: Financial services companies that emerge as pioneers in scaling the circular economy will establish a leadership position, gaining significant advantage over their peers. Says Massimiano Tellini, Global Head Circular Economy at Intesa Sanpaolo, an Italian banking group, "The financial service industry doesn't yet understand that there is a huge opportunity in being a pioneer, leading the way and creating demand for the circular economy. We need to be proactive and not just responsive."

- **License to operate and risk mitigation**: As governments and other stakeholder groups become more aware of the importance of transitioning to a circular economy, they will begin exerting increasing pressure on industries to support the shift. For the heavily regulated financial industry, investments in circular businesses now should help mitigate those risks and enable companies to secure a license to operate. Moreover, a huge advantage of transitioning to the circular economy that few financial institutions are taking into account is the mitigation of risks that will become increasingly prevalent in the future; these include the risk of virgin material dependency, the associated price fluctuations, shifting consumer demands, and the impact of stricter environmental legislation.[5,6] As Leon Wijnands from ING puts it: "Maintaining business-as-usual might in the end be riskier than transitioning to circular business models. Failure to assess the risks and adapt accordingly will cause linear risks to build up in portfolios and loan books, potentially leading to significant consequences."

Four Sources of Finance

The financial services sector and other capital providers can support the circular economy by improving access to essential credit, creating innovative products to provide those funds and providing incentives to encourage businesses to implement circular initiatives. The kind of help offered will generally depend on the type of finance provider:

- **Banks and lenders**: can provide credit instruments such as bonds or loans that link outcomes to the cost of lending: For example, if sustainability performance improves, the net interest rate decreases. That's the kind of innovative financial instrument being developed by ING. ING's

Sustainability Improvement Loan provides financial incentives for clients whose sustainability rating goes up. In 2017, for instance, ING issued a €1 billion loan to Philips with an interest rate that's coupled to the client's sustainability performance and rating.[7] Italian bank, Intesa Sanpaolo, is also working to provide innovative offerings to clients, launching a €5 billion credit facility in 2018 to support businesses adopting circular business models.[8] Intesa Sanpaolo has also established an innovation center, which helps fledgling start-ups connect with more than 10,000 investors, companies, and other players in the innovation ecosystem.[9] "Circularity means de-risking the banking sector, making it more resistant to external shocks," says Massimiano Tellini of Intesa Sanpaolo.

- **Commercial investors**: may have longer-term investment horizons, potentially making them better suited to financing disruptive circular businesses. A case in point is Circularity Capital, a specialist private equity firm, which invests in small-to-medium-sized circular businesses at a critical phase in their development. "We are constantly being told how important it is to have investors who really understand these types of business models and also to have the right network to add value to investee businesses – for example, through business development with key corporates," notes Jamie Butterworth, Partner at Circularity Capital. Another example is Closed Loop Partners (CLP), which focuses on infrastructure projects that accelerate the development of circular supply chains and on catalytic technologies to drive circularity across a range of material categories. Since 2015, CLP has invested over $44 million across 30 initiatives, which has helped to unlock an additional $105 million in co-investments.[10]

- **Non-commercial capital providers**: such as development institutions or private philanthropies can provide co-funding through grants, public capital, or government-backed vehicles that generally have less stringent requirements to generate short- or medium-term returns compared with financial instruments from commercial investors. Take, for example, the European Investment Bank (EIB), the largest multilateral development bank that makes long-term financing available for initiatives that contribute toward EU policy goals. EIB typically finances 30–50% of the total investment in circular businesses, with the goal of attracting additional financing from other public and private sources as the initiatives mature. In other words, EIB absorbs the early risks in worthwhile projects with the aim of making them more bankable and attractive to financiers over the long term. Over the last five years, EIB has provided €2.1 billion in co-financing to more than 100 circular projects in a variety of areas including water management, agriculture, and the bio-economy.[11]

"The EIB is unique in its deep technical and financial expertise and its strong track record in risk management," says Shiva Dustdar, the Head of Innovation Finance in the Advisory Services Department at the EIB. "We gain additional risk capacity thanks to our risk-sharing mechanisms with the European Commission and with our financing we pave the way for traditional banks and mainstream investors to come in and share in the risks and returns." High-Net-Worth Individuals (HNWI) are playing an increasingly larger role as private philanthropic capital providers, such as the Eric and Wendy Schmidt Fund for Strategic Innovati on which funds the "Circular Economy Learning Program" offered by the Ellen MacArthur Foundation.[12] The resources of HNWIs can also be pooled together to further impact investment opportunities, for example, leading impact investment bank ClearlySo, raising £4 million in funding for the circular start-up Bio-Bean.[13,14]

- **Corporate venturing**: involves corporate players finding, supporting, and investing in early-stage companies, typically start-ups with an innovative value proposition for their industry. Corporate venturing efforts help large companies boost innovation and potentially secure early investment access to promising businesses. In some cases, corporate ventures can act as an accelerator, providing a platform for start-ups to develop their offering and bring it to market. Take H&M's Global Change Awards, for example, an award program delivered by H&M Foundation that sources early-stage ideas in the circular fashion space, from design and production to material innovation and recycling. The program has received over 14,000 entries since 2015 and some of their winners have then worked with leaders in the fashion industry.[15]

 Case Study: ABN AMRO

A leader in circular investments, ABN AMRO actively seeks out clients that might be receptive to switching to a circular business model. The Dutch bank's path toward greater ecosystem maturity highlights a few of the steps along that journey.

In the emerging stage, ABN AMRO published a circular economy guide in 2016 that explained basic circular principles and provided a five-step process for preparing a circular business case.[16] The company also released a suite of tools that would help ease the transition to those new business models. In the established stage, ABN AMRO opened a new facility in 2017 designed to facilitate collaborations with other companies, clients, and local residents.

The building, which was developed with the help of architects, academia, and suppliers, symbolized the fundamental principles of the circular economy: Recycled materials were used in the construction (old jeans, for example, were repurposed as insulating material), and the structure was designed for easy disassembly and reuse.[17] And lastly, in the leading stage, ABN AMRO, ING, and Rabobank collaboratively developed and launched new financial guidelines in 2018 that could serve as the standard framework for investments in the circular economy. These guidelines describe the new forms of capital needed and explain the financial fundamentals of circular business models, such as pay-per-use payment structures and value creation in second-hand markets. With this information, executives will be better able to select and finance proposals for new businesses based on circular models. The goal is to help accelerate the funding of circular initiatives by providing a useful framework for their evaluation.[18]

Overcoming Obstacles

For a number of reasons, current, or traditional, financing mechanisms and systems are often not well-suited for a transition to the circular economy, for example:

- Banks are typically averse to circular risk, as it is perceived to incur greater risks than conventional or more "proven" investments
- The bond market requires a certain level of business maturity in order to scale and have a wider impact on the economy
- Venture capital and private equity favor short payback periods
- Crowdfunding has trouble mobilizing the volume of capital needed for asset-intensive circular business models
- Standards to define circular companies, products or initiatives are still being defined, so investors may struggle to find investable businesses that are both financially and environmentally attractive

Because of these and other obstacles, the size and prevalence of funding for circular initiatives are still exceptionally small, with only a handful of financial organizations having distinct circular strategies or programs. As Katherine Garrett-Cox, CEO of Gulf International Bank (UK), points out, "Circular business models are not yet widely understood within the financial services sector, and the traditional corporate finance toolkit has not been sufficiently adapted." Shiva Dustdar, the Head of Innovation Finance in the

Advisory Services Department at the EIB, confirms the trend, stating that, "Five years ago, the term circular economy was barely known in the financial services community. For instance, only in the past year or two have we seen mainstream financial outlets cover the circular economy as an emerging investment opportunity." Although there is still a ways to go to drive the circular transition within the financial services industry, there are a number of measures that can help overcome these challenges.

One solution to unlocking more financing is to find partners to maximize the impact of circular propositions, with the added benefit of sharing the risk. That's the idea behind the Circular Supply Chain Accelerator (CiSCA) which ING developed together with Accenture Strategy and Circle Economy, all as members of the World Economic Forum's Platform for Accelerating Circular Economy. CiSCA supports large multinationals and their small- and medium-sized suppliers shift to circular business models. In 2018, CiSCA announced the first round of the accelerator would be focused on the building and construction sector, given the material and energy intensity of the industry.[19] Another example is the Circular Economy Framework Loan, the largest credit line (€1 billion) for circular initiatives in Europe and the first of its kind in the Italian market.[20] Through the collaboration, Intesa Sanpaolo and EIB have been able to provide new resources to mid-cap companies and innovative SMEs, with a particular focus on investments in projects related to the circular economy in the manufacturing, agriculture, energy, and waste management sectors.[20]

Another obstacle to overcome is the way in which financial institutions assess circular initiatives: Traditional financial measures are used to evaluate the new types of business models because of a lack of an appropriate framework. But those conventional measures overlook various important factors, such as the environmental and social benefits of a circular initiative and the different ways in which value is generated. For example, circular business models could be regarded as highly risky based on traditional financial risk models, due to their limited track record, novel product offerings, or new ways of serving consumers. Financial risk modeling will need to adapt to appropriately evaluate the residual value of assets that are plugged back into the value chain and other benefits such as the higher customer retention of service-oriented businesses. It is also important for financial institutions to factor in the risks of linear models in an increasingly resource-scarce world.

"The financial services sector needs to develop better risk assessment and valuation models in order to be able to assess correctly the risks and opportunities associated with circular business models. Circular business models often involve different asset, cash-flow and risk/return profiles to linear business models. There is a need to develop new approaches to measuring and monitoring initiatives within the circular economy. A common taxonomy helps ensure investors and investees speak a common language," emphasizes Katherine Garrett-Cox of Gulf International Bank (UK). The guidelines developed by ING, ABN AMRO, and others that were mentioned earlier provide a good first step in that direction, but much more work is needed.

It's also important to note here that, although the current risk models and financial approaches tend to be conservative, multinational companies have tremendous potential to effect changes to these models and approaches and influence the sectoral shift. After all, these large corporations are the major clients of financial institutions. They can work to educate their financial services providers on the benefits of the circular economy and collaborate to develop the appropriate financial instruments. As a way to seize this opportunity, in February 2018, Danone amended its €2 billion syndicated credit facility in order to integrate environmental and social criteria into the margin payable to its banks.[21] The criteria are based on the scores provided by two independent ESG agencies as well as the percentage of Danone's consolidated sales covered by B Corp certification. The project was supported by BNP Paribas, a French international banking group acting as the sustainability coordinator for a pool of relationship banks.[22] BNP Paribas has developed this concept further by launching additional Positive Incentive Loan schemes with Solvay, L&Q, Thames Water, and Deutsche Börse Group, in the latter case financing a €750 million credit consortium in partnership with Commerzbank.[23]

 Chapter Takeaways

- By investing in circular initiatives, financial services companies can gain competitive advantage in three important ways: achieving growth; differentiating from competitors; and securing license to operate and risk mitigation.
- New types of financial metrics and instruments are needed to properly evaluate and fund circular initiatives. Financial institutions should find better ways to evaluate risk and use blended financial models to mitigate risk.
- Banks and lenders should collaborate with their clients to help them develop the business case for circular projects and better identify and quantify costs and benefits.

Notes

1. Tom Freke, "How 'Transition Bonds' Can Help Polluters Turn Green," *Bloomberg Businessweek*, January 14, 2019, https://www.bloomberg.com/news/articles/2019-07-14/how-transition-bonds-can-help-polluters-turn-green-quicktake (accessed August 13, 2019).
2. UNCTAD, "Promoting Investment in the Sustainable Development Goals," 2018, https://unctad.org/en/PublicationsLibrary/diaepcb2018d4_en.pdf (accessed September 2, 2019).
3. *The Economist*, "The EU Wants to Make Finance More Environmentally Friendly," March 22, 2018, https://www.economist.com/finance-and-economics/2018/03/22/the-eu-wants-to-make-finance-more-environmentally-friendly (accessed August 13, 2019).
4. Lyubov Pronina, "What Are Green Bonds and How 'Green' Is Green?" *Bloomberg Businessweek*, March 24, 2019, https://www.bloomberg.com/news/articles/2019-03-24/what-are-green-bonds-and-how-green-is-green-quicktake (accessed August 13, 2019).
5. ING, "Rethinking Finance in a Circular Economy," May 2015, https://www.ingwb.com/media/1149417/ing-rethinking-finance-in-a-circular-economy-may-2015.pdf (accessed August 13, 2019).
6. Ellen MacArthur Foundation, "Money Makes the World Go Round," March 2016, https://www.ellenmacarthurfoundation.org/assets/downloads/ce100/FinanCE.pdf (accessed August 13, 2019).
7. ING, "ING and Philips Collaborate on Sustainable Loan" April 19, 2017, https://www.ing.com/Newsroom/All-news/ING-and-Philips-collaborate-on-sustainable-loan.htm (accessed August 30, 2019).
8. Fonazione Cariplo and Intesa Sanpaolo, "Intesa Sanpaolo And Fondazione Cariplo Launch the First Circular Economy Lab In Italy," September 24, 2018, https://www.group.intesasanpaolo.com/scriptIsir0/si09/contentData/view/content-ref?id=CNT-05-0000000513D20 (accessed August 13, 2019).
9. Intesa Sanpaolo, "Intesa Sanpaolo Innovation Center: The Future-Proof Business Accelerator," https://www.intesasanpaolo.com/it/news/innovazione-e-fintech/acceleratori-di-imprese-e-startup-intesa-san-paolo-innovation-center-a-prova-di-futuro.html (accessed August 13, 2019).
10. Closed Loop Partners, "Closed Loop Partners 2018 Impact Report," http://www.closedlooppartners.com/wp-content/uploads/2019/03/Closed-Loop-Partners-Impact-Report-2018-1.pdf (accessed August 30, 2019).
11. European Investment Bank, "EIB's Leadership in the Circular Economy Recognized at World Economic Forum Meeting in Davos," January 21, 2019, https://www.eib.org/en/press/news/eibs-leadership-in-the-circular-economy-recognized-at-world-economic-forum-meeting-in-davos.htm (accessed August 30, 2019).

12. Ellen MacArthur Foundation, "Circular Economy Programme," https://www.ellenmacarthurfoundation.org/our-work/activities/learn-about-the-circular-economy/circular-economy-programme (accessed August 13, 2019).

13. ClearlySo, "Individual Investors," https://www.clearlyso.com/investors/individual-investors/ (accessed August 13, 2019).

14. ClearlySo, "Bio-Bean Secures £4 Million to Disrupt Markets Reliant on Use of Virgin and Scarce Resources," April 25, 2019, https://www.clearlyso.com/bio-bean-secures-4-million-to-disrupt-markets-reliant-on-use-of-virgin-and-scarce-resources/ (accessed August 13, 2019).

15. Global Change Award, "About the Award," https://globalchangeaward.com/about-the-award/ (accessed August 13, 2019).

16. ABN AMRO, "Infographic: Towards a Circular Company in 5 Steps," https://www.abnamro.com/en/about-abnamro/in-society/sustainability/newsletter/2016/january/towards-a-circular-company.html (accessed August 13, 2019).

17. ABN AMRO, "Circl, a Circular Pavilion in Amsterdam, Officially Opened," September 5, 2017, https://www.abnamro.com/en/newsroom/press-releases/2017/circl-a-circular-pavilion-in-amsterdam-officially-opened.html (accessed August 13, 2019).

18. Rabobank, "ABN AMRO, ING and Rabobank Launch Finance Guidelines for Circular Economy," https://www.rabobank.com/en/press/search/2018/20180702-abn-amro-ing-and-rabobank-launch-finance-guidelines-for-circular-economy.html (accessed August 13, 2019).

19. ING, "What Motivates Companies to Go Circular?" January 17, 2019, https://www.ing.com/Newsroom/All-news/What-motivates-companies-to-go-circular.htm (accessed August 13, 2019).

20. Intesa Sanpaolo, "From Intesa Sanpaolo and the EIB 1 Billion Euro for Midcaps and the Circular Economy," June 10, 2019, https://www.group.intesasanpaolo.com/scriptIsir0/si09/salastampa/eng_comunicati_detail_intesa_spaolo.jsp?contentId=CNT-05-000000053317E#/salastampa/eng_comunicati_detail_intesa_spaolo.jsp%3FcontentId%3D-CNT-05-000000053317E (accessed August 13, 2019).

21. Jay Coen Gilbert, "Every CFO Should Know This: 'The Future of Banking' Ties Verified ESG Performance To Cheaper Capital," *Forbes*, February 20, 2018, https://www.forbes.com/sites/jaycoengilbert/2018/02/20/every-cfo-should-know-this-the-future-of-banking-ties-verified-esg-performance-to-cheaper-capital/#2715c4da7e4d (accessed September 2, 2019).

22. BNP Paribas, "Danone's Positive Incentive Financing Strategy," August 3, 2018, https://cib.bnpparibas.com/sustain/danone-s-positive-incentive-financing-strategy_a-3-2238.html (accessed September 2, 2019).

23. BNP Paribas, "Deutsche Börse, with the Support of BNP Paribas, Launches a New Positive Incentive Loan," March 27, 2019, https://group.bnpparibas/en/news/deutsche-boerse-with-support-bnp-paribas-launches-positive-incentive-loan (accessed September 2, 2019).

22

📝 Ecosystem Deep Dive #2: Policy—The Role of Policymakers

Governments are a critical accelerator of change. In addition to developing, considering, and instituting policy measures and channeling public investment toward a circular economy, they can activate other actors to develop and scale circular economy practices which are beneficial to businesses and societies. To deploy that power in constructive ways, public policies should create a conducive environment for companies to develop and scale circular business models, with the ultimate goal of enabling citizens to thrive in a healthier, prosperous, and more equitable society. According to Erika Chan from Dell, a multinational technology company, "Policymakers have a significant role to play in driving the development of the circular economy. As work in the domain continues, we will almost certainly find obstacles and barriers preventing the acceleration of our work. Policymakers have the opportunity to help remove those barriers, either through regulation, guidelines, or investment."

A Policymaker's Circular Economy Toolkit

Policies for accelerating the circular economy should start with a clear vision, describing the circular activities that the government would like to see and the objectives it wants to achieve. Clear objectives and targets provide a framework for deciding which business activities should be encouraged (or discouraged) and they set a benchmark against which policy alternatives can

© The Author(s) 2020
P. Lacy et al., *The Circular Economy Handbook*,
https://doi.org/10.1057/978-1-349-95968-6_22

be compared to resolve any conflicts. For instance, measures to increase recycling may conflict with initiatives to scale the use of waste-to-energy.

Armed with a clear vision, policymakers can then evaluate a mix of policy interventions for bringing the circular economy to scale, each addressing different barriers that prevent circular businesses from achieving scale (see Fig. 22.1).

CIRCULAR ECONOMY STRATEGIES AND TARGETS

VISION	Resource efficiency, recycling, economic value addition, job creation		
REGULATION	Product standards	Recycled content requirements	Bans of harmful substances & plastics
FINANCING & TAXATION	Subsidies & fiscal benefits	Externality pricing & taxation	Extended producer responsibility
PUBLIC INVESTMENT	Physical & digital infrastructure	Awareness & behavior change	Public R&D
COLLABORATION	Public-private collaboration & cross-sector partnerships		

Fig. 22.1 Different policy interventions can be used to support the circular economy

National and local strategies and targets have become common in energy and climate policy, and countries are starting to develop these for their transition to a circular economy. Circular economy strategies present a comprehensive approach to sustainable resources use, setting targets, and introducing a series of measures to achieve the targets. Waste management and recycling are typically key elements, often supplemented by goals for increasing productivity, resource efficiency, and job creation. Notable examples include:

- The EU Circular Economy Action Plan presents the EU's vision on the transition to a Circular Economy. The related Directives on Waste set concrete targets for waste management, including an EU target for recycling 65% of municipal waste by 2035; a common EU target for recycling 70% of packaging waste by 2030; and a binding landfill target to reduce landfill to a maximum of 10% of municipal waste by 2035.[1]
- China's 13th Five-Year Plan, together with its Circular Economy Promotion Law, sets targets for increasing resources productivity by 15% (from 2015 levels), increasing recycling rates of major waste types to 55%

by 2020 and raising the utilization rate of industrial waste by 73%.[2,3] As Zhao Kai, Vice President & Secretary General of the China Association of Circular Economy puts it, "Cohesive national strategies are essential for accelerating the transition to circular economy, and we see this starting to have an impact in China. Best practice pilots or initiatives, such as creation of zero waste city pilots or circular industrial parks, are then needed locally to bring these policies to life and demonstrate the advantages of going circular."

Regulations and bans are used to address waste management and resource use practices with direct negative effect on the environment, human health, and/or the economy. Some of the first environmental policies involved the banning or regulation of harmful chemicals (e.g., certain pesticides), and recently the approach has been used to address waste problems, most prominently plastics waste.

- Regulations prescribing the handling and disposal of hazardous waste are common. In the United States, electronics that are hazardous must follow the Resource Conservation and Recovery Act and be managed accordingly. In Chin a, which generates the highest e-waste quantity globally (7.2 million tons), national laws regulate the collection and treatment of TVs, refrigerators, washing machines, air conditioners, and computers. However, informal waste-processing practices and illegal disposal are highly lucrative and continue to play an important role in the management of electronic waste in China, despite increased government attention.[4]

- Policymakers and regulators around the world have been introducing bans on the use of different types of plastic products, reacting to growing concern about plastics waste. Bans of different types of plastics products, mostly single-use items like shopping bags or cutlery, have been announced or are in place in the majority of African countries, the European Union, all major Asian countries, and numerous US states and cities, among others.

- For developing countries, a major issue has been the illegal dumping of plastic waste. China's withdrawal as the world's repository for plastic waste has thrown global markets into turmoil, resulting in a surge of imported plastic trash to Vietnam, Indonesia, Malaysia, and Thailand. Malaysia, for one, has recently introduced regulations to curb the import of plastic waste, and other countries could soon follow suit.[5]

Product requirements and product standards were introduced originally to regulate the use of harmful substances and content. They have evolved to set requirements on the minimal levels of sustainable content (e.g., recycled content) and performance (e.g., energy efficiency).

- The EU Eco-design Directive (Directive 2009/125/EC) provides EU-wide rules for improving the environmental performance of products. It sets minimum mandatory requirements especially in terms of energy use. The goal is to eliminate poor-performing products from the market and stimulate industrial competitiveness and innovation.[6]
- California is one of the first jurisdictions using product standards for recycled content. The Rigid Plastic Packaging Container Law, which was enacted to help decrease the amount of plastics thrown into California's landfills, stipulates that plastic containers need to be made from at least 25% recycled materials.[7] The state has also introduced recycled content requirements for plastic bags.
- Members of the G7 Oceans Plastic Charter have adopted an aspirational goal of "working with industry towards increasing recycled content by at least 50% in plastic products" by 2030.[8]

Taxes and incentives are used to price practices that are harmful (waste generation, unsustainable waste disposal, etc.) and reward practices that are beneficial.

- Incentives include subsidies for investment in circular economy solutions or for their use, as well as tax benefits, such as the UK Capital Allowances scheme, which allows for accelerated depreciation of investments in energy-saving systems.[9] In Sweden, there is a reduced value-added tax (VAT) rate for repair shops, for instance.[10]
- Taxation or pricing of negative effects of practices or products involves making polluters pay for the harmful effects of their activities. Examples include waste disposal fees, direct taxation of waste generation (for instance, through a plastic bag levy), and a carbon tax. By assigning a price to carbon through a market or tax, governments seek to encourage low-carbon solutions. Similarly, France has recently introduced a penalty system that taxes non-recycled packaging material.[11] The revenues raised by taxing harmful practices can then be used to invest in infrastructure or to provide subsidies for solutions.

Businesses have an important role in ensuring fair and reasonable regulation that recognizes the true cost of products and services on society and the environment. The costs of negative environmental impacts, so-called externalities, have traditionally not been included in the price of products and services, and this has been a significant barrier to the progress of the circular economy.

In recent years, leading circular businesses have become strong advocates of integrating the costs of negative environmental impacts, for instance, calling for governments to put a price on carbon emissions. This would strengthen their case for investing in emissions reduction measures in their business and stimulate consumers to choose their low-carbon products over alternatives. "With pricing externalities, the value of the secondary market will be even higher, because consumers will realize the real value of products and the remaining value after end-of-life," says John Atcheson of Stuffstr, a recirculation platform company.

Pricing externalities would also help provide a more accurate picture of the environmental costs involved. When considering the water pollution caused by the traditional dyeing process in the textile industry, DyeCoo, a supplier of industrial CO_2 dyeing equipment, believes that policies that make businesses pay the price of pollution would result in circular processes becoming more favorable. "Once legislation is enforced where companies have to purify their wastewater to a higher level and pay for pollution, then circular solutions will become cost competitive," asserts Reinier Mommaal, Co-Founder of DyeCoo.

- Extended Producer Responsibility (EPR) policies are a comprehensive policy approach for waste management and recycling through pricing and rewards. EU member states have introduced EPR schemes to regulate the collection, recycling, and recovery of e-waste, as specified by the Waste Electrical and Electronic Equipment (WEEE) Directive.[12] The 2018 Revised Waste legislations also introduced minimum requirements for EPR schemes. Under these policies, businesses are responsible for bearing the costs of collecting e-waste, but fees can be used to stimulate the return of electronics products at end of use. French consumers, for instance, must pay an "eco-fee" when they purchase a new electrical or electronic appliance.[13] That fee is then paid to a takeback organization (accredited by the government) that recovers used appliances to decontaminate and recycle them. EPR policies have become increasingly common around the world. India has been a pioneer of EPR in Asia, and EPR schemes are under discussion in China, with the aim to introduce these in 2025 for electronics, automobiles, lead–acid batteries, and packing products.[14,15] In Latin America, Chile was the first country to introduce an EPR scheme in 2016, and now 10 countries in the region have EPR policies in place.[16] Countries that have introduced EPR policies have generally seen recycling rates rise, provided that the fees are sufficient incentive (compared with illegal disposal) and that a reliable infrastructure for returning used products is in place.[17]

Investments in infrastructure, awareness, and technology for waste recovery and recycling are a way for governments to create a platform for effective circular solutions.

- Recycling is a key priority for circular economy and waste policy. Most countries have policies to stimulate recycling, but rates have thus far been low and the quality of material poor. In the EU, 23% of municipal waste was still sent to a landfill in 2017, and in seven member states it exceeds 60%.[18] EU Member States will have to increase targets for reuse and recycling of municipal waste from 55% by 2025 to 65% by 2035. In other countries, landfilling rates are typically above 50%. Lack of infrastructure and capacity are key challenges for increasing recycling, especially for waste separation, collection, and sorting systems. Waste separation is most effective when done at the source, that is, by the public, which is why government policies focus on consumer awareness and education to ensure that incentives in the collection process (fines and reverse collection) can be effective. New technologies, such as autonomous robots, offer enormous potential for improving waste sorting. Policymakers can invest in R&D to accelerate the development of these technologies and offer financial benefits to stimulate their deployment.
- Developing countries, in particular, suffer from limitations in waste collection and treatment infrastructure and capacity. Problems include underfunding so that waste collection only reaches part of the population, a lack of disposal infrastructure that leads to illegal dumping activity, and insufficient capacity to enforce legislation and collect waste fees that, in turn, exacerbate shortages in funding. The World Bank has helped finance projects for strengthening waste management infrastructures and capacities around the world, working with local governments and international partners. This includes investments in the rehabilitation of existing waste disposal sites (e.g., in Indonesia, Bosnia Herzegovina, and Azerbaijan), projects for increasing consumer awareness and engagement (e.g., in Morocco, Jamaica, and China), and investments in waste collection capabilities (e.g., in Nepal and Liberia).[19]
- Use of recycled materials can only improve when manufacturers have reliable data about the composition and quality of these materials. This requires investment in a digital infrastructure for collecting and tracking the relevant data. In the United States, the Environmental Protection Agency has recently set up a national system to track hazardous waste shipments, and this new "e-manifest" will affect companies across all

industries that generate hazardous waste, from leftover ink at a printer to scrap tires at an auto service center.[20]

Going forward, there will not only be a need for investment in waste collection and processing infrastructure and awareness, but also for the infrastructure that can bring recycled materials back into the manufacturing process. Waste-processing companies will see their roles change dramatically. They will no longer be businesses at the end of the value chain managing one-way disposal; they will become players connecting the value chain's beginning and end, responsible for upgrading resource streams and finding the highest value of recycled materials. Governments can support this closing of the loop by incentivizing or contributing to investment in infrastructures for reverse logistics.

Collaboration and cross-sector partnerships can be facilitated by governments to stimulate comprehensive circular solutions across the value chain.

- Along with initiating policy, governments can play a key role to help stimulate and coordinate action by businesses and other groups. Their power and perspective make them ideally placed to convene players from different sectors to encourage comprehensive solutions. When policymakers are engaged in business partnerships, they can more readily address regulatory barriers that prevent new partnerships and practices. On a local level, governments can stimulate cross-sector collaboration and industrial symbiosis in business parks and industry centers. China, for instance, operates multiple certified industrial parks that use the principles of circular economy— primarily reusing and recycling common materials including plastics—in managing their supply chains. The country's 13th Five-Year Plan aims for over 75% of national industrial parks and more than 50 provincial industrial parks to be practicing complete circular strategies by 2020.[2] Similarly, in country Export Processing Zones (EPZs) and Special Economic Zones (SEZs) can be restructured as centers of excellence for developing, testing, and scaling circular solutions, increasing the appeal of such zones for multinational companies and their suppliers.
- Governments also need to address barriers that prevent companies from developing joint circular business practices. Competition regulation can discourage collaboration, especially for businesses operating in the same sector. Policymakers can remove such obstacles by defining the conditions under which cooperation is allowed, thereby ensuring both fair competition and consumer protections. Arrangements for data sharing and intellectual property present additional hurdles for any type of ecosystem innovation. Companies are more likely to enter innovation partnerships

when there are clear rules that prescribe how data can be shared and that set out how intellectual property is shared and protected in joint initiatives.

In addition to adopting new interventions, policymakers should also regularly review and rationalize existing regulations, especially those that offer conflicting objectives or include measures with unintended side effects. A review of existing policies in light of new policy objectives, or even advances in technology or processes, will often uncover opportunities to remove barriers to circular practices while still fulfilling the original purpose of the existing policy. For instance, a food safety regulation may prevent the donation of surplus food from restaurants. Adjustment of that regulation could specify under what conditions food waste can be donated.

Global Landscape

The circular economy is clearly on the agenda of policymakers at national and local levels around the world. Policymakers in Europe, Asia, and other regions have expressed bold ambitions for moving to a more circular economy, and several countries have set concrete targets. But the implementation of circular economy policies varies widely, as does the ability to deliver on the policy objectives due to limitations in enforcement capacity and infrastructure.

 EUROPE: *leading through shared multinational circular initiatives and goals*

- The European Union Circular Economy Action Plan sets out the EU's vision for the transition to a circular economy with the ambition to extract the maximum value and use from all raw materials, products, and waste, fostering energy savings, reducing greenhouse gas emissions, and creating new business opportunities and jobs. It lays out 54 concrete measures that member states and public authorities must implement to achieve the vision.[21]
- A recent report on the implementation of the Circular Economy Action Plan confirms the business benefits: In 2016, circular activities such as repair, reuse, or recycling generated almost €147 billion in value added from around €17.5 billion worth of investments.[21,22]

- Collaborative platforms have been established to coordinate action among public authorities, think tanks, universities, businesses, and trade unions.
- Two countries at the forefront are **Finland and the Netherlands**, which have each devised roadmaps of concrete actions that can fast-track their transformation to a competitive circular economy.[23]

ASIA: *increasingly strong national waste and resource efficiency strategies and laws, galvanized by concerns about plastics waste, electronic waste, and air pollution*

- **China**'s 13th Five-Year Plan sets out the country's targets for the circular economy, and the Circular Economy Promotion Law (2009) introduced measures to increase efficiency and reduce waste and pollution in manufacturing.[2] It is supported by rules for financial institutions to give credit support to energy-, water-, land-, or material-saving projects; tax preferences to industrial activities promoting the development of the circular economy; and requirements for businesses to deploy recovery technologies to comprehensively use the wastewater and heat generated in production processes.
- The government in **India** has introduced EPR schemes to stimulate the development of the formal waste management system and encourage the integration of workers involved in informal waste collection and processing. The first EPR system was introduced for lead–acid batteries in 2001, and since then it has been applied to e-waste and most recently packaging through the Plastic Waste Management Rules (2016).[14,24] However, limited enforcement capacity and fragmented implementation across states have slowed the impact of these measures.[14]
- Countries across Asia have been taking action to reduce plastics waste and marine litter. **Indonesia** has introduced the National Action Plan on Marine Debris (2017–2025), aiming to reduce 70% of its plastic debris (from a 2017 baseline) by the end of 2025, and the government of the **Philippines** has drafted a National Strategy on Marine Litter, which provides the basis for a subsequent Master Plan on Marine Plastics Management.[25] The impact of these initiatives, though, is stalled by the availability of waste management infrastructure and capacity at the local level.

🌍 **AFRICA**: *building up waste management capacity, while addressing direct negative impacts of plastics and electronic waste to the environment and human health*

- Many African countries have waste laws in place, generally prescribing collection and treatment of waste, and sometimes setting targets for recycling. Implementation and enforcement are often difficult, however, due to a lack of resources and capacity at the local government level. Countries have therefore introduced mechanisms to finance the formal waste sectors through waste management fees or taxes. Additionally, they are building capacity by integrating informal waste workers into the formal waste management system. **Morocco**, for example, has worked with the World Bank to formalize the roles of 20,000 waste workers.[26]
- African countries have led the way in addressing plastic waste; more than 30 countries in **sub-Saharan Africa** have either banned plastic bags or imposed taxes on their use. As one of the most extreme examples, Kenya's ban includes possible jail time or a hefty fine.[27]
- African countries have long been a destination for discarded hazardous electronics, often resulting in harm to the environment and human health, as open dumping, burning, and landfilling are the predominant disposal methods being used. The Bamako Convention (1998) aimed to address this by banning the import of hazardous and radioactive waste into Africa from other countries. But the dumping of e-waste is still occurring because of a lack of follow-up at the national level. An investigation by the Basel Action Network suggests that hundreds of metric tons of electronic waste from European countries are still being exported to developing countries each year, despite European regulation banning the practice.[28]
- Recent years have seen the emergence of supranational initiatives for driving economic development through the circular economy. **Rwanda**, **South Africa**, and **Nigeria**, for instance, are working with the United Nations (UN) Environment Program and the World Economic Forum to develop a continent-wide alliance to spur Africa's transformation to a circular economy, with a focus on e-waste.[29] As Peter Desmond, Founder of the African Circular Economy Network, emphasizes, "The implementation of circular policies in Africa has the potential to open up a better development path, building on the defining characteristics of resilience and resourcefulness, and enabling Africa to leapfrog to a sustainable, equitable, prosperous and circular economy."

🌏 **AUSTRALIA and NEW ZEALAND**: *moving beyond waste laws to broader policies for a circular transition*

- The federal government in **Australia** updated its National Waste Policy in 2018, prioritizing waste avoidance, improved material recovery, and the use of recovered materials. A framework was provided for the environmental management of products, including voluntary, co-regulatory, and mandatory stewardship.[30]
- **New Zealand** has established accelerator programs and funds for initiatives that will spur the country's circular transition. The Waste Minimisation Fund supports projects that promote or achieve waste minimization, resource efficiency, reuse, recovery, and recycling.[31]
- New Zealand has issued a nationwide ban on single-use plastic bags, starting in July 2019. Similarly, single-use plastic bags of certain thicknesses have been banned in Queensland, Western Australia, South Australia, Tasmania, ACT, and the NT, with Victoria set to follow in November 2019.[32,33]

🌎 **NORTH AMERICA**: *establishing state and regional leadership in public–private circular collaborations*

- In **Canada**, circular economy policy is created at the provincial and local level. Ontario initiated a "Strategy for a Waste Free Ontario: Building the Circular Economy" in 2015, and multiple provinces have adopted recycling targets.[34] The City of Toronto aims to achieve zero waste, starting with diverting 70% of waste produced from landfill, as set out in its 2016 Long Term Waste Management Strategy.[35]
- Canada is a frontrunner in promoting public–private circular partnerships, such as the Circular Economy Lab.[36] In addition, the National Zero Waste Council has been bringing together governments, businesses, and NGOs to advance waste prevention.[37]
- In the **United States**, circularity is gaining traction in the business community, with strong momentum in supporting the circular economy at the state and local level.[38] More than 20 states have introduced EPR regulations for electronic waste, and states like California, Colorado, and Washington have set targets for waste minimization and resource efficiency. New York City is committed to becoming a worldwide leader in solid-waste management by achieving the goal of zero waste by 2030.[39]

- The Federal Resource Conservation and Recovery Act (RCRA) regulates the management of hazardous and non-hazardous solid wastes in the United States.[40] It also encourages waste minimization and recycling through a focus on sustainable materials management, creating partnership and award programs to incentivize companies to modify their manufacturing practices to generate less waste and reuse materials safely.

LATIN AMERICA and THE CARIBBEAN: *starting to define objectives for a circular economy*

- Latin American countries have set national policies for energy, waste, and the environment. Uruguay, Chile, Brazil, and México have developed circular economy roadmaps with the assistance of the United Nations Industrial Development Organization (UNIDO) Climate Technology Centre and Network.[41]
- **Chile** was the first in the region to introduce EPR and the first to ban plastics bags.[42,43] Moreover, in 2018 the Chilean Economic Development Agency (CORFO) and the Ministry of Environment of Chile created the first public finance instrument in Latin America to help entrepreneurs and companies implement circular business models.[43] Carolina Schmidt, the Environment Minister of Chile, highlights the crucial role of policymakers in driving progress: "Policymakers are fundamental in generating the right incentives and in establishing the new rules of the game so that private sector can move from a linear to a circular economy. We are convinced that circular economy policy must be addressed in a comprehensive manner and with various complementary instruments. In Chile, we have combined multiple policy approaches, including regulation, for example with the implementation of the Extended Producer Responsibility scheme, and prohibitions, such as the law that banned plastic bags. Additionally, we have articulated voluntary agreements with the industry such as the Chilean Plastics Pact."
- In **Brazil**, the Ministry of Industry, Foreign Trade and Ministry of the Environment, and the National Confederation of Industry are part of the Forum of Production and Sustainable Consumption and are committed to achieving the competitiveness of the national industry and the sustainability of its operations.[44]
- The Circular Economy Forum of the Americas aims to create a supranational policy framework to drive the circular economy in the Americas.[45]

What's Next for Policymakers

Although new and updated policies and regulations have encouraged the adoption of circular business models, this in turn has led to a range of new policy questions. As we move forward, policymakers should address the following five areas:

- **Waste definitions**. Waste regulation typically defines when materials are considered waste, secondary material, or by-product. These classifications determine the value of a material, as well as whether it can be exported. For instance, discarded electronic equipment classified as waste may face export limitations, even if it could serve as a source of secondary material abroad. To address such barriers, policymakers should review all waste classifications and restrictions in light of the new circular economy policy targets and latest technological possibilities.
- **Application of material use and waste hierarchies**. Policymakers should steer regulations toward practices that yield the highest value use of scarce materials and waste. Consistent application of priority frameworks, like the waste hierarchy of "reduce, reuse, repair, recycle, recover, dispose," will help ensure coherent policy measures and settle potential conflicts between policy objectives (e.g., between circular economy objectives and climate policy).
- **Taxation changes to incentivize circular behavior**. Existing taxation designed to achieve other objectives (e.g., job creation or economic growth) may discourage the efficient use of resources. Policymakers should thus review the impacts of taxation on resource efficiency and, when possible, consider shifting taxation toward resource use. To prevent the total tax burden from rising, increases in taxes on the use of materials can be accompanied by reductions in the taxation of labor, stimulating new, circular activities that create jobs and contribute to more inclusive economic growth.
- **Product quality and safety regulation**. These types of regulations typically place limits on how products can be used after disposal. They can restrict secondary use altogether (e.g., donations of food waste even when still edible) or decrease the value of the secondary product. Policymakers can reduce this barrier by clarifying when secondary resources can be used while also continuing to guarantee quality and safety. The presence of hazardous chemicals is an area of particular concern, and it is important

that policymakers and regulators take a prudent approach to reviewing the applicability of product safety regulations to recycled material, especially those that contain hazardous substances.

- **Infrastructure investment**. One of the biggest challenges we hear from local businesses is the lack of infrastructure for collection, sorting, recycling, composting, and so on. It remains critical to free up and direct funds to develop, strengthen, and expand waste infrastructure, and new infrastructure is needed so that recovered and recycled materials can be integrated back into production processes. As policymakers recognize the potential of the circular economy for development and economic growth, they should take a more active role in prioritizing and facilitating investment in circular economy infrastructure, as they would for other critical infrastructure.

Given the continual innovation in circular initiatives, additional changes in government regulations and laws will more than likely be needed in the future. To spur continued growth of the circular economy, businesses should continually engage with policymakers, and help identify gaps and barriers in current legal and regulatory frameworks, as well as share information about the potential and implications of new circular economy practices and solutions.

 Chapter Takeaways

- Governments have a crucial role in accelerating the transition to a circular economy through policy measures and public investment and by convening other actors to develop and scale circular practices.
- Policies for accelerating the circular economy should start with a vision and clear targets, supported by a mix of measures involving regulation, financing and taxation, public investment, and actions to facilitate cooperation.
- The circular economy is on the agenda of policymakers around the world, but the implementation and effectiveness of circular economy policies vary across regions.
- To facilitate circular initiatives, policymakers should address the following five areas: waste definitions, waste hierarchies, taxation, product quality and safety, and infrastructure investment.

Notes

1. European Commission, "Implementation of the Circular Economy Action Plan," https://ec.europa.eu/environment/circular-economy/index_en.htm (accessed August 16, 2019).
2. Central Compilation & Translation Press, "The 13th Five-Year Plan for Economic and Social Development of the People's Republic of China, 2016–2020," http://en.ndrc.gov.cn/newsrelease/201612/P0201612076457 65233498.pdf (accessed August 9, 2019).
3. Jinhui Li, "Role of Circular Economy in Achieving SDGs – Case of China," United Nations Centre for Regional Development, December 26, 2016, http://www.uncrd.or.jp/content/documents/4414Background%20 paper-Jinhui%20Li_Final-PS-1.pdf (accessed August 16, 2019).
4. International Institute for Environment and Development, "Clean and Inclusive? Recycling e-waste in China and India," March 2016, https://pubs. iied.org/pdfs/16611IIED.pdf (accessed August 12, 2019).
5. BBC News, "Why Some Countries Are Shipping Back Plastic Waste," June 2, 2019, https://www.bbc.co.uk/news/world-48444874 (accessed August 16, 2019).
6. European Parliament, "Report on the Implementation of the Ecodesign Directive (2009/125/EC)," May 7, 2018, www.europarl.europa.eu/doceo/ document/A-8-2018-0165_EN.html (accessed August 16, 2019).
7. Cal Recycle, "Recycled Plastic Products and Materials," July 26, 2018, https://www.calrecycle.ca.gov/plastics/recycled (accessed August 9, 2019).
8. Plastic Action Centre, "G7 Ocean Plastics Charter," https://plasticactioncentre.ca/directory/ocean-plastics-charter/ (accessed August 9, 2019).
9. Gov.uk, "Claim capital allowances," https://www.gov.uk/capital-allowances (accessed August 9, 2019).
10. Richard Orange, "Waste Not Want Not: Sweden to Give Tax Breaks for Repairs," *The Guardian*, September 19, 2016, https://www.theguardian. com/world/2016/sep/19/waste-not-want-not-sweden-tax-breaks-repairs (accessed August 16, 2019).
11. The Telegraph, "France to Set Penalties on Goods Packaged with Non-recycled Plastic in 2019," August 12, 2018, https://www.telegraph.co.uk/ news/2018/08/12/france-set-penalities-goods-packaged-non-recycled-plastic-2019/ (accessed August 16, 2019).
12. Organisation for Economic Co-operation and Development, "Extended Producer Responsibility (EPR) and the Impact of Online Sales— Environment Working Paper No. 142," 2019, www.oecd.org/official-documents/publicdisplaydocumentpdf/?cote=ENV/WKP(2019)1& docLanguage=En (accessed August 16, 2019).

13. Eco-systemes, "French Regulations," https://www.eco-systemes.fr/en/french-regulations (accessed August 16, 2019).

14. EU-India Action Plan Support Facility—Environment Sponsored by the European Union, "Waste Electrical and Electronic Equipment the EU and India: Sharing Best Practices," European External Action Service, http://eeas.europa.eu/archives/delegations/india/documents/eu_india/final_e_waste_book_en.pdf (accessed August 16, 2019).

15. *China Daily*, "China Unveils Extended Producer Responsibility Plan," January 3, 2017, www.chinadaily.com.cn/china/2017-01/03/content_2785 1701.htm (accessed August 16, 2019).

16. Gob.cl, "President Bachelet Enacts the Recycling and Extended Producer Liability Law" May 26, 2016, https://www.gob.cl/noticias/archivo-president-bachelet-enacts-the-recycling-and-extended-producer-liability-law/ (accessed August 16, 2019).

17. Organisation for Economic Co-operation and Development, "The State of Play on Extended Producer Responsibility (EPR): Opportunities and Challenges," 17–19 June 2014, https://www.oecd.org/environment/waste/Global%20Forum%20Tokyo%20Issues%20Paper%2030-5-2014.pdf (accessed August 16, 2019).

18. Eurostat, "Municipal Waste Statistics," June 2019, https://ec.europa.eu/eurostat/statistics-explained/index.php/Municipal_waste_statistics (accessed August 9, 2019).

19. World Bank, "Solid Waste Management," April 1 2019, https://www.worldbank.org/en/topic/urbandevelopment/brief/solid-waste-management (accessed August 9, 2019).

20. EPA, "The Hazardous Waste Electronic Manifest (E-Manifest) System," June 27, 2019, https://www.epa.gov/e-manifest (accessed August 9, 2019).

21. European Commission, "Report from the Commission to the European Parliament, the Council, the European Economic and Social Committee and the Committee of the Regions," March 4, 2019, http://ec.europa.eu/environment/circular-economy/pdf/report_implementation_circular_economy_action_plan.pdf (accessed August 12, 2019).

22. Eurostat, "Private Investments, Jobs and Gross Value Added Related to Circular Economy Sectors," August 17, 2018, https://ec.europa.eu/eurostat/tgm/refreshTableAction.do?tab=table&plugin=1&pcode=cei_cie010&language=en (accessed August 12, 2019).

23. Ellen MacArthur Foundation, "Achieving 'Growth' Within," https://www.ellenmacarthurfoundation.org/assets/downloads/publications/Achieving-Growth-Within-20-01-17.pdf (accessed August 16, 2019).

24. *The Economic Times*, "Government Notifies Plastic Waste Management Rules," https://economictimes.indiatimes.com/news/economy/policy/government-notifies-plastic-waste-management-rules-2016/articleshow/51459885.cms (accessed August 16, 2019).

25. World Bank, "World Bank Statement at the Special ASEAN Ministerial Meeting on Marine Debris," March 11, 2019, https://www.worldbank.org/en/news/speech/2019/03/11/world-bank-statement-at-the-special-asean-ministerial-meeting-on-marine-debris (accessed August 16, 2019).

26. The World Bank, "Solid Waste Management," April 1 2019, https://www.worldbank.org/en/topic/urbandevelopment/brief/solid-waste-management (accessed August 9, 2019).

27. Reuters, "Kenya Brings in World's Toughest Plastic Bag Ban: Four Years Jail or $40,000 Fine," *The Guardian*, August 28, 2017, https://www.theguardian.com/environment/2017/aug/28/kenya-brings-in-worlds-toughest-plastic-bag-ban-four-years-jail-or-40000-fine (accessed August 9, 2019).

28. Basel Action Network, "Holes in the Circular Economy: WEEE Leakage from Europe. e-Trash Transparency Project," 2018, http://wiki.ban.org/images/f/f4/Holes_in_the_Circular_Economy-_WEEE_Leakage_from_Europe.pdf (accessed August 12, 2019).

29. Platform for Accelerating the Circular Economy, "African Circular Economy Alliance," https://www.acceleratecirculareconomy.org/african-circular-economy-alliance-index (accessed August 16, 2019).

30. Australian Government, "National Waste Policy 2018," https://www.environment.gov.au/system/files/resources/d523f4e9-d958-466b-9fd1-3b7d6283f006/files/national-waste-policy-2018.pdf (accessed August 9, 2019).

31. Ministry for the Environment—New Zealand, "Circular economy—Ōhanga āmiomio," https://www.mfe.govt.nz/waste/circular-economy (accessed August 9, 2019).

32. Swati Dubey, "New Zealand Issues Nationwide Ban on Single-Use Plastic Bags, Apna Time Kab Aayega?" Storypick, July 1 2019, https://www.storypick.com/new-zealand-plastic-bags-ban/ (accessed August 9, 2019).

33. Ministry for the Environment—New Zealand, "Single-Use Plastic Shopping Bags Are Banned in New Zealand," https://www.mfe.govt.nz/waste/single-use-plastic-shopping-bags-banned-new-zealand (accessed August 9, 2019).

34. Ontario, "Strategy for a Waste-Free Ontario: Building the Circular Economy," March 8, 2019, https://www.ontario.ca/page/strategy-waste-free-ontario-building-circular-economy (accessed August 9, 2019).

35. Toronto, "Long Term Waste Management Strategy," https://www.toronto.ca/services-payments/recycling-organics-garbage/long-term-waste-strategy/ (accessed August 9, 2019).

36. Circular Economy Lab, "About Us," https://circulareconomylab.com/about-ceil/ (accessed August 16, 2019).

37. The National Zero Waste Council, "About the Council," http://www.nzwc.ca/about/council/Pages/default.aspx (accessed August 16, 2019).

38. Office of Energy Efficiency and Renewable Energy, "Energy Department Announces up to $70 Million for New Remade in America," June 23 2016,

https://www.energy.gov/eere/articles/energy-department-announces-70-million-new-remade-america-institute (accessed August 9, 2019).

39. NYC.gov, "Zero Waste," https://www1.nyc.gov/assets/dsny/site/our-work/zero-waste (accessed August 9, 2019).

40. United States Environmental Protection Agency, "Summary of the Resource Conservation and Recovery Act," https://www.epa.gov/laws-regulations/summary-resource-conservation-and-recovery-act (accessed August 16, 2019).

41. Petar Ostojic, "Latin America Goes Circular," Medium, May 26, 2019, https://medium.com/@petarostojic/latin-america-goes-circular-5d1b73a96c27 (accessed August 9, 2019).

42. Petar Ostojic, "Chile's Journey to a Circular Economy," Medium, September 11, 2018, https://medium.com/@petarostojic/chiles-journey-to-a-circular-economy-8ea601c829ec (accessed August 9, 2019).

43. Bnamericas, "Chile Unveils Draft Climate Change Law," June 19, 2019, https://www.bnamericas.com/en/news/chile-unveils-draft-climate-change-law (accessed August 9, 2019).

44. Ministry of Economy—Brazil, "Circular Economy," June 29, 2018, http://www.mdic.gov.br/index.php/competitividade-industrial/sustentabilidade/economia-circular (accessed August 9, 2019).

45. CEFA 2018, "Building a Circular Conscious Continent," https://www.cefa2018.com (accessed August 16, 2019).

23

Toward a Circular Future

We are fast approaching a tipping point, where our consumption patterns and demand outpace our planet's ability to safely regenerate, let alone thrive. We've been locked into an unsustainable system of production and consumption over the last decade. While technological advancements have enabled more efficient use of natural resources, we continue to take and waste more than we grow. A shift to the circular economy is a powerful opportunity for business to innovate and create new markets while also reducing harmful environmental impacts and improving socioeconomic outcomes. When adopted strategically, the circular economy can create significant financial and economic value for business and society. This is what we call the circular advantage.

By no means is this shift easy or straightforward. While the fundamental concept of circularity is simple—turn all waste into something valuable—disrupting our current linear models of both production and consumption is a massive task. As demonstrated throughout this book, there are impressive examples of where private and public organizations of all types and sizes are successfully navigating the transition. But to turn this tipping point into an opportunity, we need to scale circular economy efforts across every industry and every geography.

To capture the $4.5 trillion value at stake, companies will need to evaluate their current linear models, core assets, and customer preferences to determine how, not if, they will transition to the circular economy. The five business models we presented—Circular Inputs, Sharing Platform, Product Use Extension, Product as a Service, and Resource Recovery—serve as a

P. Lacy et al., *The Circular Economy Handbook*,
https://doi.org/10.1057/978-1-349-95968-6_23

blueprint for that transition. Enabled by the 27 physical, digital and biological technologies we described in these pages, leaders can now replicate and scale circular innovations at pace and with financially attractive returns. This approach can suit any industry, as our industry profiles show. Each industry will shift away from their linear systems in different ways, depending on current waste streams, expected demand for natural resources, consumer preferences, and industry maturity. The journey to becoming a circular company is as wide and varied as companies themselves, which opens up a world of possibilities for innovation and reinvention. Therefore, an integrated approach that considers Operations, Products & Services, Culture & Organization, and Ecosystems is needed to pivot wisely from linear to circular.

We hope that *The Circular Economy Handbook* has helped you understand the fundamentals of the circular economy, and that it has provided you with practical tools and insights to begin charting your organization's course for transformation. While the purpose of the Handbook is to act as a practical "toolkit" for leaders, we hope it also inspires readers and those just embarking on their circular journey to join the numerous companies, governments, NGOs, consumers, the public, and others on this movement toward a more regenerative and positive future. It's a future where novel business models and technologies will lead the way to robust growth and profitability, where production and consumption are redefined, and where environments and societies can prosper. As William McDonough, one of the original drivers of the movement, emphasizes, "Enough. For all. Forever."

Appendix A:
The $4.5 Trillion Value at Stake

Purpose

Waste to Wealth (2015) included an estimate of the total value at stake in 2030. It came out at $4.5 trillion. In the process of writing *The Circular Economy Handbook,* there was a desire to revisit this analysis and do three things:

1. Bring it up-to-date based on the latest available data,
2. Understand what, if anything, had changed in the intervening period,
3. Determine whether it was possible to do anything additional.

The purpose of this analysis is to provide an estimate of the potential impact to Global GDP of an increasingly resource-constrained environment and, in turn, understand the potential of the circular economy to reset that relationship.

This appendix outlines the headline findings, a detailed six-step methodology (including sources) and limitations to the study.

© The Editor(s) (if applicable) and The Author(s),
under exclusive license to Springer Nature Limited 2020
P. Lacy et al., *The Circular Economy Handbook,*
https://doi.org/10.1057/978-1-349-95968-6

Headline Findings

- Since 2015, when *Waste to Wealth* was published, we have revisited our calculations and found no substantial change in the scale of that opportunity; in fact, this estimate is probably fairly conservative.
- $4.5 trillion of Global GDP in 2030 is at stake from resource constraints; this is equivalent to the current size of the German economy (the world's 4th largest).
- If adopted at scale, the circular economy has the chance to unlock this value and continue world on its current economic growth trajectory.
- Currently, the global economy generates demand for natural resources equivalent to that required by 1.7× planets.
- The estimate of the value at stake is predicated on the assumption that the world needs to become a "one-planet economy" (only using resources that can be replenished in a single year) by 2050.
- If this transition is forced to happen sooner than 2050, due to increased awareness of irreversible damaged being caused, then the value at stake will increase dramatically.

Detailed Methodology

Given this work constitutes a refresh of the analysis conducted previously, it has remained consistent in terms of sources and methodology used. This has involved six steps:

1. Forecast global population and global GDP
The model is predicated on understanding the potential impact of resource imbalances to future GDP. This requires a Global GDP forecast to 2050, based on three things:

   i. OECD historical data and projections of global population,[1]
  ii. Historical GDP (at USD 1990 PPP) from Total Economy Database,[2]
 iii. Projected GDP (converted to USD 1990 PPP) based OECD and HSBC forecasts.[3,4]

This provides a consistent view of Global GDP and GDP per capita from 1970 to 2050.

2. Understand relationship between GDP and resource consumption
Using the historical data, the model determines the relationship between
GDP and resource consumption. This is based on a dataset collected by the
UN Environment Programme that tracks Domestic Material Consumption
(DMC) across four categories of materials (measured in metric tonnes):

- Biomass,
- Fossil energy carriers,
- Ores and industrial minerals,
- Construction minerals.

In 1970, the world consumed a total of 26.54 bn tonnes of materials. By
2017, that total had risen to 41.66 bn tonnes.

Using this data, it is possible to determine the relationship between DMC
and GDP as a ratio. For every ton of material extracted, how much GDP is
generated? As technology improves, humanity has become more efficient at
extracting value from resources. In 1970, 1.95 kg of materials were required
per dollar of GDP. By 2017, that ratio had dropped to 1.08 kg per dollar.

3. Forecast resource demand
Historical data illustrates the rate of improvement in this material input to
economic output ratio. The model calculates these rates of change for each
of the four material categories on decade-by-decade bases, weights the rate
of change in favor of more recent decades, and determines four potential
scenarios:

a. **No change:** This assumes that the ability to improve how much value can
   be extracted from a single unit has peaked and that there will be no additional improvements.
b. **Baseline:** The improvement in the input/output ratio will continue at the
   historical weighted average.
c. **Pessimistic:** The improvement in the input/output ratio will continue,
   but at lowest end of the range of historical weighted averages.
d. **Optimistic:** The improvement in the input/output ratio will continue,
   but at highest end of the range of historical weighted averages.

Because these scenarios are about varying the rates of change, the difference is compounded for each year that they are applied. This means across these four scenarios, total resource demand (based on a consistent GDP forecast) varies significantly:

Scenario	Total resource demand (bn tonnes 2030)
No change	112
Baseline	106
Pessimistic	121
Optimistic	95

As a final assumption, total resource demand is reduced by partially excluding construction minerals (leaving 10% of total). This is because these resources, such as sand, are abundantly available and therefore not subject to the same scarcity dynamics.

4. Forecast resource supply

Having understood historical and project resource demand, the next step was to determine the availability of resources. This was done in a top-down fashion, based on three core elements:

i. **Biocapacity**: An estimate by the Global Footprint Network of the total number of hectares of productive land the world has. This is currently 12.2bn hectares. The model assumes that number is fixed until 2050.[5]

ii. **Footprint**: The Global Footprint Network also estimates the hectares that current human activity requires per year.[6]

iii. **Footprint Intensity**: Finally, it is possible to convert footprint (in hectares) into "DMC allowance" (in tonnes) through understanding the historical footprint intensity ratio. This determines how many hectares were required to support one tonne of material consumption. In 1970, this figure was 0.55 hectares per tonne. By 2014 (last available date), it was 0.43 hectares per tonne.

With these three elements, it is possible to project future resource supply. This requires two further critical sets of assumptions.

The first is that the world will eventually need to return to a state in which annual ecological footprint does not exceed biocapacity. This is referred to as a being a "one-planet economy." Today, ecological footprint is

21.33 billion hectares or $1.7\times$ biocapacity. The model assumes, in line with all UN agencies, that the point of parity must be reached by 2050. It also assumes there will need to be a transitionary period. This is modeled as a linear progression from $1.7\times$ to $1.0\times$ in two stages. By 2030, the world will be 20% of the way to the target, and by 2050, it will have achieved the goal.

The second key component is forecasted footprint intensity. Again, this is done using scenarios. The baseline scenario assumes that the improvements in the hectares to tonnes ratio continue based on weighted average historical rate of change (0.6% per annum). The high and low scenarios rely on data from the IPCC. These projections of global CO_2 emission can be used to create a view of emissions per tonne of DMC per capita. The pessimistic scenario (RCP 2) assumes no improvement in the ratio whereas the optimistic scenario (RCP 1) assumes a rapid improvement (1.5% per annum).

Given all five of these components, it is possible to understand global resource supply (or allowance) based on each of the scenario (defined in section #3 above). This can be expressed in billions of tonnes. The result for each scenario is:

Scenario	Total resource allowance (bn tonnes 2030)
No change	48.4
Baseline	44.3
Pessimistic	42.4
Optimistic	53.5

5. Determine resource imbalance

Having computed the total resource demand (implied by GDP) and the total resource allowance (implied by a transition to a "one-planet economy"), it is possible to determine the total resource imbalance for each scenario in any given year. This analysis looks at 2030 as the target year. Once the total demand figures are discounted due to the abundance of construction materials, the supply imbalance implied for each scenario is as follows:

Scenario	Total resource allowance (bn tonnes 2030)
No Change	24.1
Baseline	7.0
Pessimistic	18.7
Optimistic	Nil

6. <u>Translate into economic impact</u>

The final step is to translate this resource imbalance into an economic impact. To do this, the model uses the production function produced by the World Bank and determines the per unit change in GDP per unit change of resources.[7] This is done at four key thresholds:

Reduction in resources of (%)	Per unit change in GDP (%)
<20	−0.33
20–50	−0.37
50–75	−0.43
75–92	−0.55

These multipliers have been applied to each scenario to produce an estimate of total impact on world GDP (in % terms) in 2030 and the corresponding USD$ value.

Finally, a weighted average of the two most likely scenarios (baseline and optimistic) was taken to find a single overall estimate. Given the significant technological and societal changes required to deliver the optimistic scenario, it is weighted at a 10% likelihood. This is in line with the upper end of IPCC estimates.

Limitations

- This assessment is entirely reliant on the assumption that humanity must stop unsustainably consuming resources.
- While this position can be rationalized, it is important to recognize that it would also represent a marked change from the historical trend of ever-increasing annual consumption.
- It is also not likely that this change will be necessitated by physical scarcity in most cases and will, instead, need to be driven by changing social, political, and regulatory expectation.
- This is a top-down analysis, focusing on the relationship between GDP and resource consumption, and it does not attempt to examine the current or future contribution of the circular economy to economic output.
- It does not have any direct relationship to any of the models performed elsewhere in *The Circular Economy Handbook* (e.g., industry-level opportunity assessments).
- No assessment has been made of the maturity of circular economy technologies or business models or their readiness to address this future gap in GDP growth.

- This assessment does not attempt to understand the investment that would be required to underpin this transition or to look at any potential GDP upside from the stimulus this investment would require. As a point of comparison, the Marshall Plan ($100bn in 2018 values) is estimated to have increased GNI by 2–3% and the American Recovery and Reinvestment Plan (2009, c.$750bn) increased US economic output by 2.5%.
- The analysis has been done on a global basis, to reflect the fact that resources can be increasingly shared internationally. It is possible to look regionally (or at major world economies), but more work would be required to refine the methodology and findings.

Notes

1. OECD Statistics, "Welcome to OECD.Stat," https://stats.oecd.org/ (accessed August 30, 2019).
2. The Conference Board, "Total Economy Database™—Key Findings," https://www.conference-board.org/data/economydatabase/ (accessed August 30, 2019).
3. OECD Data, "Real GDP Long-Term Forecast," https://data.oecd.org/gdp/real-gdp-long-term-forecast.htm (accessed September 2, 2019).
4. HSBC Global Research, "The World in 2050: Quantifying the Shift in the Global Economy," January 2011, https://www.hsbc.ca/1/PA_ES_Content_Mgmt/content/canada4/pdfs/business/hsbc-bwob-theworldin2050-en.pdf (accessed September 2, 2019).
5. Global Footprint Network, "Measure What You Treasure," https://www.footprintnetwork.org/ (accessed August 30, 2019).
6. Global Footprint Network, "Open Data Platform," http://data.footprintnetwork.org/#/ (accessed August 30, 2019).
7. World Bank, "Where Is the Wealth of Nations?" http://siteresources.worldbank.org/INTEEI/214578-1110886258964/20745221/Chapter8.pdf (accessed August 30, 2019).

Appendix B:
Industry-Level Opportunity Assessments

Purpose

The industry-level opportunity assessments consider the impact of circular initiatives on the contribution margin of various industries, in turn aiding our understanding of industry-level opportunities from the circular economy.

These analyses supplement the industry chapters by quantifying circular opportunities within each industry which result in either the migration of value or the addition of value through increased revenues or reduced costs.

Detailed Methodology

The analysis has consisted of five steps:

1. <u>Size the industries</u>
The industry size is calculated as the sum of revenues in 2018, from relevant companies in the industry, according to Bloomberg Industry Classification System (BICS). An average industry growth rate is applied based on external research, to estimate the potential size of the industry in 2030.

2. <u>Estimate current cost structure</u>
The cost structure of each industry is estimated by taking the median of various cost items, such as Cost of Goods Sold (COGS) and Sales, General,

and Administrative (SG&A) expenses, as a percentage of revenue, for all companies with more than >70% of revenue in the industry.

3. Identify circular initiatives
The key circular initiatives in the entire industry are identified by exploring circular investments made by companies alongside industry research trends and forecasts.

4. Identify value levers of the initiatives
The impact of each initiative is categorized based on whether it generates:

- **Value Migration**: A shift in the share of value within the industry, via either market share shift or product substitution,
- **Value Addition**: An increase in total value captured by the industry, via either new revenue generation or cost reduction.

5. Calculate benefit of each initiative
The EBITDA impact of an initiative is then estimated by multiplying:

  i. The size of the industry,
 ii. The size of the value lever that the initiative is impacting, as a share of the industry size,
iii. The impact of the initiative on the respective value lever, based on industry research, expert opinion, and leading company targets.

Breakdown of "Value at Stake"

"Value at stake" is driven by two key levers, defined as Value Migration and Value Addition.

   Value Migration: This is the EBITDA impact of initiatives that cause revenue to shift from one player in the industry (who is not or less circular) to another player in the industry (who is more circular).

   This shift could be driven by:

1. **Brand value**: Initiatives that lead to a shift in revenues from environmentally conscious consumers who value a circular product portfolio or circular supply chain.
2. **New business models**: New business models such as resale or rental that lead to a shift in revenues from products within the industry to higher premium products in the same industry.

Value Addition: EBITDA impact of initiatives that increase the total size of the industry or reduce the costs in the industry. These increases or reductions could be driven by:

Revenue Addition: Initiatives that increase revenues to the company (or industry) by

1. **Pricing premium**: Initiatives that enable companies to charge higher for a product due to its circular value,
2. **New revenue streams**: Initiatives that create new revenue streams in the industry and steal share from adjacent industries.

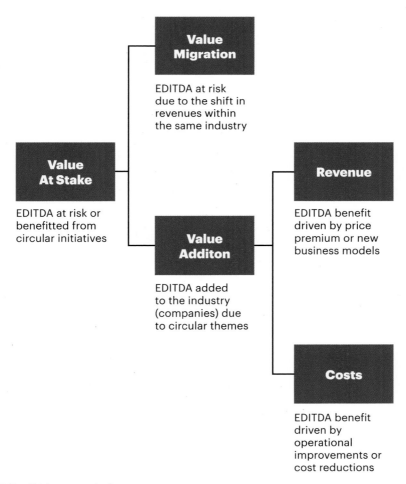

Fig. B.1 "Value at stake" tree

<u>Cost Reduction</u>: Initiatives that reduce cost to the company (or industry) by

1. **Circular design**: Designing circularly to use less material/energy or reuse waste,
2. **Produce less**: Forecast better to produce accurately and reduce wastage,
3. **Sustainable inputs**: Reduce input costs by sourcing cheaper recycled inputs,
4. **Smart operations**: Reduce waste by improving efficiency in operations (Fig. B.1).

Index